Mission
Focus
Current
Issues

Mission
Focus
Current
Issues

Wilbert R. Shenk, Editor

Foreword by Arthur F. Glasser

Herald Press
Scottdale, Pennsylvania
Kitchener, Ontario

1980

Library of Congress Cataloging in Publication Data
Main entry under title:

Mission focus.

Includes bibliographical references and index.
1. Missions—Addresses, essays, lectures.
I. Shenk, Wilbert R.
BV2070.M555   266   80-15686
ISBN 0-8361-1937-1 (pbk.)

15 14 13 12 11 10 9 8 7 6 5 4 3 2 1

Contents

III. Strategy and Policy

Foreword

One of the delightful surprises of the latter half of the twentieth century has been the prophetic vigor of the Mennonite tradition. Increasingly, through public witness and facile pen its leaders have entered the arena of public debate. They have not defended a narrow, encapsulated evangelicalism. Nor have they reduced "The Gospel of the Kingdom" to a vapid Christian humanism. Indeed, they have shown themselves capable of critical and constructive independence of Roman Catholic, Orthodox, mainline ecumenical, non-conciliar evangelical, and charismatic approaches to the issues facing the church in our day.

I have personally been greatly enriched by the writings of my Mennonite colleagues particularly in the field of mission. Some time back I began subscribing to MISSION-FOCUS, a five-times-a-year Mennonite publication deliberately beamed "For Mission Leaders." In no time at all I was writing for copies of all back issues. I found them scholarly in conception, biblical in orientation, and penetrating in their insights. Hence, it is with a real sense of delight that I welcome the publication of this collection of MISSION-FOCUS essays. They speak to the times in which we live and to the church which we serve. And no leader within church or para-church structure can afford not to listen to what our Mennonite colleagues have to say out of their rich and growing worldwide involvement in mission.

Arthur F. Glasser, Editor
MISSIOLOGY, An International Review
and Dean, School of World Mission
Fuller Theological Seminary
Pasadena, California

February 19, 1980

Introduction

This volume brings together articles on missiological themes written during the period 1972-78. In introducing this collection I wish to comment briefly on what missiology is and how the work of the missiologist relates to the Christian mission. The term "missiology" (missio + ology) refers to the science/knowledge of mission. Contrary to the popular stereotype of missionaries as people in such a hurry to save the world that they have no time or interest in reflection, wherever missionaries have gone, since the earliest days of the Christian movement, they have had to face questions of such size and importance that they had no choice but to ponder many aspects of their work.

The term "science of missions" first began to be used about 100 years ago, signaling a growing awareness that the missionary task deserved, indeed demanded, that it be undergirded by systematic study. One of the earliest advocates of specialized missionary studies was also the man elected to occupy the premier professorship of missions in Edinburgh in 1867. Alexander Duff (1806-1878), the famous Scottish missionary educator, wrote and spoke in favor of such an innovation for many years before the General Assembly of the Free Church of

Scotland acted. Duff's appeal to the General Assembly is interesting. He noted that during his four years as a theology student at St. Andrews he had never heard so much as an allusion to the task of world evangelization. Since Duff considered this to be the foremost purpose of the church in the world, he found this lack indefensible. Duff contended that *according to any just conception of the Church of Christ, the grand function it has to discharge in this world cannot be said to begin and end in the preservation of internal purity of doctrine, discipline and government. All this is merely for burnishing it so as to be a lamp to give light, not to itself only but also to the world* (William Paton, *Alexander Duff,* p. 186). Duff's plea for institutional recognition of the importance of the study of mission finally won approval and this example stimulated similar developments throughout the Western world.

In addition to winning a place for the study of missions in seminaries and universities, missionary leaders founded several journals during the latter half of the nineteenth century which provided a forum for missionaries and scholars to present their findings to a wider public. Major world missionary conferences—Liverpool, 1860; London, 1888; New York, 1900; Edinburgh, 1910; plus conferences in India and China—gave impetus to research, writing, teaching, and training.

The task of missiology divides into four parts: (1) study of the biblical-theological foundation of mission; (2) history of the encounter of the Christian gospel with the world; (3) reflection on the present-day encounter; and (4) discernment of emerging directions in world mission in the light of the first three areas of study. The horizons of each of these areas constantly expand and no one can conclude that missiology is a static field of study. In such a dynamic situation, the task of the missiologist is to aid the missionary in coming to terms with the context in which the witness is being given in such a way that the message might be received with the greatest possible clarity.

We have recently passed through a period of intense criticism of the missionary movement—as well as the church. Criticism turns destructive when it begins to obscure the original point of concern. That past generations of missionaries made mistakes should come as news to no one. Yet the force of recent criticism has created the impression of wholesale mistakes due to willful arrogance. The upshot of such a misreading of the record has been that some people have concluded that any movement which leads to such a bad performance is itself wrong. We urge that this question be considered from another point of view.

These essays proceed on the assumption that the missionary task is incumbent on the church of Jesus Christ at all times and in all places. At the same time we need to come to terms with the record of past missionary action, explore and clarify its biblical and theological foundations, and study seriously the world in which we now live and will live within the next few years. What are the "redemptive analogies" whereby the gospel of Jesus Christ can penetrate post-industrial society? How do missioners maintain credibility when they hail from the rich northern tier but are attempting to share a message of love and forgiveness with people who feel themselves to be the victims of those missioners' homeland? One can go on posing the questions which any honest apostle must confront.

We share these essays with you, praying that these fragments of reflection and search might contribute to the quest for a more obedient missionary response by the people of God in the remaining two decades of this century.

Wilbert R. Shenk
February 13, 1980

Part I
Biblical and Theological

Biblical Perspectives for Mission

1

Willard M. Swartley

During visits in 1975 to numerous cities of first-century Christianity, I frequently asked myself: By what power and vision did the Apostle Paul dare to preach to the famed Athenian philosophers, to confront Ephesian and Corinthian civil religion, and to challenge imperial Rome's political sovereignty? Who was this Paul anyway who headed for the cultural, commercial, and political urban centers and dared to defy the sacred cows of the Roman empire, whose emperor himself claimed to be "the august son of the august god." Did the sending churches back home at Jerusalem and Antioch know what a powerful "guerilla-bomb" their missionary Paul really was?

Reflection upon these questions prompted insights into several areas of thought crucial to the Christian's missionary task, Apostle Paul's and ours.

The Pattern for Growth: Jerusalem to Rome

The Book of Acts tells the phenomenal story of how Christianity, beginning in Jerusalem as a localized religion with few adherents, grew into a worldwide movement claiming disciples throughout Palestine, Asia Minor, Greece, and Rome. The structure of Luke's story accents the remarkable growth of this messianic movement. As Bruce Metzger suggests, the Book of Acts consists of six periods of church expansion, each period concluding with a summary-statement of church growth (1965:172):

Period I: 1:1-6:7. The gospel spreads throughout Jerusalem. Summary: "And the word of God increased; and the number of disciples multiplied greatly in Jerusalem, and a great many of the priests were obedient to the faith" (6:7).

Period II: 6:8-9:31. The church is extended throughout Palestine, including Samaria. Summary: "So the church throughout all Judea and Galilee and Samaria had peace and was built up; and walking in the fear of the Lord and in the comfort of the Holy Spirit it was multiplied" (9:31).

Period III: 9:32-12:24. The gospel moves beyond Jewish boundaries. Cornelius becomes a believer and the church begins in Antioch. Summary: "But (despite persecution) the word of God grew and multiplied" (12:24).

Period IV: 12:25-16:5. Cyprus and Asia Minor receive the gospel and new churches are founded. Summary: "So the churches were strengthened in the faith, and they increased in numbers daily" (16:5).

Period V: 16:6-19:20. Through Paul's second and third journeys the gospel is carried into Europe with churches established in Philippi, Athens, Corinth, and Ephesus. Summary: "So the word of the Lord grew and prevailed mightily" (19:20).

Period VI: 19:21-28:31. Paul's missionary labors culminate in Rome through his arrest and appeal to

Caesar. Summary: "And he lived there two whole years at his own expense, and welcomed all who came to him, preaching the kingdom of God and teaching about the Lord Christ quite openly and unhindered" (28:30-31).

Who Enters the Kingdom?

Underlying this pattern of phenomenal church expansion is the important theological issue of first-century Christianity: Who gets the kingdom of God? The "kingdom of God" functions as a key term in Acts. During the forty days between the resurrection and the ascension, Jesus, when he appeared to the disciples, spoke concerning the kingdom of God (1:3). Hence the disciples' question in 1:6: "Will you at this time restore the kingdom of Israel?" Tucking away the question of time into the Father's sovereign purpose, Jesus answered: After receiving Holy Spirit power you will be my witnesses (1) in Jerusalem (1:1-8:3), (2) in all Judea and Samaria (8:4-12:25), and (3) unto the ends of the earth (13:1-28:31).

Not until the gospel arrived in Samaria does the key term, "kingdom of God" occur again. Then **in Samaria,** Philip is preaching "the good news of the kingdom of God" (8:12). The term does not occur again until Paul takes the gospel to **the Gentile world** (13:1ff). Then the phrase occurs three times! At the end of his first missionary journey, blessed by Gentile believers, Paul warns "that through many tribulations we must enter the kingdom of God" (14:22). In his Ephesian ministry, Paul spent three months "pleading about the kingdom of God" (19:8). And in his farewell speech to the Ephesian elders gathered at Miletus, Paul describes his missionary labors thus: "I have gone about preaching the kingdom" (20:25).

When the book reaches its climax, so also does the author's use of the term "kingdom of God." After arriving at Rome, the capital of the empire, we are told that Paul is "testifying to the kingdom of God" (28:23). Four citations gifted for a new task. Further, it appears that this group of leaders functioned as the representative body in commissioning this team for missionary work.

At the end of the first journey (14:26), the missionary team returned to Antioch. They called the church together to hear their report on God's work among the Gentiles (14:27).

Again, the sending church was vitally involved in the missionary enterprise even though this sending church may have thought of itself as a new congregation formed by missionary assistance from Jerusalem. The missionaries also recognized the role of both Antioch and Jerusalem.

Later in Paul's ministry, Ephesus became the headquarters of his labors. For three months Paul taught in the synagogue, pleading about the kingdom of God. When opposition arose, he found a new center, the hall of Tyrannus, in which he continued teaching for two years. From this ministry, the gospel spread throughout all Asia (19:10). In his farewell speech to the Ephesian elders, Paul indicates that his ministry in Ephesus lasted for three years (20:31). His letters to Corinth (and possibly the Galatian epistle) were written during his stay at Ephesus.

While Ephesus is nowhere designated as the sending church for Paul's missionary team, it is clear that it became an on-the-field center for the missionary movement in Asia Minor and Europe. Seven Asia Minor churches are mentioned in Revelation 2-3 with Ephesus listed first. This may suggest that Ephesus functioned as a recognized originating center for the gospel's spread.

In all of these cases—Jerusalem, Antioch, and Ephesus—the role of any given Christian center was not static. Although the specific role of each congregation was determined by the dynamic of the missionary movement itself, each congregation was involved in the missionary cause in a continuing role. So it must be for congregations today if they are Spirit-led, gift-discerning, mission-oriented congregations.

The Power for Growth

The Book of Acts indicates that Christianity's growth from Jerusalem to Rome came through the power of the Holy Spirit. Acts 1:8 says: The spread of the Christian witness will happen after you receive the power of the Holy Spirit. Pentecost heads the story of the Christian mission (Acts 2).

The missionary significance of Pentecost is threefold: the release of new power, the perception that Jesus is both Lord and Christ, and the formation of a new community which through the miracle of tongues overcame historical linguistic boundaries. Throughout the Book of Acts we are reminded of fresh outbursts of the Spirit's power, usually by the term, "filled with the Holy Spirit" (Acts 2:4; 4:8, 31; 6:5; 7:55; 9:17; 13:9, 52).

In the Book of Acts this spiritual power was not a nebulous good feeling. It was integral to the messianic scandal, the bold conviction that a specific man, Jesus of Nazareth, is both Jewish Messiah and universal Lord (Acts 2:36). The goal of the missionary, therefore, is to call for belief in this messianic scandal, an offense to both Jews and Greeks (1 Cor 1:22-24) and then expect the formation of a believing community.

Standing in the ruins of ancient Corinth or sitting upon the rocks of the Areopagus (Mars Hill) under the shadow of the Acropolis, one of humanity's greatest cultural achievements, one feels overwhelmed by the boldness and courage of the Apostle Paul. Paul proclaimed a gospel not of noble ideas or social betterment but a gospel of a new political reality. Jesus is Messiah and Lord of all; he calls all people into full allegiance to his Lordship. Jesus is Lord because God raised him from the dead. The resurrection of Jesus, therefore, is the foundation for all missionary motivation and vision. Paul's speech to the Athenian philosophers makes this point unmistakably clear: Paul was of Old Testament Scripture then follow, all stressing that God's sovereign purpose has been accomplished in the Gentiles' acceptance of the gospel. The concluding verse notes that Paul spent two years in Rome, "preaching the kingdom of God" (28:31).

Quite clearly and precisely, the missionary vision of Acts is that the kingdom of God must no longer be considered Israel's private possession. It is a liberating power calling all people—Jews, Samaritans, and Gentiles—into a common fellowship under Christ's Lordship. The Christian church, originating in Jerusalem, must grow until it is found throughout the empire and especially in Rome. Paul himself must contribute to the gospel's growth in the capital city. For Paul, Rome symbolized the center of world power and culture. Not until the gospel reached the capital was his mission complete, his task fulfilled.

The Role of the Sending Church

In reflecting upon this rapid spread of first-century Christianity, one does well to ask: What was the role of the sending church in this missionary enterprise? Which was the sending congregation: Jerusalem, Antioch, or Ephesus? Each center plays a significant role in the missionary task.

Five considerations show how Jerusalem took initiative in the missionary enterprise. (1) On the occasion when the gospel first moved beyond Jewish geography into Samaria, Peter and John went from Jerusalem to Samaria to extend the Pentecost-community of faith to the new believers (8:14-15). (2) Upon hearing of the birth of the church in Antioch, the Jerusalem church sent Barnabas to Antioch to affirm the Lord's salvific work and thus firmly link Antioch to Jerusalem as common centers of God's peoplehood (11:12-24). Barnabas also sent to Tarsus to get Paul to assist the continuing missionary work in Antioch

(11:25-26). (3) In the description of the first Pauline missionary journey, two textual notes indicate the importance of Jerusalem in the team's missionary origin: (a) Barnabas, Jerusalem's missionary to Antioch, is mentioned first in the selected pair, Barnabas and Saul (13:2). (b) John [Mark], also from Jerusalem, goes with them as their *huperetes* (the Greek word in 13:5), which means an officially appointed "minister of the word" (compare Luke 1:2). John Mark's presence on the missionary team was Jerusalem's guarantee that the gospel would be faithfully transmitted and proclaimed.[1] (4) The Pauline mission among the Gentiles was accountable for its ecclesiastical authority to the church in Jerusalem (Acts 15). (5) Paul's determination to take the relief gift to Jerusalem (Rom 15:16, 24-33; Acts 21:7-15) symbolized both his commitment to the unity of the church and his awareness that Gentile Christianity stood indebted to Jewish Christianity. For these convictions he was willing to live and die.

From beginning to end in Acts, Jerusalem played a key role in the missionary enterprise. This mutual responsibility, both in financial resources and discernment of the practical meaning of the gospel for church life, should be instructive to us today.

Antioch also played a crucial role in the Pauline missionary enterprise, developing into a leading center for Gentile Christianity (11:20ff). The church at Antioch, equipped with prophets and teachers (13:1), became the commissioning body of the first missionaries. The text indicates that the Holy Spirit initiated the missionary movement (13:2). The perception that Barnabas and Saul should be set apart for the missionary task apparently came not to the whole church but to the prophets and teachers as they were worshipping and fasting. It may well be that these leaders sensed an oversupply of prophets and teachers and discerned which ones among them were best preaching "Jesus and the resurrection" (17:18) and, according to the final words of the sermon, God "has given assurance to all men by raising [Jesus] from the dead" (17:31b). Verse 32 then says that some mocked when they heard about the resurrection of the dead.

This reality of the risen Christ, infused by the dynamic of the Holy Spirit and the vision of a new universal peoplehood, supplied the power of the missionary movement. Neither mocking nor persecution could halt it. Beyond Paul and his colleagues was the Lord himself—the Lord of a new people, the Lord over the emperor, and the Lord of the gospel the missionaries preached.

Courage to Confront and Conquer

Only by coming to terms with the unique power behind Paul's work can one begin to comprehend how Paul confronted the three major pagan bulwarks of Roman society (and ours).

Confronting human achievements

In Athens Paul confronted the proud achievements of human intellect. Close to where Paul stood to address some Stoic and Epicurean philosophers towered the famed Parthenon, a showcase of architectual excellence. To its left were the well proportioned Propylaea, the small graceful temple of Wingless Victory, and the Erechtheum with its exquisite beauty. In the midst of these monuments to Athens' cultural grandeur stood the large statue of Athena, the goddess of beauty and perfection. Further, these philosophers could boast of Plato, Socrates, and Aristotle. To entertain themselves, they listened to what this new babbler, Paul, had to say.

Hats off to Paul! He took the opportunity. While recognizing the validity of some philosophical insights, Paul nonetheless stood firm, both in denouncing Athenian idolatry and in affirming that history—past, present, and future—hinges upon an appointed person whom God raised from the dead.

It is customary to say that Paul's effort failed, implying that we should now know better than to confront philosophers with the gospel. Yet the text reminds us that some believed—Dionysius the Areopagite and a woman named Damaris, among others. The fourth-century Christian historian, Eusebius, tells us that this Dionysius became the first bishop of the church at Athens. This indicated that Paul's effort met with greater success than is usually acknowledged. And likewise, it indicates that Paul's encounter with philosophy should urge us to speak the gospel courageously to today's esteemed philosophers, artists, and scientists. If this point is taken seriously, it will mean that our church's educational enterprise will also be part of our church's missionary commitment.

Confronting civil religion

In Ephesus and Corinth Paul sabotaged first-century civil religion. Early in the first century, a trend began which developed into an open clash between the Roman government and Christianity. After his death in A.D. 14, Augustus Caesar was acclaimed as son of the deity. Within several decades the emperors were regarded as gods worthy of worship throughout the empire.

In order to facilitate this new emperor cult, many temples were built in major cities from Rome to Baalbek. Both Ephesus and Corinth were among these centers selected to promote the new imperial cult. But this emperor worship did not replace the earlier cults oriented to the fertility cycles of life, both human and agricultural. The older worship of Ashtarte, Aphrodite, and Venus continued. Cultic prostitution was commonplace.

With this joining of emperor and fertility worship, a powerful civil religion emerged, functioning as the economic infrastructure of the economy of the Roman cities. This combination of sex, politics, and religion was a winner for human desire.

Into the midst of this political playboy paganism Paul came with the gospel of the risen Lord Jesus Christ. So effective was the gospel against this civil religion that a riot broke out in Ephesus (Acts 19:23-41). Demetrius' protest indicates that Paul's Ephesian ministry, two to three years long, had created an economic paralysis. Fewer and fewer people were buying the pagan cultic products. In Demetrius' words, *This Paul has persuaded and turned away a considerable company of people, saying that gods made with hands are not gods. And there is danger not only that this trade of ours may come into disrepute but also that the temple of the great goddess Artemis may count for nothing, and she may even be deposed from her magnificence, she whom all Asia and the world worship* (19:26b-27).

In Corinth also, Christianity apparently had effect upon the local economy, at least upon the city treasurer, Erastus. Acts 19:22 reports that Paul sent Erastus into Macedonia to visit young churches. In Romans 16:23 Erastus is mentioned as the city treasurer, presumably of Corinth, since Paul wrote Romans while at Corinth. At the site of ancient Corinth is an inscription on the pavement in front of the first-century theatre which reads: "Erastus, the treasurer of the city, personally paid for laying this pavement." It appears that the Erastus of Romans 16:23 is the same Erastus mentioned in this inscription. Since the event of Acts 19:22 is several years later, it is quite likely that this Erastus quit his job as city treasurer, involving complicity with Corinth's civil religion, and took up the new task of assisting Paul in his missionary work.

From these two incidents we can observe two models of Christian confrontation of civil religion: (1) in Corinth, by calling a given person out of the system, and (2) in Ephesus, by changing the religious allegiance of a sufficient number of persons so that economic crisis and paralysis resulted.

Challenging Rome's political supremacy

In Thessalonica and Rome Paul challenged the political supremacy of Rome. According to Acts Paul went to Rome as a prisoner to appeal his case to Caesar, but we are not told what happened to that appeal. Eusebius, quoting Tertullian, tells us, however, that both Paul and Peter were beheaded and crucified under Nero.

Paul's earlier troubles in Thessalonica forecast this imminent clash between Christianity and Rome. In Thessalonica the Jews accused Christians of inciting the people against the empire, "acting against the decrees of Caesar, saying that there is another king, Jesus" (Acts 17:7; cf. Lk 23:2). To preach as Paul did—that Jesus is Lord—was a political put-down for Rome, for if Jesus is Lord, then Caesar is not Lord. No one can serve two masters.

Within the next several decades many Christians were killed because they refused loyalty to Caesar. Christianity became a subversive irritant to Rome's political arrogance. Polycarp's martyrdom, dating from 155 A.D., clearly indicates that the issue was a political one of whether Jesus was Lord or whether Caesar was Lord. This missionary movement from Paul to Polycarp shows that the gospel threatens any nation that demands unconditional allegiance from its subjects or citizens.

Conclusions

1. The pattern for missionary work and church growth is to begin at home and push outward and onward until all people have opportunity to become members of the kingdom of God.

2. There must be sending congregations who identify gifts and missionary candidates and who maintain relationships with missionaries sent out. This supporting

role in the missionary enterprise must be adapted to the changing needs of the missionary movement.

3. The power for church growth comes from the Holy Spirit who enables faithful missionary witness. The gospel centers on the risen Lord and inspires the vision of a believing community composed of persons from all nations and walks of life.

4. The New Testament missionary gospel will challenge and dethrone idolatrous claims upon human lives, whether these claims come from intellectual philosophy, appealing civil religion, or arrogant political powers.

[1]John Mark's return to Jerusalem (13:13) and Paul's later chagrin (15:39) are quite understandable when one regards John Mark as a "bridge" between Peter and Paul. In this writer's judgment, John Mark functioned as a vital link between Jewish Christianity and Gentile Christianity; he thus appropriately wrote the first Gospel to assist the Gentile missionary program. This view is developed in chapters 1 and 11 of my book, *Mark: The Way For All Nations* (Herald Press, 1979).

Reference Cited

Metzger, Bruce
  1965 *The New Testament: Its Background, Growth, and Content* Nashville: Abingdon

Jesus at Nazareth: Jubilee and the Missionary Message

2

Don Blosser

In Luke's gospel, the public ministry of Jesus opens with an appearance in the synagogue at Nazareth (4:16-30). It is significant that Luke should select this event, for it does not in fact "begin" the ministry of Jesus. He had been preaching in the synagogues of Galilee and had already developed a rather substantial reputation (4:14-15). This Nazareth incident must have had special importance for Luke to have used it in this way, because Luke wrote with a specific purpose in mind, and he selected his materials carefully (1:1-4). This event is given programmatic significance, laying the foundation for the rest of the gospel story.

This account is not without its problems. Some of the language and the sentence structure do not match Luke's normal fluent Greek. Several rather specific, yet diverse themes seem to be thrown together, leading some to believe that Luke created the story from a variety of different synagogue appearances in order to make a particular theological point. As scholars identified these themes,[1] only rarely did anyone ask, "What is the unifying element which holds this story together?" It was assumed that there was no such element, thus it must be a Lukan fabrication.

This study—which assumes that the event actually did happen—seeks, first, to show that there is a unifying element to the story, and second, to see what insights this theme provides for our understanding of the missionary message.

The Year of Jubilee
When Jesus came to Nazareth, He was invited to read the prophet lesson in the synagogue service. The text which He read (Is 61:1-2) provides the initial key for understanding the event. The references to "good news to the poor; release to the captives; liberty to the oppressed; the acceptable year of the Lord" all have unmistakable connections with the jubilee. Thus, Isaiah 61 directs us further back in Israelite history to Leviticus 25.

At that time Israel was standing at a crucial point in its history. Basically a nomadic, wandering people, they had just been freed from slavery and were now approaching the promised land, where they were to begin a new way of life in agriculture. This new way of life required new laws. Included in these laws were regulations for sabbath year (seventh year) and jubilee year (forty-ninth year) observance. The basic elements provided that:

1. Every sabbath year the land was to lie fallow (Lev 25:1-7; Ex 23:10-11).

2. In this sabbath year all persons who had been sold into slavery (normally due to debts) were to be set free (Ex 21:2; Deut 15:12 & 18).

3. All debts among Israelites were to be canceled (Deut 15:1-11).

4. The seventh sabbath year was designated as a year of jubilee. All the usual sabbath regulations were observed and all land was restored to the original owners (Lev 25:8ff).

There are few references to the jubilee in the Old Testament (Num 36; Ruth 3-4; Jer 34; etc.), indicating that observance was sporadic at best. During the Babylonian captivity there was a temporary resurgence of religious interest. Priests revised many of the laws in hope that when Israel returned home, these revised laws would have a better chance of acceptance. Among the jubilee laws those controlling the release of slaves were most affected. Emancipation was moved from the seventh year to the jubilee year.[2] But only the regulations affecting the fallow fields and the debt release were observed with any consistency, and it was not long until complicated "legal" ways were devised for circumventing even these laws. In the process of rabbinic discussions, the jubilee gradually moved from literal obedience into the realm of speculative theology—a symbol of that special time when God would redeem Israel. So Israel settled back, waiting for God to act on their behalf by bringing the jubilee to them.

During the intertestamental period, the Jews were dominated by foreign powers. Attempts at self-liberation involved huge loss of life and widespread suffering, but brought only temporary freedom. Israelites were certain that God's Spirit had departed from them, and they longed for the day when a true prophet of God would once again be in their midst (1 Macc 4:46; 9:27; 14:41; etc.). In their despair their hope that God would soon redeem them began to fade, and jubilee became even more firmly enveloped in future, spiritual meanings that had little contact with their present situation.

Jesus Announces Jubilee

Thus the stage was set for Jesus to appear in His hometown synagogue, publicly claiming to be God's anointed spokesman and announcing that the jubilee had come. The evidence supporting the jubilean content of His opening proclamation is summarized as follows.

1. At the jubilee everyone was to return to his family (Lev 25:10, 13). Matthew (13:54), Mark (6:1), and Luke

(4:16) each report this return to Nazareth as part of Jesus' ministry. Luke strengthens the connection to jubilee by describing Nazareth as the place "where he had been brought up," thus explaining why Jesus came to Nazareth for this occasion rather than going to Bethelehem.

2. The jubilee year began on the Day of Atonement (Lev 25:9). There was in Jesus' day a set cycle of Torah texts (Old Testament law) to be read in the synagogue. These were followed by a Haphtarah (prophet) reading which supported the Torah. The specific Haphtarah texts were only suggested, and within certain guidelines the reader was free to make his own selection. Jesus was given the scroll of the prophet Isaiah (Lk 4:17). Isaiah 61:10-11 was the suggested Haphtarah for the final Consolation sabbath which came just before the Day of Atonement. When Jesus was given the scroll of Isaiah, already opened to this text, He used the freedom of selection allowed Him and chose to read instead from Isaiah 61:1-2—also a very appropriate Consolation sabbath text. From this Consolation text we conclude that Jesus must have appeared in Nazareth just prior to the Day of Atonement, in order to make His jubilee announcement in accordance with the Leviticus requirements.

3. Working from references within Luke (1:5; 2:2; 3:1), from datable events provided by first-century historian Josephus, and from Roman records, we can determine that the year was most likely AD 26. This becomes especially interesting when, working from Josephus and Jewish intertestamental literature, one discovers that AD 26 was the beginning of a sabbath year.

4. Since the jubilee was never observed with regularity, most scholars stop here, saying it is impossible to determine whether or not AD 26/27 (the Jewish year overlaps the Christian year) was in fact a jubilee year. But Dr. August Strobel, a German professor of New Testament, does not quit so easily. He argues on the basis

of calculations going back to Ezra, that if the jubilee had been observed regularly, AD 26/27 would in fact have been the seventh sabbath year.[3]

5. We have already referred to the jubilean character of Isaiah 61, but additional comment is warranted. The text is actually a combination of Isaiah 61:1-2 and 58:6. The mixing of these texts gives strong indication that such "jubilee texts" were commonly used by Jesus and were identified with His ministry. Isaiah 29:18-19; 35:5, 6, 10; 42:6-9; 49:8-13 are also possible "jubilee texts."Luke, quoting the Septuagint from memory, unintentionally inserts 58:6 into 61:1-2 because each text had been used frequently by Jesus, and there is substantial similarity.

Thus the timing, the location, and the Old Testament Scripture all point to the jubilean content of the announcement. But will this theme serve to unite the various elements of the story?

After reading the Scripture, Jesus announced that it had been fulfilled (4:21). He declared that the "acceptable year of the Lord" is NOW. In doing this He brought the jubilee out of the vague, spiritual, other-worldly realm of the future where first-century Judaism had lodged it; He made it something to be observed in their own immediate social and economic circles.

The people responded with a call for proof. The "physician, heal thyself" (4:23) statement shows that they recognized the jubilean content of the sermon.[4] Speaking out of their own understanding of jubilee, they wanted evidence of its presence. "If this is the jubilee, prove it by showing us some of the blessings that are to come with it; then we'll believe you." As is so often the case in man's relationship with God, they passed over their responsibilities of obedience, going directly to the blessing which God had promised them—if they were obedient.

Jesus responded immediately to this faulty understanding of jubilee (4:24) by firmly refusing their demand. "No

prophet is acceptable. . ." is His way of telling them,
"I'm not going to work miracles just to make you accept
what I say, because jubilee is not a miraculous act of
God." He was returning the jubilee back to its original
Mosaic terms. He was telling the synagogue worshipers
that jubilee is not something God does for them while they
just sit there. It was to be their response to God's
continuing grace by correcting the injustices which had
developed among them.

Finally, Jesus also redefined who is to be included in the
jubilee celebration (4:25-27). From their own history He
showed how God has never limited Himself to only the
Jews. In fact, He has on occasion withheld His blessing
from them and given it instead to the Gentiles. Jesus was
rejecting the "God will bless us because we are children of
Abraham" argument, defining the children of God in
terms of living faithful obedience, not parental heritage.

This was more than the Nazareth Jews could take
(4:28-30). This was not the familiar reassurance of their
standing before God which they had hoped to hear from
their popular favorite son. To be told that God does not
automatically favor them and that they must share
salvation with the Gentiles was too much. Forced to
choose between Jesus and their own secure interpretation
of the Scriptures, they chose to stay with their own past.
Jesus, with His radical new ideas—which were, in fact,
merely a fresh statement of the Mosaic law—was rejected
and expelled from their synagogue.

This jubilee theme occurs over and over again in Luke's
gospel. Several representative texts will be identified
simply to illustrate its presence.[5]

*Luke 6:20-25. The woes and blessings identify the
changes which occur at the jubilee.

*Luke 7:18-23. When asked by John to restate the
evidence for His Messiahship, Jesus answers with jubilee
language.

*Luke 22:31. Anxiety about the necessities of life is answered in terms closely paralleling Leviticus 25:20-21.

*Luke 19:1-10. Salvation comes to Zaccheus as he makes restitution.

Implication of the Jubilee for the Missionary Message

Jesus' use of the jubilee theme should not be seen as an end in itself. Rather, it is a paradigm, presenting the fundamental concern of God for wholeness, peace, and justice among His people. The jubilee message is revolutionary in nature, but it is a revolution brought about not by force or by seizing political power. It is brought about simply by putting it into practice. The heart of the gospel message is the invitation to participate with God's people—and thus with God—in this new kingdom which Jesus described in the jubilean terminology of forgiveness, justice, peace, and wholeness.

Several observations are offered here in an introductory way. Each is deserving of more attention than it is given here.

1. One is impressed with the similarities of religious belief between the time of Jesus and our own day. Faith has been spiritualized and given a primarily futuristic significance, detached from the ethics of everyday life much as it was in Jesus' day. But Jesus gave the gospel a specific, identifiable expression in daily life. He proclaimed a message of obedience which was radically different from the popular beliefs of the day which promised that sometime in the future God will save us out of this mess.

Much of traditional Christianity finds itself sitting in the Nazareth synagogue, expecting the affirmation of God's love upon them, and then objecting vehemently to the words of Jesus which make obedience the heart of the faith response. To separate such direct jubilee themes as money, labor relations, use of natural resources, use of industrial capital, treatment of the poor, etc., from the gospel—even to claim that they belong to an important "phase two" of gospel proclamation—is a severe distortion of the Jesus message.

2. When Jesus announced that the kingdom is here (4:21), He was announcing the activity of God in and through His own ministry as God's servant. From that perspective, there is nothing we can do to bring in the kingdom, for God in Jesus has already brought it in. It is for us to decide whether or not we will live in it and to invite others to live in it with us. The parallel with Leviticus 25 is fascinating. The reason for observing the jubilee is given several times: "I am the Lord your God, and I brought you out of Egypt" (vv 38, 42, 55). First century Judaism had the belief that if all Israel would keep the law perfectly for just one day, that would bring the kingdom of God. But Jesus allows no possibility for any thought of self-salvation through personal achievement. The salvation of God, as was the jubilee, is firmly rooted in God's saving grace. To argue that ethics do not belong as part of the gospel proclamation (or the faith response) indicates that one has not comprehended the full meaning of the presence of the kingdom which Jesus announced in Luke 4:21.

3. The jubilee theme is saturated with forgiveness. But the forgiveness is specific: slaves are set free, debts are canceled, property is restored. The presence of this strong forgiveness element in the jubilee theme challenges the common assumption of Christianity that forgiveness is rooted solely in the cross. Luke anchors forgiveness in the nature of God and His work, as revealed in the total life and ministry of Jesus, of which the cross/resurrection is the culmination. This holistic approach to the Jesus-event is important for Luke in His telling of the gospel story. Luke presents an integration of the complete Jesus ministry that is sadly lacking in most Christian theology.

The reason the Jews wanted to get rid of Jesus—and it begins with this very first episode at Nazareth—is because of the things He taught and did (4:28-30; 6:6-11; 11:54; 19:47; 22:2; 23:2, 5). The events of the ministry of Jesus provide the reason for His death, and His death and resurrection give authority to His ministry. Already in this first recorded public appearance, the present availability of God's grace is forcefully declared and jubilee living is given as the proper response to grace. God's grace is not tied exclusively to the cross of Jesus. The good news which Jesus proclaimed is not primarily the cross, but the present reality of the kingdom of God. Jesus proclaimed forgiveness and salvation as a live option in response to his announcement of the presence of the kingdom. The possibility of salvation—participation in the kingdom— was a reality before Jesus died. His word to Zaccheus says it succinctly, "Today, salvation has come to this house" (Lk 19:9). Using one of Isaiah's "jubilee texts," Paul in 2 Corinthians 6:2 also emphasizes "today."

Therefore, to load all our "salvation theology" on the cross does not give proper significance to the revelation of God in the ministry of Jesus. Luke, from the very beginning, builds a holistic theology which says that the death and resurrection of Jesus do not **by themselves** constitute all there is to God's saving event in Jesus. He sees the entire presence of Jesus (public ministry, death, resurrection, and ascension) as a unified confrontation of the saving God with the human race. Jesus does not reject the validity of God's past redemptive activity. Instead, He affirms it and uses it as the foundation upon which to build the proclamation which He is making of God's present saving grace.

There are other themes present in this text which cannot be developed here:

1. The Christology of 4:18-21 has positive implications for Jewish and Christian dialogue.

2. The proclamation of jubilee to Jesus' home synagogue at Nazareth raises the question of the kind of gospel we preach in our established congregations. Do we interpret the missionary message differently at home so that it does not speak so directly to our own disobedience and idolatry?

3. The jubilee theme has sobering implications for much of Western Christianity, for we are the rich and powerful of the world. For us, is the jubilee proclamation good news—or bad news?

4. Jesus refused to perform miracles in order to gain a hearing, because in performing them He would have denied the very message He was proclaiming. Are we always clear about the methods we use in order to gain the opportunity to be heard? Do we sometimes identify too completely with those in control so that our security is not threatened?

The jubilee theme is exciting because it illuminates many of the things Jesus said. But it is also troubling because most of Western Christianity is wealthy and powerful, and we have become spiritually comfortable with that wealth. We have redirected the gospel message to accommodate our economic status. Perhaps the most striking implication of the jubilee message for Western Christianity is in its message to us: we who have for generations been the missionaries, taking the gospel to others, may now need to allow that function to be reversed, so that our brothers and sisters from Africa, Asia, South America, etc. can come to us with the Jesus-call to repentance, restitution, forgiveness, and participation in the kingdom which was announced at Nazareth.

Notes

1. Jesus and the Spirit, v 18; Jesus and the Old Testament prophets, vv 18-19; the announcement of the kingdom of God, v 21; faith as a basis for miracles, vv 22-24; mission to the Gentiles, vv 25-27; rejection by the Jews (symbolizing his death) vv 28-29; his ultimate victory, v 30. All these have been given as the reason Luke tells the story.

2. This extended the term of slavery from six years to a possible 48 years. Compare Ex 21:2-6 and Deut 15:12, 18 (the earlier form of the law) with Lev 25: 39-41, 55 (the later form).

3. I am presently corresponding with Dr. Strobel on various details of his work. He believes the jubilee is the fiftieth year, coming one year after the seventh sabbath (Lev 25:10), thus he concludes that AD 27/28 was the jubilee year. While identifying the jubilee year would be helpful, the validity of the theme itself does not depend upon proving the date.

4. This statement probably originated as a challenge given by a member of the congregation. By the time Luke received the material, it had been switched to Jesus and made part of the sermon.

5. John H. Yoder, *The Politics of Jesus,* pp. 64-77, provides the best concise summary of this material, but his list is not intended to be exhaustive.

Bibliography

Because few writers deal with the jubilee theme, preferring to develop one of the themes listed in footnote 1, it is difficult to suggest further reading. The following may be useful:

Eltester, Walther, et. al.: *Jesus in Nazareth*. Berlin: DeGruyter, 1972.
A collection of four studies—three in German—on this one event.
Erich Grasser, *Jesus in Nazareth;* August Strobel, *Die Ausrufung des Jobeljahres in der Nazareth-predigt Jesu;* Robert Tannehill, *The Mission of Jesus according to Lk 4:16-30;* Walther Eltester, *Israel im lukanischen Werk und die Nazareth-perikope.*

Kraybill, Don: *The Upside-Down Kingdom*. Herald Press, 1978. Good, popular approach to subject, built on solid foundation.

Trocmé, André: *Jesus and the Nonviolent Revolution*. Herald Press, 1973. Not as good as Yoder, but covers more territory.

Yoder, John Howard: *The Politics of Jesus*. Eerdmans, 1972. Basic foundation.

The Great Commission

3

Wilbert R. Shenk

In the popular mind Christian missionary activity arises from the Great Commission. This command represents Jesus' final words to His disciples—His last will and testament. Never mind where these words are found in Scripture. The missionary mandate is a straightforward order which the faithful carry out.

When one turns from the popular notion to scholarly theologies of mission, one finds that the Great Commission plays a minor—even insignificant—role. What accounts for this disparity? Has scholarship failed to serve the needs of the masses, in this case missionary enthusiasts, by doing its work in isolation from the rest of the church? Historically, however, middlemen have "brokered" between ivory tower and pew. Missions promoters and propagandists have popularized the slogans and concepts which have guided the missionary movement.

Two new books give occasion to reflect on the Great Commission and the way it has functioned both in the theology and the practice of mission. Max Warren, one of the most influential missionary leaders in this century, has written of his abiding commitment in *I Believe in the Great Commission*.[1] Richard R. De Ridder's exegetical study of Matthew 28:18-20 first appeared in 1971 in a limited edition as a doctoral thesis under the title *The Dispersion of the People of God*. It has now been issued and retitled by the American publisher as *Discipling the Nations*.[2] Warren's book is responsible popularization while De Ridder's is solid biblical scholarship.

The Great Commission has been used improperly in the interpretation and promotion of Christian mission in at least three ways.

The Great Commission has been misused when it has been seen as a proof-text. The Matthew 28:19a phrase, "Go ye therefore," or Mark 16:15, "Go ye into all the world and preach the gospel to every creature" (KJV), were the basic texts. The imperative voice appealed to an activist people. Popular support rallied around a vision of conquering unknown territory, of pioneering on distant frontiers. Western culture applauded the hero who overcame hardship to win. Such an approach fails because it neglects too much that is vital and basic. Warren insists that we cannot understand the Great Commission apart from Jesus Christ Himself in whom the Commission was first enacted.

Another mistaken approach treats the Great Commission as a separable part which can be acted on without reference to all that has gone before or that is to follow. De Ridder devotes more than half of his book to a survey of the Old Testament background and Jewish proselytism as preparation for understanding Jesus and His commission to the disciples. This historical-theological perspective is indispensable.

A third error is to read the text inaccurately. Missionary promoters traditionally stressed "Go ye" whereas the original text centers on "make disciples." The Great Commission, according to De Ridder, focuses the entire missionary action on winning people to be disciples of Jesus Christ. The Great Commission becomes the new covenant God makes with His people. It gives no license for geographical exploration or preoccupation with the exotic elements of strange peoples in faraway places. "Go" is subservient to "make."[3]

Warren begins his study by summarizing what the New Testament says about mission. Next he surveys the course of mission during nearly two millenia since Pentecost. He concludes with a section on the Great Commission in action today. This approach helps highlight the fundamental importance of the commission in structuring the church's entire existence.

Early in His ministry Jesus dispatched His disciples on missions. Although the Old Testament vision of mission anticipated that through Israel's obedience and example the nations would eventually be drawn to worship Yahweh, the Jewish people in exile started a missionary movement. Even while denouncing Jewish proselytism (Matt 23:15; cf. Rom 2:17-24), Jesus did not hesitate to send His disciples out as witnesses. He drew a distinction at the level of substance rather than form.

Each of the four Gospels plus Acts records a version of the Great Commission. In the Gospels it immediately follows the resurrection. The missionary mandate is integrally related to the resurrection for the missionary is to witness to the resurrection. The fact that the commission appears in each Gospel is already important, but there is more. Each Gospel emphasizes a different aspect of the Great Commission, thus enriching its meaning and enlarging the vision.[4]

The Gospel of Matthew opens with a genealogy which establishes Jesus within the Jewish royal line. John the Baptist prepares for Messiah's coming by calling the people to "repent for the kingdom of heaven is at hand." Jesus begins His ministry by announcing that the kingdom is near. Matthew maintains this emphasis on kingdom throughout. When Jesus gives His last command, it is based on the authority of the kingdom. Under this authority the disciples are mandated to go to all the peoples of the world inviting them to enter into covenant with the Messiah. Discipleship is validated only as we "make disciples of all nations." Those within the covenant are responsible to witness to those outside. As people accept the witness, they are to be baptized as a sign that they have also entered into the covenant (i.e., now live under God's rule) and are consecrated to live the life of discipleship. Teaching is the means of growth in discipleship.

Of all the Gospels, Mark depicts most vividly the struggle between the powers of love and evil. When Jesus sent the disciples out the first time, Mark reports that He "gave them authority over the unclean spirits" (cf. Matt 10:1 and Luke 9:1f which give more elaborate forms of the commission—including "authority over all demons"). The Markan Great Commission emphasizes the authority of liberation. The gospel of Jesus Christ represents to all people release from the bondage of sin and the demonic powers. To live under the reign of God is to live in freedom.

Luke's Gospel, with his eye for human interest, is focused on forgiveness and new relationships. The Lucan Great Commission is based on the authority of forgiveness. The story of the Prodigal Son (Luke 15) summarizes much that Luke has to say about the basis for this new community of faith. The Great Commission becomes the call to live in a community based on love and forgiveness.

The Gospel of John is unified by an emphasis on the unity of the Son with the Father. In John 17 Jesus indicates that because of the authority of continuity He was commissioning His disciples to go into the world in the same manner as He had been sent. Following the resurrection, Jesus appears to the disciples and informs them "As the Father has sent me, even so I send you"

(20:21b). Not only is there a direct link between resurrection and commission; but the disciples are called to travel the same way the Master has trod—the way of suffering and self-sacrifice. The Johannine Great Commission conjoins the highest possible authority with the ultimate service.

A fifth version of the Great Commission appears at the beginning of the Acts. In connection with the ascension, Jesus assures the disciples they will be specially empowered to carry out their commission. The authority of power characterizes the Acts 1:8 Great Commission.

Matthew most clearly describes the centrality of the kingdom of God. This is what the disciples witness to. The Matthean Great Commission is based on the authority of the kingdom. Mark depicts the decisive struggle between the power of love and evil powers. The Great Commission in Mark's Gospel emphasizes the authority of liberation. Luke's Gospel portrays new relationships, and the Great Commission highlights the authority of forgiveness. In John the unity of Father and Son and disciples is stressed and the Great Commission has the authority of continuity. Finally, the Acts form of the Great Commission underscores the authority of power. Kingdom, liberation, new relationships, continuity and power—each is a part of what we call the Great Commission. What does this mean for us today?

1. The Great Commission is God's blueprint for a new order, a new creation. It is not a travel permit for the adventurous. It is Christ's mandate to His church under which it is to witness to the power of the resurrection until the end of time to all peoples throughout the world. The Great Commission forms a permanent structure for the life of the church. If the church is faithful to the Great Commission, the disciples will be a people in dispersion, a pilgrim people.

2. The Great Commission is not to be carried out

legalistically.[6] The early church did not appeal to the authority of the Great Commission directly because they were living it out. The Holy Spirit energizes and empowers the people of God to be a missionary community.

3. The Great Commission extends the ministry and witness of Jesus Christ. Jesus' style and example are definitive for His disciples. He proclaimed that the reign (kingdom) of God had begun and demonstrated what it meant to live under that reign by rejecting all power except love. He confronted evil but suffered rather than retaliate with violence. The Great Commission can be carried out faithfully only by rejecting all attempts to ally the kingdom of God with a particular nation, race, class or economic-political power. In the confrontation between the kingdom of God and demonic powers, the disciples must take the way of suffering love and sacrifice. For that is the Master's way.

Notes

1. Wm. B. Eerdmans, 1976; Hodder and Stoughton, 1976.

2. J. H. Kok Co., 1971; Baker Book House (reprint), 1975.

3. Karl Barth failed to clarify this point in "An Exegetical Study of Matthew 28:16-20," in Gerald H. Anderson, *The Theology of Christian Mission,* McGraw-Hill, 1961, 63. Cf. De Ridder, *op. cit.,* 174, 180-96.

4. Johannes Blauw, *The Missionary Nature of the Church,* McGraw-Hill, 1962, 88, points out these contrasts in the Synoptic Gospels but does not develop them.

5. Cf. Jim Wallis, *Agenda for Biblical People,* Harper and Row, 1976, 23-29, for an exposition of the radical nature of the Great Commission and a critique of Evangelicalism's faulty and superficial understanding. Cf. John Driver, *Community and Commitment,* Herald Press, 1976, Chapter 6.

6. Roland Allen first drew attention to this point in his writings. Harry R. Boer subjected it to systematic examination in *Pentecost and Missions,* Eerdmans and Co., 1961.

Paul and Mission

4

John Driver

Paul's missionary methods are sometimes conceived of in terms of strategy, as if it were primarily a program for accomplishing the task. Obviously this is one way of focusing the question of method or strategy. This orientation, of course, has proved to be attractive, especially in the Western church. I believe that we cannot really understand Paul's missionary methodology when we approach it from this perspective. My thesis is that Paul's methods grew out of his understanding of the nature of the gospel. It is the nature of God's relationship to men; the form of His incarnation in Jesus of Nazareth; the meaning of His message of salvation to mankind which determine Paul's missionary methods as well as his own discipleship. Paul's methods and his understanding of the Gospel are mutually elucidating.

Therefore Paul's methodology does not respond to the accidents of history, nor is it optional in its character. They are not methods which can be added or dropped according to the time or place of mission. Since they communicate the nature of God and of His gospel given through Jesus, His Messiah, they become normative for Paul, and for anyone else who understands the gospel of Jesus as Paul did and would faithfully carry out God's mission in the world.

Far from being the most "efficient" ways of carrying out the Christian mission, Paul's methods will probably be judged inefficient by modern secular standards. But efficiency and success dare not be the criteria by which we determine missionary methods. What counts is their faithfulness to the nature of God's revelation in Jesus Christ.

Method

1. Paul understood his mission to be divinely ordained within the prophetic tradition of Israel and, as in the case of Jesus, specifically determined by the vision of the Servant of Yahweh.

Paul's understanding of mission can scarcely be grasped apart from his extraordinary commissioning on the Damascus road. Rather than conceiving of this experience primarily in terms of "conversion," we can better understand it as a call to mission. Or perhaps the experience could be called a "messianic conversion" which in turn shaped his understanding of mission. In reality Paul's Jewish cosmology, anthropology, theology, and even his morality to a certain extent, remained basically untouched by his Damascus road experience. However, his Christology was transformed beyond his wildest expectations, and this furnished the point of departure for his participation, in deed as well as word, in God's mission in the world. According to Paul's own testimony, his commission to the Gentiles arose directly out of this experience (Acts 9:15; 22:17-21; 26:17; Gal. 1:16; 2:7,8).

This extraordinarily strong sense of being divinely commissioned is further reflected in Paul's own writings. "But then in his good pleasure God, who had set me apart from birth and called me through his grace, chose to reveal his Son to me and through me, in order that I might proclaim him among the Gentiles" (Gal. 1:15,16a; cf. Gal. 2:7; Rom. 1:1; 15:15b,16; I Cor. 1:1, etc. NEB). In describing this divine commission in Galatians 1:15 (lit., "having separated me from the womb of my mother"), Paul used a direct allusion to the prophetic vocation of Jeremiah (1:5) and to the divine commission given to the Servant of Yahweh (Is. 49:1). Paul's call linked him to the prophetic tradition of Israel and charged him to continue the mission of God's Messiah in the world. Elsewhere in his writings Paul indicates that he understood himself to be divinely commissioned to continue Christ's saving mission to the ends of the earth. The statement of Paul and Barnabas in Antioch of Pisidia, "I have set you to be a light for the Gentiles, that you may bring salvation to the uttermost parts of the earth" (Acts 13:47) is a direct reference to the second of the Suffering Servant Songs (Is. 49:6). The assurance which Paul received from the Lord in his Corinthian vision, "Do not be afraid, but speak and do not be silent; for I am with you . . ." (Acts 18:9b,10a), is an allusion to Isaiah 41:10 and 43:5. In Paul's third report of his Damascus road vision, the words of Jesus, "I send you to open their eyes and turn them from darkness to light . . ." (Acts 26:18 NEB) are a direct allusion to Isaiah 42:7,16. In his appeal to his Corinthian readers to appropriate God's grace, he quotes from Isaiah 49:8, "In the day of my favor I gave heed to you; on the day of deliverance I came to your aid" (II Cor. 6:2).

Paul understood his task to be to continue the mission of

the Messiah who is a "light to the nations," spreading his salvation to the ends of the earth. In both Acts and the Epistles the Isaiah texts which apply directly to the Servant of Yahweh are applied to Paul. Paul's understanding of his mission is not characterized merely by his extraordinary sense of divine commissioning. He also understands himself to fall within the prophetic tradition of Israel. But what is even more noteworthy is the way in which he understands his mission to be a continuation of that of the Messiah. He is the Servant of Christ, empowered by Christ himself to carry out his mission which, in a sense, remains unfinished. Paul understands his mission to have been prefigured in the person of the Servant of Yahweh, predestined to be "a light to the nations" (Is. 42:6; 49:8). Paul, like Jesus, understood his mission in terms of suffering servanthood. In fact he explicitly refers to his suffering as a continuation of the Messiah's suffering: "In my flesh I complete what is lacking in Christ's affliction for the sake of his body, that is the church" (Col. 1:24).

2. Paul's call to mission can best be understood as a charismatic experience—in the N. T. sense of the term.

According to Paul's own testimony, his knowledge that Jesus of Nazareth is indeed the Messiah came to him by revelation. Paul's vision on the Damascus road initiated his ministry as an "apocalyptic" or "charismatic" prophet. Through a spiritual vision (lit., apocalypse), Jesus was revealed to him to be the Messiah (Gal. 1:12,16). And even beyond this initial spiritual or charismatic experience, apparently spiritual visions were not uncommon to Paul. (See Gal. 2:2; Eph. 3:1-6; I Cor. 2:4; 14:6,26; II Cor. 12:1,7, etc.). Acts reports that in Antioch he functioned as prophet and teacher, and according to I Cor. 12:8,10,28, Rom. 12:6,7, and Eph. 4:11 these are charismatic ministries. Of course, in the context of his discussion concerning the relative usefulness of prophecy and tongues, Paul reports that the gift of tongues has also been granted to him (I Cor. 14:18). According to Acts, Paul must also have received the gifts of the apostolate, of exorcism, of discernment of spirits and of healing. Under the influence of the power of God's Holy Spirit, Paul's earlier religious enthusiasm for the traditions of the Fathers gave way to the consuming passion of messianic mission.

Paul was not simply a charismatic missionary. He sought to reproduce the authentic experience of God's grace in his hearers. In his letter to the Christian community in Corinth, Paul expressed thanksgiving for "the grace of God" which had been given to them in Jesus Christ; and more specifically for the fact that in every way they had been enriched in Him. In fact, confirmation of the testimony to Christ in their midst is seen in the fact that they are "not lacking in any spiritual gift (charismata)" (I Cor. 1:4-7). To the Roman church, whose members he did not know personally, he wrote, "I long to see you, that I may impart to you some spiritual gift (Charisma Pneumatikon) to strengthen you" (Rom. 1:11). These *charismata* are, of course, the result of the activity of the Spirit of God in the midst of His people and are therefore a sign of the church's supernatural life. These gifts, Paul wrote, are to be ardently desired in the church (I Cor. 12:31; 14:1).

Paul appreciated fully the powerful intervention of the Holy Spirit in the fulfillment of his mission. To the Thessalonians he wrote, "For our gospel came to you not only in word, but also in power and in the Holy Spirit . . .

for you received the word with much affliction, with joy inspired by the Holy Spirit'' (I Thes. 1:5,6). He reminded the Galatians that it was the Spirit who worked signs and miracles among them, awakening a response of faith (Gal. 1:2,5). Paul recognized that churches were not founded by human rhetoric or persuasion, but rather by what Christ had wrought through him "by word and deed, by power of signs and wonders, and the power of the Holy Spirit" (Rom. 1:18,19). The charismatic character of the messianic mission which Paul carried out, produced charismatic communities in which spiritual gifts abounded for the common good and whose flowering contributed to the fulness of the body of Christ (Eph. 4:13).

3. Paul considered Jesus' life of obedience to the Father as paradigmatic for the believer's new life in Christ. And this becomes not only a part of his missionary message, but also a basic element of his missionary method. Called to be imitators of God, of Jesus Christ, and of the apostolic missioners, as well as themselves becoming examples to be imitated blend together in Paul's writings. Perhaps the clearest example of this blending is I Thes. 1:5-7. "You know what kind of men we proved to be among you for your sake. And you became imitators of us and of the Lord, for you received the word in much affliction, with joy inspired by the Holy Spirit; so that you became an example to all the believers in Macedonia and in Achaia."

Paul frequently indicated that, like Jesus, his life too provided a model to be imitated by those who received the gospel. "Be imitators of me, as I am of Christ" (I Cor. 11:1). Paul was not being arrogant. He was simply following Jesus and expected recipients of the gospel to do the same. Later we shall return to the question of the concrete ethical content of this imitation. But here it is sufficient to point out that Paul's missionary method (and of the N.T. in general) was fundamentally that of modeling the new life which had come in the Messiah. When we read the testimony of Paul from this perspective, the evidence becomes quite impressive.

Paul's farewell charge to the elders of the Ephesian community is prefaced by the statement, "You yourselves know how I lived among you all the time from the first day that I set foot in Asia" (Acts 20:18). Following this we find references to his humility, suffering, persecution, verbal testimony (vss. 19-21), warnings (vs. 31), and fraternal economic practices (vss. 33-35)—in contrast to the false leaders who are described as "fierce wolves" (vs. 29), probably a reference to their lifestyle. One is impressed by the fact that the missionary message was not so much a matter of unincarnated doctrine as it was the proclamation and demonstration of a new way of life and a system of values rooted in the Messiah.

In response to the arrogance manifested among certain elements in the Corinthian congregation Paul writes, "I have applied all this to myself and Apollos for your benefit, brethren, that you may learn by us to live according to the scripture, that none of you may be puffed up in favor of one against another. I urge you, then, be imitators of me. Therefore I sent to you Timothy, my beloved and faithful child in the Lord, to remind you of my ways in Christ, as I teach them everywhere in every church" (I Cor. 4:6,16,17). Apparently this insistence on giving attention to the concrete form in which Paul modeled the gospel was his universal practice (vs. 17).

Paul also suggests that being "co-imitators" of him is an alternative to living as "enemies of the cross of Christ." "Brethren, join in imitating me, and mark those who so live as you have an example in us. For many, of whom I have often told you and now tell you even with tears, live as enemies of the cross of Christ. Their end is destruction, their god is the belly, and they glory in their shame, with minds set on earthly things. But our commonwealth is in heaven, and from it we await a Savior, the Lord Jesus Christ'' (Phil. 3:17-20).

Communication of the gospel in propositional as well as exemplary forms blend together in Paul's missionary methodology. ''What you have learned and received and heard and seen in me, do; and the God of peace will be with you'' (Phil. 4:9; cf. I Thes. 2:9-12).

Apparently the recipients of the Pauline mission understood from the beginning the fact that Paul's observable activity in their midst was not neutral. His example, even in the seemingly ordinary affairs of life, carried gospel meaning. ''For you yourselves know how you ought to imitate us; we were not idle when we were with you, we did not eat any one's bread without paying, but with toil and labor we worked night and day, that we might not burden any of you. It was not because we have not that right, but to give you in our conduct an example to imitate'' (II Thes. 3:7-9; cf. Eph. 4:28).

These representative passages point to the fundamental role of Paul's example in his missionary methodology. (Cf. I Tim. 1:16; II Tim. 1:13; 3:10,14; etc.). Of course Paul also expected that other missionaries would use the same methodology (I Tim. 4:12,15; Tit. 2:7,8; cf. I Pet. 5:1-3; Heb. 13:7). Paul was not content merely to witness to Christ's life in general, but he demonstrated certain specific traits and characteristics of Jesus' life. We shall return to this theme when we consider aspects of Paul's missionary message.

4. Because of its far-reaching consequences, probably the most important element in Paul's missionary methodology was his vulnerability, or "weakness" (I Cor. 1:25,27; 2:3). His voluntary renunciation of coercive power in the fulfillment of his mission is evident at a number of points in Paul's life and thought. The fact that the rise of the modern missionary movement has largely paralleled movements of political and economic conquest has served to keep this basic aspect of Paul's stance hidden from our view. Western missions have continued to ride the crest of economic imperialism right up to our own times. Practically all of the sending is from the West and the North. Much has been made of Paul as an example of missionary fervor and strategy, but hardly anyone has noticed that while Paul moved from the oppressed colonies toward the centers of imperial power in his day, from Antioch and Jerusalem to Athens and Rome, the opposite has been the case in the modern missionary movement. Naturally, in this situation missionaries were not inclined to raise penetrating questions about what this difference in the direction of movement might mean for the missionary enterprise. Was being sent from Palestine to Rome any different than being sent from Rome to one of the oppressed colonies of the Empire? We have come to view the flow of missionaries from England to India and Africa, from Holland to Indonesia, from France and Belgium to Black Africa, from the U.S. to Latin America as normal. And then we have pretended to apply Paul's methods without noticing this fundamental difference. Small wonder that Paul's basic suffering servanthood stance has been overlooked. It has scarcely occurred to us to ask if a rich and powerful church can really communicate the gospel of Jesus Christ. Instead of

coming to grips with this problem, the churches and their missionaries have done an un-Pauline thing. They have made peace with the generally accepted dichotomy between the exercise of coercive power in its various forms, on one hand, and the gospel message they verbalize, on the other.

The revolutionary situation of the last decade has alerted many to the distance which separates the orientation of the modern missionary enterprise from the Pauline stance. But we still have a long way to go. I suspect that the distinction which Jim Wallis makes between "establishment Christianity" and "practitioners of biblical faith" can also be applied to missions. Even believers church missionaries have been seduced into roles determined by establishment power and influence.

Paul's Damascus road experience convinced him that Jesus of Nazareth was indeed God's Messiah in the world. This meant that suffering servanthood was to be God's strategy for mission among the peoples of the earth. It is therefore natural that Paul's missionary stance should be characterized by weakness, by suffering and by sacrifice.

a. I Corinthians 1:17-2:5 is a fundamental passage for grasping Paul's understanding of his stance as one of weakness. "And I was with you in weakness and in much fear and trembling; and my speech and my message were not in plausible words of wisdom, but in demonstration of the Spirit and power, that your faith might not rest in the wisdom of men but in the power of God" (2:3-5). The power of God is found in the cross of His Messiah (1:17). The suffering servant Messiah is the power and the wisdom of God (1:24), in contrast to the exercise of power and the intellectual arrogance of the Jews and the Greeks of the first century. It was Paul's understanding that in the incarnation God had, in reality, restored His value system which had been inverted by fallen mankind. This accounts for Paul's insistence on weakness, or vulnerability, as the fundamental stance of the messianic community. That is why Paul in effect calls his stance of weakness "triumph" (II Cor. 2:14). Furthermore, Paul refers to the crucifixion of Christ "in weakness" as the rationale for his own weakness (II Cor. 13:4).

I Corinthians 1:17-2:5 reminds us that this stance of vulnerability was no more acceptable in the first century than it is in the twentieth. For that reason Paul's—and the early church's—insistence on maintaining this stance is all the more remarkable.

I Corinthians 9:19-23, which is sometimes interpreted in terms of evangelistic strategy, is actually a remarkable illustration of Paul's vulnerable stance. Although Paul enjoyed the status of a free man, he voluntarily made himself a slave to all (19). Although Paul had been freed from the narrowness of nationalistic legalistic Judaism, he was willing to submit to legalistic Jewish requirements (20). Although Paul by birth belonged to the covenant community, he voluntarily became as a Gentile (lit., lawless) (21). Although Paul was of a strong conscience, he willingly accommodated himself to his brethren with weak consciences (22). "I have become all things to all men, that I might by all means save some" (22).

The course of action described in these verses is no mere strategy of missionary accommodation, nor a methodology of psychological identification. On the contrary, he did it "for the sake of the gospel that (he might) share in it" (9:23). He did these things because it is of the nature of the gospel to live this way. All of these steps are voluntary acts of subordination which partake of the nature of the gospel. Jesus himself had set the precedent for Paul: ". . . though he was rich, yet for your sake he became poor, so that by his poverty you might become rich" (II Cor. 8:9); He "who knew no sin [was made] to be sin . . . so that in him we might become the righteousness of God" (II Cor. 5:21); "Who, though he was in the form of God . . . emptied himself taking the form of a servant" (Phil. 2:6,7).

This is the only kind of social mobility which is consistent with the gospel of Jesus, downward mobility in conformity with God's mission in the world. We do violence to both Paul and the gospel when we interpret "becoming all things to all men" to cover prayer breakfasts with officials, or golf with the major, or hunting trips with the generals on the pretext of witnessing. This is no license for the missionary to hobnob with the embassy crowd or the foreign business community. In fact this passage points in the opposite direction.

b. A closely related characteristic of Paul's mission was the suffering and persecution it brought him. In fact this is the other side of the weakness-vulnerability coin (II Cor. 11:30). The apostolic stance means vulnerability. And the world's certification of this apostolate is persecution. Of course we should have expected this in Paul from the moment when he understood his mission in terms of suffering servanthood. In fact, he explicitly refers to his suffering as a continuation of the Messiah's suffering. "Now I rejoice in my sufferings for your sake; and in my flesh I complete what is lacking in Christ's affliction for the sake of his body, that is the church" (Col. 1:24).

II Cor. 4:10-12 expresses this fact with extraordinary clarity: "Always carrying in the body the death of Jesus, so that the life of Jesus may also be manifested in our bodies. For while we live we are always being given up to death for Jesus' sake, so that the life of Jesus may be manifested in our mortal flesh. So death is at work in us, but life in you." The grammatical construction of this passage makes it clear that it is not with the death of Christ understood in some mystical sense that Paul identifies himself, but rather "the killing of Jesus:" "Always carrying in the body the killing of Jesus." The forms which the historic suffering and killing of Jesus took also aply to Paul's understanding of the apostolic mission as a continuation of suffering servanthood (cf. II Cor. 1:5).

The sufferings to which Paul refers over and over again are not merely the dangers inherent in first century travel, although these should not be underestimated. "Three times I have been shipwrecked; a night and a day I have been adrift at sea; on frequent journeys, in danger from rivers, danger from robbers, . . . danger in the city, danger in the wilderness, danger at sea . . ." (II Cor. 11:25-26). It was more than hardships inherent in an itinerant ministry, although it certainly included that. "In toil and hardship, through many a sleepless night, in hunger and thirst, often without food, in cold and exposure. And, apart from other things, there is the daily pressure upon me of my anxiety for all the churches" (II Cor. 11:27-28).

It was in effect a "cross," the world's verdict in response to his revolutionary activity (Acts 17:6,7 Jerusalem Bible) and to his life and message which so patently contradicted the generally accepted social values. The sufferings which Paul bore were basically those of a prophetic dissident at odds with the prevailing system. It was precisely because of the gospel that Paul wrote "I am suffering and wearing fetters like a criminal" (II Tim. 2:9). Persecution, suffering, imprisonment became practically an apostolic characteristic in the N.T. But we are reminded that this is not only a characteristic of the apostle. It has also been the lot of the prophets (Mt. 5:12). Jesus said that it would also be the portion of His followers (Mt. 5:10,11). And Paul expected his followers to suffer the same fate (II Tim. 1:8; 3:12; I Thes. 1:6; II Thes. 1:4,5; etc.).

Although he reports it with considerable hesitation, the record of Paul's experience at the hands of the Law is impressive. "Fettered like a criminal." "Far more imprisonments, with countless beatings, and often near death. Five times I have received at the hands of the Jews the forty lashes less one. Three times I have been beaten with rods; once I was stoned" (II Cor. 11:23-25; cf. 6:4,5).

All of this should lead us to read with more realism Paul's allusion to himself as "an ambassador in chains" (Eph. 6:20). Being ambassador for the kingdom of God among the "nations" entailed repression and suffering at the hands of the "powers." The "powers" respond to the gospel in the form of "chains." In spite of the care taken in Acts to avoid blaming the cause of persecution on the Roman authorities and transferring it rather to the Jews and satanic opposition, we are left with the inescapable impression that apostolic mission in the world of the first century necessarily implied suffering and persecution. Apparently there was no other way to authentically communicate the gospel of Jesus Christ.

c. Paul furthermore insisted that the apostolic mission calls for personal sacrifice, even including those benefits which he rightly could have claimed for himself. Note especially his attitude toward self-support and even suffering poverty in the interests of the unhindered fulfillment of his mission. Although he was rightfully entitled to economic support from those whom he served, he did not claim it because, as he said, "we endure anything rather than put an obstacle in the way of the gospel of Christ" (I Cor. 9:18). Work, in order not to be a burden while preaching the gospel, was simply a part of the way in which Paul communicated "kingdom living" in his mission (I Thes. 2:9-12). Paul makes it clear that his practice of self-support was essential to his communication of the gospel. "You yourselves know that these hands ministered to my necessities, and to those who were with me. In all things I have shown you that by so toiling one must help the weak, remembering the words of the Lord Jesus, how he said, 'It is more blessed to give than to receive'" (Acts 20:34,35; cf. Eph. 4:28, etc.).

5. Paul's methodology included his concern for the unity of the Body of Christ. He roundly repudiated denominationalism. In effect Corinthian Christians had been forming groups under various "names" or "denominations" (I Cor. 1:10-12; 3:3,4). Paul could have taken the easy course by ignoring the other factions who probably would have eventually withered away. Or he could have promoted his own "denomination," a thing which he refused to do. Instead he insisted that the richness of diversity which contributes to "the fulness of Christ" must be built upon the only foundation there is, Jesus Christ (I Cor. 3:11).

Peter, Paul, and Apollos had their differences in terms of Jewish Law, Greek wisdom, styles of preaching, and matters of personality. Paul did not seek to smooth over these differences or give the impression that people were free to choose one or another according to their personal preferences. On the contrary, he wrote of a foundation upon which all subsequent missionaries were called to build (I Cor. 3:5-15). In this particular case Paul had laid the foundation (3:10) which by its very nature is unique (3:11). This oneness of the church is indispensable to its being and according to Paul the ultimate survival of a missionary's work depends on his respecting that foundation (3:11) and building upon it in a way consistent with the nature of that foundation (3:12-14).

Paul's conviction that the church of Jesus Christ is essentially one led him to collect funds among the Hellenistic churches for the brotherhood in Jerusalem. He opposed pressures which would have forced all Christians into a Jewish mold (Judaizers) or who would have simply allowed the Jewish branch to wither away (Hellenists). Paul went out of his way to maintain relationships with Greek and Jewish elements of the church and did so at the considerable price of persecution and personal suffering because of his conviction that the essence of the gospel lies in the destruction of the barrier between Jews and Gentiles through the creation of a new humanity in which the old causes of separation are overcome (Eph. 2:11-22; Gal. 3:28).

6. Finally, one notes that in the Pauline experience of mission the role of the local congregation is fundamental. Paul and Barnabas were commissioned and sent out from the congregation in Antioch (Acts 13:2,3), and at least twice Paul returned to the congregation to give an accounting of his work (Acts 14:26,27; 18:22,23).

Both Acts and Paul's epistles bear witness to the fact that invariably the Pauline mission led to the formation of a local messianic community. Each of these local communities was fully the church. In Paul's thought it is not the sum of individual congregations that produces the total Christian community. Each community, however small, represents the total community. Even a small fellowship such as a house church can be called a church (Rom. 16:5). And it can be listed together with other larger congregations (I Cor. 16:19; Col. 4:15,16). In fact Paul can write of the "church of God," referring to a single congregation (I Cor. 1:2), as well as in the plural of the "churches of God." It apparently does not occur to Paul to make a qualitative distinction between the total church and the individual congregation.

This fact underscores the importance of Paul's church planting mission. He does not understand his apostolic activity as simply contributing to the growth of the total church (although he does conceive of the church in terms which are universal and even cosmic (Cf. Col. and Eph.), but as leading to the emergence of the church of God (or Christ) in its particular local expression. While a brotherly sense of responsibility led Paul to report back to Antioch "all that God had done" (Acts 14:27), the new congregations in Iconium, Lystra, and Antioch of Pisidia were the "church of God" in the same sense that the congregation in Antioch of Syria was the church.

Message

It is certainly un-Pauline to attempt to distinguish between method and message in understanding his apostolic mission. As we have seen, the rationale for the particular methods which Paul employed rests in the content which these communicate. The **way** the gospel is communicated determines **what** is communicated, and vice versa. In order to understand more fully Paul's concept of his mission, however, we should also view it from the perspective of content or message. This will complement what we have already learned through approaching it from the perspective of missionary method or posture.

1. Paul's message was concretely Christological. His call to imitation was not merely a general appeal to follow the heavenly Christ. It was also a call to imitate Paul, as he imitated Jesus, in certain specific ways. Jesus of Nazareth, the Messiah incarnate, is the example which lies behind Paul's invitation to imitation.

We must not underestimate the importance for Paul of the humanity of Jesus. Paul's apostolic activity following the Damascus road vision was profoundly influenced by the historical career of Jesus the Messiah. In his use of the term "Kingdom of God," Paul surely echoes the proclamation of Jesus himself. Acts uses the term five times with reference to Paul, and it appears some 14 times in Paul's writings. Paul refers at a number of points in his writings to specific teachings of Jesus, granting to them an authority comparable to that which Caesar demanded in the secular realm.

In Rom. 15:1-6 Paul bases his appeal "to bear with the failings of the weak, and not to please ourselves" squarely on the example of Jesus, who did not please himself but suffered the reproaches of others. He concludes with an appeal to live in harmony with each other "after the manner of Jesus" (NEB). Paul makes a similar appeal in I Cor. 10:24-11:1: "Let no one seek his own good, but the good of his neighbour." In support of this Paul speaks of his own concern to "please all men" (vs. 33) in everything he does, not seeking his own advantage. This is the context of the call to imitation in 11:1, "Be imitators of me, as I am of Christ."

Paul also notes that Jesus is a model of forgiveness. "And be kind to one another, tenderhearted, forgiving one another, as God in Christ forgave you" (Eph. 4:32; cf.

Col. 3:13). Jesus is also a concrete example of the form which love takes. "Walk in love, as Christ loved us and gave himself up for us" (Eph. 5:2).

In I Thes. 1:6,7; 2:14,15 Jesus, along with the prophets and the Christian communities in Judea, is presented as an example to be imitated. But, again, it is notable that this is not a call to imitation in some general and vague way. There is rather one clear and specific point to be imitated: patient and loyal obedience even in the midst of suffering (Cf. Heb. 5:8,9; 12:1ff). The invitation in Phil. 3:17, "Brethren, join in imitating me," according to the context also points to this particular concrete aspect of Paul's (and Jesus') life—suffering for the sake of obedience. "That I may . . . share his sufferings, becoming like him in his death" (Phil. 3:10). According to I Cor. 4:16,17, Paul's readers are urged to imitate his "ways in Christ." Here again the context supplies us with the specific content of this imitation. They are to imitate the servanthood stance of Paul (4:1), which means, according to Paul, "to live according to the scripture" (4:6).

Finally, the well known passage in Phil. 2:3-11 can be cited as another example of the concrete way in which Paul expected believers to imitate the example of Jesus Christ. Messiahship according to the suffering servant model, with all that it means in terms of self-giving, vulnerable, sacrificial service, is God's way to authentic exaltation and lordship. Paul's appeal to the form of Jesus' messiahship gives concrete form to the humility and unselfish interest in the welfare of others that Paul commends to the Philippian Christians.

Paul's missionary message calls for concrete conformity to the words and deeds and Spirit of Jesus the Messiah, and especially to His suffering servanthood and what this means in terms of social relationships among the citizens of his kingdom.

2. Paul's message was essentially eschatological. Paul, as well as other N.T. writers, speaks of "this age" or "the present evil age" (Rom. 12:2; I Cor. 1:20; Gal. 1:4) and "the age which is to come" (Eph. 1:21). Paul's understanding of "this age" and the "age to come" does not have to do primarily with time sequence, although the temporal aspect is not entirely absent. They are basically qualitative categories which describe distinct realms. The "coming age" is the realm of God's power inaugurated in the event of Christ's life, death, and resurrection and is already present and effective in the world in the person and activity of God's Spirit. The "present evil age" is the world which God has created but which is held in bondage by hostile evil powers. The two ages are seen to co-exist between the incarnation and the parousia. The "present evil age" in which man stands enslaved by the powers of this world, alien to God and hostile to His purpose, is the sphere in which the Pauline mission is carried out. And it is the proclamation of the gospel which opens up the new possibility of life in "the age to come."

Paul uses a rich variety of terms to describe man's possession by the evil powers of this age, his alienation from, and his hostility to God, and, finally, his bondage to the powers of sin and of death. On the other hand, "the transcendent power" of God (II Cor. 4:7), operative in and through the power of his Spirit which participates of the "age to come," will one day destroy fully and finally the evil powers of "this age." Therefore the salvation to which Paul's mission points will be future.

But even though God's power transcends the present

age and stands over against the powers to which this age is in bondage, God's power is nevertheless already effective for men in Christ. The two spheres meet, as it were, in Him through whom God is already in this present time reconciling the world unto himself (II Cor. 5:19). Paul describes the saving effects of God's power in terms of a "new creation" (Gal. 6:15; II Cor. 5:17). Man's existence is "new" by virtue of a new relationship with God through Jesus Christ. Therefore Paul understands that the "eschatological" power of God is already operative. In Christ a "new creation" has come about. There is a sense in which the old age has passed away and the new age has dawned (II Cor. 5:17). So in addition to being a future hope, salvation for Paul is also a present reality. Paul declares with emphasis, "Behold now is the day of salvation" (II Cor. 6:2). By this he does not mean that it has been manifested in all of its fullness, but rather that it has already occurred and is effective.

In the O.T. (Joel 2) as well as in late Judaism, the sign of the coming of the eschaton was to be the coming of the Spirit of God with power. For Paul also, the presence of the Spirit of God signifies the coming of the new age. But in his understanding of the work of the Spirit, one observes again the dialectic in Paul between the present and future aspects of salvation. On one hand, the Spirit represents the actual entry of the eschaton into the present age (Rom. 5:5; Gal. 4:6,7). The Spirit "gives life" (present tense, II Cor. 3:6). On the other hand, the Spirit is also a harbinger of that which is yet to come. In Rom. 8:11 Paul says, "If the Spirit of the one who raised Jesus from the dead dwells in you, he who raised from the dead Christ Jesus will give life (future tense) also to your mortal bodies through his Spirit dwelling in you." The Spirit makes present that which belongs to the "age to come," as well as certifying by His present activity that which is still to come with the full flowering of the kingdom.

Paul uses metaphors to express this dialectic truth. He speaks of the "firstfruits of the Spirit" (Rom. 8:23). The firstfruits represent the full harvest which is coming. The Spirit does not merely precede the "coming age," but actually bears it and represents the power of that age, i.e., of God Himself, already at work. A second metaphor speaks of the Spirit as a "guarantee" given by God (II Cor. 1:22; 5:5). *Arrabon* is a Semitic term which literally means "down payment," or the first installment of what has been promised. Just as the down payment is a part of the total sum that will be forthcoming, so the Spirit, present already in God's new creation, is a guarantee of that which is yet to come.

For Paul, "in Christ" does not merely describe a mystical relationship, purely spiritual or invisible, but rather the concrete sphere in which believers live. It is the "age to come" in which Christ's lordship is recognized and obeyed. Physically, the believer lives in the world and has no other alternative but to be subjected to the material limitations of "this present evil age which is passing away." But spiritually and morally he lives on another level. "In Christ" he participates already in the "age to come."

The characteristic juxtaposition with which Paul begins some of his epistles ("To the saints in Christ Jesus in Philippi," or "in Colossae" and "Ephesus" illustrates perfectly the eschatological context in which Paul carried out his mission. "In Christ" a new creation had been achieved. The age to come had already dawned. By the power of the Spirit, men and women were already coming to experience the life of the kingdom. Meanwhile "in Philippi" and "in Colossae," life in this "present evil age which is passing away" was still going on. But Paul and his followers were convinced that it was an existence which had no future. The object of the Pauline mission was nothing less than the formation in the power of God's Spirit of communities of the future, of the new humanity. They are the eschatological people of God whose life is determined not by the values of the present age but by those of the age to come.

5

George R. Brunk, III

The Missionary Stance of the Church in 1 Peter

Just as Saul's armour was unfit for God's servant David, so also not all forms of mission and witness are appropriate for God's servant people. Too much of the search for right method and successful technique is generated by imitation of secular propaganda and publicity patterns. This may take place in ignorance of the implications or in unconscious compensation for the lack of a genuine Christian spirit that seeks out its own fitting form of expression. In any event the mission of the church is debased by a style of mission and evangelism in which the medium (form) is not in harmony with the message (spirit).

The small epistle of 1 Peter illustrates this principle both explicitly and implicitly. The writer expressly advises his readers that in the defense of the gospel, "do it with gentleness and reverence; and keep your conscience clear" (3:15, 16). Elsewhere in the epistle the author extolls these particular virtues as essential characteristics of the follower of Christ. As the context clearly shows, the power of witness is contingent upon the consistency of **what** is defended with **how** it is defended (3:16b).

The epistle of 1 Peter invites consideration as a statement of missionary strategy for another reason. The letter addresses a minority community in a hostile atmosphere. The church is a pilgrim people that lives most keenly the distinction between a believing fellowship and the unbelieving society. More and more this is the context in which the contemporary mission of the church must be carried out. The passing of colonial securities, the increase of political confusion and revolution, and the reawakening of non-Christian religions are creating a world in which the church finds increasing identity with first-century believers.

In spite of the difficult circumstances, 1 Peter reveals an inextinguishable optimism about the penetrating power of the gospel proclaimed by a faithful church. The writer does not describe a high-profile form of mission. In fact, with the exception of the classical text of 2:9, this New Testament writing is not used as a basis for missiological concerns. This is because we fail to appreciate a low-profile mission that seeks to integrate mission and life-style and because we are not aware that many believers today live under conditions that preclude a high-profile mission. The epistle makes the significant point that "low-profile" mission can at the same time be "high powered" mission. The purpose of this essay is to uncover the understanding of mission which determines this viewpoint and to disclose its unique dynamics.

The Wider Angle of Vision

The pastoral letter of Peter contains a theological perspective that is both developed and incisive. Several dimensions of this vision of faith are crucial for our study.

1. The central themes of faith have a marked eschatological character. Salvation is primarily future (1:5) and progressive (2:2). The gift of the new birth is preeminently the gift of hope (1:3). The whole of Christian existence is conditioned by hope. The expression, "set your hope fully upon the grace that is coming to you at the revelation of Jesus Christ'' (1:13) illustrates the future orientation of grace in the context of an appeal to appropriate behavior. This suggests that a clear vision of the goal of redemption inspires obedience to the will of God. The eschatological hope becomes a direct norm for present living in the exhortation to bless because, as a believer, blessing is the anticipated outcome (3:9). Here the motivation to transformed living is: be now what you hope to become. Hope strengthens the people of God in their present suffering (1:6; 4:13; 5:10). Therefore, a living hope both leads to an alternate lifestyle in the midst of a society trapped in the past (1:18) and present (4:4), and at the same time steels the nerve for the conflict that results between the old and the new. As we will see more fully, Peter sees the mission of the church rising like a spontaneous flame ignited by the friction between a world that is passing and another that is coming. In this case the awareness of the end (1:20; 4:7) does not merely excite the redeemed community to ''work for the night is coming,'' i.e., work fast for the time is brief. Eschatology is part and parcel of the missionary stance of the church in its very nature and every action.

2. The integral character of theology and ethics is also a conspicuous feature. The author moves freely between the saving action of God for believers and the saved action of the believer before God. In all instances where the saving benefit of the cross is stated (1:18; 2:24; 3:18), the setting is one of ethical exhortation. The work of the crucified Lord is the ground of upright behavior. In a form similar to the Pauline mode of expression, the relationship between the indicative of the saving fact and the imperative of righteous act is the key linking word—therefore (see 1:13). The action of God on behalf of believers is the foundation of all holy living. On the other hand there are indications in the epistle that obedience itself is the basis for new actualization of Christian being (1:22). Perhaps this is the way to understand the enigmatic affirmation that suffering contributes to the cessation from sin (4:1). Suffering, as the consequence of righteous living, marks out in the believer an even greater separation from unrighteousness. The integral nature of Christian existence extends also from ethics to mission. In Peter it is the church suffering because of its uncompromised holy conduct that has a missionary impact upon society (2:12, 15; 3:1, 2, 16). This observation leads to another essential consideration.

3. The church as portrayed in the epistle lives in an unrelaxed, unresolved tension between distinctiveness and involvement in relation to the world. On the one hand the right doing of the believer is so counter to pagan behavior that the latter reacts negatively (4:4). Rightdoing is treated as wrongdoing (2:12). Those who represent God are a distinct people (2:9). Thus a counter community is set up in the midst of the general social structure: a distinctive people with a distinctive life. On the other hand, this special people deliberately maintains its involvement in the "Gentile" structure. They are among the nonbelievers (2:12) and recognize the civil order as applicable to themselves (2:13). Apparently they are not expected to set up counter economic systems but participate in the larger system (2:18). This dual movement is the key to faithfulness. On one side the result is suffering; on the other it is evangelistic penetration. The relaxation of distinctiveness would avoid suffering. The relaxation of involvement would compromise evangelism and service. Either way the integrity of the vision would be lost. Now what is so significant is that Peter sees evangelism as one dimension of the dynamic encounter between a special people and a hostile world. The progress of the gospel takes place in the crisis triggered by the nonconformist, believing fellowship confronting the world. The crisis is inevitable. The evangelistic result, however, is dependent upon the consistency and perseverance of the distinctive way of life of that fellowship. The kind of mission here envisioned is powerful but costly. It demands a high quality of discipleship, a high commitment to engagement, and a high tolerance of suffering. Peter seems to demand both nonconformity and contemporaneity in the church's relation to society. The church must take a stand for God over against the world, but that stance must speak prophetically to that world in which the church presently lives.

The Specific Aspects of Mission

One might well speak of mission in our epistle as a quite natural aspect of being the authentic people of God in the world. Mission and evangelism are not sharply distinguishable parts of the church's life; they do not constitute a special program or strategy in isolation from other activities. They are two facets of Christian existence. In particular, mission can be said to begin at the place where Christian behavior becomes responsive, productive activity in relationships with neighbor and society. This interaction has several aspects.

1. Demonstration

It is characteristic of 1 Peter to speak of the behavior of Christians in their relationships with those who do not obey the word (3:1) as upright conduct. Among the Gentiles, or pagans, they "maintain good conduct" (2:12) cf. 3:16). Even in the domestic setting "reverent and chaste behavior" is the key to redemptive relationship (3:1, 2). The latter case is of special interest. The example is that of the wife relating to the husband. The adornment used to impress the mate is not outward artificiality but inner spirit allowed to blossom in action. Adornment as witness—the metaphor is apt! (cf. 2 Cor 2:15). This is not an ethic repressive of human nature but creative of righteousness not only in oneself but also in others!

In 2:13-18 the writer develops the general case of good conduct among the Gentiles under the concept of servant-hood. The vocabulary of subjection, honor, fear, and love in human relations expresses the essential commitment to enjoy Christian freedom in service to God (2:16). Since service-in-love is the basic feature of relational ethics both within the brotherhood (1:22; 2:17; 3:8; 4:8-11) and outside, the characteristic Petrine unity of ethics and evangelism again comes into focus. Peter sees service to one's fellowmen as the complement to evangelism.

The evangelistic impact of "good conduct" begins in the act of observing [out of] the good deeds (2:12). Observation leads to understanding. The ultimate outcome is either winning to the faith (3:1) or putting to silence or shame (2:15; 3:16). The epistle carefully notes the kind of behavior that elicits such a response.

Christian living is impressive for its uniqueness, persistence, and consistency. The peculiar style of life is rooted in the source of that life: it is God-like (theological) in essence (1:16); it is Christological in shape (2:21 ff.); it is eschatological in power (3:9), that is, the life of total blessing is motivated out of the expectation that the ultimate bliss will have just that form. Be now what you hope to become! The witness to this novel, "futuristic" life is protected from ruinous compromise by persistent zeal in right (3:13) and by rigorous consistency because even one's form of defense must reflect the same character as one's other conduct—with gentleness, reverence, and clear conscience (3:15c).

Peter reflects in his own way the "signs" theology of the wider New Testament. Jesus and his followers witness to the divine action — the power of the kingdom — among them and through them. In Acts 14:3 this is keenly referred to as God's own witness to the human word of witness. Interestingly however, Peter does not accent the miraculous aspect of signs and wonders even though he apparently knows that is possible (2:9?). Rather, the power to live the kingdom life is itself the greatest sign and wonder. The criterion of a demonstrative sign is not its "supernatural" appearance, but its "unnatural" particularity—it points to the intrusion of a new order of things into the "natural," present order.

The epistle, as the rest of the New Testament, points to the essential role of demonstration in mission. The inevitability, the credibility, and the clarity of the gospel message are conditioned on it. For Peter we would not be too wide of the mark to say that "the messenger is the message."

2. Explanation

The natural correlate of demonstration is explanation. Explanation presupposes something that already is present and known but not understood. The word of explanation points to the act or fact that is demonstrated. It builds on the strengths of demonstration in mission and adds its own. First, it avoids the tendency to manipulate by overpowering intellect or impassioned rhetoric. Proclamation of the gospel in isolation from the gospel's power depends entirely on sheer verbal power. Second, explanation witness sets the stage for learning to take place. The interest and curiosity of the observer-listener is a given. The implied openness is the first step to understanding. The witness takes the offensive even when forced to appear before the world's judges.

Such is just the case in 1 Peter. The believer may be called to account for the hope of the community of faith (3:15). (Note that a comparison of hope in v. 15 and righteousness in vv. 13 and 14 underscores the point that the demonstrated life reflects the expected life-to-come.) It is true that in some instances the word of explanation is dispensable (3:1). The text uses the point to emphasize the primacy of demonstration. Elsewhere the author implies that verbal defense easily degenerates into counterproductive unfaithfulness (2:22, 23; 3:15c, 16a). Yet explanation remains essential both because others may require it and because demonstration needs it as a complement.

The nature of the gospel is such that its meaning, in terms of its transcendent points of reference, is not self-evident. Peter does not develop this point explicitly. The passages dealing with the verbal announcement of the message imply it (1:12, 25; 2:9; and see below). Furthermore, a correct understanding of the classical text in 2:9 may affirm the fact. The Old Testament precedent would suggest that the wonderful deeds are not exclusively the great acts of God in antiquity; they include the acts of God right up to the present moment of the children of God (see the Psalms). The text defines this active God in the subsequent clauses in terms of His acts for the Petrine churches—from darkness to light, from "nobody" to a "somebody" people. To declare the behavioral pattern of this God is to explain the demonstrable effects of His mercy in a new people whose task it is precisely to do that declaring. But this leads into a new focus point.

3. Disclosure

The divine deeds in the contemporary moment are certainly related to the great central deeds of God in the long history of revelation. The latter events and their interpretation in Scripture serve as the norm by which the believers of all times interpret the contemporary deeds of God among them and in their world. Without this key no proper basis would exist for the explanation of the current deeds of God. Explanation needs both the present event to which to point and the comparison and analogy from the past. The expression, "declare the wonderful deeds of [God]," points to this, not by distinguishing these two aspects, but by emphasizing the equally important fact that the process is a continuous line of unfolding action and proclamation. Consequently, the contemporary witness is linked solidly to the chain of divine purpose that unites all history and gives the new people roots (2:10.)

The reader can detect the two aspects in sequence by noting the emphasis in chapter one on the proclaimed word centered in the prophetic promise and its fulfillment in the death and resurrection of Jesus (1:10, 11, 23-25), the all-inclusive reference to "wonderful deeds" in 2:9, and finally the specific demonstration-explanation form of witness in the 2:11 ff. section.

The crucial role of the foundational acts of God is reflected in the concept of canon, i.e., Scripture. For Peter it was the Old Testament as promise (1:10) plus the apostolic proclamation of Christ (1:12b); for us it is simply the whole of Scripture. Scripture interprets contemporary life in the light of the acts of God for our salvation.

At the heart this is a function of disclosure. This is more than explanation. It is informational in the deepest sense, for in it God reveals Himself and His will. The paragraph, 1:10-12, states this clearly by attributing to the Spirit the prophetic insight (11) and the apostolic announcement (12) regarding the action of God in Christ. Without this essential datum, this given, no light would be shed on human existence. What Heidegger said of language in general—it is a disclosure event—is eminently true of revealed truth. The word received is like a clearing in the forest where light breaks through. The figure of light and darkness is, of course, a basic biblical motif. Peter uses it in the key passage defining God's missionary people (2:9). This people has been called from darkness to light. Here is expressed that disclosing power of the good news that comes from without (calls) but penetrates within (born anew, 1:23).

Thus the place of proclamation—announcing the facts of salvation—is secured in the missionary life of the church. These data must be fed into the mixture of demonstration and explanation in order to be the catalyst of genuine faith. The life-containing, life-preserving quality of this word is underscored by our epistle (1:23-25). The disclosing power of these words, the gospel message, endures through time and place. It is irreplaceable.

4. Visitation
The focus on disclosure highlights the divine involvement in mission. This note is intensified in the concept of visitation. The day of visitation signifies the time when the Gentiles observe the good conduct of believers and acknowledge God ("glorify God"). In line with prophetic usage in the Bible, this term can refer either to an intermediate or the final occasion when God intervenes in human affairs in judgment or vindication. Which is it here? Does Peter see it as a moment of crisis in life or as the time of final judgment?

In light of the obvious dependence on Matthew 5:16 and the parallel expression in 3:3 where the husband is "won" (the same unusual Greek word is used for "see" in both contexts in Peter), the balance of evidence points to the moment of divine intervention in the course of life. A parallel would then be the observation of Jesus that Jerusalem had not known the time of her visitation by the Messiah (Lk. 19:44). The reference would be to those moments when God breaks through the wall of human indifference and the individual or nation is confronted with spiritual need. This is the day of opportunity for salvation.

The people of God in mission who are aware of God's way with His world will take a dim view of any stance that presumes to "conclude" the evangelistic call by using persuasive gimmicks or pressure tactics. Recognition of

God's sovereignty and respect for the individual's readiness are important to serving as midwife in true spiritual birth. Furthermore, one must note that the day of witness is not necessarily the time of opportunity for emerging faith. The implication of Peter's words is clear: live an open and consistent life before unbelievers so that whenever the opportune time arrives, the "other life" of the Christian will point the searching individual to the better way. If the Christan community's "visit of witness" is to connect with the divine visitation, it must be made with great sensitivity. On the other hand it frees the community from false guilt in assuming that it bears responsibility for success.

5. Apologetic

2 Peter pays brief attention to one other aspect of mission. The role of the church in mission is also that of unmasking and judging the senselessness of unrighteousness. Doing right "should put to silence the ignorance of foolish men" (2:15). Those who revile good behavior in Christ "may be put to shame" by the believer's nonvengeful response to abuse (3:16). This example relates evangelism and the peace witness. We are probably to understand these responses of the nonbeliever as occurring in the present life.

The picture is one of a mix of gentle means and aggressive impact. Witness is not smooth dialogue but debate. The world calls the church to account and finds itself shamed and wrongheaded—an anticipation of God's call of the world to account (4:5). Here is truly a form of almighty meekness. Given the minority status of these churches in a time of suffering, the call to fearless (3:14) action is striking. Even then it is no occasion for heady pride; judgment stands first over the household of God (4:17).

Given the context of the statement in 2:15 which refers to the political authorities one might well speak of a political witness. Interestingly, here that witness is done in the demonstration of subjection. On the other hand as noted, the legal setting implied in 3:15 is one in which the tables are turned and the believer confronts his accusers— still in a spirit of reverence. In this instance the world initiates the confrontation. The believers' lifestyle causes irritation (cf. 4:4). One might venture the guess that Peter, if he addressed the church today, would say that what is at issue in "political witness" is not so much whether the gospel is relevant to the political arena or whether the Christian has a right or duty to speak there, but whether the church is faithful enough to provoke being called to account, out of hostility or perhaps admiration, for the transformed life of messianic discipleship.

Conclusion

1 Peter is not a comprehensive treatment of the biblical themes of mission. Yet it remains remarkably complete in its all-too-brief assertions of mission as an integral part of the church. Mission is thoroughly at home in true Christian existence as the people of God in the world. In this epistle the missionary stance reflects the self-understanding of the believers church: the voluntary church of disciples embraces the way of separation and holy living and finds in its tension with the world not a threat to mission but its heartbeat.

6

Howard H. Charles

The Gospel and Mission Strategy

Gospel and mission strategy belong together. One speaks of message; the other is concerned with communication. Both are needed. The gospel is good news that exists to be shared. But the order of the terms in the title is significant. Gospel stands first not only because there must be something to share before ways of sharing can be discussed. There is a more fundamental reason. Mission strategy must be rooted in and have integrity with the gospel. If it is not, then the gospel itself may be distorted or even falsified in the process of sharing.

Gospel Defined

Gospel then is the prior term. But what is the gospel? It may seem late in the day to ask this question. Don't we all know what the gospel is? Perhaps until we try to define it. Then it suddenly becomes elusive. The more we think about it, the more complex it becomes. If we seek help from others, we receive diverse answers.

Some would define it as essentially **a body of belief.** The gospel becomes an intellectual abstraction. Even the earthly Jesus or the glorified Christ is reduced to an idea in an intellectual system. Orthodoxy is of prime concern. When the gospel is understood in this way, mission strategy is devoted to the transmission of information. Indoctrination with a view to correct conceptualization is a logical correlative of a propositional view of the gospel.

Others would see the gospel primarily in **experiential** terms. The emphasis gravitates toward what has happened in personal religious experience, on life in Christ or in the Spirit, or on feeling. Jesus is viewed as the spiritual Christ who is the key to the desired inward experience. Frequently the experience is stereotyped with Paul, Luther, Wesley, or Pentecostalism furnishing the model. Mission strategy then turns to the matter of reproducing the stereotype.

Still others would find the gospel consisting chiefly in **a style of life.** Jesus is regarded as a teacher and exemplar of a pattern of conduct. The locus of the gospel is no longer in a theological system or in spiritual experience but in ethical injunctions in the New Testament letters. Mission strategy in this case is devoted to securing the proper action response. Conduct must conform to the code.

While there is a modicum of truth in each of these ways of viewing the gospel, there are also serious limitations which are then reflected in mission strategy. The gospel is more than a set of ideas for the mind, or a catalytic agent for galvanizing emotions, or a code addressed to the will. Its referent lies elsewhere.

The Bible points us to the arena of history. To be sure, the gospel does not emerge out of history as though it were its product, but neither can it be understood apart from history. It has an "event" character. It can best be told in story form.

Christ-Event Is Central

The story begins with Abraham (Gal 3:8), but in the thick of the plot stands the figure of Jesus. He was bone of our bone and flesh of our flesh. Yet the heavens were open to him and he was full of the Spirit of God. The path he chose was that of the lowly servant of the Lord serving faithfully in a ministry of word and deed. Then came the cross and darkness, followed by the triumph of life over death. The New Testament as a whole makes it abundantly clear that Jesus not only proclaimed the gospel (Mk 1:14f.) but that in the totality of his ministry, he was himself the gospel (Rom 1:3f.; cf. Acts 10:36ff.).

When the gospel is seen as focusing in the advent and ministry of Jesus, none of our first definitions is adequate. Not only is each too fragmentary, but they both miss what is most distinctive: Jesus in the wholeness of his ministry. In this larger whole are held together both word and deed, the Sermon on the Mount and the cross and all that lies between. What is more, the gospel is seen in relation both to what preceded and to what follows the ministry of Jesus. That ministry marked a decisive stage in God's pursuit of his purpose in the world. That purpose is the gathering of a people for himself. God wishes to establish community between himself and humanity, and among people. That goal is magnificently portrayed in a closing vision of the New Testament (Rev. 21:1-22:5). The Christ-event is a fresh beginning in an effort to reach the goal, an effort repeatedly frustrated by human recalcitrance. Jesus is the second "Adam" (1 Cor 15:45ff.; Rom 5:12-21). He is the nucleus of a new community upon which his Spirit was poured out on the day of Pentecost. The story of the spread and growth of that new community is told in the pages of Acts and in the annals of later church history.

The People of God: The New Creation
To put the understanding of the gospel in the context of the dynamic outworking of God's purpose to create a people for himself is to place its meaning in a new framework. The elements of belief, experience, and action noted at the outset of this discussion are not discarded,

but they are repolarized. They are caught up in a larger living unity and are given new significance. The gospel, for example, has to do with understandings and beliefs. It is not a foe of theology. But its theology can no longer be that of a cold and sterile scholasticism. It is rooted in a story of what has happened in history and is an attempt to expound its meaning. It is more like a living organism than a dissected corpse. It is more of a commentary on a narrative than an exercise in logic. It is a creed to be sung, not merely signed.

Again, the element of experience is not ignored or minimized. But when it is seen in the framework of the gospel story, certain safeguards are provided against its distortion. This might be illustrated in various ways, but space will allow only one reference. The gift of the Spirit is part of God's beneficence toward us in the gospel. As Christians we are to be full of the Spirit (Eph 5:18). But the category of "Spirit" in and of itself is a rather nebulous one. It is like a wax nose that can be turned in any direction desired. It is like the wind without form or shape and unpredictable. All sorts of inexplicable and bizarre experiences can be attributed to the Spirit, if the Spirit is largely severed from rootage in the gospel story, that is. When the Spirit is seen as tied firmly to the figure of Jesus, then definite structure is given to our understanding of the Spirit and his work in our lives. Experience is prevented from being swallowed up in the morass of subjectivism.

Ethics, likewise, do not lose their importance but are seen in a new light when they are rooted in the gospel story. Abstracted from that context, the ethical injunctions of the New Testament may be reduced to a "do it yourself" morality. The door stands open to move on the one hand in the direction of a legalistic moralism or on the other toward a flabby "situation ethic." But Christian ethics in the New Testament sense are not like flowers that can be cut and arranged at will. They are potted plants with sustaining roots. They are response ethics to what God has done in the Christ-event. They take their shape and derive their motivation from the particulars of that action. They flow from grace and are meant to be energized by the gift of the Spirit. They are designed to make evident in the midst of the old age the contours of the new. Seen in this light, ethics are not the whole gospel, nor an adjunct to it. They are an integral part of it.

Thus far we have been trying to establish a point of reference for understanding the gospel, a way of viewing it. To focus, as we have, on the "event" character of the gospel is to keep it oriented toward the realities of history. It is to emphasize as of first importance what has happened (Christ-event) in order to put what is happening (experience) and what ought to happen (ethics) in proper perspective.

Our proposal is that we seek the gospel as God's free and gracious action in the Christ-event to create a people who in fellowship with himself and one another will achieve their true destiny. This is to think in personal (not to be equated with individual) and relational categories which are appropriate to the dynamic complexities of the gospel. It is to assign a unique and decisive role to Jesus. It is to look not only upward and backward but also forward if we hope to understand the full dimensions of the good news.

Strategy of Mission

To see the gospel in its historicity has certain implications for mission strategy. To these we must now turn. Only three have been selected for brief comment.

Style of Presentation. First, there is the matter of the mode of presenting the gospel. Christians, although obviously interested in getting a favorable response to the gospel, cannot be propagandists in the sense of manipulating people. They must be concerned about three matters: They will offer content (the facts of the gospel and their meaning); they hope to arouse interest in and get assent to the gospel; they must respect the freedom of the individual to make his or her own decision.

One of the most difficult problems in evangelism, at least on the American scene, is to arouse interest in the gospel. Declaratory assertions and dogmatic pronouncements are often met with indifference. They dampen rather than create curiosity. They appear to coerce decision rather than invite it. Perhaps we can learn something from the form in which the gospel was first wrought out in history that may be helpful in presenting it in our situation.

The historical figure of Jesus as portrayed in the Gospels is not free of enigma. He attracted certain people and repelled others. His presence, speech, and conduct were not such that faith was inevitable. On occasion he might perform miracles, but when they were demanded of him, he refused. He spoke in parables. He challenged conventional ideas and practices. He fitted no stereotype. He invited investigation. In short, there was enough light and enough darkness to stimulate curiosity and give faith a chance.

L. E. Keck in his book, *A Future for the Historical Jesus,* has suggested that today Jesus needs to be presented in the form of a question rather than a dogmatic answer. People must be allowed to keep company with him in such a way that he provokes again the ancient question: "What sort of man is that?" (Matt 8:27). To be sure, there is room for witness about what faith has found in Jesus both from the pages of the New Testament and from contemporary experience. But a declaratory mood which provides only answers and does not invite exploration does not do justice to the historical mode in which the gospel first came to us.

Unity of Word and Deed. Second, to see the gospel in terms of the totality of Jesus' ministry means, as we have already noted, that it consists of both word and deed. It will not do to regard the miracles as merely seals attesting to the truth of a gospel that finds its essence in a non-miraculous ministry. They too are a part of the gospel of the new order that was breaking into the old. Jesus was concerned about the abuse of the temple and took action to correct it. He warned against the dangers of wealth. He spoke out in defense of the poor and the helpless. He defied the conventions of the day that robbed men and women of the freedom and fullness of life intended for them.

This means that the familiar antithesis—between evangelism as a soul-saving function and social involvement in the so-called non-spiritual aspects of human existence—breaks down. To perpetuate this dichotomy is to misunderstand the meaning of the incarnation as the expressed form of the gospel. The particular shape of our involvement with the physical, social, political, and economic needs of men and women cannot be spelled out in the abstract. It must be tailored to specific situations. It should be said, however, that the methods employed in these areas will need to be consistent with the spirit and goals expressed in Jesus' ministry. The means must not invalidate the gospel that seeks expression through them.

Translation. Third, taking the historical character of the gospel seriously involves translation so that it speaks meaningfully to contemporary people. The warrant for this is found in the New Testament itself. Interesting changes can be discerned both in the way in which the gospel was conceptualized and in the forms of its cultural expression as it moved out from Palestine and into the broader Roman world. To some extent this was inevitable because of the change in the linguistic medium. No translation from one language into another can be made without the risk of some loss or distortion of meaning.

Beyond the shift from Aramaic to Greek were some deliberate changes in conceptualization. Jewish Christians, for example, made use of the category of "Messiah" to express the significance of Jesus. In the Greek world this was a meaningless term. Consequently, among Greek-speaking Christians the term, insofar as it was retained, was used not as a title but as a proper name. The title "Lord" was more meaningful and, therefore, preferred. One might speak also of the different ways in which the person of Christ and the meaning of his work are articulated in Colossians as compared with Hebrews. The former presents a historic-cosmic Christ as the Christian answer to a syncretistic theology. The latter offers an interpretation of Christ in the framework of the Jewish cult for a Jewish-Christian audience.

The Jerusalem conference represents an attempt to distinguish between the gospel and Jewish ethnocentric piety. It was decided that Greek Christians need no longer become Jews, by adopting circumcision and all that it stood for, before they could be good Christians. The gospel could now be expressed in appropriate Hellenistic cultural media.

The process of translation begun by the early church must be continued today. The crucial matter is to determine the criteria and to discuss the appropriate categories under which it can be carried forward. Then it will remain the gospel although expressed in new forms.

7 The Dynamics of Mission

Wilbert R. Shenk

The mission of the people of God has its origin in the intention of God himself. It can be placed in its proper perspective only if we understand this to be the means by which God is achieving his purposes in history. A deformed understanding of mission allows it to be viewed as a special function for which special personnel and financial resources must be recruited. This understanding stems from a long process throughout church history by which the church accommodated itself to the purposes of the worldly order and was seen as the chaplain to society.

The Message of Jesus: "The Kingdom of Heaven Is at Hand"

The Synoptic Gospels characterize Jesus' ministry from the outset as messianic. They link his ministry directly to the messianic expectations expressed in Isaiah 61. These, in turn, were based on the proclamation of Jubilee (Lev 25:10ff). "The acceptable year of the Lord" was understood as the time when God's reign—or kingdom— would literally begin. When John the Baptist sent a delegation to Jesus to inquire whether in fact Jesus was the Messiah, Jesus quoted Isaiah's description of the Messiah's work and suggested that they "go and tell John what you hear and see . . .'' (Matt 11:4-5).

Matthew, Mark, and Luke each describe in essentially the same way the inauguration of Jesus' ministry: first the baptism, then the manifestation of the Spirit, the temptation experiences, and finally he began to preach. In baptism Jesus publicly indicated his identification with God's purpose in the world. The visible coming of the Spirit upon him was the confirming sign that he was the Messiah, for the Messiah was to be the one in whom God's Spirit was fully sovereign.

It was no accident that Jesus was then faced with a decisive period of testing. The launching of the messianic reign through the word-deed of the "kingdom of God" immediately brought on a challenge from the kingdom of this world. In this brief sequence the issue of the ages is depicted: the two kingdoms are utterly incompatible. No accommodation can be made, and ultimately one will be victorious over the other.

The length of the encounter between Jesus and Satan and Jesus' exhaustion afterwards indicate the reality and gravity this held for him. Satan's suggestions are universally plausible. They not only placed Jesus in a genuine dilemma, Satan's ploys continue to be live options for the people of God today. These strategies of Satan appeared to be consistent with God's purposes, but in fact they were of a different order and would lead to another outcome. Instead of realizing the reign of God through these strategies, Jesus would have contributed to solidifying the reign of Satan.

Not only did Jesus denounce Satan's suggestions directly to him, but he moved immediately from the temptation experiences into his public ministry. In defining what his ministry was about, Jesus used Isaiah 61. In quoting from Isaiah's description of the work of the Messiah, Jesus left out a phrase crucial to his Nazareth audience'' . . . and the day of vengeance of our God''

(Isa 61:2b; cf. Isa 35:4b). Thus he not only rejected the strategies Satan suggested during the temptation experiences, he countered with a new strategy. The kingdom of God will be constituted without recourse to violence or force. To put it positively: the characteristic of this kingdom is its utterly new basis. The Jubilee which had never been proclaimed by a king during Old Testament times was now being inaugurated by the Messiah himself. It was to be carried out in an utterly unconventional way— by a Servant-Messiah through suffering love and self-sacrifice.

The Kingdom of God Is Eschatological

The way we view the present is profoundly shaped by the way we view the things to come. Latin has two words for future: *futurum* and *adventus*. *Futurum* signifies the unfolding of that which was already inherent. The meaning of *adventus*, however, is the appearance of something new which was not present before. Our view of God's reign among people—his kingdom—will be decisively affected by our vision of the present and the future.

Christian thought in the Western world during the past 200 years has been strongly influenced by rationalism and an evolutionary view of human progress. Unprecedented economic and technological progress throughout these two centuries has given modern Westerners an unusual sense of self-confidence and optimism about human potential— notwithstanding the occurrence during these years of the most costly wars in human history. This basically optimistic view has had obvious effects on the way we have read our Bibles and have gone about theological reflection. We have tended to see the future as *futurum*, as an unfolding of what is already present, a projection of our own desires and designs.

But the biblical orientation is different. The kingdom of

God is the divine incursion into history, the *adventus*. It is not a reformulation of what has been; rather it represents "the new creation." The establishment of God's reign among humanity began with the Christ-event and will be brought to completion in the final coming of Christ. The resurrection itself was an eschatological event. In the resurrection we have already been given the final answer about what the outcome will be (1 Cor 15:12-28). Therefore, in the Christ-event, revelation became history and present experience is now illumined by hope in Christ Jesus. Our instructions about how to carry out the establishment of God's kingdom, consequently, are drawn from this assured final victory.

The kingdom of God is already present in judgment and redemption. The presence of the kingdom judges the existing world order and its rebellion against God, but that judgment holds within it the possibility of repentance and therefore redemption. Those who accept God's reign are assured of continuity within his purposes because of the resurrection.

Although the kingdom of God is already present and we know the outcome of history, it is not yet completed or fully established. The demonic forces are still at large, doing their work. Thus the work of establishing God's reign is a frontal attack on Satan's kingdom, with the consequence that until the consummation conflict and tension will be part of human experience, individual and corporate.

The Kingdom of God Is Mediated by the Holy Spirit

The mission of God is the establishment of his reign among people, and the Holy Spirit is the agent of the mission. The presence and action of the Spirit is our "guarantee" (2 Cor 5:1-5) that the work is God's, as is the final victory. The Spirit's work among the people of God is the down payment on the divine promise, the fulfillment of which we eagerly await.

Christ's presence in the world throughout this eschatological age is mediated to us by the Spirit. His role is to represent to men and women the person and work of Christ, for it is through acceptance of Jesus Christ as the Messiah that the reign of God is established in the people's lives. In those who have made that fundamental response in grace to the Spirit's bidding, the Spirit continues to work to bring about the "fullness of Christ," in anticipation of the final consummation. The Apostle Paul concludes his exposition on this point by saying that we "are being changed into his likeness from one degree of glory to another; for this comes from the Lord who is the Spirit" (2 Cor 3:18b).

Finally, the Holy Spirit inspires and equips the people of God for their role in the mission of God. He accomplishes this by giving gifts to his people. The "fullness of Christ" (Eph 4:1-16; cf. 1 Cor 12-14; Rom 12:4-8) is to be experienced in this eschatological age by using the Spirit-given gifts bestowed on every member of the people of God. This endowment of gifts is universal. Every member shares in receiving a gift or gifts and each is to be available to the entire body in exercising those gifts. The endowment of gifts is based on differentiation. Each gift is unique as each individual is unique. Gifts are complementary because they are given for the benefit of the body and not simply for private welfare. When members of the body employ their gifts competitively or use them to exclude others, the "fullness of Christ" is obviously not being achieved and the effect destroys the body rather than building it up. The endowment of gifts is strategically ordered. The people of God have a purpose and the gifts facilitate the achievement of that purpose.

The Kingdom of God Is Actualized in God's People

The people of God are those who have accepted God's

reign in their lives and exist as a part of this new community or the new humanity. They have confronted the fundamental difference between the kingdom of this world and the kingdom of God, and they have made a choice. They are now living self-consciously as part of a new people, though they remain very much within the world.

The significance of the people of God lies not simply in the fact that they are a people, for this world has many peoples. Rather they are distinguished by the fact that they have been constituted into this peoplehood by God himself. Allegiance to him requires a completely new orientation which places his people in tension with their environment in the world. In human communities the basis and boundaries of communal relations tend to be egocentric and ethnocentric. Gods become nothing more than tribal deities. The God revealed in Jesus Christ calls his followers to be self-emptying, and his appeal is to all people. John's Revelation discloses that God's will will be achieved and his people will be comprised of persons from all languages and peoples (Rev 5:9-10).

Furthermore, this peoplehood is a matter of choice. God's grace alone is the basis for the existence of this new people, and that grace does not contradict itself by coercing men and women. Because the hallmark of this peoplehood is God's grace, the only instrument and the appropriate posture is servanthood (Phil 2:5-8). God's people confront a hostile world with a strategy of deliberate powerlessness. This example and message makes the gospel a "stone of stumbling, a rock of offense."

God's reign is being actualized through his people because they exist as a missionary people: they are sent by God into the world to achieve his purposes. God intends that his reign be extended ever more widely until it encompasses all who will follow him and be joined to his people. The proclamation of God's kingdom is done precisely by those who are already members, living examples of its meaning. To be a missionary people is to be set apart, with a distinctive style of life and unique values. The people have crossed the boundary from unfaith to faith in God.

The fundamental task of mission is to persuade others to cross over into a new way of living—to exchange an old way of life for a new one. In our recent growing awareness of cultural differences and the complexities of intercultural communication, we have been tempted to dilute or blur this point. But an important distinction needs to be made. The missionary's duty is to make every effort to identify with the culture of the people to whom he or she goes. He or she must learn to understand their thought patterns and idioms so as to communicate the message as accurately and fully as possible. But missionaries must not minimize the fundamental and drastic choice before their listeners. The Book of Ruth makes this point with beauty and poignancy, when Naomi warns Ruth about the risks and costs of "crossing over" and joining an alien people.

In Conclusion
The dynamics of mission originate in God himself. Mission is the focal point of God's action in the world where his reign confronts the forces of the demonic and decisive struggle occurs.

The coming of Jesus Christ as Messiah inaugurated God's reign. Jesus' resurrection guaranteed that during this eschatological age God's kingdom will be established and finally brought to consummation. The Holy Spirit, the continuing presence of Christ in the world, is the agent for accomplishing of God's reign among men and women. The people of God already share in the blessings of God's reign while also being the instruments through which this "gospel of the kingdom" continues to be preached wherever Jesus Christ is not yet recognized as Lord.

8

Virgil Vogt

Rediscovering the Apostolic Ministry

We are living in the most exciting era in the world mission of the Christian church. During the past 250 years, the emphasis on "foreign mission" has been so successful that Christian churches have now been established in almost every nation on earth.

We are now entering a time when the evangelization of the nations will be carried primarily by local churches and local leadership. We can expect to see dramatic growth on the part of these younger churches. What has happened in Indonesia or among Pentecostals in South America is an example of growth which I expect to see repeated in many parts of the world.

For churches in North America, the success of foreign missions requires a shift in our thinking about missions:

1. We need to discover a more adequate style of spontaneous growth for churches which are indigenous to North America in this latter third of the twentieth century. Because North America plays such a central role in world politics and world economics, the reformulation of Christian mission within this continent is a strategic contribution which we can make to the whole world. This

is a fundamental part of our world mission responsibility at this particular stage in history. The advanced nature of our highly organized society will require churches of great spiritual power and organizational creativity. They must be stronger in shaping the lives of their members than the combined influence of the university, the White House, the news media, General Motors, and the Pentagon. No small task! But already we have a number of promising examples.

2. The church worldwide still needs missionaries in great numbers. The spontaneous growth of local churches does not eliminate this need. In fact, the United States and Canada have great need for missionaries, not to mention all those nations in which the Christian church is an even smaller minority.

However, we have come to a point in world missions when a more careful and profound understanding of the missionary task will be necessary. The definition of "missionary" which was good enough fifty years ago is inadequate in most situations today. Hence, those groups which have not sharpened their understanding of the missionary role are finding that missionaries seem almost obsolete in the current world scene. All kinds of specialized workers are now being sent out, often with little awareness of the fact that being a missionary is a unique specialization, with specific requirements that are at least as exacting as those of other professions.

Clarifying the Missionary Role

The primary purpose of this paper is to suggest the lines along which we might clarify the missionary role. **We should begin to equate "missionary" with "apostle"** as we study our New Testament.[1] The two terms are synonymous. Our concept of missionary would be helped a great deal if we identified it more closely with the role played by the apostles in the New Testament church.

In the New Testament the term apostle describes people who carried a particular ministry within the larger Christian movement. We find this term listed by Paul as one of various spiritual gifts which God has given to his church (Eph 4, 1 Cor 12). While the original twelve apostles had a unique role in history, never to be shared by others, most biblical scholars agree that the term apostle has a broader application. There were other apostles in addition to the twelve. There is an apostolic gift which, along with the gifts of teaching, prophecy, evangelism, and all the others, is given to the church in every generation. Let me share a few ideas about what this apostolic gift is, and how people who have it function in the expansion of the church.

People like Peter and Paul were apostles in the New Testament church. The most gifted and most experienced leaders in the whole movement were the ones sent out by the church to the frontiers on missions—the apostolic ministry. This is in striking contrast to much current practice. We tend to send the young and inexperienced to do missions. They are more mobile. When we do this, however, we demonstrate that we have grossly underestimated the nature of the task.

2. The root of the term apostle means "to send out." These are people who have been sent out by the church. Apostles do their work away from home. Theirs is by definition a traveling ministry. Again, we can see the contrast with much current policy. Today's missionaries are sent out, but they often settle down in their new environment. Peter and Paul never did. Their home base remained in Jerusalem and Antioch. At other places they were always transient. Their apostolic ministry was an itinerant ministry. Sometimes they stayed as long as two or three years; most often it was a matter of weeks or months. This transient quality is important, for it distinguishes the apostolic ministry from the pastoral

ministry. We have frequently sent pastors from one country to another and called them missionaries. But a church built around a foreign pastor has great difficulty in learning to function with indigenous leadership.

3. The unique gift which the apostle exercises is in laying the foundation of the church: "So then you are no longer strangers and sojourners, but you are fellow citizens with the saints and members of the household of God, built upon the cornerstone" (Eph 2:19-20). The Apostle Paul's personal testimony is given in 1 Corinthians 3:10: "According to the grace of God given to me, like a skilled master builder I laid a foundation, and another man is building upon it." An apostle is empowered by the Lord to lay this foundation. For this reason the apostle does this with particular effectiveness. The apostle's gift of establishing the church differs from that of an evangelist. The evangelist is gifted in leading persons to faith in Christ. But an evangelist is not gifted in gathering a group of believers and forming them in such a way that they constitute the foundation for a new church.

This apostolic gift is also different from the gift of pastor (or elder/overseer). Pastors are gifted in gathering believers together into an experience of church, but they are an essential ongoing part of that church. For this reason pastors who have gathered churches around themselves in some foreign country—just as in the homeland—have so much difficulty leaving those churches to other leadership. But apostles have the gift of gathering individual believers and creating a church fellowship which can function in the apostle's absence. This is a unique and highly specialized task. It always includes identifying and empowering local leadership (Acts 14:23; Tit 1:5).

4. In order to perform this unique function, an apostle has always been given the possibility of exercising a variety of spiritual gifts. In fact, during the early stages of

laying the foundation, apostles with their helpers must exercise all of the more important gifts. Special mention should be made, however, of the gift of faith which is necessary for an apostolic ministry. Apostles are those who have learned to trust God in many situations. They have learned to have complete faith in God to provide for all the economic needs of the ministry. This is made especially clear in Matthew 10, a set of instructions given by Jesus to his first apostles, but obviously preserved in their present form because of their relevance for later apostles. Apostles have faith to perform "signs, wonders and mighty works," as a testimony to the message they proclaim (2 Cor 12:12). Most important of all, apostles have faith that a new people will be created and new leaders empowered where these realities have not existed before.

5. The apostles who are instrumental in founding new churches also have an important role in the care and training of such churches. The New Testament gives abundant evidence of this. In this role, however, the apostles take their place alongside a host of other workers (1 Cor 1-3), all of whom build on the foundation which has been laid. Apostles do not hold any exclusive right or power over the churches which they have helped to establish. In fact, the apostolic authority, which was total authority over the new church in its founding, diminishes dramatically as the local church grows in the exercise of its own authority.

6. Paul, in his apostolic ministry, directed a team of other people who functioned in supportive roles. Timothy and Titus were not apostles. They were Paul's helpers. Paul enlisted and directed a large number of individual workers. Even though none of them on their own could have done the work of an apostle, by working with Paul they were able to enhance and enlarge his apostolic ministry. The same holds true today. Persons with other

gifts, such as teaching or evangelism, may be ineffectual in establishing new churches if sent out on their own. But if they work with someone with an apostolic gift, their labors can play a strategic part in founding new churches.

Policy Implications

Let me try to summarize some of the implications which this understanding of the missionary task would have for current church policies and programs:

1. Being a missionary is a highly specialized task which can be carried out only by those particular persons whom God empowers for this ministry of establishing new churches. The church should be sensitive to confirm and support those who have been called by God to perform this ministry. Because of the nature of this task, we should expect that the most experienced and gifted leaders of the church will be the ones called upon to fulfill this itinerant missionary role. In my observation, the emergence of full-fledged apostolic ministries is most frequently found in those sections of the church which are involved in the charismatic renewal.

2. We should be more careful and more modest about the kinds of assignments that we give people who are going overseas. We should not send pastors and evangelists to do the work of an apostle. We should not send young and inexperienced workers to exercise spiritual gifts which they have never been given opportunity to employ in their home churches. Sending young, dedicated Christians to overseas assignments is a fine thing. This should be continued, even increased. But when they go overseas such people should have a job description which does not overestimate their spiritual capacities.

3. Missionaries who have the gift of establishing new churches in a relatively short period of time are continually and urgently needed in all parts of the world. This concept

and this need should be kept in the awareness of the church.

4. With indigenous churches now existing in almost every nation, there is a great need for sharing people and money among churches in various parts of the world. This exchange of resources should not, however, be equated with apostolic ministry, except where an apostolic ministry is really involved. The church-to-church sharing of resources should continue and grow. So should the sending out of apostles. Both the sharing and the sending of apostles is hindered when we fail to understand the difference between the two.

5. Mission organizations could be most useful in this new era of world mission by focusing more specifically on the support of apostolic ministries. At the very least, they might begin to distinguish more clearly in their assignment of people and money, between church-to-church sharing and the apostolic ministry.

Note

1For more detailed discussion of the apostolic ministry, see Watchman Nee, *The Normal Christian Church Life,* International Students Press, 1969.

Proclamation and Service

9

J. D. Graber

I propose to challenge the traditional, perhaps easy, answer to the question of what is the most effective and the most biblical method of propagating the gospel to the world. I was jolted upright by a recent statement by a Catholic missionary in Africa who "thinks the contemporary Church neglects its real mission by confusing it with the teaching of arithmetic and the principles of cattle management" (Donovan 1969:6). Later in the same review he shocked his listeners by saying that when he goes on a missionary tour he doesn't carry penicillin or sulfa drugs, even though he knows he will meet someone who needs them, because his experience has taught him that being a medicine man is a sure way of avoiding the tougher job of being a missionary.

We Mennonites, in recent years especially, have taken as axiomatic that the proper way of opening a mission work is to begin with relief and social service. We have accepted uncritically such cliches as, "You can't preach to a person who is hungry"; or, "Our message is to the whole person—physical, mental, emotional, and spiritual"; or again, "The word and the deed can't be separated." We have almost gotten to the place where it smacks of heresy even to call into question such statements. I am not denying the validity or the truth of these statements, but I believe we have made them carry too much baggage in our present-day missionary thinking. I propose to open questions such as these to wide examination and evaluation.

My mental reservations on this aspect of mission strategy are not all of recent origin. In 1960 I wrote in *The Church Apostolic:*   *A timeworn, and we may say naive, concept in missionary thinking on the relation between service and witness needs to be called into question. In many quarters it had been taken for granted that the missionary cannot approach a people directly with the Gospel; that we must give them physical benefits, which they appreciate and for which they have a felt need, and only then can we begin to tell them the Gospel story. It has been taken for granted that people will be so appreciative of material and physical benefits received that out of sheer gratitude they will accept the Gospel. Unfortunately this is not the case* (1960:58).

We have become long on relief and service and have neglected a strong emphasis on gospel proclamation. We have banked much on what we might call "the silent witness." I wrote in 1960, "Are we not in danger, when we try to preach after we have served, of creating misunderstanding and confusion?" I also quoted Dr. H. D. Northfield in that same context: The missionary "must and will have to proclaim God's truth . . . to those around him; he may, of course, do so quite effectively without opening his mouth at all, but generally, in such instances, **the message becomes neutral and feeble**" (emphasis mine).

What I am reaching for is not a negative mission philosophy that says the church should not engage in social service to the needy. I am trying to see the relation between the concern of the Christians in their world on the one hand and the missionary strategy of the church on the other. Are these two aspects of the task of the church really different and can we distinguish between them? This requires hard thinking and the answers are not easy.

I honestly feel there has been confusion in our mission strategy; and, by the pragmatic test, we cannot say that our strategy has been effective. To excuse our ineffectiveness by saying that even Jesus was not successful in winning large numbers of followers is begging the question. The early church, where Jesus Christ was the center of all faith and loyalty, was eminently successful in gaining a wide acceptance for the gospel. The growth of the church in that era was nothing short of phenomenal. Father Donovan describes Paul's success as follows: *In the year 47 Paul started on the first of his three famous missionary safaris. In that year Christianity did not exist in any of the places to which he was to go. His first safari was about 1200 miles. He worked in an area of about 15,000 square miles. . . .*

His second safari was 2650 miles. The area to work in was 30,000 square miles. He worked five months in one place, one and a half years in another and then went home again; his work finished in the second place. . . . His third safari was 1400 miles. He had nine other missionaries with him. The area of work was 50,000 square miles. He worked in one place for two and a quarter years and then went home for the final time. . . .

The year was now 57 A.D.—10 years later. And in those ten years he had planted Christianity in four provinces of the Roman Empire. He is not remembered for any schools or hospitals that he started, or for any social program he initiated. As a matter of fact he hardly seemed to advert to the slavery all around him. But he is remembered, as St. Paul, for the work he did in those four provinces, for the foundation of the churches we know as the churches of the Thessalonians, and the Philippians, the Corinthians, Ephesians and Galatians (*ibid*).

We have had many voices crying in the wilderness, as it were, insisting that Acts is our textbook for missions and that Paul's strategy and method should be imitated and emulated. One of the best-known authors stressing this point of view was Roland Allen, an Anglican missionary to China. He felt strongly that the standard missionary strategy of the colonial period he saw and lived with in China was wrong because it had no biblical foundation, nor was it effective in establishing the New Testament kind of churches. So in 1914 he wrote and published *Missionary Methods—St. Paul's or Ours?*, and some years later, *The Spontaneous Expansion of the Church and the Causes Which Hinder It*.

The tragedy is that no one paid much attention to what he was saying. I read his books in the late twenties in the atmosphere of colonial-type missions in India. Although the ideal was intriguing and challenging, the method seemed idealistic and unrealistic. It simply did not seem feasible or possible to repudiate and to change the method so firmly entrenched and so well in harmony with colonial period thinking. Allen sensed this mind-set when he wrote to his son a strangely prophetic word saying it would probably be 1960 before his mission philosophy would be accepted.

This was an uncannily accurate prediction because it was about that time that the breaking up of colonialism drove the missionary thinking of the churches away from the old accepted patterns back to biblical foundations. New editions of his books were published in Great Britain and in America, and Roland Allen's views on the work and place of the Holy Spirit in the founding of Pauline-type churches are receiving new attention.

In contrast to the service and institution-centered mission approach, Allen stressed the power of the gospel to convert people and a radical dependence on the Holy Spirit to build up and guide these new believers into living churches. Paul emphasized charity, hospitality, and mutual aid for "members of the household of faith especially." But his missionary efforts did not utilize the benefits accruing from such services as a missionary approach. Rev. Donovan expresses it vividly when he says:

> He really had a lot of nerve going into a world of circus and gladiator cruelty, degradation of women and whole-sale slavery, and doing nothing about it except planting the idea that some day might do away with these evils. He must have been appalled by the sickness and beggary and prostitution of the sailor town of Corinth. But he just preached the Gospel—the good news, as it came to be known (ibid).

He then describes his experiences among the Batomi people of East Africa: *The Batomi people are a people suffering from a good deal of underdevelopment, and a state of womanhood that would undoubtedly shock most of you, plus a few other things thrown in. It is not an easy thing to decide what to do. Christian missionaries have been among them for 16 years, dispensing charity on an enormous scale, but their underdevelopment has not changed an iota, nor has the condition of Batomi women. It is a difficult decision to make, to coolly plan that you will do nothing directly about their underdevelopment, to their view of women or their other problems. To make matters worse, every outsider who has ever been among them has spoiled them by perpetual hand-outs. They have come to expect this of outsiders, and they have become the most dependent tribe in East Africa. . . . The Gospel had better be enough for the*

Batomi people. God help me, I have nothing else to offer them (ibid).

So we have by this time raised a lot of questions about the traditional missionary approach. But there is still more to come, and from an unexpected quarter. William Stringfellow, a lawyer, an Episcopalian, grew up with a tremendous sense of social concern. This concern led him to take a room in a terribly decrepit apartment house on one of the worst streets in Harlem. He felt compelled to live among these depressed people and to share life with them. His description of life in Harlem and of the degradation and poverty of these people is literally hair-raising. He identified fully with the people. He sought to help raise them up to better things. He was a missionary, but certainly of an untraditional type. After several years of involvement and so-called missionary attempt he concluded, as he wrote in *My People is the Enemy: What is requisite to mission, to the exposure of God's Word within the precarious and perishing existence of poverty, is the congregation which relies on and celebrates the resurrection. . . .*

*The Churches have been beset by a false notion of charity. They have supposed that the inner city must become more like the outer city before the Gospel can be heard. They have thought that mission follows charity. They have favored crusades and abandoned mission. I am all for challenging the face of Harlem, but the mission of the Church depends not on social reformation in the neighborhood, as desperately as that is needed, but upon the presence of the Word of God in the society of the poor as it is right now. If the mere Gospel is not a whole salvation for the most afflicted man, it is no comfort to other men in less affliction. Mission does **not** follow charity; faith does **not** follow works, either for* *donor or recipient. On the contrary, mission is **itself** the only charity which Christians have to offer the poor, the only work which Christians have to do.*

The promise of most urban church work, it seems, is that in order for the church to minister among the poor, the church has to be rich, that is, to have specially trained personnel, huge funds and many facilities, rummage to distribute, and a whole battery of social services. Just the opposite is the case. The Church must be free to be poor in order to minister among the poor with nothing to offer the poor except the Gospel, except the power to apprehend and the courage to reveal the Word of God as it is already mediated in the life of the poor.

*When the Church has the freedom itself **to be poor among the poor,** it will know how to use what riches it has. When the Church has that freedom, it will be a missionary people again in all the world* (1964:49).

The question of how to meet the crying social needs of people is always facing the missionary. The standard response to human need in foreign missionary work has been to establish institutions. Are people illiterate? Establish schools. Are they sick? Open hospitals and dispensaries. Are they orphans? Establish orphanages. William Read in *New Patterns of Church Growth in Brazil* discusses this missionary dilemma at length. His research led him to see that Pentecostal-type churches have had nothing short of a phenomenal growth during the past several decades while the standard, old line churches, with the standard, old line institutional approach, have grown scarcely at all. Read writes regarding mission institutions and their failure to produce the climate for church growth: *While institutions still liberalize commu-*

nities, the extension of the Church no longer depends on them. An epoch is passing, and institutions suddenly find themselves in a completely new situation unable to realize that a new day calls for a new vitality and a new emphasis (1965:102).

When educational institutions founded by missions are mentioned, Brazilians tend to classify them in the same category as public utilities—and the cry is often raised, "We're being exploited by foreigners. . . ." In the event that the spirit of nationalism continues to increase, this tension might develop to the place where these institutions could possibly do more harm than good to the cause of the Gospel (ibid:103).

Thus, more and more, the institutions have only marginal value for the Church, for believers are usually not wealthy people. Their children cannot buy educational opportunities in such a complicated institutional setup. Years ago they could, but not today. Things are different; times have changed (ibid:105).

There is no way to escape the gnawing appetite that institutions have for missionary finances. Institutions, once organized, grow and demand more and more of men, mortar, machines and money. It is useless to speak of institutions being able to support themselves eventually—it is merely an idle dream (ibid:106).

Read's message is clear: mission institutions do help a few people, but they do not solve the problems of the people at large. They help what we feel are the fortunate few to acquire an education and to raise themselves out of the lower social classes to a middle-class bourgeoisie, thus cutting themselves off from sympathetic communication with their erstwhile brothers and sisters, making them sterile as Christian witnesses, and often arousing jealousy and resentment against themselves and against the gospel, while the social problems of the people remain as they were. William Read finds a much better pattern among Pentecostal-type churches. First of all the grace of Christ is proclaimed, leading people to accept Christ and to become members of the Christian fellowships. Although they receive no handouts and no direct financial aid, especially not from a foreign mission, converts do get new hope, a new motivation, and a better pattern of life. Thus begins a steady climb out of poverty, hopelessness, and degradation. Here are a few random quotes from Read on this subject: *The Assemblies win thousands of the masses and attract countless artisans who compose the lower middle class of Brazilian society. These Pentecostals then march on into higher echelons of the Brazilian social class structure. . . . Peasants drift into the cities and almost over night large slum areas appear. The Assemblies preach the Gospel to these people, and many respond, swelling the churches (ibid:130).*

Humble attain higher social status: In the fellowship of the Assemblies there is a constant challenge to live a better life. It is necessary to learn to read, find a way to educate one's children, be economical, frugal, live simply, and maintain a high spiritual level. Old, expensive vices are renounced, and all of life changes into something better. Something has happened and eventually these Christians find themselves attaining a higher station in the social structure, especially when their children have the opportunity of an education and are able to enter respected vocations that pay higher salaries and wages (ibid: 137).

There is social revolution in Brazil today, and all govern-

ments are certain to make better and better provision for the common man. I believe he will win his revolution through the instrumentality of the Church which gives him a chance to rise with God's help to new hopes, positions, and happiness in relation to his God and to his fellow men. The Assemblies present Jesus Christ to the masses as their only hope of achieving God's gracious plans for them. . . . They are rising everywhere into new levels of character and godliness. God is blessing them with income, education and status (ibid:143).

To the hopeless the Gospel is something new and challenging. In it they find help where there seemed to be no help (ibid:211).

If we need more evidence, we can find a rich lode in Dr. Donald McGavran's writings. Of course we know him as the man who has for years been tirelessly proposing the radical idea that in the gospel we are commanded to harvest and not merely to plow and to plant. In one of his earliest books, *The Bridges of God,* he writes: *Under the present strategy Christian leaders tend to think of missions as a conglomerate mass of mixed chicken-raising, evangelism, medicine, loving service, educational illumination, and better farming, out of which sometime, somehow a Christian civilization will arise. The treatment for all such splendid and self-sacrificing* **mission work** (emphasis added, JDG) *is the same: pray for it and support it* (1955:103).

Dr. James A. Scherer of Chicago Lutheran Seminary in his most perceptive book with the unfortunate title, *Missionary, Go Home!,* analyzes the historical development of the institutional approach to mission during the colonial period and highlights its ineffectiveness in producing New Testament-type churches on the apostolic pattern. To quote him: *Christians have differed in their understanding of the purpose of service in relationship to the total missionary program, but they have never taken the attitude that feeding the hungry, clothing the naked, healing the sick, and caring for the helpless was not Christ's will for His people.* [Is he here differentiating between the universal task of the Christian citizen and of the Christian community and the **mission strategy of the Church?**] *During the colonial period Christian missions received encouragement to develop educational, medical, and welfare institutions to the fullest extent* (1964:114).

Even the revered three-self formula may prove to be a Trojan horse—doing more to extend the institutional pattern of Western Christendom into the younger churches than it ever did to promote real indigenization (*ibid:*100).

And again: *The younger churches cannot be blamed if they accuse western missions of prejudicing their future by saddling them with the institutional baggage of western Christianity. When the indigenous church movement came into full swing a century ago western Christianity had nothing better to offer* (*ibid:*101).

To recapitulate my argument:

1. The primary mission of the church in the world is to declare the gospel of God's grace in Christ Jesus, and to announce to all his absolute Lordship.

2. If a missionary approaches an underdeveloped people first of all with a social service program, the impact of the gospel will be dulled and the message will be confused.

3. Let our missionary strategy begin with the gospel itself. Social service is best accomplished as people get new hope in Christ and new motivation to better living. This kind of inner-motivated self-help is more effective in solving social ills than the conventional institutional approach.

4. We recognize that love, unselfish service, and charity are cardinal Christian virtues incumbent on every individual Christian citizen. **But we distinguish between this duty common to every Christian citizen and the missionary strategy of the church.**

5. Evangelism, gospel proclamation, and bringing people to faith in Christ need to be placed in the forefront of our missionary strategy, thus giving social services and charity a secondary place—**not in Christian living but in mission strategy.**

References Cited

Allen, Roland
  1962 *Missionary Methods: St. Paul's or Ours?* Grand Rapids, Michigan: Eerdmans

  1962 *The Spontaneous Expansion of the Church and the Causes Which Hinder It* Grand Rapids, Michigan: Eerdmans

Donovan, Fr. Vincent
  1969 "Missioner With a Message" *National Catholic Reporter,* June 25, 1969

Graber, J. D.
  1960 *The Church Apostolic* Scottdale, Pennsylvania: Herald Press

McGavran, Donald
1955 *The Bridges of God* New York: Friendship Press

Read, William
1965 *New Patterns of Church Growth in Brazil* Grand Rapids, Michigan: Eerdmans

Scherer, James A.
1964 *Missionary, Go Home!* New York: Prentice Hall

Stringfellow, William
1964 *My People is the Enemy* New York: Holt, Rhinehart & Winston

10 The Shape of Mission Strategy

David A. Shank

As a technical military term, "strategy" speaks about the deployment of people and material in order to defeat and force capitulation of the enemy. In the context of the mission of the people of God, the term is highly loaded and its use fraught with danger. There is first of all a built-in notion of conquest, of triumphal imposition, of imperialism. But in it also inhere the ideas of planning, structuring, and commissioning of "special forces" for the jobs of conquest. It seems that, "although God works in history through a comprehensive people-nation, and strictly speaking not through a missionary army, the latter must be organized for the avant-garde work of the total people."

This second danger is illustrated by Christian history, including our own times. That history is replete with the exploits of Christian crusaders and their conquests, proof abundant of an effective strategy. Whether the results were those sought by the Servant of the Lord who is to "bring forth justice to the nations," cannot be examined here. The subtle dangers inherent in the term, however, lead us to expect distortion, and amply justify a new look at the shape of strategy for Christian mission.

How does one avoid distortion? What precedents are

valid for today? To what do we turn for criteria? What is the understanding that governs our discernment of a strategy?

The Cross as Strategy as Well as Message

The Abrahamic pilgrimage of faith was fulfilled in the Lordship of the life-giving Spirit released through the crucial ministry of Jesus of Nazareth. From his ministry emerged a new people from and in the midst of all nations. Through that strategy of persuasion through his suffering Servant, God created a like-minded people who are servant to all peoples for their blessing and salvation. The strategy of Christian mission is nothing more—nor less—than participation in carrying out God's own strategy. Its shape is that of a cross.

Paul's appeal to ''Christ and him crucified'' is essential to the missionary thrust. Even more basic as a clue to strategy is the apostle's appeal to the **mindset** of the Crucified. Any note of triumph, or conquest, or empire based on the essential and primitive confession of faith that Jesus is Lord must be seen in the light of that prior mindset which conditioned that Lordship and shaped its strategy.

The shape of strategy that you should have is the one that Christ Jesus had: He always had the nature of God, but he did not think that by force he should try to become equal with God. Instead, of his own free will he gave it all up, and took the nature of a servant. He became like a man, he appeared in human likeness; he was humble and walked the path of obedience to death—his death on the cross. For this reason God raised him to the highest place above, . . . so that in honor of the name of Jesus all beings . . . will openly proclaim that Jesus Christ is Lord to the glory of God the Father.

The persuasive appeal continues to be addressed to the church of Christ in the world today as the *sine qua non* of mission strategy. If, as Emil Brunner once wrote, "The church exists by mission as fire exists by burning," we can add—with 2,000 years of history to substantiate the apostolic word—Christian mission is shaped by the cross as both strategy and message. The Lordship of the life-giving Spirit is the same as the incarnate servanthood of the self-denying, obediently humble, crucified one. Our strategy should also be shaped by the same understanding. The Johannine great commission parallels the Pauline appeal: "As the Father has sent me, even so I send you" (Jn 20:21).The appeal addresses the whole people of God, both in the Philippian letter and in the resurrection-word given to the disciples. The whole people of God is the special force to accomplish God's mission by the cross-strategy.

The Elements of a Cross-Strategy
1. Self-denial, the prerequisite
The normal mindset behind the strategy of the individual, the social group, the institution, the religious body, the nation, is fundamentally: "What do I get out of this?" "How will this enhance my existence?" "How does this participate in my sense of fulfillment?" "How will this permit a more perfect self-realization?" "How shall I use privilege for my development?" But all of these questions are in contradiction to the cross mindset of Jesus, who "always had . . . , but of his own free will he gave it all up."

"Go from your country and your kindred and your father's house to the land that I will show you. . . . And he went out not knowing where he was to go . . ., for he looked forward to the city which has foundations, whose builder and maker is God" (Gen 12:1; Heb 11:8-10). Abraham's faith was the self-denial of pilgrimage, and not the adventure of self-fulfillment. This is the place, says von Rad, where the Babel confusion of primeval history opens into the strategy of a new people. "If any man would come after me, let him deny himself. . . ." (Mk 8:34). The people of God learn to renounce privilege; "baptism into his death" is their point of departure.

The call to renounce and give up what constitutes a basic cultural identity (country, family, home) leads to the disturbing cross-cultural experience of discovering new identity. This new identity comes through faith in God who promises the creation of a universal family of those with a faith like that of Abraham. The test of that faith through the sacrifice of Isaac (the denial of his identity and continuity in the future descendants) is evidence of his reaffirmation of that mindset, his readiness for God's newness, and mission. The evidence of that readiness in God's people will always be their "No" to legitimate privilege. Without that strategic denial, their mission will always be haunted by the specter of a smothering paternalism. "Look what I gave up for you" really means that nothing was given. "Why don't you appreciate what we are doing for you?" is always blurted from a standpoint of privilege. As is our "bringing them up to our level." The greater the **apparent** sacrifice (giving without giving up), the greater will be the paternalistic follow-through; the imperialism is to be found in the attitude.

The kingdom will break through the mission of God's people in the faith-discovery of new life in new forms, not a reproduction of the false absolutes of human privilege that have been renounced—economic systems, ideologies, political institutions, nationalism, racism, ethnic religions. Abraham and the people of Jacob who are his descendants were completely opposite when the latter said to Samuel, "We will have a king over us, that we also may be like all the nations, and that our king may govern us and go out before us and fight our battles" (1 Sam 8:19-20). The greatest of the church's missionaries in the Abraham-Jesus tradition expressed the cross-strategy when he wrote: "But whatever gain I had, I counted as loss for the sake of Christ" (Phil 3:7). This is the cross in life; the medium is the message.

The basic strategy is a "No" to privilege, without which all other strategies become expressions of a betrayal. It is not a once-for-all denial. As with Jesus, the tempter returns ever again seeking a more appropriate season.

2. Servanthood, the stance

Without a fundamental "No" to privilege, the self-giving "Yes" leads to self (group, institution, nation) exaltation and lordship. But the self-denying "No" opens the door to a "Yes" of servanthood. It was to this that Abraham's descendants were called as "a light to the nations." The prophetic word in the Isaiah servant-songs points clearly to that intention. But this servant is always seen first as servant of the Lord. Without the relationship to the Lord of justice and peace, the servant to the nations would only serve their own self-exaltations, ambitions, and lordships. The oft-quoted "the world writes the church's agenda" is a faithful reading only when the church—in the steps of Jesus—is the suffering servant of the Lord. With the important condition laid down, servanthood is best understood, it is true, in terms of availability, the second important element of mission strategy.

Servants allow others to dispose of them; they turn themselves over to the ones being served. In this they are completely vulnerable. The ones being served define the situation, the condition, the need, the ambitions. They write the agenda for the servants of the Lord who serve with the Lord's strategy. "I am a free man, nobody's slave; but I make myself everybody's slave in order to win as many as possible." The basin and towel of the servant who washes the other's feet is without doubt a foretaste of the cross and an essential part of its strategy.

Now it is clear that the doctor is not a crippling master but a true servant when he performs an appendectomy on the patient who pleads with him for a laxative. But even where "doctor knows best" the diagnosis is based on the patient's complaint, a thorough examination of the patient, and a thorough consultation with him or her. Such a parable helps us to see how servants of the Lord are clearly oriented and qualified by him in their service to the nations. But this does not make them *ipso facto* experts with all the answers to every situation. In the service of the church to the world, it is expert only in that in which it is the most vulnerable—in its own faith, hope, and love-expression, which it maintains only as it gives them away as servant.

Another parable? The maidservant from Israel who attended Naaman's wife, and the prophet of God, Elisha, give an image of a people who are servants of healing to the leadership of one of the nations, because they are first of all servants of the Lord. The leper provides the agenda, the servants are available—in the Lord. The leper refuses the word of the Lord's prophet and dictates his own terms in the light of his own understandings. The servant is still available, but he has shown that it is not subject to the personal whims of the leprous master. Other servants will persuade the Syrian officer to listen to the prophetic word; his obedience will bring the healing of the Lord through his servants who served him. This is what men and women saw in Jesus of Nazareth, who "took the nature of a servant." The apostle who said that he was nobody's slave will unashamedly call himself the slave of the one who reoriented his service. This is elementary to all of the people of God.

3. Identification, the risk

The servant-son of God put himself in the human situation: "he became like a man." Thus by virtue of this identification with humanity, the strategy of the people of God is also defined as putting one's self in the other's place. For Jesus it meant experiencing Zealot ambitions to reestablish the Davidic kingdom, violently struggling with Pharisaic desire for purity that could choke out the human, knowing the Sadducean appeal to compromise and conformity as his own. This could be a risky thing; but Jesus was the servant of the Lord.

"Sitting where they sit" will always be fundamental to mission strategy if it is a cross-strategy. We never have a guarantee that the risk will not fail! Israel was a part of God's risk when she settled in Canaan and lost out in the midst of these national baals. The well-known artist Vincent Van Gogh took the risk as an evangelist in the mining area of the Belgian Borinage, and lost. The worker priests of the Paris Mission took the risk, until the Roman hierarchy intervened and said the risk was too great. But precisely this risk makes servanthood possible. Identification with the ones being served, living faith, temptation, and love in this context and from their perspective is the hallmark of service. The writer to the Hebrews understood the incarnation as one "tempted in all respects as we are yet without sinning." This kind of servanthood is at the heart of God's strategy.

One of the classical heresies with regard to the incarnation was that of docetism, which taught that Jesus appeared to be a man, that for all practical purposes he **seemed** to be a man, but he was not **really** human. The doctrine presented Christ as one who was only "playing man." In a similar way we must face the fact that much of what we have traditionally called missions has been heretically docetic. Missionaries seemed to want to identify, but they didn't really. Often by definition they were structured into the place of privilege from which they came. Factory workers in Paris told the worker-priests that they were just playing being working-men, because at any moment they could decide that they had had enough of a laboring man's life and return to parish church or convent. For a true working man in Paris this was not possible, for he had no other place to go.

This docetic missionary stance—apparently almost inevitable—only points more clearly to the way in which the total body of the people of God is called to mission. In fact in the deepest sense of the word it is the "everyman" of the church that is in true identification—in the shop and factory, in the school and classroom, in the office and business. It is the so-called "special forces" sent into new and strange and other-cultured contexts that are docetic. This is the reason they work as rapidly as possible to create "a new people of God in this place" so that there will be authentic identification. It is the docetic character of this pattern which should more than ever make missionaries suspicious of automatic transfer of their own cultural values to other people. It reduces the people's identification with their own milieu, and thus reduces the heart of God's strategy—incarnation—to a docetic non-redemptive mission.

Naaman said to Elisha, *'Henceforth your servant will not offer burnt offering or sacrifice to any God but the Lord. In this matter may the Lord pardon your servant: when my master goes into the House of Rimmon to worship there, leaning on my arm, and I bow myself in the House of Rimmon, when I bow myself in the House of Rimmon, the Lord pardon your servant in this matter.'* [Elisha] *said to him, 'Go in peace'* (2 Kings 5:17-19).

And what if the risk should fail? It is no worse than that of refusing to take the original risk Christ took in identifying with humanity. At the same time the docetic threat is always there. The Apostle Paul was aware of this as a mobile and flexible missioner, yet he worked hard at overcoming it. *To the Jews I become as a Jew in order to win Jews; to those under the law I become as one under the law—though not being myself under the law—that I might win those under the law. To those outside the law I become as one outside the law—not being without law toward God but under the law of Christ—that I might win those outside the law. To the weak I become weak, that I might win the weak. I have become all things to all men, that I might by all means save some* (1 Cor. 9:20-22). Was he "playing" Jew, or Gentile, or weak?

He was anxious to see that the bridges of God in cultural identification not be absolutely broken through cultural transfer. *This is my rule in all the churches. Was anyone at the time of his call already circumcised? Let him not seek to remove the signs of circumcision. Was anyone at the time of his call uncircumcised? Let him not seek circumcision. For neither circumcision counts for anything, nor uncircumcision, but keeping the commandments of God. Every one should remain in the state in which he was called* (1 Cor 7:17-19).

We always risk failure, docetic or otherwise, when we seek to identify with others. Yet the people of God take the risk. "The Son of Man came eating and drinking and they say, 'Behold a glutton and drunkard, a friend of tax collectors and sinners.' Yet wisdom is justified by her deeds" (Mt 11:19).

4. Humble obedience, the contradiction

The servant of the Lord is characterized by obedience to the Lord. The servant in the midst of the nations is characterized by humility—submission to the human context of need, learning from it, and obedience to that situation. The description of the servant stance has already pointed out in passing what is here underscored— the contradictory situation of the person who commits him or herself to people in their situation. Yet in spite of identification with them the servant obeys the Lord in another Spirit, with another Word, with another means, with another strategy. And this latter can often be interpreted as being the opposite of humility.

We must admit that docetic missions have often—and this is the perennial problem—confused the "will of the human context from which I come" with the will of the Lord. Thus what has been honestly discerned as "obedience to the Lord" by the servant has often been "obedience to my own points of reference." The people of the nations often correctly discern that this is not a humble obedience but a proud imposition of the foreign.

Yet, taking into account this serious distortion, a true obedience to the Lord, the life-giving Spirit, can and will still be interpreted as a proud intrusion of the foreign. This "foreign" element of Spirit and Word is, however, the real reason for being and his ultimate meaning. This contradiction is built into the heart of mission; it can be no other way. Docetic missionaries, because of the possibility of these facile distortions, will therefore do their "sorting-out" **with** the new people of God and not **for** them. It may be that the missionaries' sense of identity and integrity will require of them that they cannot accept for themselves that discernment. Nevertheless, they will not impose their commitment to their own sense of identify on those of the new people of God who have discerned otherwise, even in a learning process. One can be a true servant of the Lord, fully respectful of his other servants in mutual respect and humble obedience.

5. The cross, the consequences

This built-in contradiction leads to the cross—the consequence of faithful obedience to the Lord. Those who are still moving in the stream of self-fulfillment, rather than the fulfillment of the Lord's purposes, oppose God's servant. Their opposition may take forms of mistrust, rejection, persecution, or liquidation. This is not in any sense to be confused with a false cross of bearing up under necessary deprivation, or what is the lot of suffering humanity (war or famine), or the consequences of a bad character and temperament, or national identity. The cross is the consequence of obedience in identification, particularly when obedience is revealed in the refusal to use self-fulfillment and its offensive and defensive tools as a strategy—either for the servant's sake or by "profiting" from that stream in others "for the sake of the gospel." The servant announces and works for the salvation of justice and peace—reconciliation in community—that Christ gives, in the way that he did, as a suffering servant. This means that results and effectiveness must always disappear in the dust behind the thrusting toward faithfulness and the cross, experts on church growth notwithstanding.

Final Remarks

A strategy-of-the-cross is fundamentally personal and derives meaning through personal commitment. It explains the personal character of this description. "Israel" is a personal reality; "the servant" is a personal reality; the "body of Christ" or the "new person in Christ" is a personal reality, even when they imply collective personalities. The individuals who symbolize or represent such collective reality, even though plagued with the contrast of their personal cross-strategy with that of the rest of the group, can resolve the conflict only by putting that too in the light of the cross. For this the Spirit is given, but that would be another chapter. Even if this should mean failure before men and women, that too is another chapter, also written by the Lord—called "Resurrection."

Biblical Foundations for Interdependence

11

John E. Toews

Introduction

Interdependence concerns mutuality and reciprocity in mission. It involves the legitimate inculturation of the gospel.

How does one ground such a theology of missions in the New Testament? I have chosen to anchor such a theology in one text, Ephesians 2:11-22, rather than in numerous themes with references to many texts. On the basis of the Ephesians text, I suggest two foundations for interdependence: First, the Christ event; and second, Christ's creation of a single new man, the church.

The Outline of the Text[1]

The structure of Ephesians 2:11-22, which represents the high point of the letter, is clear. Verses 11-12 provide a description of human alienation. Verses 13-18 offer praise for Christ's reconciliation of the alienated. Verses 19-22 describe the shape of the reconciliation Christ has effected.

The central section of praise, and the longest unit of the text, is based on what most scholars recognize as a Pauline or even pre-Pauline hymn which was sung in the Christian community. This hymn describes the purpose and effect of Christ's work as peace among enemies, the creation of "a single new man," reconciliation, and common access to God. The time of this work is defined by Christ's coming. The cost and means of Christ's work is indicated by a series of phrases: "in His blood," "in His flesh," "in His person," "in one body," "through the cross," "through Him," "in one Spirit." The sign of Christ's work is pictured as peace between Jews and Gentiles. Significantly, this sociological peace precedes the description of peace between God and man in verse 16.

The final unit of the text defines the shape of Christ's peace in terms of the church as a growing body. Three images are used. First, architectural metaphors reveal the foundation and the high point toward which it is being built. Second, the building process is described as a communal event that resembles physical growth. Third, the purpose of the whole process is dwelling in the presence of God.

Reflections on the Text
Reflection on this text suggests several observations.

First of all, the Christ event, or the reconciliatory work of Christ, is described in political language. I use the word, "political," deliberately as a technical term that denotes how a group of people defines its identity and meaning by selecting leaders, structures, and processes that will embody its vision of reality. Thus, I am using a familiar term in an unfamiliar way; it is used technically and not colloquially. The Christ event was a political event in and of itself. Christ's life, death, and resurrection was a political event. It both modeled how to be and how to live as the people of God in the world, and it confronted and defeated the principalities and powers of this world.

The Christ event also was political in its effects. It created an alternative sociopolitical reality in the world, the church, as the new way of the people of God to be and live together in the world. Christ is praised in verses 14-18, not for bringing peace to individual souls, but for bringing two alienated peoples together. The peace Christ brings in this text is a social and political peace; it reconciles different and antagonistic people into a new political reality.

The political nature of the Christ event is intensified by the use of Isaiah 57:19 to bracket the Christ hymn (vv. 13, 17). In the Isaiah text "far away" and "near" designate Jews in exile and Jews in Palestine. The anticipated union of the two is an eschatological-political union, the messianic, reunification of the people of God. When Paul designates the "far away" and "near" as Jews and Gentiles, he is not inventing an entirely new interpretation, for "far away" had come to designate proselytes in Jewish literature. In other words, Isaiah 57:19 had already been understood as a reference to the incorporation of Gentiles into God's people. But two elements distinguish Paul's use of this text in Ephesians 2. First, it is Christ's blood, not Gentile circumcision blood, that is the means of incorporation. Second, the "far away" are sinful Gentiles, not God-fearers who participate in Jewish religious life but who have not yet formally entered the Jewish community via circumcision. The "far away" here are those people described in Ephesians 2 as "dead in lapses and sins," sons of rebellion, living in hostility against Israel and God (vv. 1-2, 14, 16).

Christ reconciles the irreconcilable, those so "far away" that they cannot be brought near. He reconciles them and makes them one. Such an act of reconciliation is a highly political activity. It disrupts all prevailing patterns of thinking and reality. It creates a new paradigm, a new perspective through which to perceive reality. Shifts in social paradigms are fundamentally political events because they alter the way people think, relate, and live.

Significantly, the reconciliation and unification of Jews and Gentiles is not due to the absorption of one into the other, but rather is a function of their inclusion in the Messiah. He is the one who came proclaiming peace (v. 17). The single new man is created in His person (v. 15). The enmity against God was killed in His person (v. 16). He united both races into one body and brought them back to God (v. 16).

Secondly, the new social reality Christ creates is described as "the new man" and "the house of God." The new social reality is an act of creation. It is not a transformed or improved reality, nor a unification of diverse elements around a new common denominator. God creates something new in Christ. This is especially evident in a comparison of the first creation account and the creation described here. In the first creation man is the last being created. But here the new man is the first being created. The church is the first fruit of God's creation in Christ (2 Cor. 5:17). The rest of creation waits for the liberation to come through the church (Rom. 8:18-22).

The new creation is called "a single new man." It is not a combination of things, but a new reality. This new reality is explicitly identified as the church in Ephesians 5:23-32. And the term church, *ecclesia,* defines an eschatological-political reality. It denotes the eschatological people of God discerning together how to live before and with God in the world.

The new reality or new man is "one . . . out of the two" (v. 15). A new reality is created, but the historic distinctions and identities remain true and recognized. The Jew may observe the law if it is not used for division or imposition. But the Gentile is free from the Jewish "yoke." In other words, Ephesians 2:15ff asserts that the people of God is different from a syncretistic mixture of Jewish and Gentile elements. The members of the church are not so equalized, leveled down, or straitjacketed as to form a third race that would be different from both Jews and Gentiles. Rather, the church consists of Jews and

Gentiles who have been reconciled to one another by Christ. The "one new man" is by origin and constitution a community of several persons. He is not an individual, nor a conglomeration of identical individuals. Instead, he is an organic body consisting of distinct members.

The existence of this new man is based upon liberation from "the wall"—all forms of nationalism, religious conceit, and individualism—and upon resurrection to a new social behavior—love, including love of enemies. Jew and Gentile alike enjoy this liberation and resurrection in the church.

The composition of the "new man out of the two" safeguards the rights of Christians to be different from one another, to remember their distinct histories (Eph. 2:11), to respect priorities (Rom. 3:1-2; 9:4-5), to enjoy unity in diversity (1 Cor. 12; Eph. 4:7, 11-12, 16). The same composition also prevents Christians from imposing the privileges and preferences of one group upon the other; it creates genuine tolerance in the context of the church.

The joining of the two peoples into one whole reveals that neither of the two can possess salvation, peace, or life without the other. One of the most startling things in this text is the consistency with which reconciliation between men precedes reconciliation with God. First the relation to men is mentioned, and only then their relation to God. Not that the two are separable; one presupposes and interprets the other. But the point, I suggest, is that he who has no people has no God. In Christ no one enters the kingdom except in the company of fellowmen. There is no resurrection to newness of life except together with one's neighbor. There is no salvation of individual souls except in the community of those confessing "by grace" we "have been saved" (Eph. 2:5, 8).

Verses 18ff. indicate that the reality of the new man means membership in God's family and gives the members of the family access to the Father. They are no longer sojourners, those living outside the house. In Christ no one lives outside. All are now members of God's household. And all in the household have equal access "in one Spirit to the Father." The word "access" here denotes worship. All that is said of peace and reconciliation in verses 14-17 is introduced and concluded with words that speak of worship, (vv. 13-18ff). The new man is centered in the worship of God. That which sets the new social reality off from all other realities is its access to the Father and its worship of the Father.

In addition Paul asserts that the new man is founded on the apostles and prophets. The church is grounded in the proclamation, witness, and confession of its leaders. The church is constituted by an event, the Christ event. It lives as the presence of this Christ is proclaimed and embodied by apostles and prophets.

The center which ties together the new man and holds it together is Christ, the keystone. He constitutes the new social reality in the world, He gives it access to the Father, and He keeps it going until all things are united in Him.

Conclusion

Ephesians 2:11-22 provides an impressive theology for grounding interdependence. Christ entered a divided world to bring peace. He brought that peace by His own life and by creating the church as His people to demonstrate to the world the reality of the new order of reconciliation in the world.

The mission of the church is the incorporation of new people and peoples into the new order of reconciliation in ways that are compatible with the nature of the new social reality and its founder, Christ. That way leaves no room for triumphal ecclesiology, nor for national imperialism, nor for paradigmatic imperialism.

What does this text say to our missionary concern for

interdependence. I submit several comments as hypotheses to be tested in the Mennonite brotherhood.

First of all, true interdependence is possible only by incorporation into Jesus Christ.

Secondly, true interdependence is possible only if we recognize the legitimacy of cultural-historical differences and identities. Negatively, this means overcoming nationalism, religious conceit, and individualism. Positively, it means affirming the diversity of the cultural manifestations of the Christian faith and community. We must affirm different Christian histories and priorities. In short, we must be tolerant and respectful of different cultural forms of the gospel.

Thirdly, interdependence will be a reality when we receive as many missionaries as we send. We need to recognize that we are a First World culture concerned with interdependence with Third World cultures. We are rich and satisfied. We are a post-Auschwitz, -Vietnam, and -Watergate people. We are a verbal culture poor in gestures and symbols. We are dominated and pervaded by technology. We are experts in national and ecclesiastical triumphalism. We represent a value-bankrupt culture. What we are causes doubt about our ability to disciple. I am more confident about our need to be discipled. Interdependence calls us to become disciples of missionaries who embody the gospel in different forms and value systems which are capable of "turning us round."

Fourthly, interdependence is for "us" more than for "them." It calls American Christians and missionary agencies to repentance, that is, to change paradigms. We need to become open and committed to being discipled rather than discipling. We need to listen rather than teach.

Interdependence calls us to define missions as the creation of a genuine new social reality, a church without racial or national superiorities, that is grounded in Christ.

Such an understanding of missions is extremely difficult for North American Christians. It is possible only if our missionary efforts are genuinely grounded in the reconciliatory work of Christ of which Ephesians 2:11-22 speaks and if we recognize that the reconciliatory focus addresses First World Christians more forcefully than Third World Christians.

Note

1 The detailed exegesis for this study is based on Markus Barth's *Ephesians,* 2 volumes, Anchor Bible (Doubleday, 1974).

Towards an Understanding of Christian Conversion

12

David A. Shank

Introduction

Ex-opera singer N. "came to Christ" out of total suicidal despair; somehow she understood that there was hope for her in Christ. Teenager A., in conflict with his family, "came to Christ" in his search for personal identity and for an "absolute" to which he could commit himself. Middle-class "riser" L. "came to Christ" out of a deep need to replace a religious system that for him was neither adequate nor consistent.

Each of these persons in a different context perceived what it meant to be "outside of Christ." What they had in common was their conversion to Christ as known in the common life of the same congregation. Each had turned from a previous condition to what was a consciously different life in a new community; yet the so-called Pauline experience of law and grace (Romans 7), or the Lutheran experience of condemnation and justification by faith was not an obvious functional part of their conversions. How do we understand conversion?

The "Pauline"-Lutheran paradigm of conversion has colored traditional Protestant understanding. The style and message of evangelism and mission have consciously sought to effect conversion as defined by a particular mental and spiritual context. This is not, however, the paradigm that we find in the gospels where there is a call to follow and become a disciple. Neither is it the paradigm of the Old Testament, nor that of the Book of the Acts. And yet in the Old Testament, Gospels and Acts, as well as the rest of the non-Pauline authors, conversion is considered absolutely essential to salvation. Thus A. D. Nock in his classic study of conversion in the first Christian centuries[1] points out that it is something found uniquely within the prophetic tradition of the Hebrew and Christian faiths. Other religions had adherents who "used" the religious thought, or system, or celebration, or priest without being wholly committed in faith to them; nor were they expected to be. Judaism and Christianity, however, "demanded a new life in a new people."

Judaism was oriented by the monotheistic, anti-idolatrous, and strongly ethical orientation which contrasted with contemporary religious climate. Hebrew youth knew when they were integrated into the covenant with God that a different community was their home. Christianity was centered in the Lordship of a Saviour Christ whose Kingdom was based on his death, resurrection, and coming judgment. Nock points to the novelty in "the **motive** which it supplied for good conduct and the abhorrence of past bad conduct which it demanded. [It was] devotion to Jesus who had suffered so that sinlessness might be within man's reach and . . . love of the brethren, altogether more lively and far-reaching in Christianity." Further, "it claimed to give **power** to satisfy its requirements; . . . grace . . . and the special gift of the Spirit."[2]

Biblical Materials

The Jewish and Christian communities were constituted by conversion, which is essentially a "turning from and turning to."

With Abraham it was **from** "country and kindred and father's house" **to** "a land that I will show you" ("he looked forward to the city which has foundations whose builder and maker is God," Heb. 11:10).

With Moses and Israel in Egypt, it was **from** "sitting with the fleshpots and eating bread to the full . . . and dying in service to the Egyptians" **to** "going into the wilderness to serve Jahweh."

With Caleb and Joshua it was to have been **from** "dying in the wilderness" **to** "receiving from the Lord a land which flows with milk and honey." But conversion was refused. So they died. . . .

With Samuel it was an appeal to convert **from** "a king to govern us like all the nations" **to** "Jahweh's being king over them." But conversion was refused. So they were given a king. . . .

Jesus' own appeal was the conversion **from** "an evil and unbelieving generation" **to** "the kingdom of God [which] is at hand." That conversion response was typified by Peter: "Lo, we have left everything and followed."

Peter's appeal, on the occasion of the coming of the Holy Spirit, was **from** "this crooked generation" **to** "forgiveness and . . . the gift of the Holy Spirit [in] . . . devotion to the apostle's teaching, and fellowship, breaking of bread, and prayer . . . (and no one said that any of the things which he possessed was his own) . . . . ''

Should we have mentioned Elijah on Mt. Carmel, and the appeals of Jeremiah (3:2; 32:40), Ezekiel (e.g. 18:30), Joel (2:12f) where the prophetic thrust is on returning **to** God with whom they are in covenant relation?

And should we make more explicit the specific context of the exceptional kind of conversion of Saul of Tarsus in his turning **from** being a ''circumcised Benjamite Hebrew, Pharisee zealous to the point of heretic hunting, and blameless in righteousness under the law'' **to** ''knowing Christ Jesus my Lord, and [being] found in Him with a righteousness of God through faith in Christ?''

It is ever again the crucial response of ''turning around'' in repentance (most often *metanoia* in Greek), or ''turning'' or ''re-turning'' to covenant with God (*shubh* and its derivatives in Hebrew—a verb of motion) that determines a future of salvation for Israel and the nations in the fulfillment of God's purposes. The shift **from** ''away from God in judgment of death and destruction'' **to** ''with God and His righteousness in the salvation of life and peace, and fellowship in the Kingdom'' is at the heart of conversion reality. Here there is neither ambivalence nor ambiguity; only an either/or possibility.

Biblical Versus Modern Understanding
The word ''conversion'' itself is used only once in the Revised Standard Version of the New Testament. When

Paul and Barnabas passed through Phoenicia and Samaria enroute to Jersalem, they reported "the **conversion** of the gentiles" (Acts 15:3), the main subject of the Jerusalem conference. There James spoke of that same reality as the "Gentiles who **turn to** God." Where the 1611 King James version translated "to convert," the RSV most often uses "to turn." The modern understanding of conversion emphasizes the psychological and affective aspects of inner experience (emotion, release, feeling, self-consciousness) as over against the biblical accent on reversal of direction, transfer of loyalty, and change in commitment. It is this latter biblical emphasis on what Nock calls "a new life in a new people" which should orient our understanding of conversion.

Biblical conversion is typified in the story of Jonah's ministry at Nineveh. Jesus used it as a type of His own ministry. A whole population of the capital city of an empire was so wicked in its greatness that it was brought to the bar of the universal judge. He responded to the case with a call addressed to a prophet to "go and cry against it." When Jonah answered finally, the Lord sent him to "proclaim to it the message that I tell you," more specifically the overthrow of the city within forty days.

Scripture reports that the people believed God, proclaimed a fast and put on sackcloth. Under the numinous impact of the word of judgment, they became as nothing. In reality this was a self-imposed "overthrow" in response to God's presence as experienced in the ministry of Jonah. Ultimately, the king himself in sackcloth and ashes proclaimed a dry fast for man and beast as total response to God: " 'Let them cry mightily to God; yea, let every one turn from his evil way, and from the violence which is in his hands. Who knows, God may yet repent and turn from his fierce anger, so that we perish not?' When God saw what they did, how they turned from their evil way, God repented of the evil which he had said he would do to them; and he did not do it'' (Jonah 3:8-10).

Faithfulness to the Word of the Lord through Israel's unwilling prophet changes history because it results in the temporal salvation of a city normally seen to be outside of God's covenant with Israel. Because a people turn collectively **from** wickedness and violence **to** God, He in His holy freedom turns **from** anger and judgment **to** pity and mercy. His turning is salvation; theirs is conversion and . . . salvation.

Here, then, is the type of Jesus' own ministry. Foreseeing the destruction of Jerusalem, He knows that it is **possible** to save it; Nineveh is the precedent. He proclaims the imminence of the kingdom of God (judgment and salvation) and the call to repent—a massive appeal to turn to God, to conversion, even to the extent of sending out of seventy apostles to **all** the cities. If Jerusalem would not turn, the coming of the kingdom of God could only mean judgment and destruction. The Ninevite salvation only heightens Jesus' sense of outrage at His own people, who refuse His appeal. He sees the Jonah-converted Assyrians among the accusing witnesses of the Judgment Day who will condemn Israel for refusing to turn to God when invited by one "greater than Jonah" (Matt. 12:40f).

As Peter so boldly pointed out at Pentecost, Jesus' death was due to Israel's refusal of conversion. But the events between His death and Peter's sermon (resurrection, ascension, Pentecost) show God's turning in pity and mercy. Thus Peter appeals for repentance. As in the Jonah story, in God's mercy a new Nineveh was created through a popular conversion, so in Jerusalem a new Israel is created through the conversion of the three thousand. It is that new people, the new community of faith, that becomes the evidence and vehicle of salvation in Christ for Judea, Samaria, and the nations. The old Jerusalem which refused Jesus' strategy of overthrowing itself in conversion was overthrown later in the Zealots' fight with Rome in 70 A.D.

The future belongs to the converted who respond to God's mercy in the prophetic word and ultimately in His Messiah who is seated at the right hand of God "till I make Thy enemies a stool for Thy feet" (Acts 2:34f). From Abraham to Peter, as typified by Jonah and fulfilled by Jesus, conversion is seen to be essentially eschatological. It means a moving into and a participation in "the last days."

But it is not enough just to turn from the past to **any** future; rather it is from the past judged by God to that future offered by God in and through the Messiah. This Messiah Jesus, interpreted throughout all of the New Testament as the **Servant (Ebed, in Hebrew)-Messiah,** and even more as the **suffering** Servant-Messiah of the Servant-songs in the Isaiah writings, is "to establish justice in the earth" (42:4). It is the new and different posture of that Servant as fulfilled by Jesus that makes Him the "greater" (than Jonah or even John the Baptist) one, the beginning and the ending of the "last times."

The early Christians' awareness of the uniqueness of the servant-stance was what made them out to be a new people in the new times. They saw themselves to be "servants" in the wake of "your holy servant Jesus" (Acts 4:29f).[3] The same Spirit that was upon the Servant in Isaiah 42:1 (and 61:1 where He is seen as proclaimer of

Jubilee) was upon Jesus (Mark 1:9-12) and now upon them (Acts 2-3). Justice and peace are being fulfilled in the new community. Peter calls it the "times of refreshing . . . from the presence of the Lord [until He] send the Christ appointed for you, Jesus, whom heaven must receive until the time for establishing all that God spoke by the holy prophets" (Acts 3:20f). Conversion is **to** that fulfillment and expectation. Paul will understand that same Spirit coming upon the Gentiles as the new people being created in the major cities of the northern Mediterranean. This is the ultimate fulfilling in Jesus the Messiah of what was promised to Abraham in his blessing of all nations (cf. Galatians 3:14).

Henceforth, conversion is seen as a turning in total faith to the reigning and coming Servant-Messiah, Jesus. This new life is fulfilled in the Spirit by baptism and is the ultimate movement in history. Conversion is eschatological but also total in the sense of being for all peoples; the converted model a pattern intended for all—a new shape for human life and community based on Jesus.

Personal Conversion in the Biblical Context

This universal people's movement of conversion is nevertheless seen to be personal, for persons are the **locus** of the turning. Those who in Christ are integrated into His Servant-community can say, "The old has passed away; the new has come." The New Testament recognizes that personal context; indeed, it is a part of the uniqueness of that picture that so much recognition is given to individual persons as such (Cf., e.g., Rom. 16). Yet little accent is put upon the description of the subjective—spiritual and psychological, affective and emotional—aspects as Western peoples are wont to do. Western culture is preoccupied with the psychological and affective. Manipulation and control of these realities has become a multibillion dollar science and industry. It is studied in order to give market dynamic to an economy of abundance.

The personal character and context of conversion is underlined in John's gospel: "born again" to Nicodemus, "drink the water I shall give" to the Samaritan woman, "eat my flesh" to the crowds filled with bread, "not walk in darkness but have the light of life" to the crowd on the last day of the feast, "enter by me—the door."

This same diversity in personal conversion contexts is evident in Paul's ministry as reported, for example, in Acts 16. There was Lydia, whose heart "the Lord opened." Then there was the slave girl with a spirit of divination which Paul charged "in the name of Jesus Christ to come out of her." In contrast to both, there is the jailer "about to kill himself. . . . Trembling with fear, he fell down before Paul and Silas. . . . He washed their wounds and was baptized at once." And finally, closely related and yet much different, there are the "households" of both Lydia and the jailer. But more important Paul uses great variety in language in his epistles. Here the appeal, teaching, conceptual explanations and interpretations will be somewhat different from his missionary message and call to repentance in the Book of Acts. The latter will almost always have the thrust seen in the Jonah-Jesus type while his epistles will speak of the real **experiential** diversity of the peoples who have turned **to** Christ **from** their personal (spiritual, social, ethical, religious, political) contexts outside of Christ. An examination of that language only emphasizes the fact that the existential and experiential reality of conversion seen as justification is one of many Pauline descriptions.

Context of Conversion	From	To	Through Jesus
Justification	Sin	Righteousness	the Just
Reconciliation	Enemy	Friend	Mediator
Resurrection	Death	Life	Resurrection-Life
Regeneration	Corruption	Incorruption	Life-Spirit
Salvation	Distress	Deliverance	Saviour
Salvation	Lost	Found	Saviour
Communion	Outside	Access	Head
Election	Nations	Kingdom	Messiah
Forgiveness	Debt	Cancelled	Sufferer of Loss
Recapitulation	Old Creation	New Creation	Lord
Hope	Despair	Assurance	Hope
Redemption	Slavery	Freedom	Redeemer
Adoption	Foreigner	Son	Heir
Victory	Hell-Satan	Heaven-God	Conqueror
Grace	Guilt	Pardon	Grace
Healing	Sickness	Health	Healer-Doctor
Deliverance (exorcism)	Possession	Self-possession	More Powerful One
Sanctification	Sin-profane	Holiness	Holy One

JUSTIFICATION

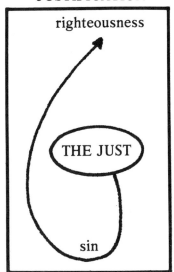

Each one of these lines is a precise, personally experienced context (sometimes collectively, as with Jews in general as typified by Paul). The personal conflict between sin and righteousness is resolved by Christ the Just, and that conversion is known as justification. It is Christ through justification who frees Paul from his sin.

The different aspect of the Word of Christ that becomes effectively functional within each "box" is variable. Here it is cross, there it is the resurrection; elsewhere it is both together. It may be His obedience, or in another place His "in the flesh"-ness, or His reign, or His coming, or His anointing by the Spirit. Each aspect obviously is a part of the whole; yet the Word comes into specific contexts in specific ways so that Christ is apprehended through the filters or grids of those who have turned to Him.

It is of course much easier to see if we look through biblical language and words rather than contemporary missions and understandings of conversion. The writers of *The Lonely Crowd*[4] make the enlightening observation that "tradition-directed" societies tend to express alienation in terms of shame; "inner-directed" societies with increasing accent on individuation tend to express relational alienation in terms of guilt; and "other-directed" modern mass societies tend to express such alienation in terms of anxiety. This can be a fruitful understanding for those involved in the Christ-given mission of the Servant-Community.

For example, F. B. Welbourn[5] points out that the missionary brought to Africa the gospel of justification and grace whereas the societies to which that message was taken were not guilt-oriented. He asks what it would mean to preach the gospel to a shame-oriented people? Or again, Jacques Ellul[6] demonstrates remarkably how

Western (especially French) philosophy and thought have literally come to an impasse in anxiety-creating despair and hopelessness. This is not seen as a theological concept or category, but an actual, existential state of humanity. Neither of these illustrations—the one from a context of pre-Christian religion and the other from Western secular thought—begin with the need for justification. Conversion is hardly functional in the context of that "box."

Reading Riesman, Welbourn, and Ellul together could easily suggest that Western Christian missions to Africa, living out the anxiety of a mass-industrial society, tried to convert a shame-oriented people in pre-modern contexts, through a gospel appropriate to an individuated guilt-oriented society. Modern Western society needed freedom from guilt and this shaped Western Protestant under-standings of Paul. But this was not necessarily where the crunch came for the Africans; in fact Western mission structures tended oftentimes to increase shame as understood by Africans. Thus, we can understand partially how the separatist, independent, spiritual congregations in Africa—without excluding Christians in mission-created congregations—have "heard" a different gospel than that being preached, have been "converted" in terms of a different mental-spiritual-social "box" and have sorted out biblical emphases other than those which were mission taught.[7]

Personal Conversion in Contemporary Western Context

Just as there has been in the West a dominant theology of justification by faith, so there have justifiably been other theologies for other contexts. Could we even suggest that the Lord-disciple theology, in contrast to Luther's, that functioned within some of the sixteenth century left-wing reformation movements, was also contextually defined by the strong hierarchical ordering of society?[8] in this vision the direct relation to the new Lord practically eliminated the socio-political, hierarchical structures yet functioned creatively in new holistic (social, political, religious, economic) communities that threatened the sacralism of the time. Given the biblical view, the crucial question about conversion is not the personal (or collective) contexts that give rise to modes of conversion in types of theologies, but the type of human community a particular theology of conversion creates.

Today we recognize the legitimacy—and even necessity because of the nature of incarnation—of liberation theology, Black theology, theologies of contestation. Theologies of hope, of humanization, of self-fulfillment, etc., all attempt to speak to experiential and existential realities. Following the New Testament, we can in fact make a list of "boxes" which define contemporary contexts of conversion.

Context of Experience	From	To	Through Jesus
Acceptance	Rejection	Acceptance	Love
Direction	to err about	to aim at	Call
Festival	Boredom	Joy	Feast-giver
Meaning	the absurd	the reasonable	Word
Liberation	Oppression	Liberation	Liberator
Becoming	Nobody	Somebody	Invitation
Fellowship	Solitude	Community	Presence
Creation	Chaos	Order	Creator
Breakthrough	Blocked	Open	Future (Omega)
Order	Confusion	Peace	Structure
Dialogue	I-it	I-you	You
Conversation	Monologue	Dialogue	Other
Decision	Indecision	Choice	Unique
Fulfillment	Nihilism	Becoming	Being
Solidarity	Exploited	Defended	Leader
Humanization	Inhuman	Human	Human
Growth	Infantilism	Maturity	adult

Conscientizacion	Powerlessness	Action	Sustainer
	Fatalism	Hope	

Conversion and Syncretism

It must be noticed that when we shift to contemporary human contexts of conversion it is easier, in contrast to biblical language, to observe how the gospel can be turned into religion similar to the first century rivals of Christianity. Using these modern "boxes" we can see how easy it is to "bring Jesus into my box" to make Him "mine," to "use Him" for my purposes. Thus conversion can become a thing that happens strictly within the self, a personal experience with no particular relationship to God's purposes "for the establishment of all things,"— the Kingdom come and coming. What we have not always seen is how this is possible also with the use of the biblical categories. When justification (or any of the other boxes, biblical or modern) is seen to be the goal of the gospel and the intent of conversion (e.g., turning **to** justification), the apostate character of syncretism becomes apparent (cf. the "box" on page 146). Happily, it was the Lutheran theologian Bonhoeffer who best helped the past generation to see this with his classic description: "justification of sin rather than that of the sinner."[9]

Not all "justification" is Christ-centered, if we review it in the community of the Spirit of the suffering Servant who as Lord fulfills history with "the almighty meekness of the Lamb."[10] Nor is all election Christ-centered, in the Servant (**Ebed**) sense. Nor is all redemption, or healing, or hope. And in the modern context we can say that all self-fulfillment is not Christ-centered, in the **Ebed** sense of the word,[11] even if the word "Christ" is used. But neither is all solidarity, nor liberation, nor blackness, nor openness.

The Axis of Conversion: The Servant-community of the Servant-Messiah.

Each of the contexts or boxes are potential syncretistic religious realities unless Christ is seen as the one who translates persons out of those specific personal (or collective) boxes into new community where justification, redemption, election, healing, hope, self-fulfillment, solidarity, liberation, blackness, openness become functional in a new community defined by Jesus the suffering Servant-Messiah.[12]

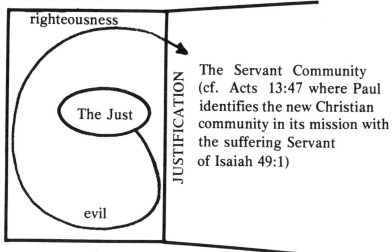

righteousness

The Just

evil

JUSTIFICATION

The Servant Community (cf. Acts 13:47 where Paul identifies the new Christian community in its mission with the suffering Servant of Isaiah 49:1)

Of all these contexts it must be said, as Paul wrote of the expressions of the Spirit in the church at Corinth: "There are varieties of working, but it is the same God who inspires them all in every one. To each is given the manifestation of the Spirit for the common good" (I Cor. 12:6f) ". . . so that the church may be edified" (I Cor. 14:3,4,5,12,26).

Conversion means in terms of understanding God, a turn **from** the many gods, or from no god, or from "belief in" a distant, unknown, or inactive god **to** "the living God." In an understanding of the religious, it means turning **from** myth **to** event and history (covenant, exodus, exile-return, Jesus-event, church in conflict with the powers. . . .) It includes turning **from** the periodic shift in sacred and profane (ritual, initiation, festival) **to** holistic sacred lifestyle (charism, forgiveness, service). In relation to time, it means turning **from** past **to** a new linear future; and **from** the "old age" **to** the (christological) "new age." In terms of spiritual power, it means turning **from** its use for primarily material orientation (fertility, success, prosperity) **to** primary ethical preoccupation on the one hand; it means turning **from** prayer as manipulation of power **to** prayer as discernment for decision and release of redemptive creativity. To be human means turning **from** instrumentalism (i.e., people are to be used) **to** personhood (i.e., unique value of person in creation, redemption, gifts, development) and a turning **from** balance of powers, and equilibrium in roles, **to** mutuality (forgiveness, gifts, service, subordination). Conversion in specific regard to community, means turning **from** ethnicity, tribalism **to** open covenant based on Jesus' lordship (within the church) and **from** geographic and temporal parochialism (nationalisms) **to** the universal (present and coming) Kingdom.

All this, it seems to me, is clear in Jesus' fulfillment of the Jonah type. Yet more basic than all this is a foundational spiritual turning. This change is of the very essence of conversion, effected according to the biblical witness by God, the Holy Spirit. And it is at this level of ethos that it seems to me that all of the other aspects of "turning" have to be ultimately discerned and judged. Reality divides into either the "Promethean" or

"**Ebed**-ist" mentality. Roger Bastide[13] suggests that all "development" today in the third world or anywhere requires a "promethean"[14] mentality. This signifies man's perpetual state of dissatisfaction in spite of his increasing achievements in mastering and apparent control over his world and destiny and his compelling ambition to push further and further into the unknown, but presumably open, future. Today conversion is **from** such a "Promethean spirit." It is **to** a mentality that I have chosen to call "**Ebed**-ist" in order to follow Isaiah in accentuating the suffering-servant quality. The current concept of "servanthood" is distorted by modern notions of service growing out of commerce and industry, on the one hand, and patronizing notions of charity, on the other. **Ebed** defines that quality brought to us in Jesus the Messiah. The "**Ebed**-ist" spirit would be reflected in human renewal of covenant with God in His purpose for reconciling all of humanity in justice and peace through Jesus Christ. This is the basis for a covenant among men and women of solidarity in repentance and hope. It is expressed in Holy Spirit-endued service, in confident meekness, through the liberating proclamation and protest of His Word, healing for wholeness, suffering for righteousness, total participation in freely restored community, as experienced in a local congregation of people where Jesus is confessed as Lord. It is that difference which can give Christian mission today its either/or quality and restore radical meaning to conversion. Thus resurrection does not form the starting-point of revolution from which anything becomes possible, and for which the future is completely open, as Roger Garaudy says. But God's incarnation in Jesus, His active obedience for justice and peace, His suffering unto death, His resurrection, His reign through the Spirit, His coming again in fulfillment of all things, all announce, on the contrary, that human community is possible under God in Christ, in the shape of Jesus of Nazareth. Because of Him such community is at the very crux of history, as well as its end.

"The Kingdom of God is at hand; be converted, and believe the gospel," is yet the essential cry of that community.

Notes

[1]A.D. Nock, *Conversion: the Old and the New in Religion from Alexander the Great to Augustine of Hippo.* Oxford: Clarendon Press. 1933.

[2]Idem, 218 ff.

[3]Henri Blocker, *Songs of the Servant: Isaiah's Good News* (London: Inter-Varsity Press, 1975), 21, underlines what is not often seen: "the need to recognize the pattern laid down in the songs *for our own service.* . . . Jesus Himself recalled the last Servant song when teaching the disciples the way to glory; and Peter quoted from it with the comment that 'you should follow in his steps' (Mark 10:41-45; I Peter 2:21)." (italics added)

[4]David Riesman, Nathan Glazer and Reuel Denney, *The Lonely Crowd,* Yale University Press, 1967 (13th Printing), 9-26.

[5]F. B. Welfourn, "Some Problems of African Christianity: Guilt and Shame," in C. G. Baeta (ed.), *Christianity in Tropical Africa,* Oxford University Press, 1968, 131-38.

[6]Cf. Jacques Ellul, *Hope in Time of Abandonment,* Seabury Press, 1974, especially "Self-critical Interlude," 156-66.

[7]John V. Taylor, *The Growth of the Church in Bugunda,* SCM Press, 1958, 253, illustrates how this happened in the Ugandan context. But it is also true that any minister or teacher of the Word knows how many messages his hearers have "heard" that he or she has never "preached."

[8]I was impressed by and reported this aspect of the context of conversion in "Faith and Doubt in Menno Simons," an unpublished seminar paper submitted to Fr. John Dunne, Notre Dame University, 1967.

[9]Cf. D. Bonhoeffer, *The Cost of Discipleship,* Macmillan, 1946, Chapter 1, for his discussion of "cheap grace" and "costly grace."

[10]Norman Grubb used the happy and significant phrase "Almighty Meekness" as title for chapter 7 in *As Touching the Invisible,* Lutterworth Press, 1966, 34-41.

[11]In fact it is probably the myth of self-fulfillment which has defined most totally the religious context of conversion in the contemporary West. See especially Jeremy Zwelling, "Religion in the Department of Religion," in Myron B. Bloy (ed.), *Functions of Faith in Academic Life (Religious Education,* 49:3-S, May-June 1974) S94-S137. John Dunne has effectively pointed this out in his writings where "self-fulfillment" is seen to be the contemporary Western myth, as definition of what life is, given the fact of death.

[12]This "religionizing" through emphasis, as compared to the major biblical thrust, is illustrated within the contemporary scene by Kenneth Kantzer's description of evangelical self-understanding: "[Evangelicals are] people who have received God's cure for the haunting and indelible guilt of sin and that corrosive emptiness of the heart for which Christ is alone the enduring solution. For this reason they have a message to share." (David F. Wells and John D. Woodbridge (eds.), *The Evangelicals: What they believe, who they are, where they are changing,* Abingdon Press, 1975, 41.) Such a tack can be one of the very real entries into Kingdom reality (which I have myself used in preaching, e.g., in *Who Will Answer?,* Herald Press, 1969) as conversion structure; but to define the gospel impact by a

single emphasis or reduction is precisely the individualizing and existential spiritualism which ignores in its emphasis the fundamental biblical thrust. To the materialists of His time Jesus warned about "gaining the whole world and losing one's soul." Here the word might well be a warning about "gaining one's soul, and losing the Kingdom." For the biblical message has a different accent than that.

[13]Cf. Roger Bastide, "Messianism and social and economic development," in John Wallerstein (ed.), *Social Change: The Colonial Situation,* John Wiley and Sons, 1966, 467-77. Bastide here expands an idea put forward by Georges Gurvitch.

[14]Prometheus, we recall, was the god of fire in Greek mythology who stole the fire from heaven in order to animate human life; but he was punished by Zeus by being nailed to a mountain where a vulture kept on eating out his liver.

Part II
Mission and the World

Which Paradigm for Mission? 13

Wilbert R. Shenk

Christian missions today are still in the throes of transition from one era to another. This crisis of missions cannot be separated from the larger crisis of Western civilization. From the time of the Enlightenment the West was fired by a spirit of manifest destiny which was expressed in technological achievement, geographical exploration and territorial conquest. The morality of manifest destiny taught that the West was trustee of the rest of the world. Whether "Britannia ruled the waves" or Uncle Sam's B-52s controlled the air, political and economic power centered in the West. And with power went the prerogatives of guardianship.

Western domination eventually came under attack. Democracy and empire proved to be incompatible allies in the end. Western morality turned out to be a self-condemned pretentiousness.

Christian missions have been conditioned by these same forces and ferment. The missionary enterprise, from one angle, is an extension of a burned-out Western civilization. Bonhoeffer sensed the depth of the problem forty years ago when he wrote that "The church is church only when it exists for others." The German church's cultural captivity during the Nazi reign has dramatized the problem. To be self-giving is not to prostitute one's integrity or destroy one's real vocation. Servanthood and prophecy demand a strength of character which is incompatible with compromise and compliance.

What we are confronted with today is no simple loss of missionary nerve. Statistics show the total Protestant missionary force remaining fairly constant. What has occurred is a decline in the number of missionaries sponsored by agencies related to the conciliar movement and an increase in missionaries from other quarters. Missionary initiative has, consequently, passed from the hands of Protestants most worried by the ambiguities and moral failures of Western civilization to the conservative-evangelicals—the element which is still the most enthusiastic and uncritical purveyor of Western culture to the rest of the world (Cf., *inter alia,* Rogers, *Confessions of a Conservative Evangelical;* Quebedeaux, *The Young Evangelicals;* and Wallis, *Agenda for Biblical People.*)

In missionary circles attention has been focused recently on the need for new models of mission. This search is notable chiefly for its preoccupation with pragmatic and structural insights rather than a fundamentally fresh theological vision. Yet mission is nothing if not theological. To seek solutions at the pragmatic level alone is to condemn the missionary movement to continued cultural enslavement.

The Bible presents us with two paradigms for mission. These two models have much in common but there are decisive differences. I shall suggest that the modern missionary movement has found greatest affinity with the first paradigm but the second should be normative for the Christian church.

Mission in the Old Testament

Most sixteenth-century Protestant reformers believed the church no longer had any active missionary responsibility. Eventually Protestants joined Roman Catholics and the Radical Reformation in affirming that the church did have a missionary mandate. It is only in this century, however, that scholars have helped all of us to see that the people of God have always been called to be a missionary community. The roots of Christian mission are in the Old Testament.

The Old Testament portrays Israel as a people on the way to salvation. In moments of worship and through the voices of the great prophets a vision broke through that the **shalom** given to Israel was also for the whole world. "May God be gracious to us and bless us, and make his face to shine upon us," sang the people of Israel, "that thy way may be known upon earth, thy saving power among all nations" (Psa. 67:1f). Isaiah anticipated a time when the nations would flow to the house of the Lord (2:2f) and once the messianic age began ". . . the earth shall be filled with the knowledge of the Lord as the waters cover the sea" (11:9). Isaiah gives the clearest statement of Israel's missionary call to be "a covenant to the people, a light to the nations" (42:6).

The missionary vision was thoroughly theocentric. Israel was conscious that it was by God's grace she had been called. Yahweh was a righteous God who had special concern for the poor, the weak and the foreigner. He was Lord of creation and of history and intolerant of idolatry. **The goal of mission was the creation of a people who lived all of life according to the will of God.**

Israel's identity was based on election. The call of Abraham was primordial (Gen. 12:1-3). The chosen people began with the choosing of one man. Yet election was not to be interpreted as favoritism. Israel's apostasy was to make Yahweh a tribal deity. Israel was not the object but the subject of election. Through Israel's election the peoples of the world were to be blessed (Gen. 12:3). Election was election for service. It was not based on race, tribe or nation. (As if to discourage Israel from thinking along these lines, God assured her she was "the least" among the nations.) The Old Testament emphasizes, not Israel as a people but Israel as **the people of God.** There is no concern for racial purity or cultural uniqueness. Provision was made for new adherents to be incorporated.

The message to Israel was the message to the nations. The Old Testament does not state that the election of Israel meant the rejection of other nations. Rather, other nations were viewed in relation to Israel as the people of God. Surrounding peoples were frequently a political threat or religious temptation to Israel. God did not hesitate to use other nations to judge and punish Israel's infidelity. On occasion He provided for Israel's welfare through the intervention of another nation. When Israel was faithful, that faithfulness became a testimony to the nations concerning Yahweh. The challenge to Israel was to set an example of social righteousness and authentic worship which would call other nations to recognize Yahweh as their God also. Increasingly the prophets expected that the messiah would bring about the gathering in of the nations.

This messianic message was the basis of Israel's hope. Through the prophets Israel received a vision of the coming messiah as the bearer of salvation. The messiah was expected to be a universal figure as well as Servant of the Lord. The messiah would be uniquely qualified by his

(1) absolute surrender to the service of Yahweh, (2) special authoritative relationship to Yahweh, (3) mandate to establish Yahweh's rule and demonstrate his sovereignty. The prophets expected that the messiah would not go out to the nations but the nations would be brought to him as tribute. The nations were a fitting gift to the Servant of the Lord.

Mission moved centripetally. The people of God were called to serve; the word of God which came to Israel was addressed to all peoples; the messianic servant was looked for as the bearer of God's shalom; and it was expected that all the nations would ultimately recognize the authority of the messiah and acknowledge Yahweh as sovereign. But the thrust of mission in the Old Testament was centripetal. Israel was to be a "light to the nations," and the peoples of the world would finally journey up to Jerusalem to join in the great messianic banquet. The geographic center was important.

In this atmosphere Israel did not launch an evangelizing mission. Israel's vision of a faith for the nations—glimpsed in worship and through the prophets—was not translated into action. During the inter-testamental period, however, Israel's self-understanding underwent change. Israel in dispersion began to engage in missionary activity, and Judaism became a missionary faith. Jewish missionary action reached its greatest intensity at the time of Jesus. Both Jesus and Paul sharply criticized it (Matt. 23:15, Rom. 2:17-23).

Mission in the New Testament

There are important points of continuity between the Old and New Testament interpretations of mission. But mission is also altered in crucial ways.

Jesus began His ministry by announcing that the kingdom of God had come. The gospel was that God was now acting to fulfill what had been promised through the prophets. Jesus proceeded by bringing the messianic character of the kingdom into sharper focus. He not only proclaimed the kingdom; He was the kingdom. Social righteousness and personal wholeness were placed at the heart of His ministry (Matt. 4:17, 23; Luke 4:18-19).

Although Jesus did not personally direct his ministry to non-Jews, He laid the basis for His universal messiahship. The prophets expected the messiah would bring the peoples together in a new relationship. Jesus created that new community by founding it on a radically different basis—suffering love and self-sacrifice. Every other society is based on self-preservation, and order is maintained by coercion. Jesus rejected conventional power and means as the foundation for His kingdom.

The inauguration of the messianic age marked the beginning of a new period in history rather than the end of history. The messianic age introduced on the plane of human experience a new order and a fresh historical possibility. Although Jesus sent out messengers to tell about the kingdom during His lifetime, the apostles became "missionaries" only after Pentecost (Acts 1:8; 2). Their function was three-fold. (1) The apostles were **proxies** for the messiah. In His name they proclaimed and demonstrated the end-time salvation. (2) They were also **first fruits** and representatives of the messianic community. And (3) the apostles were **witnesses** to Jesus' resurrection while carrying on His work in the world. The Holy Spirit empowered them for this task.

The church is the messianic community (Eph. 2:20, Gal. 3:28, John 8:56). The apostles do not witness as individuals in isolation. They speak out of a living context where the kingdom is being experienced.

In contrast to the Old Testament, Jesus deliberately directed the mission to the peoples: the centripetal pattern gave way to the centrifugal. This restructuring, mentioned in the various forms of the Great Commission, called the people of God to be a dispersed people. The Gospels end with the resurrection and the call to mission. This reformulation desacralized the land and holy places. God's people were freed to move across the face of the earth announcing the good news of the messiah and forming new centers of messianic reality. (Cf. W. D. Davies, *The Gospel and the Land.*) Territoriality is superseded by universality.

To summarize: Mission in the New Testament was based on the message that the kingdom of God was being fulfilled as promised. This message was for all peoples. The establishment of the kingdom marked the beginning of a new epoch—the messianic age when the Holy Spirit carries out the will of Jesus Christ. The church as the messianic community had a key role to play both as a living expression of messianic reality and a witness to it. Jesus restructured mission from a centripetal to a centrifugal pattern, from a passive existence to an active reaching out, from being only a sign and presence to sharing the good news through self-sacrifice and suffering love. God's people are to face outward and send out members in missionary obedience.

Meaning for Contemporary Mission

The modern missionary movement has had a strongly geographic orientation. The Constantinian character of the Western church assured a close alliance between missions and state. It was natural for the missionary to seek to bring into existence a church patterned after the sending church. Terms like "national" or "indigenous" church indicate an uncritical acceptance of Constantinian forms of church life. (There is no discernible contribution from the "Free Church" tradition to missiological thinking in this respect.) Comity arrangements among missionary societies were a logical extension ecclesiastically of what had been done politically.

Missionaries not only reflected the Constantinian background and pattern of the Western church but also did their pioneering during a period of geographical exploration and political expansion from the West. William Carey and other budding missionaries were greatly influenced by Captain Cook's *Journals* and similar accounts.

The Bible does not refer to a national congregation but a congregation from among the nations or peoples. Indeed, we moderns have imposed on the Bible a concept of nation alien to the biblical period. This territorialism has inhibited a vision of the new messianic community which might overcome the natural divisions among the peoples of the world.

The emphasis on territory led to a corollary: Western missions proceeded to universalize a particular (Western) cultural expression of the faith rather than expecting the messianic reign to transform cultural and political particularities. To be sure, missions eventually recognized the problem intellectually. Practically, little progress has been made in overcoming the consequences for theology, worship patterns, architectural styles of church buildings, ministerial support, etc.

This problem is a direct parallel to the situation facing

the primitive church. The great debate between the Apostle Paul and the Judaizers turned on this issue. In that case Paul's viewpoint prevailed. In the long run the Judaizers have dominated church history.

Not only have Western forms and thought dominated the development of the younger churches, but Western distortions of the gospel have been transmitted as well. One of the clearest illustrations of this is the failure to provide younger churches with an adequate theology of the church. It has been observed, for example, that the Chinese were not given a theology of the church and its missionary obligation. "The first full-orbed doctrine which the Chinese received is Marxism. We did not give them a doctrine of the church in the purpose of God" (Goodall, *Missions Under the Cross,* 139). The list could be extended.

The modern missionary movement has become a judgment on war even though this is not generally recognized. One major result of missions has been to extend the Christian church into nearly all corners of the world. It is one thing for so-called Christian lands to conduct war against the infidels. It is quite another matter for Christians in an ecumenical age to acquiesce quietly and support their governments in waging war when there are invariably Christian brothers and sisters on "the other side." (This fact has been dramatized in the recent war in Vietnam when a Mennonite service worker noticed a cross on a Northern soldier's canteen. When the Vietnamese acknowledged he was indeed a Christian, the two men embraced, momentarily recognizing they were bound together by a transcendent bond, and the Vietnamese assured the American that there were other Christians fighting on the side of the North.) The context for

Christian ethical decision-making has been radically
altered during the past 200 years even if most Christian
ethicists have yet to recognize it. Kingdom ethics
inevitably require that we reconsider the methods which
Jesus pioneered for establishing and maintaining the
messianic kingdom.

Modern missions have been marked by pragmatism. It
is frequently observed that the missionary movement has
been motivated more by how than why. Theology of
mission, as a division of theology generally, did not
emerge until late in the nineteenth century. Missionary
writings were dominated until this century by questions of
method and principle. During the past several decades the
contribution of the social sciences to missiology has
probably been more influential than that of theology.
Some of the most vigorous applications of social scientific
methods to the study of missions has been made by
conservative evangelicals. This leads to an uncritical
pragmatism.

Conclusion

The Bible describes two paradigms for mission. Israel
was elected to be the people of God in order that she might
serve God. Religious, cultural and political particularities
all distorted Israel's missionary obedience. Jesus introduced a new missionary vision of religious, cultural, and
political transformation which led to the creation of a new
people who were free to live by the will of God. The
modern missionary movement has followed the first
paradigm far more than the second. But it is the second
which contains the true seeds of the kingdom of God.

Authentic Witness—A Call for Reappraisal

14

C. Norman Kraus

The most obvious factors in the world situation remain change and unrest. Such a statement is almost a cliche, but it still remains a basic, dominating fact. Old cultures and patterns are breaking up at an almost unbelievably rapid pace under the onslaughts of industrialization, technology, new communications systems, and the demands of the newly emerging cadres of politically aware and discontent young people. Curfews, barbed wire and soldiers guarding public buildings and airports, student demonstrations, war, and constant turnover of governments across Asia and East Africa—all witness to the profundity of the disturbance.

The changes as they affect the course of missions can be analyzed briefly under three categories. First, there is **nationalization.** The political consequences of this process can be readily traced on the constantly changing map of Asia and Africa—especially Africa at present. All missionaries were asked to leave Burma in the mid-sixties. India has slowly increased her regulation of propagandistic missions from abroad, whether political or religious. Nepal and Bangladesh keep a constant eye on missionaries. In all these countries a new national self-consciousness has created a new climate for missionary work.

If nationalization describes the political process, **liberation** characterizes the psychological and social release from the old political and religious dominations. There is a new self-identity and self-respect; and if not an immediate self-reliance in every case, at least there is much less inclination to tolerate economic exploitation and social discrimination than was formerly the case. This new spirit is reflected in new attitudes of nationals toward "teachers" and administrators from the West. The old obsequity is fast disappearing. For example, one sensitive and honest Asian Christian leader broke with the American mission at great personal risk in order to begin a truly indigenous work saying, "I did not want to be a 'boy' all my life." And the new quiet self-confidence and ability of younger African leaders is truly impressive.

Perhaps not quite so obvious, but just as important, is the changing motivation for accepting Christianity. Becoming a Christian is less and less tied to socio-economic upward mobility. There must be more personally satisfying reasons to become a Christian. Two examples will illustrate what I am referring to. The first is Japan which has achieved the technological standards of the West without adopting Christianity. And the second is the Independent Churches of Africa who are adopting a satisfying indigenous expression of Christianity without adopting Western civilization.

Along with this new independence, we have seen the emergence of a more self-confident, aggressive posture by various national religions. In the Philippines the Ecclesia ni Christo is a homegrown nationalistic (perhaps bastardized) variety of Christianity which is neither

Catholic nor Protestant that has built an extensive and impressive religious organization. In Japan the lay renewal movements within Buddhism have had a phenomenal appeal. Hinduism not only is more aggressive in India, it has itself become a missionary religion. Also in India there are stirrings of renewal among the Muslim community, and Islam of an aggressive fundamentalist variety is being exported from Pakistan and Kuwait.

The third aspect of change is **secularization**—the shift from sacral (religious) cultures and governments to a recognized separation of political life from the traditional national religion. The effects upon culture are profound. It hastens the disintegration of traditional social patterns—customs and morals. The old forces for social cohesion and order, the patterns of social relationship such as the extended family, and economic classes are fluid and in transition. Pluralism is the new shape of technologically dominated cultures.

One example must suffice to represent this phenomenon. Forty years ago Kagawa correctly described Japan as one of the most religious nations on earth. Today it is a secular technocracy—probably one of the least religious in terms of outward religious forms and continuity of a religious tradition.

Implications for Missions

Such social and political revolution inevitably brings with it changes in missionary strategy and goals. Old methods no longer seem effective. The changing structure of relationships and responsibilities within national churches leaves missionaries uncertain of their roles. The missionary's self-understanding has become much less clear. Is s/he evangelist? teacher? fraternal worker? pastor?

The uncertainty reaches crisis proportions in some cases.

The official responses of sending agencies to this revolution range from stubborn standpattism to calls for the secularization of the mission. At the one end of the continuum are those who view these developments as demonic and call for increasing the effort and money to undergird the old strategies. At the opposite end of the continuum there are those who advocate the politicization of the church in the service of rightful demands of developing nations for liberation from exploitation and a fair share of the earth's resources.

And to complicate all this, the grass-roots supporting constituency's conception of the missionary role and its expectations of "results" from contributed missionary dollars have not kept pace with changes on the field. This causes real tension for both missionaries and home boards who are generally much nearer to the situation on the field and must interpret it to the supporting constituency at the same time they appeal for funds. Such rapid and profound change is accompanied inevitably by confusion, unclarity, and uneasiness. One senses among missionaries and boards an ambiguity of purpose and a loss of focus on central goals—and little wonder. To say the least this is hardly a time for slogans that gather up purposes into overly simple, ringing statements to stir us to action. The situation is understandably unnerving and drains much emotional energy on the field.

We need to give priority to reevaluation of goals and strategy. But how does one give priority to such long-range considerations when ten things in a wildly fluctuating situation are clamoring for attention, and when the supporting constituency threatens to reduce funds unless old methods and goals are not prosecuted with greater vigor? We of course cannot begin **de novo.** Our job is to shift from one institutionalized strategy and set of goal expectations to another. We must **un**-do as well as **re**-do—a task that is more than doubly difficult.

Perhaps we have no choice. Or do we subscribe to the old philosophy that somehow the human race will muddle through, and the church will come tagging on behind? Frankly, I am not ready to settle for that. The church may have turned into a taillight rather than a headlight, as Ralph Abernathy lamented in 1964 in the midst of the civil rights movements, but I cannot simply accommodate to that. And if it is true that we should be headlights, I see no alternative to putting some priority on long-range, careful rethinking of goals. That means theology as well as pragmatic strategy. We need serious theological work to inform and undergird strategy.

Three Stages

It has been pointed out that in the development of missions we move through **dependency** and **independency** to **interdependency.** This analogy from human growth helps us understand the historical development of the missionary enterprise as well as the maturation process of any given mission project.

In the first stage the model for mission was one of Christian civilization seeking to enlighten the primitive heathen—teacher to pupil, rich(er) to poor, wise to ignorant. The "heathen" were thought of as children who were dependent upon fathers. It was assumed that they could not be entrusted with the mission of the church until they had mastered Western civilization. The expatriate missionary was initiator, overseer, policy maker, pioneer evangelist, medical doctor, etc. The national Christian was deacon, lay evangelist, etc. An **institution of dependency** upon a continuing supply of missionaries, message, and supplies from the West was created.

Then came the modern movements for national political independence from the colonial regimes under whose umbrella missions had begun and which to a certain extent they had taken as a model. It was not long until the ideal of political independence began to be felt in the churches. National churchmen also wanted an independent religious movement under their own discretion and control. The big word in missions at this stage was **indigenization**— creation of national churches independent from the mission in organization and finances. More recently from the side of the nationals has come the call for a "moratorium" on missionaries (but not funds), so that the indigenous churches may become truly independent.

Now we have begun to enter the third stage of interdependency in which the watchwords are **partnership** and **brotherhood.** World mission is conceived as the work of the worldwide church, and there must be genuine cooperation between the older and younger churches.

My concern is not to discuss these stages further, but to use them as three models for a comparison of goals and strategies involved. I believe that interdependence is the proper relationship between expatriate and national in the world mission of the church. Thus a comparison, again schematic, is for the purpose of helping us analyze more clearly our goals for the future, not for criticizing all that has gone before.

Goals and Strategies

In the first stage or model the goal was **telling.** The emphasis was upon a verbal message. Whatever else he

might have been, the "missionary" was "evangelist."
The message was a Western import, and the strategy
aimed to make converts to Christianity.

In the second stage/model the goal was "**servanthood.**"
Institutions were turned over to the national churches as
much as possible, and organized "leadership" was
transferred to local hands. While the model of servanthood
was good, it was difficult for missionaries not to develop a
"helper-helpee" relationship in which the "helper"-
servant defined the need and prescribed the solution.
Furthermore, especially in ecumenical circles, service
began to be defined as service to the world—the church as
servant helping underdeveloped nations gain liberation.

Now, both evangelism and service are excellent, but we
are coming to see that they need a context of
interdependence and partnership if they are to be in a
Christlike pattern. The new emphasis, so it seems to me,
needs to be **embodiment in a community of salvation.**
Interdependence requires a new theological stance and a
new strategy—a strategy of identification with, or if you
please, incarnation. And does not incarnation bring us
back to the center of the gospel?

While it may seem obvious on the surface that this
emphasis on incarnation is theologically correct, as a
matter of fact it has not been obvious. Many missionaries
who went out as evangelists to save people from sin and
hell did not think of incarnation as the center of the gospel.
They would have held crucifixion as sacrifice for sin to be
central. If this is considered a theological subtlety, I must
insist that it is one which has made a significant difference
in the way missions have been carried out. The shift in
third century Roman theology—which put more and more
emphasis upon sin, guilt, and juridical models for dealing

with sin—brought with it a whole pattern of theology and mission. This pattern, which was inherited by the Protestant reformers, leads to a different strategy than a theology of incarnation might indicate.

In a theology of incarnation we also deal with sin and reconciliation; but we do it, not by preaching a juridical transaction accomplished on the cross, but by taking up the cross and following Christ in discipleship and witness. As Canon Fairbairn put it, we incarnate Christ as He incarnated God, i.e., we are His embodiment or "body." The church is to be a community of forgiveness through whom the healing love and grace of Christ continues to be offered to the world—not in institution and sacrament, but through fellowship in Christ's suffering.

During the last 150 years of Protestant missions, most evangelical missionaries assumed on theological grounds that it would be a sin to identify with, to "incarnate" in the "non-Christian cultures" to which they went. They viewed these cultures as antagonistic and not just neutral. They thought of them not only as non-Christian but anti-Christian because they incorporated and reflected "heathen" religions. This attitude is far from dead on mission fields.

An emphasis on incarnation indicates a theological attitude which has significant implications for the psychological approach to missions. While I do not profess to know all the implications, I am convinced that this is a fundamental watershed and that the Apostle Paul's incarnational approach remains valid. Paul's greatness lay in the fact that through personal embodiment and message he was able to present a Jewish Jesus, the Messiah, as a live option for Graeco-Roman culture.

Western missions have by and large taken the position

that the way to spread Christianity was to multiply duplicates of themselves. "Church planting" was a transplanting of what Van Leeuwen has called "duplicate churches." The whole style of missions was to induce the convert to embody the missionary's culture, not vice versa.

Authentic Witness

Some will take exception to my term "identify with," but I have not found a better way to express the necessary attitude and approach. Let me explain what such an approach entails.

First, to identify with does not mean to imitate. Imitation is not authentic identification. Neither does it necessarily imply an exact adopting of cultural roles— "getting inside" the culture. Speaking from the perspective of anthropology or sociology the missionary may identify as an "outsider."

To identify with means, in the first instance, **to listen** to and **learn** from the adopted culture. It means to learn that culture so well that one as an outsider might understand it better than insiders. Of course, knowing a culture this way is still a secondhand experience so I must add that identifying with means further that one tries to **feel with** the adopted culture. This is extremely difficult, and one must simply do the best he can. A genuine caring attitude covers a multitude of sins in this area.

In Addis Ababa I talked to a young couple who were studying the language for one year before being sent out to do development work. We began talking about the problem of identifying with the culture, and I said to him reverently, "For God's sake do not do anything on the field for the first year." Having had some previous experience, he agreed with me, but he asked, "What am I going to write back home during that year?" I suggest that we should not expect missionaries to "do anything" for five years. Of course they would be doing something. Probably they would be doing the most effective thing possible. They would be relating and listening. They would be getting into a position where someone would hear and understand what they were saying.

Jesus, the Christ, who is our model for this kind of activity,took 30 years to become incarnated for His mission of two and a half years! The very suggestion sounds preposterous, does it not? But at the least, it strongly suggests the relative allotment of time and effort that ought to be given to identifying with others. In my judgment we have seriously erred in this regard. We have expected people to start producing reports almost immediately when they get to the field.

In the second place, to identify with means **to respect** the adopted culture, to give it the best interpretation possible, not the worst. In too many cases we have used "heathen culture" as a foil or straw man. Unless we have a message that is better than the very best that they have already, there is not much reason for us to have gone in the first place.

I do not mean to suggest that one should be totally uncritical of an adopted culture any more than he should of his native culture, but this is a delicate point. Perhaps we can indicate the proper direction by saying that one should not criticize the adopted culture until the criticism is genuinely felt as self-criticism. Of course Christ stands above every culture as both savior and judge, but in both roles He comes as the incarnate one.

In the third place, identification with implies a dialogical stance. Many evangelicals are afraid of the word dialogue because they assume it implies that the truth of the gospel may be compromised. But dialogue does not demand compromise of truth. It does imply that we may not be omniscient, that there may be different ways of looking at something, that insights from the adopted culture may also throw light on the subject being discussed.

Dialogue is crucial to good communication across cultures. In all too many cases we have assumed the overwhelming superiority of our own world view, social institutions, and moral practices. We have assumed that the message of Christ could only be expressed through the thought patterns of Western culture. Thus, we have harangued and demanded conversion to the Western system rather than taking the time to consider respectfully and understand the other culture's perspective, values, and possibilities as a carrier of the gospel message.

Fourth, and perhaps most important in the attitude of identification, is the willingness to forsake our power base as visitors from a superior technological civilization. Not only have we remained independent of the cultures and people to whom we attempted to witness, we have taken advantage of that power to maintain an otherwise impossible distance and elite living standard. **But most serious of all, we have presented an ideal of individual independence and invulnerability as an advantage offered by the gospel.** We have offered the "wonders" of industrial civilization as fruits of conversion. This is the opposite of incarnation and interdependence. Read Philippians 2:5-11 again.

Instead of allowing our weakness to become the matrix of God's strength, we have insisted on our own strength and it has proved dysfunctional—a stumbling block and offense to the gospel.

In the strategy of incarnation, then, we must first identify with the people to whom we witness. A second implicit aspect of the strategy needs now to be made explicit. In order for there to be a new embodiment of the gospel, we will consciously have to dissociate the Christ from Western Christianity and the gospel from the Western theological synthesis. If we are going to work seriously at this new model, we must truly **cross** cultures.

There is good precedent for this in the New Testament itself. This process is precisely what is reflected in the letters of the Apostle Paul. The first theological matrix for the gospel was rabbinic Judaism. Its theological categories came from the Hebrew prophets, i.e., Messiah, kingdom of God, Sabbath, salvation as a national event. Its moral practice was defined in terms of the traditional classifications of "clean and unclean," i.e., holy and unholy. The New Testament as a Greek document represents a **translation** from Judaism to Hellenism. Paul, John, and even Peter to some extent, not to speak of Luke and Mark, clearly reflect a theological dissociation with Judaistic terminology and rabbinic theological categories. I hasten to add, however, not a discontinuity of message. Undoubtedly, the power and appeal of an Apollos lay in his Hellenistic style and ability to communicate, but he needed deeper understanding of the essential message.

The Apostolic Stance

In a real sense we must again take the apostolic stance in witness. This would mean at least two things: (a) to take a first generation, pre-theological and pre-institutional stance. Like the apostolic witnesses we must begin at the beginning and ask what Jesus means for the people to whom He is proclaimed , and (b) to exercise prophetic discernment under the auspices of the Holy Spirit in applying the gospel to another culture. An apostle was one who had both a direct experience with Jesus Christ and a fundamental theological understanding of the implications of Christ for human need which gave him the ability to discern the will of God for the new church. Thus what the apostle said was authentic, even though it was not a repetition of what Jesus said or even what Jewish Christian theology was saying.

Some of the adaptations that Paul made caused a great deal of tension in the church and nearly resulted in his excommunication from Jewish Christian circles. That tension is the measure of the distance that he had moved beyond the Judaistic concepts of James and Peter. But what Paul said to the Greeks and Romans had such authenticity that it makes up the greater part of our New Testament. All this despite the fact that Paul was not an associate of Jesus, and that his gospel already represents at least one step beyond the original Jewish cultural setting in which Jesus Himself came as the Messiah.

We are probably in a better position today than at any time since the first century to understand Jesus in His own historical Judean context as distinct from our own. Thus we are in a better position to make the distinctions necessary to dissociate Him from the Graeco-European-Hebrew synthesis which is our "orthodoxy."

As recent as 150 years ago, most Bible scholars read the Bible as though it were written in and to their own century. They did not first ask the question, "What did this mean in the first century context as the writer addressed the Galatian or Corinthian Christians?" We have not even conceived that question clearly until recent times because we did not have the historical and linguistic self-consciousness to do it. Such self-consciousness is very modern. Witness the artists of Holland and Italy in the 14th-17th centuries who painted biblical scenes as though the settings and costumes were those of their own time and place.

Today this historical self-consciousness along with wide cross-cultural travel has given us the perceptions necessary to stand outside our own immediate culture and to relate the Jesus Christ of the New Testament more directly to the cultures in which we are witnessing.

All this is not to fault Western Christians for working out a synthesis—a theology—for themselves. The only point is that we should not **impose our synthesis** on other cultures as **their orthodoxy.** We must let Jesus Christ be normative for them. We must let the Holy Spirit guide them in forming their theology in dialogue with the Bible. The goal is that our statement of the gospel should be the catalyst which induces the process among them. This is the ideal. It is complex and difficult, but I am persuaded that it is possible. We must let the gospel speak to their questions.

Let me illustrate. In Calcutta at Sunday dinner with a missionary publishing agent, our conversation turned to Union Biblical Seminary, Yeotmal. He reported that some missionaries were unhappy with Yeotmal because it was "too liberal." When I asked what they meant by "liberal," he said that there was some complaint that the graduates of the seminary did not know whether they were Calvinist or Arminian in their theology. The clear assumption was that Indian theological students must know the terminology and categories of a seventeenth century European theological debate in order to be properly prepared to preach the gospel in India.

Or again, in Ethiopia I found vigorous, committed young evangelists arguing about the meaning of the Genesis accounts of creation in rationalistic, modern Western thought forms and assumptions when their own culture provides a much better basis to understand the language and linguistic form of the Genesis stories than does our scientific culture.

In Tanzania and Kenya, where the significance of community as the very matrix of the individual's life and identity are intuitively understood because it is the cultural tradition of the family, we have preached the gospel in individualistic terms of Western Pietism. After several sessions of a seminar in which I was attempting to explain the biblical concept of salvation in community to the obvious uneasiness of missionaries, a young Luo pastor expressed his appreciation to me and said, "We understand what you are talking about."

In the Bihari mountains of India a missionary told me that he had difficulty arousing much concern among the aboriginal people for their **sins**; but, he said, "They are extremely concerned about demons!" I replied that I hoped that he had cast out a few. The gospel speaks to that problem also. In fact, there are more instances of Jesus casting out demons than of forgiving sins in the accounts of His ministry.

In order to do this, we will need the gift of prophetic discernment. There has never been a time in the history of the church when the Spirit of prophecy was more urgently needed. Especially in situations of cultural change, whether in social revolution or in transcultural communication, prophetic discernment is essential to authentic witness.

This brings us back to the centrality of the church as the community of prophetic discernment. The prophet speaks from within a community of the Spirit which tests and authenticates his message. He does not come as a lone individual speaking to strangers. Thus the church as the **koinonia of the Spirit** remains the focus of Christian concern. It is not the individual Christian who is the embodiment of Christ but the church of which the individual is a "member." Our concern for individuals is that they be brought into the new fellowship of salvation.

Training for Mission

If this is the nature of the task, what kind of missionaries will we need for the future? How should we go about training them? Again, we can only sketch the broad outline. First, they will need to be highly skilled specialists at communicating across cultures. This would suggest a new level of cultural sophistication—anthropological insight, language ability, etc. The new missionary will need to play a different role than the old father-evangelist figure.

Second, they will need a grasp of the gospel and a kind of theological insight into the meaning of the faith that gives them maximum freedom under the Spirit to adapt and to work out its implications in differing cultures.

All this suggests that the new missionary will need to be long-term. The picture of an integrated, interdependent worldwide brotherhood suggests the need for more than short-term technical experts to help raise the level of development in "underdeveloped" countries. It suggests to me more than simply turning over the enterprise to nationals who then run an independent project while short-term volunteers return to the joys of the American way of life. It suggests rather continuing interaction, a mutually shared task, mutual leadership, two-way translation and influence. (The early Jewish contingent of Christianity died out because it refused such interaction and mutual interdependence with Hellenistic Christianity.)

This does not rule out the contribution of short-term technical experts in brotherly interchange. But it indicates that they will not carry the major share of the continuing task. They will make the best contribution if they can fit into long-term programs under the supervision of ongoing interdependent leadership—national and expatriate.

Such a reappraisal raises the question of preparation and training for such a role, but that is a new subject which deserves attention in its own right.

15

Robert L. Ramseyer

The Gospel and Culture in Evangelism

Culture and the Gospel—Definitions

Christians can be engaged effectively in evangelism, in the sharing of the gospel of Jesus Christ, only when the gospel and culture are in proper relationship to each other both in the life of the individual Christian and in the corporate life of the fellowship of believers that we call the church. This gospel-culture relationship is seen most clearly in Jesus Christ. When this relationship is not maintained properly the church and individual Christians either become so isolated socially that they are unable to communicate the good news to those outside the church, or they become so much like the society around them that they have no good news to communicate.

Culture as it is used here means all of the things that we acquire by learning, including our language, all of the things which are handed down in our society from generation to generation. Culture has been defined as "the common, learned way of life shared by the members of a society, consisting of the totality of tools, techniques, social institutions, attitudes, beliefs, motivations, and systems of value known to the group." In other words, culture is that which binds us together as human beings into groups and communities. However, as we are bound together into groups, we are also divided from other human beings who are in different groups with different cultural traditions. Culture is not only the great unifier of human beings, it is also the great separator. Culture brings us together and it pulls us apart. As we are drawn closer to some people, we are pulled farther away from others.

Gospel as it is used here refers to the good news of the richness and fullness of what God has done for us in Jesus Christ: an act of God in Jesus Christ that occurred in our own world in the midst of the flow of human history. The gospel is something that was done within human culture, in a specific cultural setting at a specific time and place in human history. As Christians we try to understand what the gospel means, what God has done for us. In our attempts to understand, however, we are forced to use our own cultural equipment, languages and world-views which we learned as we were growing up. This is the only way that we have of understanding anything. Moreover, as we try to share the gospel with others, we are again forced to use the means which our own culture has brought to us or which we have learned from other cultural traditions. These are the only means which we possess for expressing and sharing that which we have experienced.

Because of these limitations both our comprehension and our expression of the infinite richness of what God has done for us in Jesus Christ can be only partial and incomplete. As the Apostle Paul has said, "For our gifts of knowledge and of inspired messages are only partial; . . . What we see now is like the dim image in a mirror; then we shall see face to face. What I know now is only partial;

then it will be complete, as complete as God's knowledge of me'' (I Cor. 13:9-12). There will always be tension between God's perfect gospel and our own weak attempts to comprehend it and to share it with others.

Gospel and Culture Together—Jesus Christ

Only in Jesus Christ do we see the coming together of human culture and the living word of God. We call this the incarnation. In Jesus Christ God became one with us and one of us; He became "like his brothers in every way" (Heb. 2:17) so that He could share with us. As Jesus Christ God identified with us completely, accepting the many limits that human culture imposed on His self-expression. Jesus spoke one human language, accepting the limts of that language. He did not invent a new "Christian" language which might have more adequately expressed the gospel. He used what human culture provided, limited as that was. As far as the people who lived around Him when He was growing up knew, Jesus was fully one of them. He was so much one of them that later on when He did begin to speak and teach with authority His neighbors were very surprised and wondered what had happened to this Jesus whom they had known so well.

Jesus chose to live as an ordinary human being so that people around Him felt at home. People were not afraid to bring Him their problems and concerns. They loved to hear His teaching which seemed to bring together God and their world as they knew it. In the wilderness we are told that Satan deliberately tried to persuade Jesus to abandon this course and to become a spectacular miracle worker. Jesus said no. This was not the way to share the love of God with men and women who must live in ordinary human society.

But as He identified with human beings in their society and culture, Jesus never allowed that society and culture to become the ultimate directors of His life. Jesus showed clearly that neither He nor His followers were bound by any human society and culture. The New Testament says clearly that we are pilgrims and strangers in this world, temporary sojourners whose citizenship is not here but in the kingdom of God. Jesus' authority did not come from any human society.

Guided as He was by a different authority, Jesus finally ran afoul of human authority. He refused to give the allegiance that His society demanded. He refused to follow all of the traditions which were part of His culture. For this, Jesus was hung on the cross.

Our Response to the Gospel—Faith/Discipleship

If the gospel is the good news about what God has done for us, then something more than a merely intellectual acknowledgment is called for on our part. The gospel is not some new esoteric knowledge to enlighten us; it is God's love saving us from sin. Our basic problem as human beings is not that we are ignorant but that we are sinners. To help us in this situation, God acted in love in Jesus Christ. We are called to respond to God's action with an appropriate action of our own, an action which we call faith. Faith here is not an intellectual assent to the proposition that Jesus died for us, but joining what God is doing. We join the movement, becoming part of what He is doing. In more traditional language the appropriate human response to what God has done for us in Jesus Christ is to become His disciple and join His group of followers.

If it is true that we are called upon to be active disciples rather than passive assenters, then a basic part of our response will be the sharing of the gospel with others. Jesus sent His disciples out to share the faith, to minister to people as He found them. Jesus told them that just as His father had sent Him into the world, He was sending them into the world (John 20:21). We have His direct command in Matthew and in Acts to be witnesses, to make disciples at home and abroad, all over the face of the earth.

The content of the gospel also demands that it be shared. The gospel is the good news about God's love, a love which reaches to all people. The gospel is good news about something that actually happened. It is not a pleasant story which someone invented just to make people happy. The response which people make to the gospel is of life and death significance. There is no way that a Christian can share in this gospel for himself and ignore the people around him who do not know Jesus Christ. The gospel in its very essence is a gospel which must be shared. There is no way that any Christian can be left out of the call to evangelize.

Gospel and Culture—Identification in Translation

In most discussions of culture and evangelism, the emphasis is on communication and identification. We have called this the incarnational emphasis. When I try to share the good news with persons, I want it to come alive within them and to become a part of their own lives rather than something foreign and outside their daily experience. I want it to be expressed in terms of their own culture as "Good News" rather than as some new law that is being placed on them from the outside. The gospel should come through to them as liberation in their own lives rather than as a new burden they are forced to carry. Consequently, in evangelism I try to express the gospel in categories which are familiar to the other person, using the things of everyday life in that person's environment to help that person see what God has done and is doing for us.

As the gospel is translated in this way into a new cultural setting, there is always the very real danger of so distorting the gospel that the result is no longer the Christian faith at all but some new syncretism that merely uses some Christian terminology. This has made some people who engage in evangelism afraid to do any translation at all. To preserve the purity of the faith they insist on keeping it in all of the cultural forms to which they are accustomed. This would be as if God had insisted on coming to us in all His infinite glory instead of coming to us as the incarnate Son of God. Thus when the Jesuits first came to evangelize Japan they felt that the Japanese words for God were too full of non-Christian ideas about God and insisted that Japanese Christians all refer to God by the Latin term "deus." So in Japan the Christian God became one more god among the many, a God whose personal name was "deus."

If we are afraid of translation and identification we need to remember that the first major heresy in the New Testament was that of the Judaizers, who were afraid to take the gospel into the non-Judaic world. They were people who said, "If people are to understand the gospel, they must come to us, into our thought world. Then they can become Christians. But we cannot go into their thought world with the gospel because that is not a Christian thought world and it would corrupt the gospel."

Paul made it clear that this sort of thinking is wrong.

The gospel can and must become incarnate in every cultural context in our world. When I want to share the gospel with my neighbors who are not Christians, I must try to become one with them, expressing the good news in ways that are clear and understandable to them. If Paul could live like a Jew to win Jews, like a Gentile to win Gentiles, and like the weak to win the weak (I Cor. 9:20-22), then surely we can identify ourselves with those around us in order to share the good news with them. Such identification is risky, of course, but it is the kind of risk that makes faith an exciting adventure.

Gospel and Culture—The Personal Relationship

In identification in evangelism however, it is not enough to try to be close to a group or a particular variety of people—Jews, Gentiles, village Hindus, etc. If I am to share the gospel with a person, I need to know that person. This is what Jesus did. He preached to the multitudes, but He also had time for individuals as they came to Him with their concerns and problems. He learned to know them. Then His gospel could be good news for them, answering the problems which they had. In our rapidly changing world many people feel lost and left out. They feel that no one is concerned about **them** as people, that they are merely being pushed around and manipulated as objects. If I as a Christian show that I really care about such a person, then that person may begin to see that Christ Himself cares, and the good news of Jesus Christ can become real for that person.

As we plan evangelism and evangelistic strategies, it is easy to forget this. It is easy to think about people as things and to work out strategies for maneuvering them into the kingdom of God. We stand apart from them, try to think about them objectively, and see how we can get them to believe in Jesus. But as we do this, we are treating them just as the modern world treats them. The only difference between us and merchants who are trying to get people to buy their product is that we have a better product.

But the gospel is not something to be merchandised. It is a personal message about God who became human like us in order to save us. It is a message which needs to be shared through a human relationship if it is to be received as the good news. We need to be open with people, admitting that we like them have strengths and weaknesses. And God who has come to us in Jesus Christ to help us in the midst of our weaknesses and problems will help them with whatever problems they may have. We and they are just exactly the kind of people whom Jesus came to help and for whom the gospel is good news.

In evangelism, then, there is no substitute for building personal relationships. But, surprisingly, it is easy for earnest Christian people to be impersonal in their evangelistic work. As we prepare for evangelism or talk together in conferences on evangelism, we readily prepare strategies to reach village people in India, or to reach high caste city people, or university students, or factory workers, or housewives. We may even work out more general approaches with spiritual laws or six principles of the Christian faith. All of these approaches may have validity at certain times when used in certain ways. But all of them tempt us to try to fit real flesh-and-blood people into categories which we have constructed. We manipulate people, attributing problems to them which we think they should feel, answering the questions which we think they should ask, instead of listening to the urgent problems and questions which they have and then together with them trying to hear the answers which God has for them.

We are not saying here that there are many gospels—different gospels for different people. The gospel is one. But the gospel is good news about an infinite God whose love is beyond our comprehension. It is a gospel about God's love, which is the answer to any human situation. Since the gospel speaks to us where we are, answering the problems which we have, that aspect of the gospel which is most apparent to a person will depend on the problems he is facing at that time. If I feel the burden of guilt because of my sin weighing me down, then the gospel comes to me as the good news of God's forgiving love and of cleansing from sin. If I feel that I am living in a world surrounded by evil spirits, the gospel comes to me as the good news of Jesus Christ's victory over all of the spiritual forces of evil, a victory in which I share fully as a follower of Jesus. If I am lonely, the gospel tells me that God's Holy Spirit is always with me and that I am part of a great company of Jesus' people.

Although we can never fully comprehend all of what God has done for us in Jesus Christ, as we grow in Christian faith, we see many facets of the gospel. In evangelism, I must be sensitive to the needs which my friends are feeling so that the gospel which I try to share with them can be God's answer to the problems with which they are wrestling, so that they can see that God is speaking directly to each of them and to their needs in each specific situation.

I hope that it is now clear why evangelism demands personal involvement. If I am not personally involved, if the word of God is not incarnate in the immediate environment of my friend through me, then it becomes extremely difficult for my friend to see the gospel as good news in that situation. If our friends cannot see the gospel as good news in their own settings, why should we expect them to respond and give their lives to Jesus Christ? After all, in order to share His love with us, God felt that He needed to make His word incarnate in our world as one of us. In order to share His love with us, God became a human being in the person of Jesus Christ who lived and worked among us. Why should we feel that we can share His love with a less direct involvement? This is not to say that mass approaches to evangelism are without value. They can be useful as a general introduction to the gospel, but there is no substitute for the personal sharing of a Savior who came into our society as a person in order to save us as human beings.

Gospel and Culture—Social Bridges and Faith Barriers

As Christians we have experienced the fact that it is not always easy to develop deep personal relationships with the non-Christians around us. Between Christians, the people of God, and the non-Christian world there are both bridges and barriers, and if we are serious about evangelism we need to understand these clearly.

As Christians we are different. We have committed our lives to Jesus Christ. He is our Lord and we want to follow Him. Therefore the ultimate authority by which Christians order their lives is different than it is for other people. This allegiance to Jesus Christ unites us as Christians and divides us from other people. At the same time, Christians have come from the general society to Jesus Christ. Therefore we have in common with people in general society many of the things which bind them together. Ethnically and socially we are at one with our non-Christian neighbors.

Even though the people of God are united in Jesus Christ, they are socially as diverse as the social backgrounds out of which they have come. Thus the people of God have clear and firm social and cultural bridges to the non-Christian society in which they live. But there are also barriers of faith between Christians and the society in which they live which are caused by the change in the life of the Christian that faithfulness to Jesus Christ demands. The unfortunate fact is that while these bridges and barriers may be clear when a new Christian group is forming, a group quickly begins to build ethnic-like barriers and then to compensate for the resulting loss of social contact with the world by minimizing the differences which faith demands.

But what about the faith barriers, the separateness, that faithfulness to Jesus Christ demands? Does not Paul himself warn us against getting too close to unbelievers, quoting the Lord as saying "you must leave them, and separate yourselves from them" (II Cor. 6:17)? Christ has called us to be His disciples, a radical step which demands a totally new orientation to life, to everything which we do, to the way in which we live. As a Christian I want to do everything that I do consciously under the direction of Jesus Christ. This ought to mean that we will live differently from the non-Christian people around us. Now the pertinent question for me is, how can I as a native of India, or the United States, or Japan most completely express the gospel of Jesus Christ in my native society? How shall I change my way of life so that it will more fully express the good news of what God has done in Jesus Christ? Often this emphasis may seem to be in conflict with the incarnation-identification which is so vital in evangelism. I may feel that if I make the radical changes in my life which faith would seem to demand, it will separate me from non-Christian neighbors with whom I want to share the gospel. It may make them angry with me and with all Christians so that they would not want to hear about Jesus Christ. Thus I am tempted for evangelistic reasons to minimize some of the things which faithfulness to Jesus Christ would seem to demand, some of the differences which being a Christian should make in my life. I minimize them so that I can have the respect and goodwill of my non-Christian neighbors and thus more easily share the gospel with them.

The Evangelistic Dilemma

This then is the evangelistic dilemma. How can I be as much like my neighbors as possible so that I can share the good news readily with them, and at the same time be as much like Jesus Christ as possible so that I really have the good news of victory in Jesus Christ to share?

Too often we are tempted to deal with evangelistic problems by developing new strategies rather than by dealing with the root of the problem—our manner of being as the people of God. The root problem in evangelism is not that we lack good techniques and strategies. The root problem is that all too often the church of Jesus Christ has ceased to be a group which is vitally concerned about living in faithfulness to God, on the one hand, and, on the other hand, maintaining living relationships with its non-Christian neighbors so that in its life among them it can bring them the living word of God. Instead of dealing with the root problem, we are tempted to study culture and society as if all that we needed for effective evangelism was new knowledge and new techniques to develop new and more effective evangelistic approaches. But new techniques cannot transform a church which has become an ethnic unit into a dynamic tool for sharing the gospel. When a church has become an isolated natural social unit, be that social unit tribal, factional, or communal, it can no longer transmit the good news effectively. A church which has ceased identifying with non-Christian people, a church which no longer lives the gospel in close contact with non-Christian people, cannot do evangelism no matter how much it studies anthropology and sociology, church growth and evangelistic method-ology. Studies and strategies can be helpful if the church is already present with a clear view of its separateness but also with its cultural-social bridges open. When the church is a vital fellowship into which anyone with faith in Jesus Christ can pass and feel immediately at home, then it can profit from deeper study of methods and strategies of evangelism.

I know of no real answer to the identification-separation dilemma in evangelism other than the person and work of Jesus Christ Himself. Jesus is the perfect example of complete faithfulness to the will of God in His life and at the same time the perfect example of full identification with a specific human, social-cultural setting. Jesus is the love of God fully expressed in human culture and society. This expression ultimately led Jesus to the cross because of the threat which God's love posed to the established social order. People saw God's love clearly in Jesus Christ and many responded to it. However God's love is also judgment, and this was so clear that some felt that they needed to remove Jesus from their midst. It is important to remember that those who rejected Jesus did so because they understood Him and knew that they had to make a decision about Him. They did not reject Him because they considered His message foreign or irrelevant to their situation. They rejected Him because He came to them as the light of God in the world, and they could not endure that. They preferred to live in darkness.

Incarnation and separation, faith barriers and social bridges, identification with human society in faithfulness to Jesus Christ—this is the context of the evangelistic task to which we are called. Only as we strive toward these goals as they are personified in Jesus Christ can we evangelize as the people of God.

16 Irish Theology

*Michael
Garde*

Theology is concerned with the study of the Word of God, i.e., sacred Scripture. This, one would think, would be obvious, but experience teaches that the opposite is often the case. The static nature of Protestant and Catholic dogmas hardly touched since the Reformation indicates that the Bible has been enslaved by the church.

Modern Trends
Since the Enlightenment we have seen the emergence of critical methods of study which have made the human dimension of the Bible more real. The idea of the Bible coming down from heaven on a rope has been shattered once and for all. The Enlightenment tried to shift the meaning of theology from a study of the Word of God in the words of men, to a study of the experience of God. The father of this approach was Schleiermacher. Accordingly John's gospel is not so much God's word through John, as John's experience of God's word.

On the other hand, some have reacted against this approach as if theology were a given and what God said through Paul or Peter did not arise out of a particular culture. They view the Bible as a linear work of proof texts, flowing from eternity to eternity and merely intersecting our time. The text is what is important, without regard to its context in the development of theology. This approach reacts strongly against the view we represented above which argues that theology is basically our reading our own views into the text. If we were Irishmen, for example, the only theology we could produce would be an Irish theology. If we were to look down the well of history for Jesus, we would see our own face reflected. This is the ultimate explanation of the Liberation theology of South America. Classical theology claimed to be preaching the word of God, but in fact it was upholding the status quo and its own class interests.

To shake ourselves free from such a system, we do not primarily discover what God is saying to us through Scripture, but through analysis—usually Marxist—of our situation. After this analysis we use various resources including Scripture to develop a theory. It tends to produce a "natural theology," a mirror image of its own time. The advantage of this method is that it takes our concrete existence seriously. Starting from practice and the experience of real people, it follows the model of the incarnation. Like Christ it faces such issues as unemployment and women's rights. Its drawback is that it does not take God's word as a starting point.

Classical theology, on the contrary, is idealist, Platonic and enslaved by abstraction. Unlike the writings of the early church which were written to real people with real questions, classical theology is in a "Babylonian" exile of academics sitting in studies writing for other people sitting in studies. It tends to play down the diversity of Scripture and harmonizes when it is totally unnecessary. It would find it hard to accept the possibility of an Irish theology and would say there is only the Word of God. The God of this theology is Greek, without body or passions, and bears little resemblance to the God of incarnation found in the gospels.

The Irish Situation
Theology in Ireland has to relate to two very different areas, namely, Ulster and the Republic. Both have drawn their theological language from the outside and are still in a dependent state. The Catholic south has gained national independence from Britain, and the majority Catholic church (96% of the population), which in dark days had been the servant of the people, has now become the establishment. It is satisfied with a Sadducean posture. No longer is it seen to be in charge as in former times, but everywhere the power of its institutions is victorious: schools, bedrooms, and moral law all manifest this power, as does the unprecedented 91% attendance at mass. Its theology is now leaning towards liberal Protestantism, and it never questions the confusion and identification of Irishness with Catholicism. Since Vatican II a strange blend of liberalism and conservatism coexist in the Irish church. Gradually the dogmatic certainties of the Council of Trent and Vatican I are withering away and are being replaced by Anglo-Saxon pragmatism and relativism.

The Protestant churches in the Republic drift on without aim or vision. The historian J. C. Beckett foresees the collapse of Protestantism on this island by the end of the century. The 1916 rebellion did not change the economic dominance of the Protestants; today they are 4% of the population and control approximately 30% of the economic wealth of the nation. Is it any wonder that the gospel of good news for the poor and of radical discipleship has not touched Irish Protestant churches?

Northern Ireland has until recently been a British theological satellite. Ian Paisley's "Free Presbyterian movement" attempts to formulate an alternative theology to the liberalism and formalism of other Protestant churches and has the beginnings of an independent Ulster theology. Paisley correctly analyzes the forces of history and has decided on a policy of theological and political reaction. He takes the Province of Ulster as a given absolute which can be separated from the whole history of Ireland. Ulster is the people of Israel; the Catholic Republic is the land of Baal. Paisley is Elijah, the prophet who cannot surrender. When those of us who live in the south claim that we have total freedom to be Christians and that we would view the incorporation of Ulster into the Republic by agreement as one of the greatest possibilities to demonstrate the power of God to change darkness into light, Paisley denounces us as false prophets who cry peace when there is no peace. His demand for total victory over the I.R.A. and a return to a Protestant-dominated Ulster parliament without any power sharing with the Catholic minority is the social outcome of his political theology. It represents a failure to see the newness of the New Covenant which Jesus introduced and a failure to see the diversity and development from Old to New Covenant, from B.C. to A.D. It is based on the writings of Chalmers, Dabney and in an unrecognizable way on the thinking of the Dutch theologian who became Prime Minister of the Netherlands, Abraham Kuyper (who incidentally came to power by sharing power with the Catholic party). The way then to preserve Protestantism, Paisley argues, is by the might of the state in alliance with the Protestant para military groups which will fight because Ulster is right.

This extreme Protestant attitude ignores the Irish past and denies the gospel call to give up rights, to deny oneself and follow Christ. The existence of the I.R.A. depends on this Protestant inflexibility. Majority Protestants are 60 percent of the Ulster population. Yet they are a people without an identity in the northeast corner of Ireland. Perhaps they are British; but the British government seems to believe in a united Ireland and advocates power sharing as a basic beginning. Perhaps they are Ulster people, but Ulster goes back to the very origins of Irish history, centuries before the Protestants arrived. Perhaps they are Irish people, but this produces a confrontation with the south over the issue of Irishness. As a southern Irish Christian, let me put in on record that as a minority in a United Ireland, Protestants would be compelled to act out a different role from the one they choose at present. I do not mean to give moral sanction to the activities of the I.R.A., but their very existence would be totally useless if Protestants accepted these new conditions. The Catholic dimension would have to be removed from a new Irish federal constitution, and there would need to be a system of checks and balances to protect the Protestant minority in a single, united Ireland. The southern non-Catholic population, which is currently so apathetic, would receive a massive boost to act in an alternative way. This surrender of Protestant rights would not touch the essentials held by various groups which hang or fall on the basis of the Word of God.

The evangelical church in Ulster has divided private and public morality. Generally, save for a few exceptions, it has accepted the status quo, upheld the injustices of the past, and reduced everything to getting saved or personal ethics. While Rome burns, the churches have fiddled over minutiae. They claim that being born again is a vertical relationship with God, and they have no vision of the radical movement which Jesus inaugurated. Attempting to gain their souls, they have lost the kingdom. In reaction to this, groups such as the Corrymeela Reconciliation Centre on the northern coast have emerged. Giving up on constructing a bridge between dogmatics and ethics, these groups atempt to operate together on social and practical concerns; afterwards they will work out a theory of what Christianity is in itself. One can understand this reaction, but again we must try to be faithful to the Word of God.

In both north and south, the charismatic movement is growing in strength. Will it be able to bring Catholic and Protestant together in a new body? Will its concern for devotion to Christ be spelled out into practical service? It seems to me that what started out as a radical spiritual movement is becoming the devotional wing of the official churches. The groups as they arise seem to be increasingly Catholic or Protestant in their theology, indicating that this movement is not transcending the sectarian divide.

An Alternative

It is one thing to speak one's mind, to pull everything down around oneself like a blind Samson. It is another to identify an alternative and to rebuild. If any current situation illustrates this truth, it is Ireland. What then could one find as a common source for the preparation of an Irish theology? Naturally, the Protestant would reply, this source must be the Word of God. The Catholic would certainly admit it as a source, the most important source, but still only one of several sources. But both approaches oversimplify. In Britain the Bible was part of the story of national liberation and has molded the whole development of English literature and language. Against this, in Ireland British rule used the Bible to sanction its imperialism and to destroy the dignity of Gaelic-speaking people. The form of British rule was colonialism, the content Protestantism. Even the nonconformity of the 17th century was introduced as part of the war machine of Oliver Cromwell. The English troops carried the Geneva Bible, which in its notes confused Canaanites with Catholics and thereby gave license to kill. One of the great theologians of Puritan England was John Owen, who was Cromwell's chaplain on his Irish expedition. Irishmen cannot read the theology of Protestants such as Owen in a vacuum.

Since Irish experience of the Bible has been different from that of the English, we need a sensitivity and critical awareness of our own past. We dare not forget the past, but it is necessary for us to repent and to make a common discovery of God's Word to us. Some contemporary Christians feel the need to replace the Bible with a socialist or Marxist interpretation of industrialized society, since the biblical writings are prescientific. This is especially the case in South America, where right wing totalitarian states have in the past had the backing of the Catholic church. In Ireland, as in Europe after the wars of religion, many have tended not to look for a new theology to overcome the impasse on our island, but to blame religion for the problem. Many are increasingly eager to depend on reason to explain our existence in a new "Enlightenment." Only in such a climate can socialism or Marxism flourish and make sense to the masses as in most of Western Europe, where totally different social structures exist and where only five percent adhere to religious practice.

All the available evidence suggests that the importation of Marxism into Ireland from secular cultures would be about as successful as the introduction of banana culture. In Ireland we still have a religious world view. Ninety-one percent of the Catholic population attends mass weekly. The demythologizing attempts of a liberal or Marxist variety go against the Irish context. What these attempts can do is to make us view the Bible not only as a message of spiritual salvation, but also of social liberation.

If Protestantism has bad connotations, we need to examine other historical models which radicalize our gospel without demythologizing it. One such model is the Anabaptist movement of the 16th century whose adherents were persecuted by both Catholics and Protestants. As the radical wing of the Protestant Reformation, the Anabaptists went beyond the divisive shortcomings of the Protestantism we have known here in Ireland; yet they challenged the sacral institutions of Catholicism. They are also instructive in that associated with them were also extremists of a spiritual and violent revolutionary type.

Certainly one lesson we need to learn is that the practice of sectarian ecclesiology as experienced in Britain does not necessarily provoke radicality. The movement from Rome through Anglicans, Independents, Congregationalists, Baptists, Quakers, Methodists to Brethren does not guarantee biblical faith and practice. People may move within these parameters and find that the only change is at a doctrinal level, while in social terms the nonconformists were the most conformist to the patterns of their societies. I am not arguing that truth does not matter. Rather it matters so much that if taking up these various positions does not lead to real radical Christianity, then they remain mind games. Also I am not questioning acting on the truth when we receive it, but I am suggesting that the way to be faithful will inevitably be "sectarian." It does not have to follow the historical development outlined above. The early Christians stayed in the temple until they were put out; Paul preached in the synagogue and only moved out when forced to. The task for Catholics, charismatics, Baptists, and members of the Church of Ireland is not to leave the churches they are in, but rather to confront them until they accept or reject the gospel. Only after real confrontation should any action be taken to bring a new reality into being. The church is God's creation, and for man to start a church is to incur the judgment of God.

Authority
How are we going to reach truth and what is our authority? Traditionally, Protestants have argued that authority derives from the Word of God. Catholics have stated much the same thing but have meant something different. For them the Word of God has two elements: sacred Scripture and sacred tradition interpreted by the teaching office of the church called the magisterium. Hans Küng, in his book *The Church, Infallible?*, argues that it is wrong to locate authority in its ultimate sense in either the church or Scripture. I agree. Final authority rests in the infallible God, and only secondarily in Scripture. Where one would have to disagree with Küng is on the issue of an infallible God revealing Himself through fallible scriptures. Scripture, which is an expression of God's desire to communicate as personal Being to personal beings, takes on God's quality of infallibility.

I would argue that God then is our ultimate authority,

and that we find His will most clearly and fully in sacred Scripture. A relative and subordinate authority is the tradition of the church throughout the ages. Lest we pretend otherwise, we are all subject to tradition; those who say they believe in the Bible alone often do so within the framework of the culture and times of James 1! Finally, it is God the Holy Spirit who leads us into all truth. The Scriptures are for individuals, but not for individualistic use. The Bible is given to the church as the body of Christ, and it is in this context that the Spirit gives His gifts to every member to help build up this community.

Church History

In an Irish theology church history would need to be taught from a different perspective. We Irishmen have tended to follow the history of Western Christianity through the Roman Empire, forgetting that Ireland was not part of that Empire. In the early period of Christianization we did not experience anything comparable to the Constantinian settlement on the greater European mainland where groups like the Saxons and Franks were forcibly converted to "Christ," paganism was banned, and Christianity became the established religion of the Empire.

The ministry of Patrick turned the Irish from a race of cruel conquerors, whose galleys spread terror along the coasts of Britain and Gaul, into a race whose enthusiasm was for missionary labor. Certainly the ministry of this man should be very important for any Irish theology which wants to rid itself of the near pagan accretions linked to his name. In Ireland there was a synthesis of the old pagan learning and Christianity, and the missionary method was infiltration, not martyrdom. This led to a confusion of

Irishness and Christianity. Infiltrators tend to lose their radical posture toward the rulers, as can still be seen today. ·Then we need to study the impact of Irish Christianity on Britain and Europe represented by such people as Columba, who became the patron saint of Scotland. In church history we need to develop an independent approach and see the connection between our past and our present experience. It seems that this is an area in which we Irish are not as interested in history as we claim to be.

Irish Theology—Some Themes

The main themes of an Irish theology will be to draw out the lines of the movement that God brought into existence at Pentecost. It will be a movement which has continuity with the history in which it finds itself, which is God's history; yet it will point to the culmination of messianic salvation when Christ returns. It will announce that we live in the last days, in the days of the Messiah, the Lord Jesus Christ. It will declare the need for repentance in order to receive personal and social salvation within the family of God. It will view the Body of Christ as the provisional wing of the kingdom of God which by virtue of Christ's death and resurrection is called to be an alternative people in the world. It will be a meeting place of all races and all backgrounds in which class distinctions will disappear.

Its politico-religious work will first be to be a community of sharing and then to bring about justice and peace in the world. Its theological task will combine the theme of a gospel of good news for the poor with the theme of spiritual liberation from self-love within the context of our Irish history. Irish theology will not be just an academic pursuit; it must follow the model of Jesus. It will become involved with those needing salvation—the hungry, the oppressed, and the violent; the fully integrated and the rich already have their reward. It will take the politics of Jesus seriously and will not allow institutions to get in the way of the cross. Only in this way will it be Christian.

Irish theology will not reject the universalism of the gospel, but it believes that the road necessarily passes through the particular. Particularism follows the path adopted by God in sending His son Jesus Christ through the Jewish nation. In all our thinking it is the Messiah, the only obedient servant, one particular individual, who will guide us through the successive stages of development. "The Lord says, 'Here is my servant, whom I strengthen—the one I have chosen, with whom I am pleased. I have filled him with my spirit, and he will bring justice to every nation. He will not shout or raise his voice or make loud speeches in the streets. He will not break off a bent reed or put out a flickering lamp. He will bring lasting justice to all. He will not lose hope or courage; he will establish justice on the earth. Distant lands eagerly wait for his teaching.' " (Isaiah 42:1-4).

17

A. F. Walls

Africa and Christian Identity

One of the more useful ways of grouping the ways in which men view the world is a division between primal world views, Indian world views, and Semitic world views; that is, those of most "tribal" peoples, those who live in small scale societies; the variety of views which have in common a cyclic view of the universe and causation, which find their expression in Hindu and Buddhist thought; and those linear, history-based world views characteristic of Judaism, Christianity, and Islam. It is also possible to group the faiths of mankind in another way: primal religions, which are the traditional religions of small scale societies, each binding by nature on all members born into that society, but not regarded as binding anyone else; universal religions, which make claims on all mankind; and folk religions, which result from fusions of the other two; where a universal faith is treated **as though** it were a primal traditional one. In either case, the primal religions form a major group of mankind, far more significant than the popular books on comparative religion, with their casual chapter on "traditional religions" or "primitive religions," or (still worse) "animism," might suggest. I am going to use the word "primal" more often than "traditional," partly because **all** religions are traditional, and one therefore needs to keep qualifying the phrase ("Zulu traditional religion," "Qechua traditional religion," "African traditional religions"): partly because "Primal" usefully emphasizes two important facts about them: the **historical priority** of these world views to all the great religions, and in all parts of the world, and their **basic, elemental nature.** They show man's religious responses in their most basic form.

Christianity and the Primal Religions

For Christians there is a still greater reason for taking the primal religions seriously. Historically, they have always been the most fertile soil for the gospel. They underlie, therefore, the Christian faith of the vast majority of Christians of all ages and all nations. What have been the societies which have become Christians in the mass? The multitudinous peoples of the Mediterranean empire of Rome (who had primal religions, even though they had literary expression for them); the barbarian tribes of the North and West from whom most of us are descended; and in the last three centuries or so, tribal or post-tribal peoples in sub-Saharan Africa, the Southern Americas, the Pacific. Indeed, it is hard, in the two millennia of Christian history so far, to find **large** adhesions to the Christian faith **except** among primal peoples. The modern Christian churches of southern and eastern Asia are precious sections of the world church; yet even there, what a high proportion of Christians have come from primal backgrounds, or, in India, from those circles where the expression of Hinduism is much like that of a primal religion.

For Christians, then, in the providence of God, the primal religions have a peculiar importance. When we consider the present position of the Christian world, the importance of **some** primal religions is even more greatly enhanced.

Let us consider. There have been three real turning points in church history so far when the whole balance of the church, geographical and racial, has altered. One was within the first century, when Christians, having once been an all-Jewish community, became an overwhelmingly Gentile one. One came within what Europe still calls the Dark Ages, when the church lost its old heartlands, "among the civilized peoples of the Eastern and Southern Mediterranean to Islam, and found a new base among the tribes of the north and west. The third has taken place within the lifetime of people not yet old, as the faith has again lost its hold on its heartlands" certainly in Europe (and I would guess in North America also) and again found a new base, this time in the Southern Continents, and especially in Latin America and Africa. The latter has every appearance of providing much of the greatest number of professing Christians in any continent by the end of the present century. The shape of the church, the theology that later church historians have to write about, is likely to be determined by what happens in Africa over the next few generations. And Africa's primal religions, the substratum of the religious life of the most substantial body of the world's Christians, are therefore of fundamental importance for the future of the church.

The Inescapable Christian Tension

It would be possible to write church history in terms of the interplay of two forces, each legitimate in itself, which are at work in any society which becomes affected by the gospel. One is that of making Christianity at home in the life of a people rooting the gospel in its culture, its language, its habits of thought—"indigenizing" it, in fact, making the church (in the words of the title of a well-known book about African independent churches) "a place to feel at home." The other is the conforming of a church's life to standards outside itself—standards which can cut across **anyone's** pattern, a process which reminds the Christian that he has no abiding city, no home on earth.

Both forces spring directly out of the gospel. The urge to make Christianity a place to feel at home, rooted in a people's culture, life and language, is of the heart of the gospel because it is a fundamental of the gospel that God takes us as we are, simply on grounds of what Christ has done. If He takes us as we are, He takes us in the state which all the conditions of our birth, history, and upbringing—our culture in fact—have placed us. He takes us not as isolated, detachable individuals, but as part of social complexes, with all our social relations on us. He takes us with a certain set of relationships with family, clan, tribe, nation. Inevitably—and the implications of this aren't always recognized—He takes us with our "disrelations" on us too—the sensitivities, hostilities, suspicions, prejudices, justified or not, which arise from our history and position. He doesn't wait to tidy up our ideas any more than He waits to tidy up our lives when He accepts us in Christ. It is for this reason, incidentally, that we should avoid that naive view of the gospel which suggests that all international problems, all social problems, will be solved simply by preaching the gospel: it is simply **not true;** that is not the way God in His mercy works. He takes us not out of the world but in the world, and that means as we are, as our culture and history have made us, and with all the consequent relations and disrelations. The Christian life, then, is one which will begin, flourish and abound in us "just as we are"—in our own culture and history. The fact that "if any man is in Christ he is a new creation" doesn't mean that he starts in a vacuum, or as a blank table. God has made his new creation in a particular time and place, it will be shaped by a particular time and place, and a man's Christian mind will be shaped by what was in it before he was a Christian. This is as true of churches as of people, and it means that there is not and has never been, and we cannot resonably expect there ever to be, a church which is not a culture church. All churches are culture churches, including our own.

This fact caused the first really major rumpus in Christian history. The first Christians were all Jews, and the mother church of all was Jerusalem. Jerusalem sent out the inspectors and the deputations to see whether new movements in Samaria or Antioch were really the work of God. They were the people with the largest experience of God, the deepest knowledge of Scriptures. Of course they rejoiced when they heard Paul talking about all the new converts in Asia Minor, about all those pagans seeing the light, turning to God. It was just as the prophets had spoken of the Gentiles taking hold of the skirts of one that was a Jew, saying "We will go with you for God is with you." They rejoiced in the conversions, but they made one fundamental assumption about them: that conversion meant that Gentile Christians would be as much like Jerusalem Christians as it was possible for such benighted heathens to become. And they would no doubt continue to follow Jerusalem's lead in all things; there were, after all, plenty of acculturated Gentiles. And when it didn't work out that way, there was trouble: we all know the story of Acts 15 and Galatians. Paul insists that there is **no** necessity for Gentile Christians to become like Jerusalem Christians. God has accepted them as they are. And he shouts at them—no circumcision, no food tabus, no ritual washings, nothing that would turn you into Jews or pseudo-Jews. You are not—you are Christians. Even those of you who are married to pagans—they are sanctified because of you. And to his Jewish brethren he shouts: No circumcision—only faith.

And much to the surprise, one imagines, of almost everyone at the Jerusalem Council, the future did not lie with Jerusalem Christians anyway. It lay with Corinthian and Galatian and Roman Christians, and fifty years after Paul, most Christians were like them, and not like Jerusalem Christians at all.

Christ took flesh and was made man in a particular time and place, family, nationality, tradition and customs and sanctified them, while still being for all men in every time and place. Wherever he is taken by the people of any day, time and place, he sanctifies that culture—he is living in it. And no other group of Christians has any right to impose in his name a set of assumptions about life determined by another time and place.

But to acknowledge this is not to forget that there is another, and equally important, force at work among us. Not only does God in His mercy take people as they are: He takes them to transform them into what He wants them to be.

This implies division, and the theme of division runs right through the Lord's words: he who came to bring not peace but a sword, who expected to set a son against father and brother against brother; who told his followers that a man's foes will be those of his own household. It runs through the words of His apostles, as they indicate that the Christian is not to be conformed to this world but transformed by the renewal of the mind. In other words, the Lord and His apostles—the one in Jewish society, the other in Hellenistic culture—**expected** the Lord's followers to be in a measure out of step with their societies: that there would be rubs and frictions and divisions, **whatever** that culture or society may be. The rubs arise, not from the adoption of a new culture, but from the transformation of the mind towards that of Christ.

One aspect of this is that the Christian is given a new set of relationships. He is still in the culture in which he was brought up: Christ has sanctified that culture by His presence in it. But he is also a member of a new people created by Christ, with a new set of family relationships, a new kith and kin of all families and nations and tongues, to whom he owes family loyalty and whom he must accept—as God has accepted him—with their group relations on them. Every Christian, that is, has dual nationality: he belongs to his human family based on kinship and nationality and to the faith family, which links him to people outside his own interest group and nationality—links him to those in opposing interest groups and nationalities who share his faith. His position between the two may become peculiarly difficult.

An Adoptive Past
Another aspect, and one less often noticed, is that he is given an adoptive past. He is linked to the people of God in all generations, who are his people, of the faith family. In particular, he is linked to the history of Israel, given several thousand years of someone else's history—for Israel, too, was the people of God.

Perhaps one can see this most clearly by thinking what it must have been like for the first Christian generation of the Gentiles. Paul talks about this in Romans 9-11. Notice there Paul's loyalty and pride in the culture in which he was brought up—and that that very loyalty causes him heartbreak as he thinks of his people's rejection of Christ. But he looks at Gentiles—ex-pagans, Greeks that he was taught to look down on—and sees that many of them are turning to Christ. They have been grafted into Israel—they **are** Israel: and therefore the past of Israel is **their** past.

Israel and Africa
I have already indicated the importance of African **theology** for the future of the church. Among current African theologians—John Mbiti, Bolaji Idowu, Harry Sawyerr come to mind—no question is more clamant than the African Christian identity crisis. It is not simply an

intellectual quest. This massive shift in the center of gravity of the Christian world which has taken place cannot be separated from the cultural impact of the West in imperial days. Now the Empires are dead, and the Western value-setting of the Christian faith largely rejected. Where does this leave the African Christian? Who is he? Where is his past? A past is vital for all of us—without it, like the amnesiac man, we cannot know who we are.

The prime African theological quest at present is thus: What is the past of the African Christian? What is the relationship between Africa's old religions and her new one? The writers mentioned are all scholars who are highly committed churchmen; they are also writers on traditional religion, who have sought to interpret it. Their conclusions have been called syncretistic by some Christian writers (cf. e.g. B Kato, *Theological Pitfalls in Africa* 1975); on the other hand, an African non-Christian writer like Okot p'Bitek may accuse them of rewriting the old religion in the "missionary" interest. The topic is too complex for discussion here. It is extraordinary that the safest verdict on many names for the Supreme Being all over Arica is that pronounced by Janzen and MacGaffey with regard to Kongo: "The parallel between the biblical "God" and the African **Nzambi** is sufficiently close that protracted scholarly debate has failed to discover how much the concept of **Nzambi** owes to missionary teaching, and the equivalence of the two terms has been universally accepted in Kongo for many years" (*Anthology of Kongo Religion,* 1974, 14). One reason for the search and debate is the heart cry of the African Christian to know whether the same God was with his ancestors as he calls on now, and whether both were the same as Abraham called on. It is, *mutatis mutandis,* the quest of Clement of Alexandria—and of Muhammad.

In the surviving literature of second century Christianity, it is not hard to see a similar agony of soul. By this time most Christians were no longer Jews. They were Gentiles, Greek-speaking people, with their own heritage of education and language. One can see the concerns of a man like Clement of Alexandria. He is a disciple of Christ; he is an evangelist who wants to bring people to the same discipleship. But how can he expect them to come if what is on offer is an alien cult? And what of their past? Did God have nothing to do with it all these years? Was everything in their heritage evil? Those who witnessed against evil and pointed to good before Christ—Was this nothing to do with God? I think none of us would be entirely happy about the outcome of his theologizing: but one can have every sympathy with his quest, and his firm apprehension that, as Paul put it, God was, and always had been, "the God of the heathen also."

But there were among his contemporaries other thinkers with the same quest, the people we now call Gnostics, whose concern was also to make the Christian faith acceptable to people brought up in the Greek world. The trouble was that their approach was based entirely on contemporary thinking, eliminating all the things unacceptable to educated—that is to Greek—men. For them the 'barbarian' element must be removed from the gospel; and the 'barbarian' element obviously included the Last Judgment and the Resurrection. But these things were part of a framework—the historical nature of the faith—which ultimately derived from the Old Testament.

Such thinkers played down, or ignored, or rejected, the Old Testament and the Christian adoptive past. Perhaps the most important point about the opponents of the Gnostics is that they were just as Greek as the Gnostics. They felt all sorts of intellectual difficulties which we do not feel. But they knew they must hold to the whole of the Scriptures, the adoptive part of their religion, and in doing so they turned the second important corner in Christian history. Perhaps the test between indigenization and syncretism is the capacity to incorporate the history of Israel and God's people and treat it as one's own.

For the Scriptures belong to the whole church: the trouble is that none of us can read the Scriptures without cultural blinders of some sort. Reading the Scriptures together gives a better chance of seeing things otherwise left hidden. In a cross-cultural situation it is likely that each will see things in Scripture that others will miss. The great theological fact of our time, which I believe makes this potentially the most exciting era in the history of Christian theology, is that the church now looks more like the great multitude out of all nations and kindreds than at any former point in its history: and thus has greater possibilities than at any previous time for mutual enrichment and self-criticism, as God causes yet more light and truth to break forth from His Word.

18
R. Pierce Beaver

The Mission to Native Americans

Protestant missions to the American Indians through 300 of the 350 years of their existence were carried out in a partnership of church and state absolutely contrary to present ideas about a wall of separation. The very colonial charters, such as those of Virginia and Massachusetts, professed that the evangelization of the Indians was the chief purpose of colonization both on part of the King and the companies. The word civilize was coupled with the term evangelize.

The Seventeenth Century

The colonists waited until they thought themselves to be militarily strong enough to withstand any attack by the Indians. The beginning in Virginia was snuffed out by the reaction to the Indian Uprising or "Massacre" of 1622, and only some educational work was done after that. Thomas Mayhew, Jr., son of the proprietor of Martha's Vineyard, Nantucket, and the Elizabeth Islands and newly ordained pastor of the church at Edgartown on the Vineyard, who knew the Massachusetts language, began quiet personal evangelism among the Indians in 1662 and initiated public preaching in 1664. The Mayhews did not interfere with the social and political structure of the Indians, and converts came rapidly. The Christians entered into a convenant in 1652, but the church was not organized until 1670. The evangelist, Hiacoomes, was ordained pastor at that time. Meanwhile Thomas, Jr., had been lost at sea, and his father assumed the missionary office. Six successive generations of the family engaged in the ministry to the Indians.

The more renowned John Eliot, pastor at Roxbury west of Boston, began public services in 1664, and enlisted other ministers of Massachusetts and Plymouth in the mission. Four thousand Christians were gathered into 14 towns of "Praying Indians" in 1674. They were devastated by both Indians and whites in King Philip's War in 1675-76. Thereafter the Indians in Eastern Massachusetts declined, but a tiny remnant of that early Christian community still exists.

Here is the origin of the whole Protestant world mission, and it has been continuous ever since Mayhew and Eliot. The activities of the chaplains of the Dutch East Indies Company had little influence compared with the Indian missions in arousing British, American, and European Protestants to missionary obedience. Inspiration, motivation, aims and goals, and patterns of action all were passed on to the overseas missions when they developed.

The Eighteenth Century

The second wave of Puritan missions began with the mission to the Mohegans of the Housatonic Valley in western Massachusetts by John Sergeant, a tutor at Yale College, in 1734. The town of Stockbridge was given them, and the converts were soon recognized as the Stockbridge nation. Sergeant's productive ministry was cut short by death in 1749. He was succeeded by the famous theologian, Jonathan Edwards, until 1758. Under the next pastor, Stephen West, the church was divided into Indian and white congregations, John Sergeant, Jr., becoming pastor of the Indians. Their position was very uncomfortable after the Revolution, and the Stockbridges moved west by stages to the neighborhood of Green Bay, Wisconsin.

Simultaneously with Sergeant's mission and closely associated with him was David Brainerd, Connecticut man commissioned by the Scottish Society in 1742, who worked near Albany, transferred to Easton, Pennsylvania, and then itinerated on the Susquehanna. Then in 1745 through a mighty working of the Holy Spirit, he gathered a community at Cranbury, New Jersey. He died of tuberculosis two years later.

It was in this same period that the Unitas Fratrum or Moravian Church sent a band from Herrnhut in Saxony under Christian Heinrich Rauch, locating at Shekomeko, Wedquadnach (now Indian Pond), and Scaticook on the New York-Connecticut border. Connecticut militia expelled the Moravian missionaries, and the settlers on the New York side forced the abandonment of the mission there. Some Mohegan converts remained at Scaticook, and others joined a community of Moravian Delawares near the Wind Gap in Pennsylvania. These Christians, after almost being slain by a mob in Philadelphia, were forced across the colony in stages, until John Heckwelder and David Zeisberger led them into the Muskingum country of eastern Ohio. There the mission flourished until on March 8, 1782 the 90 Christians of Gnadenhutten were brutally murdered by a company of American militia. The people of the other villages fled, and after many temporary settlements finally located at Fairfield, Ontario.

There were efforts to penetrate the Iroquois country of New York from New England. The largest and most creative scheme was that of Eleazer Wheelock. Wheelock, while pastor at Lebanon Crank, Connecticut, in 1743 took into his home the Mohegan youth, Samson Occum, and taught him for four years. This gave Wheelock the idea of training Indian and English students together so that they might learn from each other, then sending them forth as missionaries. He established Moor's Charity School for this purpose, teaching both boys and girls. Occum went to Great Britain to raise money for Wheelock's enterprise. He was lionized. Occum was ordained and spent his life as a missionary to the Mohegans, Niantics, and Montauks. The white pastors seemed always to expect far higher standards and achievement of Occum than of themselves. Wheelock was unable to work well with others, and he was often at odds with his missionaries. His most famous white agent, Samuel Kirkland separated from him. After Moor's School Kirkland finished his education at the College of New Jersey (Princeton) and became a missionary to the Oneidas, one of the Iroquois nations.

The one mass movement during the colonial era was the conversion of the Mohawks of Central New York and their entrance into the Church of England. The mission was initiated through the efforts of two royal governors of New York, sponsored and subsidized by Queen Anne, and taken under the direction of the New Society for the Propagation of the Gospel in Foreign Parts. The first missionary was Thoroughgood Moore, who arrived at Albany in 1704; but the first full-time missionary was John

Stuart, who came just as the Revolution began and was interned for the duration. The movement was not due to the efforts of missionaries, but to the influence of the paramount war chief, Joseph Brant, and Sir William Johnson, superintendent of Indian Affairs. They did not disturb the Mohawk culture. The Mohawks were loyal to Great Britain during the war, and at its end they moved to Ontario.

Missionary Motives. The foremost motive was **gloria Dei** (glory of God), for the Puritans aimed at furthering the kingdom of Christ in the western part of the earth and making the desert blossom as the rose, thus contributing to God's design for the consummation of history in the Eschaton.

The second grand motive was compassion: first for the perishing souls of the poor heathen and second for their wretched physical and social condition. This led the missionaries and their supporters to unite inseparably "evangelization" and "civilization," and their followers down into the twentieth century agreed with them. On the one hand, the Indians were regarded as men created by God in His image, possessed of reasoning minds, and capable of understanding and responding to the gospel. They could be saved by faith in Christ. On the other hand, they were regarded as "the ruines of mankind," utterly depraved, without civilization, living in barbarism, slaves of the devil. No value of any kind was seen in Indian culture. The Puritan Christian man was the model disciple of Christ and the standard of civilized humanity. The Indian was to be made over into his image. Progress in growth in his likeness would indicate the stage of growth on the path of salvation.

The only people who disagreed with this understanding

of mission aims were Joseph Brant, Sir William Johnson, and the Rev. Charles Chauncy, pastor of the Second Church in Boston. Brant and Johnson held that the anglicized converts of the New Englanders were gloomy and unfit for the hunting life of the forests. They believed that the red man could be a Christian and still remain an Indian. That was also the view of Chauncy, who said that it was wrong to try to make an Englishman of the Indian, and that this was the primary cause of the decrease of the race in New England. Let the Indian accept the gospel, and in time the gospel will effect any changes that are really necessary. These three voices could not persuade the majority. During three and a half centuries the missionaries tried to make a red WASP out of the Indian.

Missionary Methods were determined by the general objective. Evangelism was primarily by preaching. Converts were baptized and gathered into churches. They were nurtured by catechizing, teaching, pastoral care, and discipline. Education stressed farming, domestic crafts, and religion. Both English and the vernacular language were used. Eliot produced a whole "library" and the entire Bible (1664) in the Massachusetts language. Some Indians were put into the Boston Latin Grammar School. John Sergeant introduced the boarding school, which would become in Indian and world missions the favorite means of weaning converts from their native cultures. The great achievement was the raising up of a native ministry. There were 37 ordained pastors in 1700. In order to further the grand design the Indians were gathered into separate towns in Massachusetts. This was to protect them from bad Indians and bad whites and to make their nurture easier. The Moravians, too, gathered converts into villages, where liturgical piety was attractive to them. The General Court of Massachusetts gave land for the towns and built the church and school. Four English families were introduced into Stockbridge to afford an example for the Indians, and that proved to be disastrous.

The Nineteenth Century

Missions declined to a low ebb during the Revolution. They were cut off from British support, and little came out of New England. Congress subsidized some of the missionaries, especially Samuel Kirkland. Yet zeal for mission was developing, and immediately after the end of the struggle there was a great explosion of organization. Beginning in 1787, a score of missionary societies were created. They aimed at the Indians, the settlers on the frontier, and the heathen overseas. It required a student movement to bring a foreign mission board—the American Board of Commissioners for Foreign Missions— into being in 1810. The Baptist Board and the United Foreign Missionary Society followed in 1814 and 1817. Gradually others were founded. They all took responsibility for missions to the Indians. Little was achieved, however, until Cyrus Kingsbury established the American Board's mission to the Cherokees in 1816.

It was government action which stimulated the expansion of missions during the nineteenth century in a partnership with the churches which lasted until 1899. Indian Affairs were placed under the Secretary of War. The first Secretary, Henry Knox, told President Washington that there was only one alternative for the Indian: He could either be exterminated or civilized! A great step could be taken towards the latter if missionaries, who alone had the disinterested welfare of the red man at heart, were subsidized to manage agricultural and mechanical schools. But when he prohibited evangelization of non-Christians, the mission societies lost interest in the proposal.

The Rev. Cyrus Kingsbury stopped in Washington to talk with President Madison and Secretary Calhoun about his new mission, and both men enthusiastically supported the scheme. They ordered the government agent with the Cherokees to provide buildings and equipment. Brainerd Station was opened in 1817 and seven other major centers soon followed. The Cherokees had already decided on assimilation. With mission help they made great progress. They so far accommodated to Southern white society that they held slaves. The nation became literate, and the ABCFM turned over the mission's press to it. A constitution patterned after that of the United States was adopted. Despite the leadership of the American Board, the Indians adapted to the Southern style of Christian life rather than that of the Presbyterians and Congregationalists of the American Board mission. They became largely Baptists and Methodists and loved the camp meeting. Soon the War Department declared the Cherokees to be a Christian nation. They completely fulfilled the expectations of church and government with regard to assimilation. Meanwhile Kingsbury had long since moved on to the Choctaws, and the same course of events reoccurred there.

President Madison in his 1817 annual message asked Congress to set up a Civilization Fund, and the appropriation of $10,000 was made in 1818. Government provided two-thirds the cost of buildings. Meager as the sum was, the mission boards hastened to apply. Evangelism kept pace with education. Soon the participating mission bodies were investing 13 times the amount given by government, and certain tribes made gifts from their funds. Thirty-eight schools were being operated by 11 mission boards or societies in 1826 in several parts of the country. The Southern Indians made such great progress that the Cherokees, Choctaws, Chickasaws, Creeks, and Seminoles were called The Five Civilized Tribes.

However, what was achieved under and through the Civilization Fund was destroyed by the government's removal policy. Ruthless pressure was exerted to induce or force the tribes located east of the Mississippi to move to the west of that river, especially into Kansas and Indian territory. Most missionaries and their boards favored removal. They saw the tribes decimated and the churches destroyed through white aggression and exploitation. They deluded themselves with their baseless self-assurance that west of the great river and especially in Indian Territory the Indians would be forever beyond reach of the white men (other than missionaries!). James B. Finley, missionary to the Wyandots at Upper Sandusky, Ohio, is an excellent example of a pastor who tried to protect his flock from removal and who tried to publicize its terrors. Isaac McCoy was, on the contrary, the most vigorous and influential advocate of removal. After Finley's transfer the Wyandots were moved by stages, and the last group lost 100 of their number within the first year. McCoy lobbied with the Congress, the President, the Secretary of War, the General Baptist Convention and its Board of Foreign Missions, and every person who might aid the cause of removal. The missionary on several occasions served the government as agent or surveyor. He induced the Convention to endorse removal. Another influential proponent of removal was the noted minister and geographer, a leader in the American Board, Dr. Jedidiah Morse.

Even the American Board for a time approved of removal because of Dr. Morse's advocacy. But when put to the test the Board became the strongest defender of Indian rights. President Monroe first set forth the removal policy in 1825, and Andrew Jackson's Indian Removal Bill was passed by Congress in 1830. It was aimed principally at the Five Civilized Tribes. Georgia in 1829 incorporated all Cherokee lands into counties of the state and declared that Cherokee laws were void. Jackson announced that he would not enforce Federal laws and treaties where they conflicted with the claims of Georgia. The American Board designed and supported the suit of the Cherokee nation against Georgia in the Supreme Court, but the Court denied that it had jurisdiction since the Cherokees formed a foreign nation. When two of the missionaries were sentenced to imprisonment at hard labor, the Board then brought suit on their behalf, that being another way to get at the basic question of Georgia's violation of Indian rights. The Supreme Court ruled in favor of the missionaries and stated that the Cherokees were a nation under protection of the United States and free of the jurisdiction of Georgia. But President Jackson ignored the ruling and ordered the Army to remove the Indians. Segregation replaced assimilation.

When the tribes had been removed across the Mississippi, then there followed the forced location of the Western peoples on reservations. The buffalo were destroyed. The Indians had to exist on inferior rations and supplies doled out by the government.

President Grant's Peace Policy provided the second

impetus to missionary expansion in the century. The Indian Bureau was thoroughly corrupted by political patronage, and an agent hired at $1,500 a year could retire with a fortune after three years. A Peace Commission appointed by Congress recommended that the service be placed under a board of unpaid philanthropists. The Board of Indian Commissioners was appointed, but it was given no power of administration and could only inspect, audit, and advise. It was called a "Church Board," but churches had no voice in selection. The members were eminent Christian laymen. They did bring an improvement in the lot of the Indians through their watchfulness. Discovering that they possessed no power, the members resigned. Their successors had even less influence. Grant's major move was to fire the agents and to ask the mission boards of mainline churches both to nominate and supervise the agents on the reservations. They were expected to establish schools and churches. They did. The number of missionaries rose from 15 in 1869 to 74 in 1873, schools from 10 to 69, teachers from 17 to 86, and pupils from 594 to 2,690. There were 90 churches. The churches on the whole provided good agents, but politicians often prevented their confirmation, "framed them" and ousted them from office, and even appointed rascals without reference to the mission boards and called them church appointees. H. M. Teller, Secretary of the Interior under President Arthur, terminated the system.

Government support of the schools continued. The Rev. General Thomas J. Morgan put an end to that through his activities as Commissioner of Indian Affairs, Secretary of the American Baptist Home Missionary Society, and chief spokesman for the nativist American Protective Association. He charged that the Roman Catholics were taking over the Indian schools as the first step in taking control of the public schools of the nation. He brought such great pressure to bear that one after another the mission boards renounced government subsidies and the national judicatories of the churches passed resolutions calling for the most strict separation of church and state. The last government grant to mission schools was made in 1899, and the three centuries long partnership came to an end.

Only the church having supervision of a reservation was supposed to have missions on that reservation unless some church was already operating there. Reservations were declared open to all churches in 1881. That allowed for a great increase of missions, which actually developed after 1900.

The Twentieth Century

The Bureau of Indian Affairs and the missions continued in accord except while John Collier was Commissioner under President Frankin D. Roosevelt. The mission boards considered him to be a foe of all that they had striven for—Christianization and assimilation. There was no further stimulation of missions by the government. Expansion by mainline churches in the Southwest was mainly due to pressure by tourists who saw the Indians there. Slowly smaller conservative churches began missions and at length some Evangelical non-denominational societies also. In 1921 there were 26 mission agencies at work. These increased to 36 by 1950. There are more today, plus many independent Pentecostal congregations led by men with charismatic gifts. The Protestant constituency in 1950 was 140,000. At present the author of this article is making a survey but cannot yet estimate the present membership. Roman Catholic

Indians are said to number 155,600. There is a crisis in ministry and youth are being lost. An apparently successful program of Theological Education by Extension, in which Cook Christian Training School in Tempe, Arizona, is the pioneer, gives great promise. There is a new Native American Theological Association sponsored by United Presbyterian and United Church of Christ institutions. A.I.M. and other Indian activist organizations are putting pressure on the churches. Although there is still strong complaint that denominational structures hold the Indians in the stifling embrace of a paternalistic hand, some measure of self-determination is beginning to be allowed. The United Presbyterian Church, for example, has a Native American Consultative Committee, and the Episcopal Church has created the Navajo Missionary District, which will eventually have its own Navajo bishop.

A burning issue at present is the recognition of God-given values in Indian culture and the use of the religio-cultural heritage in Christian life, worship, and ministry. What is a truly indigenous church today? Having been transferred from the foreign mission boards to the home mission boards, the Indians did not participate in the great drive for indigenization and independence which characterized world mission thinking and action from about 1920 to the present. Now they are trying to find their way to renewal and to credibility with their people. Even more difficult than solutions to reservation problems is the discovery of what it means to be Indian in the industrial city and how the church may minister to the many thousands who now live there cut off from roots in the reservation communities.

Notes on the Theological Meaning of China

19

J. Lawrence Burkholder

Some of us who have visited China recently have returned in general agreement regarding China's achievements. Here are some of the more astonishing.

1. A productive, noninflationary economy, largely self-sufficient, relying mainly on domestic raw materials of coal and oil, supplying food, fiber, and employment for 900 million people, impressive technological developments in agriculture and heavy industry.

2. Socialized medicine according to preventive principles resulting in excellent health, virtual elimination of venereal disease and illicit drugs.

3. Universal education on primary level, dramatic improvement in literacy, political awareness, and social involvement, growth in technological education.

4. Revolutionary consciousness of the masses providing personal sense of identity.

5. A general social ethos of peace and tranquility, the miracle of social organization of 900 million people with minor evidences of physical strife.

6. A strong sense of national destiny in which historical realism is combined with utopian hope.

7. Unparalleled personal and national morality as evidenced by assumed honesty, low crime rate, sexual

probity. Prostitution has been eliminated.

8. A strenuous work ethic with emphasis upon manual labor, simple, unostentatious living, and sharing.

9. An egalitarian social system which precludes private wealth and abject poverty.

10. An ethic of service to society within which personal pride, aggrandizement, and "elitism" are discouraged.

11. An authoritarian social system resulting in unparalleled "law and order."

12. An alternative model for underdeveloped nations with political, social, and metaphysical implications—a world view.

One could go on and on. It is the total impact of China which so compellingly requires study and assessment on many levels. Students of history and political science have been studying modern China for years. Many writings have been ideological. Religious perspectives have varied. Some reflect a typical "cold war" anti-communist sentiment. Others reflect an uncritical, naive idealism. Few, to my knowledge, have reflected the complexity and ambiguity of China. For on the one hand, China today represents one of the greatest social, political, and moral achievements in history (900 million people lifted from poverty to relative security, peace, morality, and tranquility in thirty years). On the other hand, China represents the tightest social system in the world, a totalitarian dictatorship of the people which many of us in the democratic tradition regard as devoid of essential freedom.

I may be among those who are at once most impressed and most perplexed by China. To me China is known best in terms of irony. I am especially conscious of the irony of a "godless" nation with the highest morality in the world, a secular people less estranged than Christian nations, an anti-missions nation that is offering on a national scale the social benefits (schools, hospitals, relief) which missions offered on a local scale, a socialist system (virtually no private property) in which ordinary people feel that they "possess" the land, a totalitarian system in which most of the people feel liberated, a dictatorship of the people which operates on a "consensus basis," a humane, nonviolent system of personality transformation, criticism, reeducation, and discipline.

Even if China's achievements were not as great as they seem and even if the irony were to that extent softened, China presents itself to Christians as a problem that cannot be ignored. It is to us above all a theological problem because so many things that Christians stand for in the name of Christ, the Chinese do in the name of Mao. Since the analogies between China and the Christian ideal are so close, the question inevitably arises as to whether China is in some sense a unique fulfillment of God's purposes. To me the analogies are exciting and incredible. The analogies between Chinese Marxism and Christianity are both formal and substantial. Let us examine a few of these:

1. **The analogy of the interpretations of history.** Both see history as a struggle. For communism it is a struggle between classes; for Christianity it is a struggle between good and evil. Both systems posit a "political" order at the "end" of history which will be characterized by justice, peace, and happiness. Christianity looks to the coming of the kingdom of God; Marxism looks to the coming of the pure communist state. In the meantime, of course, both systems must come to terms with frustrations, though at the present time the Chinese seem more confident of fulfillment than do many Christians.

2. **The analogy of radicality.** Both systems are radical and revolutionary in the sense that they call for nothing less than a "new man" and a new social order operating on principles of neighbor love and selflessness.

3. **The analogy of commitment.** Both systems demand total commitment. "Seek ye first the kingdom of God," can be compared with many equally radical demands for seeking first the "Revolution." In this connection, both early Christianity and Chinese Marxism are ideologically suspicious of "compromise" (Troeltsch) and "revisionism" (Mao Tse-tung).

4. **The analogy of lifestyle.** Both espouse the simple life. Riches are repudiated; eroticism is rejected; pride is criticized. Abandonment of ostentation in the form of fancy restaurants, silk apparel, and large estates remind one of New Testament severity.

5. **The analogy of discipline.** Both systems insist that the corporate reality is prior to the individual. The Christian church and the Marxist Chinese state limit the freedom of the individual and "paradoxically" liberate the individual for service to the neighbor. There are essential differences in the disciplinary process, but both make a significant place for "brotherly rebuke" and "criticism." Christian "nurture" is analogous to "reeducation." The Chinese revolutionary system of correction appears like a secular version of Matthew 18.

6. **The analogy of heresy.** All through its history, Christianity has struggled against "false teaching." Chinese Marxism struggles similarly against "revisionism." The need for the interpretation and reinterpretation of orthodoxy over against which ideas and attitudes may be judged is felt by both traditions. Related to this are social and psychological attitudes of acceptance and rejection as saints judge sinners within the Christian community and the "politically conscious" judge the "unaware" within the communist state.

8. **The analogy of decision-making.** Both Christianity as interpreted by Mennonites and Marxism as interpreted by Mao uphold an ideal form of decision-making through "consensus." The dynamics of the "discerning commu-

nity" according to the believers church model is similar in many respects to the dynamics of the "revolutionary committee"—the basic decision-making body in cities and communes.

9. **The analogy of sexual morality.** China's attitude toward sexual morality is as it were "a page out of the New Testament." Sexual deviation is simply regarded with horror! The strictest Puritan ethic is no more conservative than the Maoist ethic.

10. **The analogy of liberation.** "Liberation" is shared by both traditions as a word describing release from bondage. It is another way of speaking of salvation. The human experience of liberation from oppression is analogous to the religious experience of liberation from sin. Chinese give testimonies in which Mao and Christ could be interchanged without violence.

There are, however, essential differences between the Chinese Revolution and Christianity. Here are a few:

1. The most glaring difference lies in the area of individual freedom. The voluntary principle in Christian faith is especially absent in Maoism. All major choices are made by the state—choices governing work, habitation, education, and political philosophy. Furthermore, in China one cannot opt out of the system. This is the major difference between belonging to the Marxist state and belonging to the church—a most significant difference.

2. Another difference has to do with metaphysics. Christianity rests upon belief in transcendent reality. Communism denies transcendence. Hence, attitudes toward the ultimate source of things differ fundamentally. Contemporary Chinese philosophy implies a secular, scientific, nationalistic world view. Hence, the "mystical" quality of life disappears. There is no theoretical place for "ecstasy" or "tragedy."

Mystery is wiped away by the steel brush of modernity. Marriage, birth, fate, and death have lost their mystical tinge. Weddings, festivals, and funerals are routine and perfunctory. Metaphysical speculation, fantasy, and superstition have been recast into a "mythology" of revolution and the "romance" of corporate productive life.

3. Another difference concerns the difference between a monolithic and a pluralistic society. In pointing out this difference between social systems I am possibly comparing totalitarianism and democracy rather than Marxism and Christianity. Christianity to my knowledge is not committed to a single social system. Nevertheless, if one rejects in principle the *corpus christianum,* i.e., the unity of Christianity and society, one is committed to a social pluralism within which the church becomes one of many groups. In China there is only one reality outside the individual and that is the state. Within the state all realms of human experience—economics, education, morality, transportation, the military, marriage, and ideology are melted together under the rubric of "politics." In China there is no escape from the impact of the whole by identification with a part. Also, there is no distinction between private and public affairs. The state does it all!

4. Another important difference concerns the use of force. Essential to China's Revolution is the use of force. China is by no means nonresistant. In the early days of the Revolution, a ruling class was destroyed either physically or socially and economically by the use of arms. The revolution occurred "at the end of the gun barrel." Admittedly, today China seems to be a most peaceful and nonviolent society. Police with guns cannot be found— only a low profile army in the background. At any rate, a theological appraisal of China must include China's use of force.

In light of the striking similarities and differences between Christianity, as we know it, and Chinese communism, one is forced to do two things: (1) One must conclude that China should be viewed theologically, i.e., it must be seen as a historical development with special relevance to the purposes of God. One dare not ignore 900 million people, especially a nation resembling the Christian ideal in so many ways. (2) At the same time one dare not identify China and Christianity as such. How then shall we think of China?

I must confess that I am not sufficiently acquainted with China to come to a conclusion. Only an intimate knowledge of that intriguing land would provide the base for a theology of China. Therefore, I can only share with you some questions which keep running through my mind.

Should we consider China under present leadership as Persia under Cyrus in the Old Testament? In the prophecy of Isaiah, Cyrus, a pagan king, is referred to as "his anointed." "I girded thee, though thou hast not known me" (45:5). Could it be possible that God may have "anointed" Mao to serve his purposes? Would it be appropriate for us to look at Mao in the providence of God as one called to "save" some 900 million from chaos and destruction? Could God have used Mao as a leader to call the church and, indirectly, the Western nations to justice, order, peace, simplicity, and morality? Could it be that God has given up the West to moral and economic disintegration and he looks paradoxically to China as the fulfillment of his purposes?

To put the question in more Christological terms, is the Spirit of Christ embodied *incognito* by the Chinese? From a biblical point of view this would be a theological possibility by way of a logos Christology. The prologue of John's Gospel and Colossians (1:15-20) identify Jesus as the logos (Word) which is the creative and ordering power of the universe. Is this power being manifest in a special way among the Chinese? Are the Chinese in this way responding to the Spirit of Christ without knowing it?

Or shall we take a completely cynical view of the moral

and technological achievements of China and simply write it off as the early phase of a revolutionary process which will eventually become corrupted as it faces the facts of history—complexity, affluence, privilege, individualism? And furthermore, is the incredible order, morality, and austerity of China inherently tied to a closed society?

The theological problem is to come to terms with the contradiction between what may be called the Christo-logical and the anthropological implications of China. That is to say, one could agree that God may be at work in bringing about a "kingdom" which embodies to a remarkable degree the principles of justice, service, morality, order, and productivity. Were one to think of God's work in terms of the "lordship of Christ" or the "Word," the way would be open for a Christological interpretation of China, adventurous and risky as that may be. However, when one reflects upon the evident lack of individual freedom within China's "closed" society, the anthropological considerations raise many problems. Quite apart from the fact that the Chinese deny in theory and in practice the existence of "free will," Chinese society makes inadequate provision for certain kinds of freedom which some of us have considered essential to humanity. To be sure it can be argued that there is a danger in equating Christian freedom with democratic freedom. Some would claim that Western society is going to pieces because democratic freedom has come to mean that "everybody does his thing." However, I feel that a far greater amount of freedom is implied by the Christian view of humanity than is granted in China at the present time. Possibly China will "loosen up" after its "greater" needs for subsistence are guaranteed.

While postponing judgment until we know more about China, I believe that China must be taken seriously—not only as a world power but as a place where God may be at work. We must remember that the God of the Bible has achieved his purposes in strange ways—much to the surprise of many of his people. And of course, we cannot overlook the fact that the Chinese seem to be acting in a more Christian manner than most professing Christians.

20 New Religious Movements

Gottfried Oosterwal

I

The sudden rise of thousands of new religions, syncretistic cults, and prophet movements is one of the most remarkable phenomena in our day, and a present formidable challenge to Christian missions. One aspect of that challenge is the sheer number of these movements, their millions of followers, their vitality and growth, and their universality. They occur from Japan to Jamaica, from California to the Congo, from Brazil to Burma. And hardly a week passes but somewhere another prophet arises or a new charismatic leader emerges who becomes the center of a new movement.

They also arise under the most diverse economic, political, and cultural circumstances: in the Buddhist world of Thailand or Burma or Vietnam, as well as in the Christian Philippines or South America. They emerge spontaneously in the isolated and marginal societies of stone-age New Guinea as well as in the affluent and pluralistic world of the American technopolis, in Muslim Indonesia or the Sudan as well as in secularized Europe, in Hindu India as well as in communist Russia, in rural Africa as well as in such metropolises as Tokyo or Sao Paulo.

In spite of these many differences in the cultural milieux in which they arise, these new religions show striking similarities in origin, form, development, and goals. Some of their general characteristics are these:

1. They usually emerge from a **crisis-situation.** In many areas the crisis is brought about by the contact between a dynamic and wealthy civilization and a more or less static, technically and economically underdeveloped population, the "colonial situation" (Balandier). But, universally, this crisis-situation is also a result of the whole technological revolution of our day, the process of modernization, rapid urbanization. The shock of the breakdown of the traditional social structures, especially of the primary groups, has neuroticizing effects on individuals. The devaluation of traditional values, economic deprivation, and a host of other social, political, and religious factors at work today cause a loss of stability and security and bring psychic stress and cultural confusion.

In many studies of new religious movements this crisis-situation has been considered the prime cause, if not the only one, of their origin and growth. It has become evident, however, that though the crisis situation works as a catalyst to stimulate or precipitate the rise of a movement, giving it a particular form and determining its development and growth, most of these so-called liberation-movements, short-circuit reactions, protest-movements, revitalization-movements, and cargo-cults are **genuine religions.** And religion is *sui generis.*

They cannot be explained by just nonreligious factors. Culture clash, anxiety, social disintegration, political oppression, and future shock don't make prophets; they don't produce a cosmic eschatology so characteristic of many of these new religions. However, these prophets and their revelations, the messianic expectations, the cult-practices, and the spirit-filled life of the believers are a challenge to the Christian churches. And as we know of similar crises that did not produce new religious movements, so we also know of cults and millennial movements that have emerged without particular crises.

But mission leaders must now ask themselves, ''Why do these millions of people find their emotional and social stability in these new religions? Why do they not flock into the established churches instead?'' Is it possible that these prophet-movements, indigenous churches, and syncretistic cults arose precisely because the churches in their life, mission, and theology were unable to offer these people the fellowship so badly needed in a time of social disintegration, meaning in life in a time of utter confusion, power in an age of depression and distress and poverty and powerlessness?

Where these crucial human needs in our ''age of crisis'' (Sorokin) have been fulfilled by Christian churches, such new religions either did not arise or they were absorbed by the established Christian community. The crisis-situation challenges Christian churches and missions to become, indeed, the body of him who preached freedom to the oppressed, offered rest to the heavy-burdened, kinship to the alienated and the lonely, a point of orientation to the confused, hope to those in distress, healing to the sick-in-body, soul, and spirit, and power to the powerless. Certainly, Christ's kingdom is not of this earth, yet it is a tangible reality. Salvation has come today.

2. These movements commonly center around a **charismatic leader.** They are not just group-reactions; nor do they spontaneously emerge out of a commonly experienced crisis. The origin and history of these religious movements is, generally speaking, the history of its leaders. They are to these movements what the condensation nuclei are to the formation of rain: the rallying point, the inspiration, the creative center. The origin of a movement can often be traced to the mystic experience of a prophet who is said to have had special

revelations from God, or a spirit, through visions, dreams, or auditions.

Often these leaders, either men or women, are said to be endowed with special gifts—prominent among them the gifts of healing, prophecy, speech, trance (i.e., of having direct contact with the spirit-world or of being a channel through which the godhead makes his will known to people), leadership, and performing miracles. As a result of these gifts, adherents often follow these leaders blindly, giving many of them great power and authority. The leader then really shapes the movement.

It cannot be denied that these charismatic persons often show schizophrenic tendencies. But rather than merely considering these men and women mentally or psychically ill, or explaining their neurotic (or psychotic) condition or behavior as a result of negative childhood conditioning, we need to take into consideration the complex whole of cultural, social, and **religious** forces to understand the charismatic person. Too few students of these new religious movements have given attention to the totality of circumstances and conditions out of which the charismatic leader has emerged.

In missionary circles these leaders have often been brushed aside as charlatans, neurotics, deceivers, false prophets, demoniacs. Anthropologists tend to seek a scientific answer to these charismatic leaders' behavior in hereditary factors and in their psychosocial conditioning. Even though there are sociocultural factors, which can be defined and analyzed, prophetism or revelation or divine powers of healing or a person's spiritual calling cannot be reduced to a purely rationalistic explanation.

It has been shown that these charismatic persons, in general, have had a more intensive personal contact with Christian missions—and missionaries—or with representatives of Western civilization than the average person. Frequently this intensive encounter has been experienced as a conflict. Sometimes the conflict is of a personal nature, but nearly always it is a clash between two cultures, two value systems. This has led many of these leaders to the ambivalent behavior for which they are noted. They do not participate fully in the experience of the new culture, certainly not on the level of those with whom they have their intense encounter: church and mission leaders, technological specialists, political authorities. But neither are they fully integrated into their own culture and society.

Out of this marginal situation the prophets and the charismatic leaders emerge. Soon they become the key figures in the rise of movements which sometimes reject the traditional values, sometimes the new culture and its representatives—including missions and missionaries—but which in general selectively adopts elements from both and develops them into a new way of life and culture. Hence the terms "importation-movements," "accommodation-movements," or even "revitalization-movements." The charismatic leader often gives the movement form and direction, though these movements commonly change in a second and third phase of their development.

These charismatic leaders are a particular challenge to Christian missions. They are key figures in the development of genuinely indigenous churches. From them people expect answers to the many problems they face in their daily needs. To the extent that these answers satisfy them and fulfill their needs, prophets and charismatic leaders are trusted and followed. They become the formulators of an indigenous theology.

No one will deny that in this process wrong answers may be given and distortions of the Christian heritage occur. But is not the whole history of the church a history of such errors? Rather than sitting in judgment upon these prophets, should not the Christian missions and churches attempt to assist them, in all humility, in the formulation of a theology that is both biblically true as well as relevant to the situation in which the people find themselves? Does not the work of the Apostle Paul teach us that true theology emerges out of the encounter with the situation in which people live, work, and suffer, rather than in isolated centers of learning, through mere transplantation, or by social heritage?

The rise of new religions challenges Christian missions to recognize the working of the Spirit in African, Asian, and Latin American leaders whom God has chosen as his instruments to advance his mission. This recognition demands new attitudes and new relations with such charismatic persons. The emergence of so many prophets and visionaries also challenges Western missionaries to discover anew that true theology, in essence, develops as mission theology, as truth that is relevant to the particular time and circumstances in which the gospel reaches people.

3. Most of the new religions find their creative center in an apocalyptic idea, a **cosmic eschatology** that inspires hope and gives believers the assurance that the present evil state of affairs will soon change. By some miraculous event, usually of a cataclysmic nature, this world will soon be destroyed, and a new age will be ushered in that knows of no sickness or sin, no tears or oppression. Soon a messiah will come who will bring a new freedom, destroy the oppressor, and establish a government of righteousness with happiness and abundance for all. The dead will return and people will live forever, happy and free. Earthquakes, floods, typhoons, volcanic eruptions, famines, diseases, wars, and increasing crime are warning signs that the destruction of the world is at hand and the coming of the messiah is near.

People differ in their ideas about how this renewal of the present state of affairs may be achieved. In some movements the Golden Age is a glorified past, and people are urged to work for the regeneration of their old paradisic tradition. The term "nativistic" is appropriate for such movements as the ghost-dance movements of the North American Indians or the Milne-Bay cult in New Guinea.

In other movements, such as the cargo-cults, it is the old culture that is rejected. Temples and other sacred objects are destroyed and people adopt and imitate the new, often without quite understanding its meaning. Mass conversions to Christianity frequently take place. These people movements toward the Christian church are not merely a story out of the past. They continue to happen in Indonesia and Cambodia, in Thailand and India, in Africa and South America. Often unrecognized by mission leaders for what they are, the movements sometimes fizzle, or they develop into new religions or prophet-movements.

Western missions with their individual-oriented approach, their institutionalism, and their lack of messianic expectations may be unable to absorb such people movements when they arise. This has been one of the real tragedies in missions the last few decades. From Oceania to Africa whole villages and tribes and communities have turned away disillusioned from established churches and missions. They did not find in them the fulfillment of their eschatological expectations and the reality of the coming kingdom, either because this was no longer an essential part of the missionaries' message or the messianic hope was ignored in the real life of the church and of the believers.

Fortunately, at a time when Christian missions may expect many more of these people movements to occur throughout the world, new insights are developing into the nature of such movements and the best ways of encouraging them to grow into genuine Christian communities. But the answer to the challenge of those new religions that center in the expectation of the soon-coming messiah, resurrection of the dead, judgment, and arrival of a new heaven and a new earth does not lie in methodology.

Success in mission always depends on the content and clarity of our message, and it is that missionary message that is challenged by these messianic movements. They stand as a corrective to the lack of hope, the lack of expectation of the soon-coming Christ, the lack of urgency, and the lack of credibility of that hope in the churches' and missions' life and preaching. The new religions challenge Christian missions to rediscover the biblical message of the coming of Christ and of the full restoration of his kingdom, and to give that message new credibility through the life of the church, the missionary, and each individual believer.

II

If the sheer rise and growth of the new religious movements, their particular message and their universality, already challenge Christian churches and missions, the fact that the majority of these movements and cults emerge from contact with Christian churches and missions presents an even greater challenge. It is true that new religious movements have arisen—and do arise—outside the contact with Christian missions or Western civilization. There is ample evidence of this in history. From the pre-Christian era until the nineteenth century many indigenous myths tell of messianic expectations among American Indians and people of Africa, Asia, and Australia before their contact with Christian missions. Evidence also comes from such movements as the poona-cult and other cargo-cults in the isolated areas of New Guinea. But the majority of the new religions do emerge out of contact with Christianity, thereby presenting a series of challenges that mission leaders must take seriously.

The epicenter of these movements is in Africa. By 1967 nearly 6,000 religious movements had emerged from this contact-situation with established churches and missions. These movements comprise some ten million followers in nearly 300 different ethnic groups. Since 1967 the process of "independentization" or "indigenization" has continued, producing some 100 new churches, cults, or prophet-movements every year with memberships totaling some 400,000 people. Today the total number of these religious movements may be estimated at over 7,000 with a membership of 20-22 million people, spread through nearly 400 different ethnic groups. If this process continues, by the end of the century these new movements will have almost as many followers as established Protestant and Roman Catholic churches. They will certainly greatly surpass them in influence, power, vitality, and missionary growth.

In Latin America the number of new movements may be fewer than in Africa, but their spread and growth is at least as phenomenal. In fact, the number of their followers is so large and their influence on society so strong that these new religious movements have become a "third force" in many Latin American nations. In Brazil, for instance, such spirit-cults as Kardecism and Umbandism have become the popular religions of the rapidly expanding urban populations. According to some conservative estimates, Kardecism has a following of nearly four million people. One of Allen Kardec's main publications, *El Evangelio segun el Espiritismo,* has sold over a million copies in just a few years. Already in 1960 the movement operated nearly 2,000 institutions (hospitals, clinics, schools, orphanages), about as large a number as the Roman Catholic Church had in Brazil and twice the number of institutions operated by Protestant churches and missions.

An even greater following has been reported from the Umbanda-cult with its great emphasis on healing and the spirit-filled life. More than half the masses of poor people in Rio de Janeiro are followers of the Umbanda-religion, over half a million people in that city alone. From a movement of about 100,000 followers in 1955, the Umbanda-cult has become a national religious movement with nearly fifteen million adherents. Umbanda has more temples and religious centers than all Christian churches and sects in Brazil combined. At the national congress of the Umbanda movement in July 1973, delegates came from more than 100,000 temples and cult centers. Each center has about 100 members.

Like the Kardecists, the followers of the Umbanda religion come primarily from the proletarian masses of Brazil, especially from among the huge city populations, the poor, and migrants in the south. With the process of urbanization continuing rapidly during the next two decades, the influence of the Umbanda religion will likely continue to increase.

These city populations, as well as the proletarian masses of society (the poor, the peasants, the lower and the lower middle classes), also flock into the many new Pentecostal movements. This is true for all of Latin America and the West Indies, but especially in Chile, where already in 1971 thirty-six percent of the population belonged to one of the new Pentecostal groups. In Trinidad this percentage was 23; the Bahamas, 21.5; Jamaica, 17.6; and Brazil, 16.5. In Chile nearly ninety percent of all Protestants belong to one Pentecostal group or another. In Mexico that percentage is already seventy. It is expected that by 1985 some twenty-five percent of the population of Mexico may be Protestant, most of whom will belong to one of the many new Pentecostal movements.

In Brazil the Assembleias de Deus shows special vitality

and a growth perhaps without parallel in the history of mission. From its origin in 1910 until 1930 the movement grew to 13,500 members. In 1957 there were already close to 700,000. Ten years later its membership had grown to 1.5 million, but since 1967 another six million have been added, giving it a membership of nearly eight million today. And the Assembleias de Deus is only one of the forty or fifty new Pentecostal groups whose membership make up some seventy percent of all Protestants in Brazil.

In Africa and Latin America the new religious movements with their many millions of adherents arose in the backyard of established Christian churches. What is the nature of these relationships? What in the established churches and Christian missions, Roman Catholic or Protestant, stimulated the rise of these new movements? What positive and negative factors have been at work that made these new religious movements grow and spread so fast?

Some of these factors, of course, are purely social and economic and cultural, such as the crisis-situation that affects all people, cultures, and nations. Others are directly related to the particular forms of the Christian churches and the nature of their mission. The relationship between Christian missions and the new religions is not simply one of cause and effect; it is not a one-way street. The new religions do not arise simply as a reaction to the proclamation of the gospel or the presence of Christian churches, either as a protest or as a corrective to a felt lack. Neither are they only conscious or unconscious attempts to indigenize the Christian church, a result of emphasizing only selected parts of the message of Jesus Christ.

All of these factors, to be sure, are significant aspects of these movements arising out of contact with the established churches and missions. All of these have also greatly contributed to their rapid spread and growth, but the challenge goes deeper. Sometimes charismatic leaders have heard a biblical message that was not—or is no longer—present in Christian churches. Often these movements are able to present the gospel of Jesus Christ in such a form that it is, indeed, good news to the millions of people who most desperately need it, but who did not hear it in the context of the established Christian churches and missions.

Each of these movements has its own characteristics, its own peculiar form and development. Though they all emerged from a Christian context, the nature of the relationships between those movements and established churches and missions shows an almost infinite variety. Generalizations are hard to make, but from extensive literature on the subject some general characteristics seem to give these contact-movements a common structure in spite of the large variety in form, content, and development. Each of these characteristics presents its own challenge to Christian missions.

1. **The new religious movements arise, grow, and spread mostly among the rapidly growing city populations** —the uprooted, the alienated, the poor, and the proleterian masses of the industrializing nations. This has been shown for South America; it is true also for Africa, Europe, North America, and Asia. The hundreds of new religions arising in Japan—though few of them do so in the backyard of Christian churches—recruit their members almost exclusively from the lower and the lower middle classes in the sprawling urban centers. The upper and upper middle classes remain almost untouched by these new religions, whereas Christianity has found most of its converts and interest among them.

These new religions are thereby succeeding in areas of God's worldwide mission today where the established churches, so far, have failed: The many millions of people now crowded together in the huge metropolitan areas of the world—Tokyo, Manila, Calcutta, Lagos, London, New York, Sao Paulo. The challenge is obvious: Why—and how—do these new religions succeed in areas where Christian missions do not? The answer to this question is important and urgent not only because the large-city population of the world is increasing about five times faster than that of the world population in general, but also because of the tragic decimation of Christian churches in urbanized Europe and North America.

If these new religions can succeed in winning the masses of the large metropolitan centers, the often repeated statement that city life and the urban mentality are incompatible with religion stands refuted. This is one of the most encouraging findings of the study of the new religions. Mission leaders are now challenged to take a hard look at their present missionary structures and at their churches' value systems. Both are usually deeply rooted in the rural society of yesteryear, and often they share an anti-city animus. Though no one can deny the difficulties involved in winning large urban populations to Christ, these new religions demonstrate that this mission to cities really starts in our own backyard. Not until churches accept this challenge and move out into the world of the cities will the mission of God be fulfilled.

2. **These new religions take a holistic view of human existence and of life in general.** In this respect many prophets and other charismatic leaders have heard an aspect of the biblical message that churches and missions coming from the West have long since forgotten. As a document from the Kimbanguist religion expresses it: "Like the gospel itself, this church considers the body to be just as important as the soul; no clear distinction is drawn between the spiritual and the secular, between the spiritual life and social life." This concept, so different from Western dualism, makes these new religions much more than doctrinal systems.

They are a way of life, a (sub)culture.

Rather than merely being sacramental bodies, these movements are new social groups that rule and affect every aspect of the believer's life, from education of children to the kind of dress one should wear, the food one may eat, and how to spend one's leisure. They give advice on agriculture, counsel on marriage relations and family life, and frequently instruct their members on social and political questions.

Because of their social, economic, cultural, and political aspects, Western scholars all too frequently have mistaken them for social protest movements, economic reform movements, nationalistic movements, and liberation movements. In most cases, however, these movements are genuine religious movements with religion at the center of the whole life of the group. Their holistic view of life resists the compartmentalization so characteristic of Western thought and practice.

This holistic view also strongly affects these movements' understandings of human illness and misery and the way people can obtain healing and redemption. In contrast to the Western view which separates the healing of the body from the spiritual dimensions of salvation, most of these new religions consider physical illness part of humanity's whole state of being before God. Body and soul are not two separate entities but inseparable aspects of one and the same person. Rather than looking at illness as merely a physical dysfunction, these movements consider it a part of humanity's oppression, loneliness, unemployment, and social disintegration.

Healing comes from God and is therefore a function of religion. This explains not only the tremendous emphasis on healing in all these new religious movements, but also the close relationship between healing and salvation, wholeness and holiness. Healing is a dimension of salvation involving the whole person. Every believer is called to participate in this process. This has serious missionary implications. To these movements, even mission hospitals appear as a horrible form of secularization.

The social, physical, and economic consequences of this holistic view have been of inestimable help to millions of people who have come into contact with these movements. At a time of cultural confusion, the new religions become a new culture where people find stability and a place to feel at home, especially those most affected by the shocks and stresses of the new age: the uprooted populations, those crowded in the cities, the proletarian masses, the lower classes have found in these religions new identity, new security, new hope, and meaning to life.

3. **These new religious movements are lay-movements.** Like the early Christian church they spread because each believer is considered a missionary and a "priest." In Latin America, Kardecism, Umbanda-cult, and the Pentecostal movements—though different from each other in many respects—all emphasize "the priesthood of all believers." Over against the traditional teachings and practices of the Roman Catholic Church, these movements stress that each believer can have direct access to the throne of God and his grace without a human mediator.

All believers share equally in the gifts of the Spirit and thereby in the Spirit's power. These gifts determine a person's status in the new community rather than family background, wealth, or education. In fact, these are considered "mundanismo," worldliness, and therefore must be rejected. This has important social consequences. In the struggles of life the socially downtrodden and the economically powerless endowed with the power of the Spirit stand as a new elite. A compensation mechanism is at work here. At the same time a powerful social protest is sounded that has revolutionary consequences for the two-strata society of Latin America.

The same characteristic is found also in the new religious movements of Africa and Asia. All people can have power as a result of their own intimate relationship with God, and they can share it with others. God is not merely a holy word, an ideal, a power in the background. His presence is real. Ecstatic utterances, dreams, visions, and miraculous healings are the tangible signs of that presence. These are not limited to a chosen few! All believers share equally in these gifts and in the power that goes with them, making for the tremendous vitality of these movements and their missionary growth.

Of special significance in the rise and growth of these new religions as lay movements has been the translation of the Bible into the vernacular and its spread among the people. When believers began to read the Scriptures, certain discrepancies began to appear between what missionaries preached and lived and what African believers felt the Bible was teaching. Certain traditional African values, norms, and even social institutions which missionaries condemned were at times found to be genuinely biblical. In Oceania people often accused the missions of not having taught them all that the Scriptures teach, of having even torn out the first or the last few pages of the Bible. In Africa people expressed the feeling that missionaries were giving them a wrong interpretation of the Bible or a truncated form of Christianity selectively chosen according to standards and particular needs prevailing in Western culture. The missions were accused of putting their authority over that of the Scriptures.

As happened before in the history of the Christian church and mission, in the hands of believers the Bible now became a powerful impetus for a lay movement. This is especially true in Africa, where not only biblical forms and names and offices and institutions and prescriptions are adopted as essential to the life of the movement, but also are certain cosmologies and images and metaphors, based on a rather literalistic-fundamentalistic interpretation of the Scripture.

The challenge to mission is obvious. More than ever before, mission leaders must begin to realize the immense difficulties involved in the transcultural communication of the gospel. Whereas in the past missionaries have seldom been aware of the fact that the Christianity they brought to Africa or Asia bore the imprint of Western culture and society, today this insight is making missionaries much more open to the contributions of Latin American, African, and Asian believers. May this greater openness also lead to the rediscovery of the biblical concept of the church as the laity, "claimed by God for his own to proclaim the triumphs of him who has called you out of darkness into his marvelous light" (1 Pet 2:9. NEB).

III

A new day is dawning in relationships between the Christian missions and churches and the new religions. The negative and often hostile attitude missionaries have shown toward these movements in the past is changing to an honest attempt to understand them.

Some independent churches have been accepted as members of Christian councils; a few mission boards are cooperating with new religious movements in the training of their leaders, in theological education and Bible study, and in other projects of common concern. Gone are the days when the study of these new religions was the exclusive domain of the social scientists (anthropologists, sociologists, historians, political scientists, psychologists) and of a few phenomenologists and historians of religion. Some of the finest studies on these movements have come in recent years from missiologists. In 1974 the International Association for Mission Studies (IAMS), at its conference in Frankfurt, Germany, chose as its theme,

Mission and Movements of Innovation, sign of the new interest on the part of mission leaders in these religious movements, and of their positive evaluation.

Many factors contribute to this shift in attitude toward the new religions.

1. The movements have become better known than before. Missions have gradually become aware that the growth of these movements is a universal phenomenon. Though each movement has its own particular ethos and form, certain characteristics are common to all. The contributions made by anthropologists to the understanding of the new religions have received great recognition also in mission circles.

2. A second factor is the recognition of these movements' many positive contributions to society and to individual believers. Notable among them are the large-scale social and moral reforms they have brought about. They introduce a new morality, often expressed in strict rules against stealing, lying, gambling, or use of alcohol and drugs, and the insistence on modesty, chastity, saving, and other such values. There is emphasis on equality and fellowship, or creating a new brotherhood that takes the place of the traditional primary groups. They establish a "third culture," where people find a place to feel at home amid the conflict between the old and the new.

"Psychological liberation" is provided so that adherents find rest and peace of heart and mind in spite of anxieties and pressures, shocks, and confusion brought about by the crisis-situation in modern times. A new universalism breaks through the traditional particularisms of class, geographical regions, or ethnic groups. New "in-groups," especially in the large urban centers, are formed where people find new identity, new security, and stability. Hope, assurance, and a new meaning to life are found in a time of depression and uncertainty.

3. **A third factor is the missionary success of these movements.** They are growing in areas where Christian missions are static or losing ground; they seem to succeed in winning people who are beyond the reach of Christian missions. Mission leaders are beginning to learn from these movements' success and are starting to apply these new theological, ecclesiological, and methodological insights to the work of mission. Among these insights are the need for indigenization and contextualization of the Christian mission, fellowship and community as a way of mission, the role of the laity in mission, the wholeness of human existence and the totality of life, the dynamics of "group-conversion" and the group-oriented approach in mission, the message of hope in clarity and credibility, and the role of the Bible (and Christian literature) in mission.

4. **A fourth development bringing about the change of attitude is rooted in the missions' genuine concern to assist the new religions.** The many positive contributions of many of these movements should not blind us to the fact that they have also many negative features that stand in need of correction. These include the movements' own selectivity in choosing only part of the whole message of Jesus Christ; a tendency to find in their own culture a source of religious inspiration and criteria for truth; a trend toward exclusivism; a spirit of noncooperation with "outsiders"; an anti-church, anti-mission attitude; over-emphasis on the expectation of the coming messiah, which leads to fanaticism, frustration, and a "falling away from the faith" when expectations are not immediately fulfilled; the inability—or unwillingness—to "distinguish between the spirits"; and an unbiblical syncretism.

As long as churches and missions continue in their negative and hostile attitude toward these movements, no help can be offered that may lead to a correction of these negative aspects. Only when missions and churches recognize their own needs and their own lacks, when they develop humility to learn from the new religious movements, can these movements in turn open themselves to the contributions that Christian missions and individual missionaries may have to offer. This mutual sharing has barely begun. But it is an urgent necessity. At stake is the truth as it is found in the whole life and work, message and mission of Jesus Christ. At stake also is the total liberation of millions of believers and of those who have not yet been reached with the message of salvation. The place to begin such dialogue and common sharing, however, is not in new institutions, not other organizations, but rather in the backyard of each church and each religious movement. Here lies the true test to the credibility of Christian love and the power of the Spirit in a world of unbelief.

For Further Reading

Barrett, David B.
  1968   *Schism and Renewal in Africa: An Analysis of Six Thousand Contemporary Religious Movements* New York (London, Nairobi): Oxford University Press

Beizais, Heralds, ed.
  1975   *New Religions,* based on papers read at the Symposium on New Religions held at Abo, Finland, September 1-3, 1974. Uppsala: Almqvist and Wiksell International

Dialogue Center
  1979   *New Religious Movements Update* Aarhus, Denmark: Dialogue Center

Earhart, H. Byron
  1970   *The New Religions of Japan: A Bibliography of Western Language Materials.* Monumenta Nipponica Monograph. Tokyo: Sophia University

Ellwood, Robert S., Jr.
  1973 *Religious and Spiritual Groups in Modern America*
       Englewood Cliffs, New Jersey: Prentice-Hall, Inc.

Hollenweger, Walter J.
  1972 *The Pentecostals* Minneapolis: Augsburg Publishing
       House

Jules-Rosette, Bennetta, ed.
  1979 *The New Religions of Africa* Norwood, New Jersey:
       Ablex Publishing

LaBarre, Weston
  1971 "Materials for a History of Studies of Crisis Cults: A
       Bibliographic Essay," *Current Anthropology*, volume 12,
       number 1, 1971

Lanternari, Vittorio
  1961 *The Religions of the Oppressed* New York: Mentor Books

Needleman, Jacob, and George Baker, eds.
  1979 *Understanding the New Religions* New York: Seabury
       Press

Oosterwal, Gottfried
  1976 *Modern Messianic Movements as a Theological and
       Missionary Challenge* Scottdale, Pennsylvania: Herald
       Press

Pressel, Esther
  1971 *Umbanda in Sao Paulo* Ann Arbor: University Microfilm

Simpson, George Eaton
  1970 *Religious Cults of the Caribbean* University of Puerto
       Rico: Institute of Caribbean Studies

Turner, Harold W., ed.
  1977- *Bibliography of New Religious Movements in Primal
       Societies* Boston: G. K. Hall and Company

The Missionary as a Marginal Person

21

Roger C. Sider

I wish to explore the idea of the missionary as a marginal person—a person who in many ways does not fit anywhere, who lives at the boundary of cultural life, and who finds that in a sense no matter where he is, he is not quite at home. In some ways none of us is ever fully assimilated to the culture to which we go to minister. Yet, after a while we do not quite fit our native culture either because we've been changed and influenced by our experiences. We need to explore the issue of life on the margin, both to look at some of its vulnerabilities and also at some of its dynamics and advantages. To do that we need to review briefly something that all of us have had in introductory sociology, the acculturation process.

The Acculturation Process

Acculturation is, of course, the process each of us undergoes as children by which we are made part and parcel of our particular society. What does it mean, for example, to grow up in North America and be acculturated here? If one compares the college student in India with the college student in Canada, one observes some striking contrasts. Cultural background produces important differences. It is highly variable in contrast to biological development. There is not a great deal of variation in our bodies whether we grow up in India, Africa, Japan, or the West. We may have slight pigmentary differences in our skin, may weigh a bit more or less, and our physical features may take on some superficially different characteristics. But, biologically, the process of growth and development is really strikingly uniform, granted that people have good conditions under which to grow.

Culturally, however, there is wide variation. Some things are learned differently in different cultures. For example, culture shapes our feelings toward authoritarianism. We learn to accept a particular stance towards authority; we learn to be competitive; we learn that it is important to strive to get ahead. We also learn attitudes and practices regarding personal hygiene and punctuality. We learn what kinds of family loyalty matter and what kinds do not. We learn, in our culture particularly, that the nuclear family, the parents and their biological offspring, are where the vast emphasis is placed in terms of family loyalties. The extended family is not nearly so important here as it is in many other cultures. We are learning all these things as we are growing up.

We even learn quite trivial things. We learn what size a Sunday morning bulletin is. We had a minor case of culture shock in moving from Baltimore to Rochester. For several Sundays we were visiting different churches. I was impressed one Sunday with the odd shape of the bulletin. It was long and narrow—about foolscap length and quite narrow. It just was not right! That illustrates another important point about acculturation. We not only learn a way of doing things, a way of thinking; we also learn that it is the right way. Bulletins are a certain size, sermons ought to be so long, ministers dress in a particular style when in the pulpit. All of these things take on a certain prescriptive value so that by the time we are teenagers we are highly acculturated. We have come to believe a great number of things about the world which are not necessarily true; but we believe them and ascribe superior value to them. That is, our way of doing things is the right way. What is merely a system of cultural conventions thus comes to be seen as possessing intrinsic correctness. Moreover, this uncritical acceptance of our own cultural conventions takes place at the deepest psychological level. The crucial aspect of the acculturation process is not what is learned, but rather how it is learned—automatically, unconsciously, uncritically.

What follows, then, is that once we have established for ourselves a cultural identity, everyone else who is different is treated as such. Anyone who has not been acculturated in this way is seen as a foreigner, a stranger, an oddball. This leads, of course, to prejudice, which is a way of protecting our cultural identity and maintaining the superiority of the way we were brought up. It is not a matter, in most cases, of malevolent motives. Looking down on other cultures, other ways of thinking or other sizes of Sunday bulletins does not come from ill motives. Such prejudice is based, rather, on deep-seated psychological reasons. We need to retain some identity with our culture and some sense that our way is the right way.

Let us examine briefly some of the psychological payoffs of being a member of a culture. One payoff is having an identity. Identity is that global concept representing who I am in terms of my self-perception and my perceptions of others. It has many parts—among them national, professional, racial, ethnic, physical, and religious aspects. All of these parts of our identity are integrated in a cultural context so that who we are is quite literally a product of acculturation. Being part of a culture is knowing who we are and where we belong.

A corollary of that is that it provides us with a great deal of security. It is nice to know what to expect. It is good for me to know that when I come to a meeting people will sit around and listen politely whether they are interested or not. That allows me to go ahead with my plans and know what is expected of me. It is very nice to know when you go to a store just exactly what is expected of you in terms of what to say and how to behave. It is nice to know how you should dress on various occasions. All of these conventions help maintain a culture. Having a culture that one belongs to is a great efficiency. It is much less exhausting than attempting to work one's way through the same small tasks when he is not at home in a culture. And it is reassuring. In our home culture we feel relatively secure in the conduct of social relations.

A third advantage has to do with the way in which our participation in our culture regulates how we evaluate ourselves—regulates our self-esteem. Most people who have not had the experience of living in another culture would be surprised to know how vulnerable one's self-esteem can become when one is away from those sources of support that we tend to take for granted in the culture to which we belong. Those persons whom we identify as people who support us, who care about us, who say nice things about us from time to time, knowing where we belong, that we matter—those things are enormously important in buoying us up and in keeping our self-confidence at a level where we can function. And, of course, if that is taken away, we become vulnerable because we do not have the kinds of emotional support that we took for granted.

Let me illustrate this with something trivial which I observed when we first got to Phumula in 1967. I discovered that a letter from my mother was extremely important even though I rarely wrote to my mother when I was at home. At home it was sufficient in terms of my identity, security, and self-esteem to telephone or visit her occasionally, but as soon as I got away from the sources of support that I was used to, a letter from my mother became very important. When the mailbag arrived, my first priority was to sort through it for her letter.

Another example shows how one's sense of identity can get confused quickly. During those first days in the hospital in Phumula, I was called out with the ambulance. One of the most important questions in my mind was, "Should I wear my white coat or not?" In retrospect, this was absolutely ludicrous, but I was not feeling much like a doctor in that situation and I was not at all sure that other people were thinking that I was a doctor. I needed some visible, tangible evidence that I was the right one. I had been secure in my role as a physician in North America because I had cultural supports. In Phumula I suddenly was not at all secure. In summary, our culture provides identity, security, and self-esteem.

The Move to the Margin

What happens when we move to the margin? What does being a missionary involve in terms of our cultural experience? It involves, in a major sense, giving up all the benefits of acculturation. We manage to retain memories. We think a great deal of what it was like back home. And when we are really feeling badly we dredge up fantasies of what we could be doing: "This evening, if we were in Mount Joy, we'd . . ." In reality, however, we leave virtually all that behind, with the exception of some slender threads. When we move to another culture, to the margin, to the farthest outpost of our culture, the reality of culture shock really hits us; and I do not think there is any way to explain that experience to those who have not had it. When you talk about it, it is much too abstract, too unreal, too vague. But when you find yourself in a world that is utterly strange in so many ways and find that—along with the strangeness—you do not know the cues, every situation is new, and you do not have the advantage of habitual ways of behaving, you become exhausted. You find that every little task is an enormously burdensome one—even buying a tube of toothpaste. You have always bought Crest and there is no Crest. What do you do? There may not even be any toothpaste that week. The fact that we are creatures of habit and routine, that we are social creatures above and beyond everything else, means that when we are wrenched away from our social nest and moved to the margin we become highly vulnerable people.

Vulnerability at the Margin

My third point deals with the vulnerabilities of people placed on the margin. Who we are depends on who other people say we are. Most of us do not realize how much we depend on other people's constant validation of us to maintain our knowledge of who we are. If that disappears, we quickly begin to wonder who we are.

Let us take the issue of missionary identity. Think back to your first understanding of what it meant to be a missionary.

Certain images and assumptions come to mind: 1) a dedicated, spiritual person; 2) one who had a high status in the life of the church; 3) a person to whom other people looked with a great deal of respect. It was that of a person engaged in public speaking, showing interesting pictures, reporting on a life of sacrifice, adventure, and faith. This was the makeup of a missionary identity to many North Americans.

When you went overseas, the people to whom you were ministering saw you, the missionary, as someone very different from what you at home thought a missionary to be.

There a missionary may be viewed as a wealthy person, or as a member of an influential minority, highly visible, and somewhat inscrutable. The missionary is an "American" with nationalistic connotations not understood here. You stop and say to yourself, "Well, that's not me. I'm the same person. I'm the missionary when I'm home, I'm the missionary when I'm here. Yet people here see me differently. Who am I? Am I what the people at home think I am? Or, am I neither? Or, do I have to be both? Do I have to start playing roles so that when I am home I do the things that people expect missionaries to do and over here do the things people expect of missionaries in this setting?" We suddenly are faced with the fact that who we are really is defined by social context. We find it hard not to adapt and not to adjust to what other people expect us to be.

On the issue of security, the move to the margin is a move away from psychological safety and familiarity toward vulnerability, exposure, and danger—in most cases psychological rather than physical. How is this so?

Security results from being in touch with the surrounding culture, perceiving cues, understanding communications, and responding appropriately. In a foreign culture correct perception is highly problematic. Thus we are never sure whether we appear as we intend to appear or whether we have observed or violated a cultural taboo. Every word, every act, every assumption in such a setting is risky. We cannot help but be gripped by the enormity of our insecurity.

There is also vulnerability in terms of our self-esteem. We have learned over the years how to protect our self-esteem, how to feel good about ourselves. But in another culture the very things that made us feel good about ourselves may backfire. For example, a remark such as "May I help you?" may connote condescension to an African rather than helpfulness. When we find that something we said reflects a condescending attitude, it reflects back on our sense of self-esteem. "Am I really that thoughtless and insensitive? Am I really missing all of this?" And so we can quickly begin to have doubts and questions that lead to feelings of inferiority.

Perhaps the most critical vulnerability is the vulnerability to cultural influence. When we move away from our culture, the process of getting close to another culture means that we are vulnerable to being influenced by that culture. Sometimes our anxieties come out more in terms of our children than in terms of ourselves. We assume we have established who we are: American expatriates, or American missionaries, or whatever. But we see our children having a different experience. They are not growing up in a pure culture, i.e., the American way of life. They are growing up at the margin and experience the influences of the culture in which they live rather than what we parents try to provide. We must face the vulnerability of not only ourselves becoming Indian, Japanese, Zambian, or whatever, but also of our children becoming "nationalized" too. We have to be willing to deal with that.

Maladaptation at the Margin

In view of this experience and these vulnerabilities, what are wrong patterns of adaptation? We can discern among all groups who have been transplanted from one culture to another three kinds of maladaptations. The first one is, "Let's make everybody else like us." This is in social/ psychological terms what colonialism is in political terms. That is the cultural analog of colonialism. Make them like us. Since I feel insecure the way they shake hands and the way they talk, and since I am troubled about not having Crest to brush my teeth, let us import Crest, teach them English, etc. I would feel much better because then I would have created for myself a cultural home away from home rather than living at the margin of my culture. I will once again be living at its center, or at least at a peripheral center, somewhere removed from North America.

We do not need to belabor the risks that are involved. But to the degree that we make other people like us, we deprive them of their own culture. We, in fact, make them marginal people. They are then the people who do not know the rules, who have to learn a new language, who have to make the transitions. We lose the opportunity to learn from them.

Another technique used by immigrants to North America is assimilation. "If you can't beat them, join them." That means you become just like they are. Make the jump totally so that there is nothing left on the other side. Become Indian, Japanese, African. Shed every vestige of what you were so that you now become what these people are. That has been the pattern followed by many immigrant groups to the United States and Canada where, because of the peculiar cultural climate and tremendous opportunities, it was relatively easy. Because of this the United States has lost much of the richness of its cultural diversity within a few generations. Many second and third generation Italians no longer speak Italian, for example. Recently, people have taken a new interest in their cultural heritage. They are now going back to find out who they were. But the process of assimilation is also a maladaptive response because we really cannot do it. One cannot become totally unrelated to what he was before. To attempt to do so is to cut oneself off from the deepest roots of one's identity.

A third response, refined to an art by Jewish culture, is the response of the ghetto. "Okay, I will live at the margin, but I will erect walls so that the vast majority of my cultural experiences—work, education, friends, and acquaintances—will occur within a closed community." There are many white man's ghettos in cities around the world, especially in Asia and Africa, where Europeans cluster together to preserve what they have and make as little contact as possible with those people who are strange. The ghetto solution is also a maladaptive solution. For one thing, we become a caricature of what we once were. For example, if I think that in England it is appropriate to have tea at four p.m. and I am living in Rhodesia and I want to retain a cultural identity as English, then tea at four p.m. will become highly ritualized and may be the most important thing in my day because that is what links me to England and to my

English identity. It may happen that in England meanwhile they no longer have tea at four p.m., but that makes no difference to me. The possibility of becoming a caricature of what I think I am attempting to preserve is a real one. The ghetto can only be preserved at the price of a high degree of prejudice against those people outside. If I do not erect those barriers of prejudice, I am going to mix. There will be nothing to prevent me from mixing, from making contact, so that I have to carry an "us/them" mentality in order to keep those boundaries sharp and clear.

The Call to the Margin

What is the call of God to us vis-à-vis cultural life? What does the Bible say to us about marginal living, about being exposed, being on the edge, not quite belonging, not knowing where our home is? The missionary must come to grips with this question in a way few Christians ever do. What does the Bible say? It says that the margin is the place for all of us—that the Christian will always live on the margin in relation to culture. Matthew 10:34-39, John 1:11, Romans 1:1 and 12:2 all speak to this. These passages—and many others—tell us that the Christian position vis-à-vis any culture is one of apartness, of being marginal, of not quite belonging. Jesus did not quite belong. It was prophesied he would not and he did not. He was not accepted by his own people. And one of the things that is special about the life-walk of the missionary is that he knows that in a way that many people do not. Those in missionary service sense the price they pay for being a person of God who is always marginal in relationship to the world. We are always exposed and vulnerable. In that sense we are always insecure. And that is the call of God to every believer.

Adaptation at the Margin

How do we adapt if that is what the Lord calls us to? Fortunately, God never asks of us anything greater than He in turn will supply. That of course is the miracle of God's intervention in our behalf. It is designed to meet us precisely at the point of our need.

We need to do two things in order to survive. First, we must be genuinely and deeply rooted in Jesus Christ.

We must be convinced that if we are at the margin, we are there because Christ is Lord and has called us. I do not know any other way to get there. If we try to go it alone, we will fall into one or another of the maladaptations. To know that Christ is Lord and that our marginal life is in obedient response to His call is the bedrock of everything else. We must come back to this when we are buffeted by the vicissitudes of marginal living. We are not there because we are masochists, because we enjoy punishment or pain. We are there because Christ is Lord and He has called us. That is the first half—the vertical half.

The horizontal half is that we must find at the margin the new community. The church is the Christian's home away from home in the sense that we are sojourners here. We are set apart and not received well by the world. In that sense we are homeless and the church is our community. But whereas God calls us to marginal life vis-à-vis secular culture, He puts us right in the center of a new culture and a new community, the body of Christ. The body of Christ is, then, a society. It is the divine society. And God provides for us, at the particular margin where we are, a new community. Now sometimes it might be pretty slim and the differences between us may seem greater than the similarities, but that is because our priorities are wrong. We are still thinking in the framework of the secular world—if they do not come on time to services, or if they stay too long—but that is not what the new community is all about.

What will this new community be like? As I tried to think through the characteristics of a new community of Christians at the margin, it seemed to me that it would have to have as its participants people of all of the surrounding secular cultures or else it would be a ghetto community again. It must transcend those boundaries. It must be diverse in its makeup. It must be embodied in structures appropriate to those constituent cultures. This may mean some rather odd compromises such as half of the songs in this language and half in that. Finally, its cultural patterns and structures would have to be evaluated by its effectiveness in promoting worship, discipleship, and brotherhood rather than how well it preserves the American way of doing things.

I believe that as we live and participate there we will find that our security, identity, and self-esteem are more and more grounded in the new community. Indeed, the Bible says this is where it ought to be. It is with our Christian brothers and sisters that we find the cultural home that the Lord has provided for us.

The Dynamic of the Margin

Why is it that God calls us to these difficult marginal places and to this kind of life? I believe it is because that is where the action is. In physics, chemistry, biology, in any physical system of which I am aware, the dynamic is always at the interface. To use a popular phrase, it is where the rubber meets the road. It is the point of contact.

If we can once find for ourselves stability at the margin, I do not think there is any other place where so much can happen because that is where life, contact, and interaction are greatest. That is the place where a tremendous amount of vitality and life can be seen. Life on the margin can be a life of rare opportunity to make a difference, to have impact, to be effective, and to be affected in return. To live at the margin is to be truly alive and vital as Jesus Christ was.

Can Western Women Adapt to Japanese Culture?

22

Sue Richard

A Japanese friend once said to Lafcadio Hearn: "When you find, in four or five years more, that you cannot understand the Japanese at all, then you will begin to know something about them" (Hearn 1928:5). After many more years in Japan, Hearn began his *Japan: An Attempt at Interpretation* by admitting, "I cannot understand the Japanese at all" (1928:6).

Twelve years qualifies me to make the same confession. Oriental culture and occidental culture are vastly different. Without a measure of understanding and appreciation for Japanese culture, a Westerner cannot make Japan his/her home.

In this article I will examine the cultural conflicts that occur when West encounters East, and more specifically when a Western missionary woman attempts to adjust to Japanese culture. The conflicts loom large if one tries to transplant values and assumptions wholesale into another culture. With some give and take, however, I believe a satisfactory measure of acculturation is possible. I want to deal with my "takings," new insights and appreciations of Japanese culture, and conclude with possible areas for "giving," areas in which I feel a Western Christian can legitimately exert influence for cultural change.

Few people go to another country equipped anthropologically to deal with all the cultural differences they will encounter. Most take the dive and then learn to swim. Cultural maladjustment is a sensitive issue. People are reluctant to talk about why they failed to adjust or how their failure could have been avoided. I recall one conversation with an American woman just before she and her husband left Japan after eight years of missionary service. She saw her husband's unhappiness as the root of the problem: too many guests, too little privacy, his need for new self-identity. But friends and coworkers said she was a loner, could not find creative outlets in Japanese society, and seemed generally dissatisfied.

Edward Hall articulates the dynamics at work when one attempts to take the plunge into another culture: **Creative use of intercultural relations exposes some very deep, highly personalized, and sensitive areas of the psyche. . . . In studying oneself by the cross-cultural technique one starts with the notion that what is known least well and is therefore in the poorest position to be studied is what is closest to oneself; . . . these are the unconscious patterns that control one's life** (1976:40).

Westerners viewing the little oriental archipelago through travelogues and history books tend to picture the Japan of tea gardens and pagodas; they suppose its people are charming and artistic. Many first encounters produce wonder and delight in the newcomer. Modesty and gracefulness are cultivated social arts. One immediately admires the serene, ritualistic movements of Japanese women in formal settings. However, a more thorough investigation of social patterns reveals that strict convention governs degrees of bows and ranks of seating. Inner compliance to a hierarchy of social relations has made it relatively easy for Japanese to defer to one another, a virtue Westerners know little of. To know one's place in Japanese social relationships is to be secure as well as polite.

Emotions are strictly guarded. Strength of character means avoiding emotional outburst and concealing one's true feelings with the ever present stoic smile of tranquility. Feminine virtues are ardently taught and exquisitely exhibited. But the glamor of oriental life soon peels away when one's Western presuppositions come into conflict with Japanese social norms. Unless one can rise above ethnocentricity and can identify elements that contribute to cultural dissonance, unresolved internal tensions insidiously build up.

The Roman Catholic anthropologist, Louis Luzbetak, writes: **To adjust one's general behavior and specialized skill to local ways will call for a recognition, appreciation and even actual adoption of numberless shocking attitudes and practices. Not the sacrifice of the luxuries of an American home or the consolations of relatives and friends but the sacrifice of one's own ways and values will be the missionary's greatest sacrifice; in fact it may even become a slow martyrdom** (1963:15).

What I had viewed as elegant and beautiful in Japanese people gradually became a source of irritation. Like other "settled in" expatriates, I secretly wondered why women in Japan needed to be bound by such incommodious social decorum. I entertained many questions: "Isn't it possible to laugh unabashedly without covering one's face?" "Why must one always avoid direct confrontation in speech?" Before my own assumptive world was threatened by conflicting values, I felt Japanese social behavior was a beautiful buttress of societal stability and harmonious interactions. Gradually conflicts mounted and guilt set in. My Western training taught me an assertive etiquette and grace that demonstrate self-worth and pride. "Stand up straight." "Keep your shoes on." "Speak out and air your opinions." These attitudes were thoroughly ingrained and did not easily succumb to opposing values of social deference.

Japan is called a country of paradoxes. World traveler Edward Hall has observed: "I can think of few countries Americans are likely to visit or work in . . . where it is more difficult to control one's input and where life is more filled with surprises than Japan" (1976:49).

"Freedom, spontaneity, optimism, activity, individualism, and self-assertion" characterize the West, whereas the East is characterized by "stoicism, pessimism, introspection, conventionality, patience, and reticence" (Gulick 1963:51). Without an understanding of the culture that esteems such qualities, conflicts arise within the person who tries to harmonize the antonymous nature of two cultures.

Cultural conflicts reach beyond the cultural environment into the physical environment. Spatial confinement may gnaw at inner contentment. Women vent their annoyance in a variety of ways: "I miss my garden and lawn." "A back yard with a little green grass would be so nice." "There is no room in our flat for my washer/dryer/refrigerator/range." Restrictions extend to the outside world as well. Standing in tight lines, shopping in crowded stores, and commuting in congested trains and buses pose an infraction of spatial rights few outsiders tolerate happily.

However, a flexible person can learn techniques from people accustomed to living in crowded conditions. The Japanese know how to exploit space; they can do the maximum in minimal space. The train station "pusher," for example, makes room for extra commuters morning and evening. Westerners bristle at being pushed and crushed. The Japanese have learned to ignore it. They reserve special respect for what is directly related to them. Social obligations are inoperative outside one's web of relationships. In domains where spatial rights cease to exist, tension is greatly reduced. "Not seeing is another way of seeing. If one can learn to ignore, then the limits of reality seem to disappear'' (Condon 1974:129).

Rooms in Japan are measured in mats—a mat is three by six feet. Many college boarding students must confine their living space to 4½-mat rooms. An old saying expresses the philosophy at work: ''Sleeping you need one mat; standing you need only a half.''

Creating illusions of space is another way of making close living tolerable. Japanese speak of practical illusions; cloth curtains give one an illusion of privacy, and paper doors that divide rooms can seem as thick as doors made of wood. Opening doors and windows expands the dimensions of a room and brings the natural world nearer. Cold weather necessitates other ways of coping.

Room decor is also crucial to comfort. Decorations should be few and simple; large objects, however beautiful, are hard to appreciate. Japanese etiquette suggests that one central motif, a piece of pottery or a flower arrangement, is enough to make a room pleasant and restful. ''A well designed space may yield a far greater sense of spaciousness than one would guess from looking only at the dimensions'' (Condon 1974:129). The woman who is willing to take her cues from Japanese interior decorating, making do with apartment-sized and fold-up items, can create illusions of space and clear rooms of clutter. Divesting oneself of American-type abundance is a first step to appreciating simple beauty Japanese-fashion and living comfortably in small quarters.

Many foreigners have a strong negative reaction to the discovery that husband and wife in Japan function in completely separate worlds. The Western wife in Japan meets a rude shock when she finds that her name seldom appears on formal invitations, and she is rarely invited to her husband's social engagements. My reactions ranged from shock to anger to questioning. This in turn led to examining Japanese women's social position. Centuries of subjugation and conformity have produced wives relatively content with their status. Vogel, in *Japanese Middle Class,* confirmed my observations: **The Japanese women do not complain of lack of companionship as American women might if the husband's business world were entirely removed from them. . . . Quite the contrary, . . . the Japanese wife prefers her husband not to encroach upon her territory, for this limits her autonomy, and she and her children need to be more reserved in the husband-father's presence** (1965:194-95). The Westerner can hardly refrain from challenging this pattern of virtuous deference.

Of all the intercultural conflicts Western women in Japan face, the greatest relate to language. The inscrutability of Japanese to the Western mind often stands in the way of facility in communication, yet language complexity may not be the heart of the problem. The meaning of words spoken by the native speaker may be perfectly clear, yet the nonverbal communication mystifies the unaccustomed foreigner. Japanese scholars refer to their language as a "terminal language" (Kunihiro 1976:273). Oriental tongues skip process to go to conclusion, whereas our Western languages emphasize logical process, answering what, why, how questions. Westerners are not accustomed to leaps in logic and find themselves wondering how the speakers came to their conclusions.

Western-style communication differs from Japanese speech in another respect. While dialogue characterizes our style of conversation, the Japanese consciously avoid confrontation and hence often engage in intermittent monologues to ensure relaxed, harmonious relations. Conversing in Japanese is like "taking a comfortably hot bath and thoroughly enjoying the warmth of another human being" (Kunihiro 1976:275). The dilemma the uninitiated person experiences may best be comprehended by observing it in reverse. "Even I, as a pure Japanese, have a strong sensation that I am another man when I give a speech in English. I feel like Dr. Jekyll and Mr. Hyde, as if somehow I have put on a disguise.'' Kunihiro goes on to say: "Expressing myself in a foreign language is not merely a passive act, but an active, creative undertaking" (1976:275). Conversely, speaking Japanese does not require close reasoning and fresh metaphors; native Japanese ears expect to hear a speaker choose appropriate forms and manipulate time-honored phrases in a smooth, emotionally warm manner.

Deprived of one's mother tongue, one must babble new, strange-sounding words. This produces particular frustration for the Westerner whose normal speech pattern tends toward impetuous, off-the-cuff responses. Automatic responses in one's own tongue speed along conversation and satisfy the need to communicate but do not lead to facility in the second language.

Larson clarifies the mysterious element of the frustration many feel. "Language is man's most precious possession, the last thing that he gives up before death, almost like breath itself. . . . To take it away even for a time in a limited way is for many a devastating experience" (1977:77). Observe the missionary who is reunited with compatriots after months of work in newly-acquired Japanese. Chatter invariably ensues until each one's need for free expression is satisfied.

Knowing how to build satisfactory primary relationships in the second culture is an adjunct of language frustration that many women face but few discuss. Acceptance and security come with being part of an in-group and finding people with whom one can share deepest joys and struggles. The first years in a new culture are crucial. Love draws the missionary close to others, yet anxieties about communication may cause anxious withdrawal to avoid the risks of misunderstanding and embarrassment. Women, more than men, are vulnerable to this particular struggle. Japanese is a language governed by strict convention. Men are permitted the use of freer, rough, shortened forms of speech, but women must use special forms and soft, sustained, even-flowing diction. Femininity is enhanced or destroyed by one's speech. Proper speech reflects proper upbringing and to a large extent determines whether a woman will be accepted by the in-group.

The person hoping to establish satisfactory psychological identification needs to reach out in many directions. Scripture offers many insightful stories about identification for the sake of mission; the book of Ruth is a beautiful story of successful acculturation. The family cluster, a sheltered enclave, can be an important source of support. Although it may slow down the process of acculturation, the family still "serves to reduce the emotional disturbances that accompany cultural contact" (Spiro 1955:1247). Compatriots, sensitive to the needs of newcomers, can also provide understanding and support. The church, the body with which one seeks to identify ultimately, is much less rigid about social convention than other relationship groups. Church members accept the stranger more readily than do others. Many anxieties are assuaged when learning to know and being known happen in the context of spiritual brother- and sisterhood.

For those whose difficulties arise from the structural rather than the cultural aspects of language, ease comes only with constant exposure, fearlessness, and commitment to mastery. Any "surrendering of arms" cuts off the possibility of adaptation and long-term survival.

In light of all the potential conflicts in intercultural adjustment, what should the transitional person's attitude be? How can one minimize the identity crisis and hasten acculturation? Adopting the position of learner stands one in good stead. **The adaptation of the newcomer to the in-group which at first seemed to be strange and unfamliar to him is a continuous process of inquiry into the cultural patterns of the approached group. If this process of inquiry succeeds, then this pattern and its elements will become to**

the newcomer a matter of course, an unquestionable way of life, a shelter, and a protection. Then the stranger is no stranger anymore and his specific problems have been solved (Schuetz 1960:109).

When inquiry grows out of a genuine desire to understand the new way of life, one gains much which will help in sharing the gospel of Christ. By studying oriental culture through the arts, the learner develops skills and gains entrance into the most natural setting for penetrating the mystery of Japanese thought and religious sentiment. "The Japanese consider every art to be a form of schooling which grants insight into life's beauty" (Herrigel 1958:xii). The Japanese regard beauty as the element of art which transcends rationality and utility thinking; art is pursued for the sake of spiritual enlightenment. One best understands the close affinities of Zen Buddhism and the arts when learning flower arrangement or tea ceremony.

Interpersonal relationships, complicated as they are in Japan, provide a further learning opportunity for people willing to submerge themselves in the society's intricate social networks. Learning to interact in a socially acceptable way affords one a deeper understanding of the meaning of subordinating individual goals and interests to those of the group. Many advocate the "servanthood role" for missionary activity. This posture is not strange to Japanese people. Society has institutionalized secular principles of servanthood to ensure harmonious relationships. The situation is thus ready-made for the missionary to demonstrate the social consequences of a dynamic, obedient relationship to the living Lord. This relationship, however, does not abdicate selfhood, nor does it passively submit to the normative pattern of static conformity in hierarchical relations.

Becoming a bicultural person requires learning and serving. The search for acceptable acculturative patterns will be most rewarding when missionary and church carry on the search together. Partnership needs to characterize the process. The missionary must shed some cultural baggage for the sake of the gospel, but the church also must kindle missionary zeal and grapple with the implications of becoming a sending body. When Christ's mandate to go and preach becomes a bilateral concern, the church gains a new appreciation for the foreigner who is trying to break into an alien culture. Together church and missionary seek to create new cultural structures as the Holy Spirit leads. The fruit of their labor will be mutual enrichment as they integrate elements of both cultures to form the new society.

In contrast, nativism is a unilateral attempt at cultural adaptation, referred to as "going native," or "snuggling" (Cleveland 1960:28,29). Although noble in its aspirations, nativism often ends in disillusionment because the total burden of cultural absorption falls on the guest. Newcomers, wanting to avoid the pitfalls of becoming part of an isolated enclave, often overreact by rejecting their own traditions and cultural values for those of the host country. Perhaps apprehensiveness about being accepted or being successful tempts one to surrender one's own identity. Luzbetak suggests that the local people's attitude is important in telling the American missionary just how American or un-American he should be (1963:9). Acculturation is not a matter of passively relinquishing one's national identity; rather it is a creative act in which both parties share in finding a new identity under the lordship of Christ. This process enables members of both cultures to discover that the command to "Let this mind be in you which was also in Christ Jesus" requires mutuality.

To what extent then can the missionary serve as an agent of cultural change? Those who see the missionary as a destroyer of folk pleasures and spreader of gloom strongly advise against meddling with other people's religions or value systems. Bob Dunham, a guest in Japan, addressed missionaries with these words: **If you attempt a one-man campaign to "convert" the people to what you feel are more modern, logical western habits you only find yourself . . . losing the battle. You will find life a bit easier if you follow instead of trying to lead, for that is the secret of the Japanese way of life** (1967:16).

On the other hand, the foreigner's presence itself suggests change. The chief concern of the missionary becomes not whether society will change but how it will change. What are the dynamics of the process? What kind of an innovator will the missionary be? Only when the missionary casts off all vestiges of arrogance about Western culture and seeks to direct change in a way that undergirds and respects existing patterns will the attempt at change be legitimate. But the real transformers of culture need to be the local people, with the Holy Spirit's power and direction.

Given the above, I believe that in several areas missionaries can rightly initiate action for change in Japan's social structures. Japanese people are internationally minded despite their tendency to differentiate between the outside world and "our world." Banquet-hall banners and speeches proclaim "worldwide friendship" and "worldwide peace." As a member of the church, a worldwide, interracial organization, the missionary faces the unique challenge of broadening the concept of worldwide friendship and peace beyond secular pursuit of self-interest. Inside as well as outside the church, people need an international peace consciousness that transcends ethnicity and stresses service in a cooperative struggle against oppression. Japan's so-called "insular mentality" regards the outside world with a view to finding ways to inculcate new ideas for economic expansion. This needs to give way to viewing surrounding nations as neighbors with whom technological skills can be shared for socioeconomic improvement. The bearer of the Christian gospel of peace, though, views service in a much broader context: the mission of reconciliation for Japan is integral to all social action in Asia.

Kurihara Akira, writing about the international consciousness of his people, concluded with a challenge that both the Westerner and the church could profitably pick up. He says old thought patterns need to be transformed in order to create a genuine international sense. The first step is to establish a "base" in the heart of a milieu dominated by artificial relationships, to cultivate a "dual consciousness" which will enable Japanese to reject old values while building new ones (1972:301).

As Westerners, we have the responsibility to shatter the typical TV/movie image which Japanese have of Americans. The pleasure-loving rich, the youth with sex appeal, the jet-setters are the models many Japanese try to emulate. The reverse values—honesty, fidelity, service— are best fostered where a nucleus of believers can flesh them out. The missionary who cares about neighbors can begin to reverse the pernicious, thing-oriented trend to a people-oriented style of living. Japan has traditionally been an imitator. In light of that fact, Westerners who have historically been model exporters need to introduce sound models worthy of imitation. The missionary soon discovers that the task of redeeming worldly models is as great as that of creating new Christian ones.

Pornography is one imported social evil that needs immediate creative counter voices and counteraction. For Japanese people with insatiable curiosity about sex, the church should prepare literature that answers questions in light of its biblical, God-intended use. Christians struggle with issues of abortion, family planning, and divorce, searching for principles to guide them in making crucial decisions. The missionary should encourage Japanese Christians to produce material appropriate to their culture to speak to these issues.

The rallying cry of many women in Japan today is

"emancipation." Sumie Mishima in *The Broader Way* echoes the words I heard so often: "economic independence." She suggests that it is "the crucial step for any social freedom of a sound and fruitful nature" (1953:211). Advocates of women's liberation voice numerous claims of injustices and press for militant action through the organization, **Chupiren.** The plight of Japanese women calls for sympathetic understanding. However, an alternative to militant action needs to be set forth, based on the biblical principles of active love lest women completely alienate themselves from mutually satisfying social relationships. The Western woman is often asked to talk about women's roles because of her unique social position. As a Christian, the missionary has special resources for responding to the questions people ask her.

Western couples can also contribute to Japanese cultural practices by entertaining guests. Family or couple entertaining is not practiced in Japan. Such entertaining helps to break down sexual discrimination and allows people to socialize outside closely knit circles. Entertaining also provides a plus element for the foreign wife; it helps to satisfy a normal socializing need and keeps her from being drawn exclusively into a foreign community.

Single people face discrimination in Japan. Traditionally they were not accorded full social status. The Westerner's heterogeneous social background can aid understanding and reduce discrimination. Small gestures of friendship and words of encouragement can build confidence and help society and church to see that single people are not "leftover blessings." We found that including single adults in our family fun from time to time filled an important social need for us and for them.

Can a Western woman adapt to Japanese society in light of all the cultural differences? Yes, but not without effort. Life in Japan is not pure adventure for the guest. The Westerner may always be regarded as an outsider in homogeneous cultures like Japan. Nida reminds the missionary that even partial identification is possible only if the person recognizes the inherent limitations of the process. Otherwise, he says, the person will spend time in fruitless questioning of others' motives and endless self-accusation (1960:168). Nida's statement does not close the door to satisfactory assimiliation, however. Cultural differences may seem like overwhelming obstacles, but because identification is an act in partnership with God, grace and strength are supplied to those who faithfully obey.

The ultimate goal of identification for Christian workers is that men and women may know and become the righteousness of God. Curiosity and eagerness for knowledge facilitate assimilation. Originality and prudence keep one a productive member of the adopted society in the dual role of priest and prophet, culture stabilizer and culture agitator.

References Cited

Akira, Kurihara, 1972. "International Sense of the Japanese" *Japan Interpreter* 7.3-4:293-301

Cleveland, Harlan, 1960. *The Overseas Americans* New York: McGraw-Hill

Condon, John, and Keisuke Kurata, 1974. *In Search of What's Japanese about Japan* Tokyo: Shufunotomo Company, Ltd.

Dunham, Bob, 1976. *The Art of Being Japanese* Tokyo: Tuttle

Gulick, Sidney Lewis, 1963. *The East and the West: A Study of Their Psychic and Cultural Characteristics* Rutland, Vermont: Tuttle

Hall, Edward, 1976. *Beyond Culture* Garden City, New York: Anchor Press

Hearn, Lafcadio, 1928. *Japan: An Interpretation* New York: Macmillan

Herrigel, Gustie, 1958. *Zen in the Art of Flower Arrangement* Massachusetts: Charles T. Bronford Co.

Kunihiro, Masao, 1978. "The Japanese Language and Intercultural Communication" *Japan Interpreter* 10.3-4:265-283

Larson, Donald N., 1977. "Missionary Preparation: Confronting the Presuppositional Barrier" *Missiology* 5.1:73-82

Luzbetak, Louis J., 1963. *The Church and Cultures* Techny, Illinois: Divine Word Publications

Nida, Eugene, 1960. *Message and Mission* New York: Harper and Brothers Publishers

Mishima, Sumie Leo, 1953. *The Broader Way* New York: John Day Co.

Schuetz, Alfred, 1960. "An Essay in Social Psychology: in Stein, Vidich, and White (ed.) *Identity and Anxiety* New York: The Free Press

Spiro, Milford E., 1955. "The Acculturation of American Ethnic Groups" *American Anthropologist* 57.6: 1240-1251

Vogel, Ezra F., 1965. *Japan's New Middle Class* Berkeley and Los Angeles: University of California Press

23 Authoritarian Governments and Mission

Wilbert R. Shenk

A decade ago revolution was one of the most pressing problems facing Christian mission. The theologies of liberation in vogue today originated under dynamic conditions where the masses felt themselves to be politically impotent. Revolutionary change seemed to be the only solution.

Now a new theme has entered the picture. Various recent study conferences have dealt with the way authoritarian governments affect Christian mission. The data documenting widespread political oppression mount up daily. Modern technology has proved to be an efficient mistress to dictators by multiplying the means of torture. Contemporary governments of all stripes depend on extensive intelligence gathering systems to help them deal with their allies and thwart their enemies. What has shocked the sensibilities of missionaries and their supporters was that they have been exploited by intelligence agents.

By concentrating discussion on the interplay between authoritarian governments and missions, the more basic question may be obscured. To get hold of the problem, questions must be asked and answered at four levels: theological, strategic, policy, and training.

The Theological Question

What is the Christian's relation to government—whatever type it may be? We should not be surprised that the Christian missionary or service worker should live in tension with society or government. This is normal. The degree of conflict will vary from one situation to another. But what is abnormal is for all tension between the Christian community and society to disappear. This was the point of the Free Church movement protest against Constantinianism—the church was servile before the state.

Quite possibly the world more accurately perceives the true meaning of the church in relation to the world than does the church itself. Christian faith poses a fundamental challenge to the world. Even when present in only weak, anemic forms, the church is an incipient threat. At its best, it asks of its members undivided loyalty. This challenges any government, but it makes the church a direct rival to a totalitarian state.

The mission of the church is not determined by the kind of government a particular country has. The purpose of mission is to lead in the formation of an alternative social order (not simply to deal with individual salvation), and the state may well perceive this as a direct attack on its existence and function.

The issue of church and state is thus joined most sharply and precisely in the missionary situation. In the act of "crossing barriers" a challenge is posed. The crossing takes place for a purpose and that purpose is to introduce change. The gospel challenges traditional, conventional, and hereditary loyalties. It disrupts the life of an individual and the community. It calls for a reordering of life in relation to family, clan, language, nation, and religion.

This new life is based on a new ultimate allegiance. This allegiance is incarnated in a movement of conversion and incorporation into a new community. In saying this, the church does not reject the state. The church is not disrespectful of the state so long as it fulfills its ordained part. But faced with threats of disorder or challenges to its power, and operating outside "the perfection of Christ," the state may abuse power and act inhumanely.

The real question is, by what power will people live? Two forces are present in human affairs. Babel and Pentecost symbolize these alternative powers. Babel displayed to us the way the spirit of this world produces chaos, disorder, disharmony, and miscommunication. The ultimate outcome is destruction and death. Pentecost showed us the power of God as love—reconciling, reuniting, and establishing communication. This new community points to the city of God.

Mission is the means by which God is establishing His reign among men and women. This is reflected in Matthew's statement of the Great Commission. The Gospel of Matthew stresses the importance of the kingdom of Jesus' ministry. For Matthew the Great Commission is a call to Christ's disciples to win other disciples. This involves overturning the conventional divisions among mankind. The new order thus takes shape amidst the disorder of the old. Because government may be one of the means by which the old order is maintained, it may oppose the church which insists on autonomy from the state.

The Strategy Question

What are the specific means by which mission is to be carried out in order to faithfully fulfill its purpose and do so in ways consistent with the ultimate objective? What light do theology and biblical studies shed on strategy? What do we learn from history?

We are evidently unsure of what our strategy should be. To be sure, the church/world relationship is filled with ambiguities. Christians have followed various strategies in the past. Some have willingly accommodated and adapted the faith to the sociopolitical order's demands. "Caesar is Lord" displaced "Jesus is Lord." Others have viewed the church as the third pillar of society—the religious prop necessary to maintain the social order. Some Christians have neutralized the church's relevance by limiting it to other worldly or "spiritual" responsibilities. By contrast, Christian revolutionaries have insisted, often in apocalyptic terms, that the old order must be swept away and a theocratic alternative installed.

Illustrations of the ways these various strategies have been applied can be found in missionary history. The cross has followed the flag many times in missionary advance. But that is only part of the story. Many missionaries have expended themselves, and some have paid with their lives, to assure the rights of indigenous peoples in opposition to colonists and traders. They combated the slave trade and worked to make colonial policies more humane. Both "guns and ointment," to borrow Kosuke Koyama's phrase, have played their role. Missions showed Christians at their worst and best.

The fact is that missionaries have lacked a clear ethical vision. But they only brought with them what they had been given by the sending church. Constantinianism could hardly have produced anything better. Consequently, no clear or consistent guidelines emerged to give strategic guidance. It is our task to work at these formulations.

As the result of a wider and profounder cultural transformation, the peoples of the world are being bound together ever more closely. The result is that the "age of innocence" is passing. This point was driven home, for example, during the Nigeria/Biafra war 1967-70. There was no possibility of relating to either side in that horrible civil conflict in a way that was purely humanitarian or disinterested. That experience and the Vietnam war have helped us to realize, in retrospect, that humanitarian assistance has seldom been entirely free of political or social implications. We have to come to terms with the politics of charity as well as the politics of development.

The emergence of the modern nation state represents new possibilities for exercising control over people's lives. Centers of power have multiplied and interrelationships have become exceedingly complex. This, in turn, has produced anti-institution, anti-government reactions. It is increasingly difficult to remain naive as life becomes more highly politicized.

What is the special threat an authoritarian government poses to church and mission? As we examine actual cases, we observe certain patterns. There are both rightist and leftist authoritarian governments. Some rightist regimes have proved to be quite congenial toward the church—on certain conditions. These governments have tolerated the church so long as it operated within limits set by the state and was supportive of the state. Leftist regimes typically are based on an ideology (Marxist, revolutionary) and are antipathetic toward religion. In this view religion represents a prime barrier to progress. Ideology is the radical or fundamental alternative to an oppressive status quo. The state is the instrument of this ideology while the church is a tool of the status quo.

Although more careful analysis is needed to show us the impact of these two types of authoritarian government on the church, we have some clues. Where a leftist government promotes overt hostility toward religion, such as in the USSR, the church turns inward. Piety is an interior experience expressed in intense worship and intimate fellowship. Religion survives only out of deep conviction since it is officially and socially discouraged. Rightist governments encourage a culture-religion mentality, lulling the church through official recognition. A thoroughly domesticated church can be valuable as a defender of a government's policies. In both cases the state has assumed complete control of society and determines the scope of the church's service to society through social ministries.

It may be quite easy to agree that the church cannot afford to be merely a handmaiden to the state, but it is another thing to settle on a common strategy of witness to the state. Some argue in favor of a strategy whereby the Christian witness *confronts* the power centers. Others favor a strategy of *infiltration.* Some people believe the church is called to *prophesy* but should not become involved in policy and administrative questions. Still others call for a strategy of *aloofness* from the specific political or social question.

But we have also introduced another set of terms: subculture versus counterculture. To be a subculture suggests acceptance of a socially recognized station within the larger society, whereas a counterculture is a group which consciously stands against the mainstream.

The first set of strategies is distinguished from the second by the insistence in the second that any ethical response arises out of a community. Rather than arguing that any one strategy will suffice, it seems more fruitful to envisage a dynamic strategy which incorporates various elements within the framework of a committed community which witnesses to its faith.

The basis of our ethical response must be clear. A strategy must be grounded in a vision. Christ is establishing and extending His reign by creating a new people. He is gathering His people from the peoples and gives to His people a continuing missionary resonsibility to all peoples. The Christian ethic, therefore, is based on this kingdom and the creation of the new community. The creation of this new community and its engagement in mission involves participation in the war of the Lamb.

The Policy Question
What program policies can be formulated which will guide the Christian worker in applying strategy? Assuming that a clear strategy is achieved, we need to move on to develop appropriate policies. These will fall into two groups.

First, we require broad policies that guide program development and decisions generally. In what situations, with what kinds of people and with which agencies shall we work? By what policy criteria do we judge whether a particular activity is an expression of Messianic reality or reinforcing worldly power structures? Unless we can ask and answer these questions, we do not have usable policy guidelines.

Second, our workers need specific policies for particular contexts. In light of our theological vision and strategy commitments, how will we witness to Christ's purposes. General policies must be applied so they become instruments of direction and evaluation.

The model for the first set of general policies may well be the ' statement *Christian Conduct in Situations of Conflict* (Council of International Ministries, 1972) designed to provide guidance to workers facing emergencies.

The Training Question

How are people prepared to cope with these complex and demanding situations? In our great hurry to get things done, we have underestimated the importance of training. Jesus himself was in training for a long time before entering on a short ministry. In a world which is becoming more complex, we can ill afford to take shortcuts in preparation. Missionaries and service workers must be trained with the world situation in full view.

The goal of training is to form individuals who incarnate kingdom values, understand the world in which we live, can cross boundaries and cope with the dynamics of intercultural communication and relationship. The kingdom calls for individuals who loosen their own cultural ties and allow themselves to be adopted by another people and culture "for the sake of the gospel."

A major component in training, therefore, is development in the individual of a large measure of self-understanding and awareness. What is the nature of the West in contrast to other cultures? What peculiar handicaps does a Canadian or American bring to the task of crossing barriers? What imprint does a particular theological/ecclesiastical heritage leave on the person and in what ways must this be dealt with as a part of the preparation for service? What kind of spirituality will sustain and enliven the Christian witness?

In the end our witness to the world depends on the people we send. Our congregations and educational institutions all share in the task of formation. The values and ideals instilled along the way will largely determine how the individual will minister "across barriers."

Conclusion

We live in a world rapidly moving toward more authoritarian/totalitarian patterns of government. Political scientists predict that by the year 2000, ninety percent of the world will live under such government. The basic strategic options open to the Christian are relatively limited. The choices made are decisive. We are called to live as citizens of the kingdom of God and sojourners in the world. The *skandalon* of the gospel is that it confounds the world by overcoming it in an unworldly way. It is the church's privilege to embody that reality and invite others to join God's people on the Way.

Politics and Mission 24

*Wilbert
R. Shenk*

From the first days of the movement, Christian witnesses have faced the "political" question. The Apostles were under no illusion. The political and religious leaders described them as the people who were turning "the world upside down," the revolutionaries. This state of affairs did not change appreciably until Constantine coopted the church in the fourth century to be a part of the establishment.

The emergence of the Christian missionary movement in modern times has reopened the question of the political meaning of the Christian church. For a long time, however, it was more implicit than explicit. During the past generation, under the impact of Marxist social analysis and various new theologies—secular, black, African, Asian, liberation—the relationship between the gospel and politics has become a dominant theme. Scholars have examined Jesus to see whether he was a Zealot and a self-confessed political leader. Did his messiahship not have political purpose? Following Moltmann's lead, a number of books were devoted to the theme of the role of eschatology in political change.

But scholars were only catching up with what had been developing for a long time. The political significance of the church has reappeared first of all because the church has spread during the past two hundred years throughout the world. If the Constantinian compromise is disintegrating, it is not because theologians finally named it for what it was. Rather the church recovered enough of its birthright as a messianic movement to become missionary once again. Even though a deformed gospel has often been presented—especially its eschatological dynamic has been missing—it pointed to Jesus Christ. In Him was the promise to "make all things new," He who was and is God-with-us. The most revolutionary confession the church has ever made or can make is: "Jesus Christ is Lord!"

We still do not have an adequate understanding of "politics and missions" as they evolved during The Great Century, to use Kenneth Scott Latourette's phrase. Most scholarship has served us poorly. Missionary insiders have frequently interpreted their work in entirely spiritual and institutional terms. At the other extreme scholars have typically treated the missionary-government relationship too simplistically. They portray the missionary as a servile accomplice of the colonial powers in their territorial expansion throughout the 19th century. Fortunately, some fresh studies are appearing which give a more balanced and accurate picture of what was frequently a troubled, unstable relationship.

One of the few policy statements defining the relationship between the missionary and politics in the 19th century was written by missionary statesman Henry Venn in 1860. As an Anglican Evangelical, Venn was thoroughly committed to the Established Church. He took the position that as a member of the Established Church, he was free, indeed under obligation, to exert influence on government to adopt policies and enact laws that furthered the Christian cause. As general secretary of the largest Anglican missionary society, he spent considerable time and energy lobbying with members of parliament and cabinet ministers to get decisions favorable to Christian missions. Traders, adventurers, slavers and commercial companies were his real opponents. In September 1860 Venn handed instructions to outgoing missionaries concerning "Missions and Politics." This statement subsequently became the official policy for the Church Missionary Society. The gist of Venn's policy was that the Christian gospel brought about change. Inward transformation in the individual led to social improvement. The gospel introduces the convert to "the true principles of justice and humanity: and so to quicken in their minds the sense of the wrongs they may suffer through oppression and misgovernment. A knowledge also of Christian duty, while it secures obedience to the sovereign powers, limits that obedience to things lawful in the sight of God as defined in His word. . ." Although the missionary is primarily a minister of the gospel, that ministry inevitably has social and political consequences. In the face of injustice, the missionary had no choice but to cry out against it, whatever the cost. And the Society would support the missionary in his witness. Venn counseled his missionaries to avoid acting in a "political spirit" even though involved in a political issue, but they were not to hesitate to witness to governments when "the great principles of justice, humanity, and Christian duty" were at stake. Venn's statement was not written in a vacuum. His missionaries in Yorubaland were faced with imminent war; the slave trade was not yet ended in Africa and the great Indian Mutiny of 1857 had left many Britishers badly shaken. Thus Venn understood thoroughly the nature, the possibilities and the limits of political action. He focused the missionary's attention on what Christian responsibility meant in the face of such a complex and ambiguous relationship.

Today's missionary confronts what may be an even more complicated and unstable world. In terms of formal relationships, the missionary must reckon with at least six groups. These include: sending church; home government, which usually has a diplomatic mission in the host country; receiving church; host government; missionary colleagues; and expatriate community, including various voluntary agencies. No missionary is an island. To take a position on an issue of the day, the missionary immediately sets off repercussions for most, if not all, of the groups to which he relates. One solution is to refuse to be drawn into debate at all. Another approach is to pretend the individual has no obligation to colleagues or other groups but to take positions on a personal basis. Both approaches are irresponsible.

Mission and Kingdom

The missionary proclaims the message of the kingdom. but how does the kingdom of God relate to the kingdoms of this world where the missionary is concerned? We can summarize several positions.

One position holds that the kingdom of God is entirely future. We preach the gospel now to win individuals to faith in a kingdom that will come in a great cataclysm at the end of history. The present world is hopeless and the Christian cannot waste time on political programs. The supreme task of the church is to preach the gospel and avoid politics. This position is based on a view of prophecy which emerged in the 19th century and which came to dominate conservative evangelical thinking. This led to the assertion that the missionary is apolitical so long as he sticks by proclamation of the gospel.

A second position sees the church bringing the fruits of the kingdom of God to bear on the larger society through a partnership between church and state and other social institutions. The church may need to assist in clarifying the respective roles of church and state in society, but we can assume that such a relationship is divinely ordered. This classical Western understanding of church and state begs many questions when transposed to a society where the church is one-half of one percent of the population and the government is based on entirely different religious and cultural foundations.

Another viewpoint calls the church to support the secular order by allowing the "world to set the agenda for the church." The church is subservient. Indeed, the church's calling is to be servant to the world.

According to the fourth type, the kingdom of God is eschatological and is being introduced into history as a messianic movement led by Jesus Christ. The missionary is in the vanguard of that movement. The messianic kingdom presents an alternative to the present world order. The church does not seek to impose this new order on the larger society but rather models the "newness" of the messianic kingdom in its common life. The world correctly perceives this as a judgment on itself and may even find the presence of the church intolerable. The messianic kingdom was inaugurated in the first coming of Jesus Christ and will be consummated at his second coming.

Each of these views leads to its own set of policies with regard to "missions and politics."

Some Emerging Lessons

Events during the past generation, beginning with the closing of China and including Vietnam, point to some lessons we must learn about the relationship between the missionary and the political order. We can offer here no more than an outline.

1. The myth that the missionary is politically neutral must be dispelled. The host government and revolutionary groups throughout the Third World know better. Until now nearly all missionaries have come from politically powerful and affluent countries and are assumed to be accessories to the political and economic designs of the Western powers. This is doubly true when a French missionary is present in Algeria or an American worker is present in Vietnam during the revolution. From the standpoint of the Algerian or Vietnamese, to be "neutral" in the midst of war is immoral and incredible. The myth has been further compounded by missionary insistence on neutrality while also urging submission to the governing power (Romans 13). In other words, the professed neutrality increasingly looked like tacit alliance with the government in power.

2. The political context is important to missions. Missionaries value security. A government which insures social and political tranquillity becomes an ally. Without government goodwill a mission cannot continue to work. But does the missionary barter his witness against injustice for personal security?

3. In the midst of conflict, it is advisable to follow a course

of positive neutrality. By this is meant, the Christian worker and agency must deliberately cultivate contacts with both sides and promote reconciliation.

4. The missionary should always be actively pro-justice. This may be personally costly when the oppressor is also the ruling power, but the integrity of the gospel the missionary proclaims depends on precisely this witness.

5. If the missionary has difficulty in coming to terms with politics, so does the local church. The missionary exerts influence in this area whether he is conscious of it or not.

Part III
Strategy and Policy

Vietnam: I Wouldn't Do It Again

25

James E. Metzler

The most intriguing yet difficult question in a review of our Vietnam experience is: Did we belong there during the decade of America's involvement? There is no doubt that the Spirit has been able to use our witness and service. We have ministered to the needs of a multitude of suffering people. And the impact of our witness is reaching to the present and holds promise for the future.

Yet I know that I feel this way largely because of an outcome that was very favorable to our position. The ending permitted us to demonstrate dramatically how we felt all along but had little chance to prove. My attitude about my involvement would be quite different if the B-52's, napalm and Smart bombs had been able to crush the people's aspirations, as the U.S. was able to do 60 years earlier in the Philippines. Yet even so, when we ever read the story of that decade of tragic suffering from the Vietnamese viewpoint, how will our presence look?

Association with the Political-Military Machine

I sense that few Mennonites in America have sufficient awareness of our identity crisis in Vietnam to grapple realistically with the question. One has to feel that overwhelming load of assumptions placed on any overseas church worker by the Vietnamese. We were yoked with a century of observations on church-state cooperation under French colonialism. And these images were being reinforced by most U.S. missionaries, diplomats and military personnel.

To most Vietnamese it was simply unbelievable that any American would be sent to their land at such a time for any reason other than to support "the cause" in some way. We could not be sure that even those who knew us best really believed that we had no Washington support, embassy directives, military privileges or CIA connections.

In a civil conflict of such intensity, we must remember that the war is the only issue. It permeates everything affecting loyalties and resources. Everything said or done becomes part of the struggle and is viewed as helping one side or the other. Our policy was to help all Vietnamese alike on the basis of need. But security and logistics made it impossible to help both sides equally. So the benefits were reaped largely by the Saigon government. Ironically, our efforts can be viewed as prolonging the war and increasing the pain.

By supplying the people's necessities, we freed the government to use its funds for more destruction. Our assistance made the war more tolerable for the victims, reducing the pressure needed to end the fighting and bring negotiations. At times I wanted to organize the refugees to protest the wanton destruction of their lives and property. It would have been no more political than building them a third or fourth house, which reduced their bitterness against the destroyers. We gave bread in the name of Christ; they saw Americans with Saigon government permits handing out U.S. surplus goods for the interests of both governments. All our work had political import.

Another implicating factor was the inclusiveness of the pacification program. Pacification means that friendship and social services are as vital as fighting. Top priority is placed on "winning the hearts and minds of the people," for the war is won or lost on the shift of loyalties. This causes the military and government to engage in the same activities as relief agencies. At times they even worked as partners. The military created the refugees and casualties, then asked the church agency to care for them—to pacify them literally!

Even one's presence is useful in pacification. Being a good neighbor and a sympathetic American built attractive images, countering the repulsive aggressor roles of other Americans. Even evangelism is seen as supporting the cause, for few can imagine a Christian not being pro-Western! In such settings there is no way one can escape being used for purposes contrary to our spirit.

What are the liabilities of citizenship? Especially in a democracy where the President claims support from the "silent majority" for his action! Can our plea of neutrality have any credibility if we continue working closely with our nation's military endeavor? Especially when that action is widely condemned by many peoples?

Some church leaders felt we ought not speak of "**our** government" or "**our** troops," which might be an important distinction for us. But for the Vietnamese, that was merely playing with words. Certainly the U.S. government considered and claimed our work as a vital part of theirs. I ask the question: Is there no situation where we should forfeit the right to represent the

Kingdom because of our nation's action in that place?

Association with American Religiosity

I now realize that another crucial aspect of our identity problem was our close association with other Protestant groups. We were unable to establish a separate self within the Christian family. And this was most critical in regards to our peace witness, which was vital to our being in a conflict without appearing as part of it.

We affirmed the way of suffering love and peace—making it central to the gospel. We regularly used opportunities to teach Christ's stance against violence. The Mennonite Church in Vietnam evidenced a keen awareness of the social implications of the gospel, emphasizing reconciliation and service in the community. And I believe that our influence on the Protestant churches definitely fostered a broader vision of the Christian life.

Yet our membership never took a stance opposing warfare for the Christian and was not seen as a "peace" group. Full fellowship was given to members in the military. An air force officer served as director of the mission's student center. I am not aware of any person who—on the basis of biblical teaching concerning the will of God—declared a readiness to face prison, torture and death rather than to kill.

Robert Ramseyer's excellent critique, "The Christian Peace Witness and Our Missionary Task: Are Mennonites Evangelical Protestants with a Peace Witness?"[1] is a good description of our self-perception. We had almost no contact with the Buddhist monks who opposed the war courageously. Nor did we attempt to seek out those who went to prison rather than to the army. Somehow it seemed easier to associate with those who said "Lord, Lord" while "praying" for more bombs on Hanoi and to ignore those who may have done God's will without saying the right words!

A Buddhist student attending an evangelistic service at our center one week and the Alliance or Baptist meeting down the street the next week would not likely have sensed any clear difference in our presentation. We saw ourselves as fellow Protestant groups, basically doing the same thing in the same way, differing mostly in degrees of concern or points of emphasis.

We were simply reflecting the theology we were raised and trained in, which divorced salvation and ethics. In evangelism we focus only on the basics for salvation, and our basics are essentially the same as others. But we expect more in the end. Mennonites include "extras" that later on require a deeper commitment. My theology was symbolized by a ladder. Our view of the Christian life has more rungs at the top—the surer to get there!

However, one doesn't start at the top rung, certainly not a rung that is rejected by most other Christians! So we had vigorous discussions when confronted with the prospect of baptizing four young men as the first Vietnamese Mennonites. The youths understood our stand for biblical pacifism, could affirm alternate service for us in America, but it just wasn't practical for them.

We knew they would likely join the army when called. Yet they were followers of Christ and were growing in their commitment. Was it not better to recognize their desire to be identified with Christ through baptism and trust the Spirit to lead them to a fuller acceptance of His will? We baptized them; and in time all four were drafted. The precedent was set and followed.

Someone asked recently—on the basis of the very same rationale—why didn't we baptize and accept as members any of the hundreds of thousands of prostitutes who felt they had to sell their bodies to support their families or find safety? Is killing more acceptable than sexual immorality even among pacifists?

My present view is that we started at the wrong place and asked the wrong questions. We overlooked the fact that the Christ who is received and followed depends on the Christ who is presented. Either peace wasn't as integral to the gospel as we thought—or it wasn't the gospel that was received!

Like most other Mennonite missionaries of this century, we had tried to attach an Anabaptist ethic to a Protestant theology of salvation and model of missions. We were calling others to a lifestyle that we were not prepared to support. We (like our other missions) not only failed to reproduce an essential element of our faith, we were all but engulfed in a hodgepodge of American Protestantism. Our associations and self-understanding greatly compromised our gospel of peace and muffled our witness against the war. Being identified with a local group who opposed the war would have increased our visibility and credibility.

Why I Would Not Do It Again
In the days of my agonizing about whether I belonged there or not, a Quaker friend shared: "Relevant Christianity is a daily practice of the art of compromise." My leaders tried to help by pointing to Jesus and Hosea who accepted vast misunderstanding. But could my suffering and possible death be redemptive if caused by identification with wrongdoing rather than for righteous-

ness? At least Jesus died as a peasant Zealot and not as a sold-out Herodian or a conquering Roman!

The question that continues to haunt me is this: Did we miss the ultimate witness? Were we brought to the stage of the world's kingdoms for that very moment—and failed to stand? A few Americans, including several Mennonites working in other agencies, gave up their right to remain and serve in Vietnam by an open protest against the war. But not one staff member of our church agencies ever made such a decision. Why?

I am convinced that there was a witness that could and should have been made. America's intervention, clearly supported by the American churches and missionaries, verified all the associations of Christianity with the white, militant, dominating West. The greatest witness we could have given in Asia in 1968 would have been a clear exception to that impression.

We would have had to do something as newsworthy as the publicized statements of Billy Graham or Cardinal Spellman. The resignation of the IVS leaders did that, but they were not recognized as a church group. Asia desperately needed one courageous act by the church— just three youth to stand unbowed inside the fiery furnace! Thankfully, that symbol of hope was raised in 1975. Yet even our staying after "the collapse" would have been enhanced if others had made an open resignation earlier.

No, I would not repeat my experience in Vietnam. Not that I regret having been there. Nor because I feel the entire team should have left. But because our witness could have been more dramatic and effective.

I would not serve again in an American organization in an area where my nation is involved in such an action. Why couldn't we have used a European office and at least a half Afro-Asian staff? Were we even open to the counsel of our European brotherhood? When we did try to recruit Japanese brothers and sisters, a typical response was: "Why help the South?" There was some effort to internationalize the staff. But there was never any doubt that we were just another American agency. If we really believe in a universal community of faith, we will find ways to lessen the liabilities of citizenship.

I would not serve again in a confusing, highly-emotional conflict without better communications and firmer support from the home base. It's a myth to think that those in the thick of the battle know best what's happening and should even be the analysts for the home church. We sorely needed a team of leaders/scholars to specialize on the conflict . . . to view both "the forest and the trees" by periodic dialogue with the staff on the field . . . and to be a voice for the staff to the home base. Such a team could give objective and specific counsel to both administrative and field personnel in a supportive way.

I would not serve again in a mission following the classical Protestant pattern. I would seek rather to extend the Kingdom by serving among the people and inviting them to live in the shalom of God with me. I would be more concerned to demonstrate a model of faithful discipleship in wholesome relationships than in verbalizing a foreign message. And, like the Apostle Paul, I'd be more realistic in choosing where and how I can be God's messenger to another culture and race.

Finally, I would not serve again in a similar setting without a keener awareness for the meaning of presence and the impact of images. I would be more ready to forfeit an institution, program or presence that contributes more to a negative, ear-stopping image than countering it. Like

Jesus, I would at times consider my absence to be as strategic as my presence. Immediate needs dare not be the only criteria for determining presence.

A striking note about the Vietnam issue has been the sudden and nearly total silence about it in evangelical circles these past several years. It's like closing completed chapters of a book: first China . . . then Vietnam . . . and next _____ . Missions seemingly find it very difficult to be self-critical. In good Calvinistic fashion, "the Lord of history" gets the blame or credit for doors that close or open. The only responsibility missions appear to accept in the matter is to decide which is which and to keep moving along with the times.

I am grateful for our church's efforts both to learn from history and to strive to shape it. We have been given a unique opportunity for influence and witness in Southeast Asia today. And if Vietnam has enabled us also to gain some political maturity, universal sensitivity and cultural humility—then our experience there has not been in vain.

1. Unpublished manuscript.

26 Walking with Vietnamese Christians

James Klassen

Halfway around the world in the little land of VietNam, I was a pilgrim. Although the path held many surprises, I was not walking it alone. Perhaps the situation was summed up best by two Vietnamese—one who followed the Jesus way and one who stood on the threshold of the Kingdom—when they shared these words of Camus with me:

Do not walk in front of me, I may not follow.
Do not walk behind me, I may not lead.
Walk beside me, and just be my friend.

Cloudy Skies

The rumors were vicious. The rumors were verified by "eyewitnesses." "An aunt and her entire family were massacred by the communists in BanMeThuot." Eyewitness substantiated. "All of the remaining students at the Bible Institute at NhaTrang who admitted they spoke English were shot on the spot by the communists." Eyewitness substantiated. "The Catholic Bishop in BanMeThuot was killed in cold blood by the communists." No doubt about it.

The setting was SaiGon. The time was April 1975—the eve of the American pullout. I was there.

The rumors went on and on. "There will be a fierce battle over SaiGon." "Just before the end of the SaiGon battle, the Thieu air force will drop asphyxiation bombs over the city, so the communists will march into a city of dead people." "Everyone who has ever worked for the Americans will automatically be killed by the communists." "Everyone who knows English will automatically be killed by the communists." "Everyone who has a high position in the military forces will automatically be killed by the communists." "All Americans will be killed by the communists." "All of the refugees who came from the North in 1954 will automatically be killed by the communists." "The blood-thirsty communists have no feelings." Fresh incredible rumors coupled with the exhaust fumes from the long years of bitter propaganda hung in the air like ominous clouds.

One option was to get out fast, to evacuate. Many Vietnamese Christians and their leaders saw no alternative.

Of course, Americans still associated with the U.S. military forces in VietNam also wanted out, and on Monday, April 28, the last President pro tem of the SaiGon government gave them 24 hours to get out. During those last days in April, another group was also departing: For a variety of reasons, all of the foreign Protestant missionaries left VietNam prior to April 30, 1975 (except for one independent missionary who voluntarily stayed at DaNang and the ones stuck at BanMeThuot). Although their leaving raises some theological (and political) questions, at least Vietnamese Christians who evacuated were not walking out alone.

We'll Stay

There was, however, another option. On April 22, 1975, at a meeting of humanitarian agencies in SaiGon, I listened as two Catholic Vietnamese nuns testified of their decision to stay in VietNam along with 100 others who jointly signed a statement to that effect. That same day, a Mennonite Vietnamese close personal friend of mine told me he had decided to stay, come what may, and drew up a statement for himself and other Vietnamese Mennonites to sign, including the following four points:

1. We will not leave our country regardless of what happens. . . .
2. We take the Word of God as the foundation for love and reconciliation between all people.
3. Because serving people is a beautiful thing, we must accept any difficulties or sacrifices.
4. Because of our strong faith in the eternal God, as Evangelical Christians we accept life as well as death.

Believe me, that came like a gentle refreshing rain in the midst of a scorching desert of irrationality.

Their option was also my option: I voluntarily chose to stay in SaiGon as did one of my colleagues. Although technically we were not classified as missionaries, we were volunteer workers for Mennonite Central Committee, a relatively small, church-sponsored relief and social work agency. Following my arrival on the scene in VietNam some two and a half years earlier, I found a variety of opportunities to share my conviction that the way of love and reconciliation is the Jesus way. Consequently, staying looked like the logical conclusion to what I had been saying and preaching. That, for me, was crucial.

The decision not to evacuate included other factors: My sponsoring organization MCC, along with family and friends in North America, supported that decision; two other colleagues had earlier decided to stay in Quang Ngai; I had not been associated with the U.S. military forces; SaiGon felt like home because I had been highly motivated to learn to speak Vietnamese and moved primarily in Vietnamese circles; and Vietnamese friends— some optimists, some pessimists, some Christian, some non-Christian—directly encouraged me to stay. According to the Bible, neither life nor death can separate us from God's love (Romans 8:38, 39), and during those last days in April 1975, I took those words very seriously. I stayed, and, in spite of the rumors, the good Lord let me go through those days with an amazing degree of serenity. The purpose of this article, then, is to share some of my experiences with Vietnamese Christians in SaiGon (now called Ho Chi Minh City) through the changeover and during the next year.

The Changeover

When April 30, 1975, dawned, no one needed a sixth sense to know that there was fighting close to SaiGon. At about 10:15 a.m. the Vietnamese radio announcer told everyone to stand by for an important announcement. At 10:30 the announcement came: there was to be a cease-fire, and the Government of the Republic of VietNam would turn its power over to the Provisional Revolutionary Government of the Republic of South VietNam. The rocketing stopped immediately. The war was over! It seemed like an answer to prayer.

Over the noon hour there was noticeably less traffic, but that was typical for that hot, humid, tropical country. In the afternoon traffic picked up again—going both directions in front of our house on Phan Thanh Gian

Street, a major one-way thoroughfare across the city. It almost looked like a carnival atmosphere: rejoicing, not necessarily because of the new government in SaiGon, but because the war was over.

Yes, suddenly the war was over. Of all the horrible rumors we had heard, not a single one was true. Praise the Lord! That aunt and her family were well and had traveled to NhaTrang. No English-speaking students at the NhaTrang Bible Institute were shot there. The Catholic Bishop of BanMeThuot held a service to ordain a Bishop for another province. And there was no bloodbath of Christians or anyone else. Perhaps truth is stranger than fiction.

The transition from one government in SaiGon to the other on April 30 was very smooth—unlike Nha Trang earlier, for example, where the bitter ARVN (Thieu government) soldiers still had guns and ammunition, and after their improvised exodus from Pleiku, took whatever they wanted. Although I had tried to prepare myself mentally and spiritually for troubled water, there never was a breakdown of public order in SaiGon, and no one tried to break into the Mennonite Center where we were staying and where our offices were located. Incidentally, our electricity and water supply continued without interruption—little blessings perhaps, but no small matter for a city of three to four million people.

Reconstruction
Since a drastic increase in rice production was needed after the end of the war and since unemployment plagued SaiGon, some of my Christian friends were among those who voluntarily moved from the city back to the countryside, but that was no easy road. Literally millions

of bomb craters needed to be filled in—the largest B-52 bomb craters being 30 feet deep and 45 feet in diameter. Yes, the war is over, but hundreds of thousands of tons of unexploded munitions still lie buried in the fertile rice paddies: mines, grenades, and bombs—ready to go off at the touch of a hoe. One member of the GiaDinh Mennonite Church on the outskirts of SaiGon moved back to his native area with his family only to be killed when his hoe struck a hidden explosive in his field. I knew him.

Religious Activities

As far as religious activities in SaiGon were concerned after April 30, 1975, the churches went right on meeting: singing, sharing, praying, and studying the Bible. More specifically, I had become rather deeply involved with a relatively young Christian fellowship at our Mennonite Center on Phan Thanh Gian Street where the first water baptism ceremonies for that group were held in February and March of 1975. When I decided not to evacuate, the earlier solidarity of the foreign Mennonites, which blurred the distinction between service-oriented MCC and evangelism-oriented VietNam Mennonite Mission, made it seem natural for me to begin teaching some of the Bible classes at the Mennonite Student Center in the early spring of 1975. On Thursday afternoons I was teaching a Bible class in Vietnamese from I Peter, and on Sunday mornings I was teaching a Bible class in English from the Gospel of John. I **continued** teaching them throughout the rest of 1975 without any interference. There I was—a foreigner, a citizen of the U.S., in the role of a teacher, teaching Bible (and English, of all things) to Vietnamese who were living under a new government that had some leaders who took Karl Marx seriously.

In mid-July 1975, the newspapers carried headlines about the registration of all meetings for security reasons. The announcement then specifically mentioned church meetings, but that is hardly surprising since many Protestants and Catholics had been fervently anti-communist only a few months earlier. Some Vietnamese Christian friends of mine sadly predicted that the registration process would be long and drawn out. They were dejected because they felt the enthusiasm for meeting would disappear by the time permission to meet would be granted. Quite the opposite took place: The Vietnamese director of our Student Center spent only three days completing the entire registration process, and during that time he was also working on some family business. Registration consisted of listing the time and purpose of our weekly meetings and was, therefore, something of a formality. The continuity of our meetings was never broken. No membership lists were submitted. No one prescribed our activities. No one ever told me what I could or could not teach in my Bible classes.

In December of 1975, I also led a catechism class in a study of the Sermon on the Mount. It was good news to my Vietnamese friends that God's love still reached them, and it was a very humbling experience for me to see God's Spirit at work. A total of 12 young people acknowledged Jesus as Savior and Lord and joined our Christian fellowship through water baptism ceremonies during my year there after the end of the war. Although I was initially "the teacher," by the end of 1975 I had stepped out of the leadership role and felt that the fellowship was able to see me more as an active Christian brother than as someone with all of the answers.

Both Catholics and Protestants had continued to exist in

the North after 1954—after the Geneva Accords drew the temporary demarcation line at the 17th parallel. During the next 20 years, however, Protestant missionaries—except for a precious few—generally supported political and military involvement of the U.S. in VietNam and consequently kept silent about the churches in the North. Perhaps you can imagine, then, how the rising and falling Vietnamese tones were emphasized as one of my Christian friends excitedly shared with our Fellowship on Sunday morning, January 4, 1976.

> Just last night at the regular weekly meeting for Christian students at the church on Thong Nhat Street we learned some history about the Protestant Church in the North. Before, all we heard about were the ones who came South (in 1954). There were thirteen pastors who stayed, as well as a few sturdy Christians who understood that God wasn't leaving them alone. Until 1959, they were regarded with some suspicion because so many of their number had already left; but, because none of them were involved in a scandal uncovered that year, they were respected. From 1970-1972, the young people got organized, and 40 attended a church youth conference. At the annual general conference in 1975, there were 600 delegates. . . . With that history in North VietNam—including the fact that there is open acceptance of Sunday and Thursday church meetings—it is clear that the Church cannot blame the government if the Church collapses. If the Church dies, we are the ones who have killed it.

Church Relationship to Government: Age-old Question

Down through the ages, one of the most persistent, perplexing problems for Christians has been the nature of the relationship between the church and the government. VietNam was, and is, no exception.

During the war, some 480 church buildings in North VietNam had been bombed. A delegation of Mennonites from the U.S. and Canada which visited North and South VietNam during May and June of 1976 learned that the Vietnamese government was giving some congregations in the North subsidies to help them rebuild their bombed church buildings. A "communist" government aiding Christians! While I rejoice with my Vietnamese Christian brothers and sisters who receive favors from their government, the question also comes to me, "Should they be accepting that government assistance?"

Lest we criticize those Vietnamese Christians too quickly and too harshly, listen to part of our Christian fellowship's dialogue on Sunday morning, January 18, 1976. The story was told of a friend who had seen a movie depicting Nixon as an airplane, with his nose as the nose of the airplane, his arms out at the side as the front wings, and his feet up in back as the tail of the plane, pulling a banner saying "Merry Christmas" while dropping bombs on HaNoi. It was a clear attempt to wrap Christianity, the bombing, and the Christmas of 1972 into one package. That was my first Christmas in VietNam: 1972—when Nixon ordered the intensive bombing. During those "Twelve Days of Christmas," enough explosive tonnage was dropped in North VietNam to equal a Hiroshima every two days. On that Sunday morning in 1976 when the film was mentioned, another Christian young lady responded,

First of all, we must recognize that what Mr. Nixon did is terribly ugly, and that, secondly, what he did is even worse because he did it under the guise of religion. It is impossible for me to remain silent in the face of that, because it's clear that Jesus is not like Mr. Nixon: Jesus wants to save VietNam, not destroy it.

Perhaps we need to repent as we recall that one famous North American evangelist stood by the U.S. President during those days and years as if to baptize the bullets and bombs that were sent to Southeast Asia.

How well I recall, too, the ecstacy and agony that went through my soul on May 1, 1975, as one of our Vietnamese staff members from the GiaDinh Mennonite Church excitedly told of meeting a newly arrived Christian soldier from North VietNam with a cross painted on his canteen! You see, many Christians in the South understood that Romans 13:1-7 meant a blind obedience to government— "support the SaiGon government and fight the communists"—(ignoring the context: Romans 12:20 and 13:8 where Paul writes, "If your enemy is hungry, feed him; if he is thirsty, give him a drink" and "Don't owe anybody anything except love"). Ironically, the Christians in the North had also been trained earlier by some of the same missionaries. Given the history of VietNam with a thousand years of Chinese rule and a hundred years of French domination, and given the admonitions by the missionaries to obey the government, Christians in the North naturally were quite willing to take up guns to drive out the "imperialistic" U.S. The bombs which destroyed church buildings in the North, to say nothing about the Christians who were killed in the bombings, also tended to unite the remaining Christians with their government's goal to "fight the U.S. to save our homeland." The result: There were Christians on both sides of the lines pointing guns at each other. They were participating in the violence instead of proposing alternatives. Surely it must have made God very sad to see people who claimed to know about his love pointing guns at each other and pulling the triggers.

I mentioned above the traumatic breakdown of public order at NhaTrang caused by the angry ARVN soldiers during the first days of April 1975. By that time, the collapse of the Thieu government and the disintegration of his military forces in Central VietNam were happening with such speed that NhaTrang experienced several days of total havoc before the PLA soldiers of the Provisional Revolutionary Government could arrive to start restoring some order. Not only were the rumors of communist atrocities there untrue, but I also learned later that the Dean of the NhaTrang Bible Institute went out to meet the "communist" soldiers and asked them to protect the Bible Institute from the looters. What would you have done? Had he sold out? Probably not. His action was simply a non-pacifist recognition of new governmental leadership in a very difficult situation and should be no more disturbing than actions by Christians in our country to call the police in times of riot or the action taken by the President of the Evangelical Church of (South) VietNam some two weeks earlier.

It was mid-March 1975 then; the Thieu government had just canceled the deferments for religious studies. The Catholics and Buddhists, along with two indigenous Vietnamese religious sects, all protested publicly. The President of the Evangelical Church, however, went to NhaTrang and counseled the students at the Bible Institute there to follow the government orders. Two days before I left VietNam, in April 1976, during a brief visit with him, he tried to make it very clear that the Evangelical Church had not been involved in politics. What did he mean by that, in a situation like VietNam where every action had political implications?

Reorientation

For Christians who were involved in the Thieu military forces, the end of the war soon brought "hoc-tap" (study-practice) sessions, not gallows. The son of one of our former staff members from the southern delta was given three days of "reeducation" and then told to go home and do something productive. That style, consistent with the new country-wide emphasis on production rather than consumerism, was typical for all of the draftees who formed the bulk of Thieu's military machine. The upper echelons of the Thieu government and military forces, however, went for a longer period of time. They studied hard, including history, politics, and economics, as well as worked hard, including raising their own food. Some reporters have noted a shortage of food at the camps—but there wasn't (and still isn't) an overabundance of food anywhere in VietNam. Those observers have also reported a shortage of Western medicines at the camps—but by the time I left VietNam there wasn't an overabundance of Western medicines anywhere in the country. Furthermore, during my entire stay after the end of the war, I heard no reports, allegations, or rumors of torture at these camps. People were returning from the camps and being reintegrated into society—including a Protestant doctor who worked at a new drug rehabilitation center on the outskirts of SaiGon.

Possible responses of Christians to the new government included a blind obedience to it, at one extreme, and a militant opposition to it, at the other. In SaiGon those numbered with either extreme were very, very few. As far as I know, the international press carried the story about the Vinh Son Catholic Church in SaiGon where guns, ammunition, radio broadcasting equipment, and a printing press turning out counterfeit money were discovered on February 13, 1976. Perhaps the "facts" will always be questionable—some of my Vietnamese Christian friends thought the affair might have been a fabrication—but at least Christians in VietNam felt that, as a result of the incident, the government was certainly going to crack down on all religious activities. But the suppression never came. The government, however, did warn Christians that they should not try to sabotage the government or misuse the freedom that was given them.

The vast majority of Vietnamese Christians, then, were grateful that the war was over, even though they still faced difficult decisions related to their involvement in the enormous task of rebuilding their precious homeland. For example, on students' days off, their idealism and enthusiasm were being channeled into constructive projects in the countryside, like digging canals and working alongside farmers, as well as projects in the city, like clean-up campaigns to help prevent epidemics. The sharing time on Sunday morning, April 4, 1976, began with a relatively young, but mature, close Christian friend of mine saying:

My class has just been cited as the top class—the exemplary class—in the whole school. Praise the Lord! That came as quite a surprise because I'm class president but haven't even joined the Ho Chi Minh City Student Union. In fact, it seems like kids who are so interested in joining the Student Union are just interested in personal gain. When some of my school's leaders asked me about the role of religion in my life, I told them, "Listen, if I weren't a Christian and if I wouldn't understand that Jesus was interested in helping people, I myself just might not be so willing to volunteer for some of those work projects of yours.''

A guest that morning, widely known in evangelical circles for her singing ability, quickly responded:

But I won't volunteer for some simple stuff like cleaning the streets. Give me some big, worthwhile job, and I'll do it.

Then another close Christian friend of mine, who had been the first one in her university group of English majors to volunteer for a recent workday in the countryside, spoke up:

But maybe you have to volunteer for some simple work, too, so that you have a perspective from which to speak. For example, sweeping city sidewalks: I volunteered to help, but not many others did. Yet we were expected to sweep the whole precinct—starting while the people were still asleep. After we were done, I told the leadership straight out that it was ridiculous for us to have done all that: if each family would keep things clean in front of its own house, the problem would be solved.

Thanksgiving for Freedom

Each year October and November dates mark the traditional national-religious Thanksgiving holidays for Canada and the U.S., respectively, when North American Christians are especially grateful for the freedom of religion which we enjoy here. In VietNam, too, Christians were—and are—grateful for the freedom that they still have and for their government's policy of tolerance toward religion. As far as we could tell, even though there has been a decentralization of power, bringing some lack of standardization and giving local officials substantial control, intolerance was the exception, not the rule. In fact, shortly before I left, a good friend of mine—a Vietnamese who received his doctorate in Bible and theology in the U.S. and who was directing Christian youth work in SaiGon besides teaching at the Evangelical Bible Institute at NhaTrang—shared these words with me in his articulate English:

> Jim, give people a true picture of the church in Vietnam as far as you know, and the freedom we still have in the country. Many are concerned and want to know the truth. They might not believe what we write from Saigon due to their suspicion that we are obliged to give them an optimistic picture! They will believe you more than what we write from Saigon.

What was the basis for his statement? Perhaps two final examples will be sufficient. First, 171 students—a very high enrollment—were finishing up the 1975-1976 school year at the NhaTrang Bible Institute, the leadership training center for the Evangelical Church in the South. (Since spring semester 1977, the Institute has not been operating, apparently pending the reunification of the Evangelical Church in the North and in the South. The country was already formally reunited in July 1976, so why not the Evangelical Church, too? Indeed, why couldn't the Evangelical Church have been the first to reunite and light the way to reconciliation for the rest of the country? But who are we to challenge them, when North America is still torn asunder by Christians with differing views on the war in VietNam?)

Second, not long after the end of the war, everyone in SaiGon, including foreigners, registered with the new government there, and on the registration forms was a place to indicate religious affiliation, if any. Government workers—civil servants—who had indicated that they were Christians were then able to take December 25, 1975, off from work as a Christmas holiday! Non-Christians— Buddhists, for example—and Christians who had been too timid to acknowledge that they were Christians had to work on December 25. It is especially amazing since Christians are a small minority in VietNam: Catholics comprise only about ten percent of the total population, and Protestants less than one percent.

Up Ahead

I didn't go to VietNam as a representative of the U.S. government, and I didn't come back from there as a representative of the new government in VietNam. I came as I went, i.e., as an ambassador of Jesus Christ (II Cor. 5:18-20). Perhaps it is understandable, therefore, why it means so much to me that my friends there are still my friends, regardless of what political system is in power. They promised to continue to pray for me and for Christians in America, and request that Christians here pray for them. It is not easy to be a Christian in VietNam, but, if we are really serious about it, maybe it is not so easy to be a Christian in North America either. Perhaps we shouldn't expect more from the indigenous Christians overseas than from the missionaries, and perhaps we shouldn't expect more from the missionaries than we expect from the sending congregations.

Near my home in central Kansas is the McConnell Air Force Base which has a huge sign close to one guarded entrance proclaiming, "Peace is Our Profession." Today, again, the fighter bombers were making practice runs overhead. In VietNam they were not practicing. When will we ever learn that war is not peace?

On my way home from VietNam in 1976, as the Boeing 747 commercial jet was taking off from Bangkok, the pilot announced, "We're at 15,000 feet now and will be climbing up to 33,000 feet. Then we'll be circumventing VietNam—staying about 30 miles off the coast." But peace is not merely the absence of war, and surely "circumventing VietNam" is not the Christian response either. The Incarnation means that Jesus was where the people were. He felt their uncertainty and their faith, their sorrow and their joy.

I believe that Christians do have good news and can light the way. For America. For VietNam. For the whole world. But only if our life and message is based on an integrity of word and deed, on a clear commitment to Christ and His Kingdom, on the centrality of His peace and reconciliation. Only one power can make people change: not guns or bombs or violence, but only the power of God's love (Zech. 4:6). If divine love can't, then nothing else can either. Because Jesus believed that He absorbed suffering rather than inflicting it. Jesus is still up ahead: calling us to faithfully follow Him, calling us to walk together in the shadow of the cross and in the light of the resurrection.

Implications of the Vietnam Experience for World Mission

27

Luke S. Martin

The Americans left Vietnam in 1975. With them went most of the Mennonite personnel who had served there. Last year a study was made of the twenty-year experience of the North American Mennonites in mission, service and peacemaking in Vietnam. This article is not a summary of the study report,[1] but deals with the implications of this experience for a North American Christian presence and witness in Asia and other parts of the world. It focuses primarily on the task of communicating the gospel message of Jesus Christ but also discusses service ministries.

The North American Mennonite effort in Vietnam was sponsored by the Eastern Mennonite Board of Missions and Charities (EMBMC), a regional mission board; and the Mennonite Central Committee (MCC), the cooperative service agency of the Mennonite churches. MCC was involved in emergency relief, medical and developmental services since 1954. EMBMC went to Vietnam in 1957 and was involved in various evangelistic, church establishment and service ministries.

I will reflect on the personnel involved in the ministries;

the mission and service objectives, strategies and programs; the relationships with governments; and dealing with societal problems and peacemaking. I also will discuss the matter of administration. While more than 100 people contributed ideas to the evaluation study, I assume responsibility for the views expressed in this report.

Missionary and Service Personnel

The selection of expatriate missionary and service workers is important; it is these people more than programs who communicate to people in other cultures. Those who are able to work together harmoniously are more effective Christian witnesses than highly individualistic persons interested in "doing their own thing." Workers should have thorough preparation for responding biblically and theologically to new life settings. As communicators of the gospel in cross-cultural settings, they must become thoroughly familiar with the local culture and sociopolitical milieu. All foreign personnel, even short-term volunteers, need to become fluent in the local languages. Workers expected to carry out crucial ministries should arrive on "field" several months—sometimes a few years—in advance of specific assignment to allow for adequate language learning and cultural orientation.

Volunteers serving two- and three-year terms have made excellent contributions in teaching and service ministries. It must be recognized, however, that individuals with longer experience can usually make greater contributions.

Personnel should normally be recruited for specific ministries. Yet they need to be flexible to adapt to program changes.

Workers should develop primary relationships with

local people rather than with fellow foreigners. Relationships with other expatriates help determine the identity of the expatriate community within the country. Close relationships with Americans identified with U.S. cultural and political concerns or with exploitative business corporations can compromise American missionaries and service workers in their identification as witnesses of the gospel of Christ and representatives of the church. This problem was particularly acute in Vietnam where nearly every American carried some marks of the U.S.A. This required that church representatives deliberately and clearly dissociate themselves from these American policies which were hurting the Vietnamese people.

The common people in Vietnam identified Catholic Christianity with France and evangelical Protestant Christianity with the United States. Since it is common in Asia to associate Christianity with the West, it is important to have an international team of missionaries to symbolize and express the transnational character of the gospel. A Christian presence and witness should not be viewed as an American presence. The MCC witness in Vietnam was significantly strengthened by the mixed team of Japanese, Indians, Canadians and Americans. In contrast, all the representatives of the Vietnam Mennonite Mission were Americans. With only American personnel, it was necessary for Mennonite missionaries to assume a stronger stance in rejecting official U.S. military policies. This had some positive values; but with a broad international team they could have maintained greater neutrality on political matters.

Beyond having an international team, it might be helpful to have an international administrative and support base. This suggests the need for new transnational mission models. The Asia Mennonite Mission Board is one attempt at international sponsorship for missionary service. Perhaps an easier way is for local churches with fairly common objectives in different countries to assign personnel and contribute funds to some shared cooperative ministry in another place. This becomes more feasible when they can work together with an already existing indigenous group.

The Vietnamese genuinely appreciated those foreign workers who lived simply and did not violate local cultural practices in living patterns and relationships. Personnel who have unconsciously accommodated themselves to the North American cultural scene in attitudes toward wealth, power, political and economic philosophy, and lifestyle— eating, living and dress habits, have more difficulty adapting to local cultural practices. To the degree that American Mennonites become assimilated into the dominant North American cultural patterns, it will become more difficult for them to associate with persons in other cultures in a sensitive way.

We must face squarely the North American Mennonite preoccupation with security. We give verbal assent to a theology of discipleship, but we are hesitant about taking personal risks for the sake of the gospel of Christ and service to others. Mission Board administrators can tell stories of families and friends overly concerned in crisis with the physical safety of persons serving in other lands. In a previous era the church's normal response in a crisis situation was for Christians to fall to their knees and commit the missionaries to the Lord. Today the normal response is to dial headquarters. The decision of several MCC men to stay in Vietnam during the revolutionary crisis of March and April 1975, had significant risks. But this became a beautiful testimony to the gospel of Christ; they gave a significant witness for some time and were supportive to local Christians in a revolutionary situation. We need to prepare volunteers, their families, and the church to more radically give up the prerogatives we so easily claim for ourselves.

MCC has tried to hold to the same standards in selecting service workers as those used for missionary personnel. Personal commitment to Jesus' way of love and peace (rather than mere humanitarianism) should be considered prerequisite for all workers. The basic motivation for service must spring from Christian commitment and find expression in life shared with other members of a local Christian community.

All field personnel should be involved in defining objectives. These objectives include both general and specific, long-range and short-term. Programs must be periodically evaluated and objectives redefined. Mature leadership is needed on field locations. Maximum local decision-making is important, especially in unstable situations. In certain areas where communication is difficult or crisis is endemic, there would be value in assigning well-trained and disciplined service teams with maximum administrative freedom.

Periodic visits by home office administrators are important.

In a situation as ambiguous as Vietnam, it is essential to assign someone not administratively involved to evaluate and analyze critically what is happening, and to suggest options, alternatives and implications. This person can be helpful both to home office administrators and to personnel on field locations to see that priority tasks are worked at.

Mission Objectives, Strategies and Programs
Mission-Church Relationships. In Vietnam Mennonite
missionaries tried to follow a plan of partnership with the
local church. They understood this to mean preaching the
gospel, teaching and baptizing those who believed and
accepted Christ as Savior and Lord, and setting up joint
structures between the mission and church so that local
Christians could gain experience with missionaries in a
local church. As the church developed and matured,
missionaries helped local Christians to assume increasing
responsibility in the church and eventually the mission
structure would fade away. Missionaries who stay on then
would become subject to the local church. This process
was followed, and Vietnamese Christians assumed full
responsibility for overall leadership in the early 1970s.

This concept of partnership has good points, for it
enables believers to become familiar with and help carry
out certain activities of the church under missionary
tutelage. But this kind of partnership has its limitations,
too. It introduces foreign patterns of church life which
might not be particularly appropriate and tends to create a
dependency which can cripple the normal growth of the
church.

It is important that the local church retain full autonomy
in leadership and decision-making at all stages in its
development. This is crucial in a revolutionary and
nationalistic society where the missionaries might not be
around long, but it might apply in most other areas as
well. Missionaries are carrying out an apostolic ministry.
They are the ones "sent" by the church and the Holy
Spirit. Missionaries and the local church both need the
freedom under the Spirit to take initiatives without being
dependent on or dominated by the other. Missionary

vision must not be suppressed by local Christians concerned with preserving their own prerogatives or fearful of moving into new areas of witness. It is also unfair to local Christians to expect them to determine the activities of foreign missionaries.

I am not arguing, however, for a complete dichotomy between mission and local church. Missionaries must be true servants of the local church and accept the counsel and discipline of the church where they are serving. One important ministry which missionaries must fulfill is in helping to teach the local church to understand the demands of the gospel. This will involve both formal and informal teaching experiences. An intimate, informal (Paul-Timothy) relationship frees both the missionaries and the local church leaders for a more faithful and fruitful ministry than where there are joint administrative relationships.

It might be helpful to note the different mission-church relationship models used by mission agencies in Vietnam. Mennonite missionaries, by 1969, relinquished most responsibilities in the local congregation in Saigon although they continued to participate in the life of the congregation. But missionaries and local Vietnamese leaders worked together in developing a total Mennonite mission strategy in Vietnam. When missionaries in 1973-74 asked that the local church assume greater leadership in this, some of the local church leaders felt that the missionaries were seeking to abdicate their responsibilities to the church.

The Vietnam Baptist Mission was founded by the Southern Baptist Convention in only 1959. The Baptists established congregations in many areas. In some congregations missionaries exercised pastoral leadership.

In others the new believers had greater responsibility while missionaries aided in a teaching ministry. Congregations led by local leadership had the most promise of developing into strong congregations.

The Evangelical Church of Vietnam (ECVN), the largest evangelical church in Vietnam, was established as an independent body in the late 1920s nearly 20 years after missionary work was begun by the Christian and Missionary Alliance (C&MA). C&MA continued as a separate and parallel organization and was able to carry out many of its objectives and concerns fairly effectively. In crucial areas such as leadership training, relations with other churches, and large-scale evangelistic programs, C&MA continued to exercise much influence on the ECVN. All local congregations and the executive committee of the ECVN were completely in the hands of Vietnamese. While recognizing significant philosophical differences between the Mennonite and the C&MA missions, I recognize the fundamental strengths in the C&MA strategy of mission-church relationships.

A mission structure should always be only an enabling organization to help establish and strengthen the church in a given area. We must recognize that missionary organizations must work with the givens in each local situation. The mission agency and the local church can be mutually supportive in the Christian witness. In Vietnam, for example, the government was more apprehensive about recognizing a new Vietnamese religious group than a foreign one which already operated in an acceptable way in another place. Thus the mission secured recognition which enabled the church to secure the property it wanted. The agency might continue as long as the local church welcomes it or as long as the sending church requests it. It should not assume that the mission structure fades away and that the missionaries will be absorbed into the local church.

Establishing a Church. One issue that Mennonite missionaries faced that never was answered with finality was the question: Do we work to strengthen the existing church (ECVN) or do we seek to establish a Mennonite church? Missionaries who taught English to Vietnamese students would generally receive a "yes" or a "no" response to an "either-or" question. So the answer to this question is "yes." Mennonite missionaries might have spent more time in teaching ministries with the ECVN (ECVN pastors frequently served the Mennonite congregation; Mennonite missionaries were sometimes invited to share at ECVN gatherings). Yet establishing new fellowships broadened the total church in Vietnam and expressed new visible church models which were instructive for the ECVN.

A practical question faced by missionaries working in a new setting is, "What are the basic criteria for determining the validity of a believer's commitment to Jesus Christ?" Some missionaries accept the basic affirmation of the new Christian: "Jesus is my Lord." Others insist on some specific response to certain life situations. It is difficult to make such judgments in a cross-cultural situation. I suggest that local Christians do the baptizing, the pastoring and the disciplining—not the missionaries. If the missionaries are part of the local church's structure, they will need to "accept" behavior among church members that they otherwise might not accept, like members going into the armed forces. If they are not a part of the church's organization, they can accept local Christians as brothers and sisters in the Lord while continuing a discerning and prophetic teaching ministry. One cannot rule out a mature church requesting a missionary to serve as pastor of a congregation or to serve in some other leadership role in the church for a period of time; this could actually express and affirm the international character of the church. When people from different nationalities and different citizenships work together as members of a congregation, one receives a foretaste of the glorified church. But this is not the norm now. There will be groups of local Christians who share a common way of life who become the church of Jesus Christ in that place. No other community tolerates foreigners serving as their leaders. It is likewise inappropriate in a church for foreign missionaries to serve as congregational or church leaders.

Evangelistic Witness. Evangelistic strategy must reflect the local situations. Mennonite missionaries in Vietnam have sometimes been criticized for giving an extremely low-key evangelistic gospel witness. It is assumed that in a place like Somalia where any verbal Christian witness is forbidden, one has to choose this approach. In Vietnam, by contrast, one had many opportunities and great freedom to preach the gospel. Yet to preach the gospel of Christ's love and peace relevant to the situation meant potential conflict with the political ideology. At this point missionaries were more hesitant than they needed to have been.

However, another political factor had to be considered. In the early years of the Mennonite mission, the missionaries took a more aggressive approach. But as Vietnam became more politicized and the government propaganda barrage increased along with the war, the missionaries became less aggressive in preaching. When American policies and programs aggressively concentrated on "winning the hearts and minds" (WHAM!) of the Vietnamese, the missionaries did not want the gospel to be confused with American propaganda. McLuhan's dictum, "the medium is the message," had meaning in Vietnam. Missionaries tried to be a Christian presence, interpreting the gospel verbally to the hundreds with whom they associated, without using pressure.

Guiding the Church. Another important area in missionary work is the shape of the church and its leadership pattern. Flexibility is called for since societal patterns may offer clues concerning structures. It is difficult to predict what future political structures will exist and what church structures will best enable the church to function in that society. The highest priority, however, is for the "equipping of all the saints for the work of ministry." Bible teaching and leadership training are of the highest priority.

Concern has been expressed about whether the missionaries did all they could to help prepare the Vietnamese church to live under a radically different political system. The Catholic Church in Vietnam had various experiences in relation to the state—periods of persecution and toleration, and briefly achieving much influence in political affairs from 1954-1963. The ECVN has generally seen itself existing alongside the state, showing little interest in the government and giving no official support to the state. Individual members of the church could involve themselves in the affairs of state, and members were encouraged to fulfill the "duties of a citizen," usually defined by the state. Members of the Mennonite Church in Vietnam frequently accepted the same stance. Others refused military service, sometimes due to Christian convictions and sometimes out of self-interest. The Mennonite historical experience and understanding of biblical theology places the church over against the state. The church does its divinely-appointed tasks while government is responsible for maintaining law and order in an ungodly society. The Christian's relationship to government is basically passive, giving only what the state asks for, provided this does not violate the Christian's higher loyalty to God.

North American Mennonites should more actively affirm the good policies and contributions of government. There are certain demonic forces inherent in the state power which Christians must reject. But we can take the main concerns and ideas of a state—left, center, or right—like freedom, independence, the pursuit of happiness, work, production, reconciliation, the "new man" and help the church to reinterpret and affirm them within a Christian theological context. For example, while the Marxists stress increasing production for meeting state goals, Christians can affirm the positive value of work in service to others. In this way the perhaps idolatrous ideological concerns of the state can be reinterpreted and accepted within the Christian community. Marxists would not support this exercise. Yet it can help Christians to be salt and light in the world and not to confront the state on the wrong issues. The church in Vietnam studied some church history, but missionaries might have given Christians more help in understanding theologically the implications of living in different kinds of societies.

Another area where missionaries were weak was in failing to prepare, publish and distribute Christian literature which would have helped the church to see how the Christian community can live within the world. This would have supplemented the literature produced by the

Evangelical Church or the C&MA. Clear interpretations of the Christian way of love, peace, reconciliation and service would have been helpful to the Mennonite community as well as to Christians of other churches. And these materials could continue to be helpful today when association with the international Christian church is more limited. Missionaries were convinced of the need for literature, staff were assigned to work at this and funds were available. But literature was never made top priority; missionaries were too busy doing other things.

The production of literature must be given much more priority wherever the church is engaged in mission. Many books have cultural biases which make them unacceptable for direct translations. Books such as John Driver's *Community and Commitment* (Herald Press, 1976) are suitable for translation into other languages. It is essential, however, that local churches produce their own materials.

One particular missionary temptation is to become so involved in "doing good" that they do not have sufficient time for the most important ministries. Service ministries to the poor and to refugees were important in Vietnam to give integrity to the gospel and were opportunites for an evangelistic witness. Yet missionaries involved in such programs were able to give less time to crucial tasks of Bible teaching. Using local people for service ministries is a helpful solution if they are committed to the same understanding of Christian service. When they do not understand or support this philosophy, their leadership of the programs creates problems.

Local staff help to create the positive and negative images people have toward the mission or service agency. Local staff relations with foreigners also affects the way they are viewed and can sometimes make them vulnerable to criticism in the community.

Training personnel for service programs or church support ministries is important. Competent staff are needed to do jobs effectively. Many of our Christian concerns and motivation can be communicated through daily association with colleagues.

The presence of the Christian church is a gracious reality in many countries. Mennonites in Vietnam were able to fellowship with those who had come to experience Christ through other churches and missions. Yet in areas where we Mennonites perceive the church to be not fully faithful to the scriptural revelation, the presence of these other church models complicates the missionary task. The biblical model of the one church means that we must accept and identify with other Christians. On the other hand, individuals who newly accept faith in Christ tend to uncritically accept those models. This requires that we share our understanding of the gospel with other Christians as well as learn from them. Above all, it requires that missionaries themselves demonstrate in their lives the gospel to which they are committed. And it is not easy for affluent North American Mennonites to demonstrate a simple and sacrificial and confident faith in God.

Service Objectives, Strategies and Programs

MCC service administrators, like mission leaders, must be thoroughly familiar with the historical, political, economic, religious and cultural situation of the area being considered. A decision to enter any country or area must be expressed in clear objectives to be attained within a stated period and include a plan for evaluation.

Working with a local organization is normally the most significant way of serving in a given area. This will frequently be a Christian church or other Christian organization with which we have much in common. Relationships with other organizations and people help create the agency's image. Mennonites both benefit from and can be handicapped by identification with these groups. Our association with other groups changes their image and patterns as well.

The services of an agency like MCC can strengthen local organizations and encourage the formation of needed structures. Helping other groups can cause them to develop patterns of dependency and contribute to a recipient mentality which must be avoided. This is more likely to happen when working with a local Christian church where we have much in common and because of the biblical injunction to help those "of the household of faith."

When a service agency works with an indigenous organization and plans to expand its ministries within that country into new geographic or functional areas, programs should be developed with other groups rather than continue only with the one organization. This will help to avoid being locked in with one organization. By working with only one organization, MCC comes to be seen as its own. Other local people who also wish to work with MCC see MCC as being co-opted by that organization. MCC's witness is expanded when MCC is able to work with other organizations.

Service workers may deeply appreciate a close relationship with Christians in a particular organization, but this can turn sour if they are limited only to those relationships. Volunteers working in a new and frustrating cultural environment may have more appreciation for local Christians when they are also able to work closely with other persons as well. MCC relationships with non-Christians or other Christian groups can also enable local Christians to see new possibilities for witness.

Although emergency relief programs are needed, a service agency needs to define objectives and develop programs which will attempt to deal with root problems in a society rather than just treat symptoms. Programs to be developed should have the potential for relating to various groups of people—sick, poor, farmers, rural, urban. Concern must be expressed for the oppressed—minority groups, drug addicts, conscientious objectors to war who are imprisoned, etc.

Programs should be designed to meet local needs rather than the agency's own needs (as, for example, MCC child sponsorship programs). In developmental and assistance programs, the agency should supplement local resources rather than provide the primary input. When objectives call for helping to develop indigenously based programs, a clear strategy for implementing a phased transition to local autonomy must be developed.

MCC sometimes can advantageously cooperate with other international agencies in working toward common objectives within a given area, as experience with Vietnam Christian Service (VNCS) has shown. This must be weighed against the limitations cooperation imposes. MCC should not limit its services to what can be done within a cooperative venture but ought to continue some of its own programs in addition.

Attitude toward Societal Problems, Peacemaking

When missionaries are proclaiming the gospel of Jesus

Christ and are relating to people who are suffering, they must also be concerned about ministering to those needs. This frequently calls for some kind of service ministry, but may also involve serving as advocates for the voiceless and powerless. There is a moral authority inherent in Christian witness. In countries with pervasive American cultural, economic or military influence, American missionaries and service workers sometimes have a kind of "Roman citizenship" which implies significant responsibility and enables them to have considerable influence in expressing concern for suffering people. This was true in South Vietnam and is likely true in many Latin American countries today. A Christian witness there does not mean that personnel will attack the local governments or advocate revolution. But they will be concerned that others are able to live as humans. Some Christian workers should be willing to run the risk of being expelled from a country for a faithful witness; this is preferable to leaving voluntarily as a public protest.

Expatriate personnel must clearly articulate their commitment to the gospel so that local people can understand it, and then they must live consistently with that commitment. When the missionaries are not involved in the local church organization, they can take positions on issues such as noninvolvement in military services which the church may not be ready to take. It is inappropriate for the missionaries to deliberately involve the local church in some issue when it is not prepared to take the consequences for a particular position.

Mennonites in Vietnam were concerned about preaching the gospel and ministering to physical need. It took a long time before they understood that the good news of the gospel included working actively to end the war. There should have been a clearer peacemaking strategy. The Mennonite churches need a multifaceted witness to confront such a monstrous evil. The peace position which we understand must be adequately interpreted within a biblical and theological framework. Even though MCC personnel and missionaries had close relationships with ECVN Christians and leaders, our biblical peace position was not widely accepted or even understood by them.

We need to develop better peacemaking models. The visits of historians, theologians, missiologists, and other church leaders to Vietnam was helpful in assisting expatriate personnel to work at some of the issues. The MCC Peace Section gave crucial leadership to the peace witness in Vietnam and in North America. Peace Section might have assigned someone to work with the personnel in Vietnam for a longer period of time.

The presence of both the EMBMC and MCC in Vietnam involved some administrative and service overlap, but the two were able to do some things—separately and together—that neither could have done alone. Their relationships to the government were different. Each organization had strengths, but also practical limitations.

A Christian witness in an area of conflict is important, not only for the service to the victims, but to keep North American Mennonites involved in helping others and to interpret the conflict to North Americans. We have the responsibility to help interpret the problems of other countries to the people and governments of North America if they are in any way responsible for the problems or have the resources for improving the situation. We then must work for change.

Much of the Christian witness for peace during the Vietnam war era in North America was given by ad hoc groups. The Mennonite churches in North America cannot expect MCC or the mission boards to do or say all that they want done or said on a given matter or issue. We must recognize also the crucial matter of timing in dealing with a live issue in the church or in society. Mennonites might have done more to emphasize the biblical basis of our peace concerns, especially among Evangelicals, when the national mood was focused on the issues of war and peace.

Relationships to Political Orders

Relationships with governments at the local and higher levels are frequently helpful. The emphasis must be on relating to the officials as human beings. The missionaries and service workers can share God's concern for the well-being of all people, both with suffering people and with government officials. Close relationships with officials can compromise the gospel message, however. Personnel who request services of the government may obligate themselves to the government. MCC should not normally give its resources directly through a governmental agency. We must recognize that our services and presence in a country frequently help build a positive image for the government among the people, even though we do not intend this. For example, in 1954 South Vietnam welcomed MCC's entry to demonstrate foreign support for their government; Hanoi likewise welcomed MCC support. Our contributed services sometimes permit governments to divert their resources to other less noble purposes. We should not ignore or suppress information on social injustices in order to maintain the good graces of any government. It is helpful to develop clear guidelines about relating to governments and military organizations within the countries of service.

When working in a conflict situation, the church can be a reconciling force. It should seek to communicate with all parties. Normally all parties should be informed of the nature of association with the others. For instance, MCC might have informed the government of South Vietnam of assistance to areas controlled by the National Liberation Front. The Mennonite decision and attempt to work with both sides in Vietnam was rewarding. Yet we still have much to learn about ways of carrying out Christian witness and service ministries with integrity where involvement by our personnel is restricted.

MCC should minimize relationships with the U.S. and Canadian governments. When support is needed for developmental programs, MCC should seek help from local governments or international agencies. North American Mennonite agencies should not accept funding from developmental agencies of their governments such as USAID or CIDA since it can easily compromise their identities. Some Mennonites might be encouraged to work directly for developmental programs of their own governments. Or they might work with indigenous organizations in other countries that have negotiated developmental assistance from North American governmental organizations.

If a Mennonite agency cooperates with a council of voluntary agencies in a country, care must be taken that it represents the legitimate local concerns rather than outside political interests.

In our complex world with many oppressive governments and systems, the mission or service agency is often tempted to support or approve an oppressive political or economic system which permits a continued missionary and service presence in the belief that a change would likely result in the installation of a more repressive system. In the case of Vietnam, it would have meant advocating continued fighting as a better alternative than having a Marxist government. This view represents little faith in God's sovereignty in the world. We are called to give a faithful witness for Jesus Christ today and trust the tomorrow to God.

Note

1. For a complete report of the Vietnam Study Project, see "An Evaluation of Mennonite Mission, Service and Peacemaking in Vietnam, 1954-1976."

28

David A. Shank

Comment on Vietnam Appraisal

The "Vietnam issue" of *Mission-Focus* (VI:2, November 1977) can become an important contribution to missiological reflection for those who feel the suffering servant stance is essential to the mission of the church of Christ and His kingdom. You have effectively pointed out four very different views behind missionary practice in relating to particular political contexts.

One has the feeling that Metzler has come to understand your "fourth type" (quoted near the end of this letter of comment) **since** his Vietnam experience and thus judges that time from a perspective he did not then hold. Klassen, sensing Christian continuity in the midst of ambiguity, does not feel the need to identify with that kind of guilt. Then finally, Martin gives a resume of lessons learned, almost a discussion of problems to be aware of the next time around.

I read these reports while studying church planting in West Africa from 1875 to 1925. In West Africa, there was on the one hand mission work in the midst of Black American colonizers among the Glebo of Cape Palmas, Liberia; on the other hand French Catholics and English Methodists (with the help of French Methodists and Reformed) worked among the coastal peoples within the "pacification" structures of the French colony, the Ivory Coast. The parallels with the American Vietnam experience are so striking that one is tempted to take the latter as a short replay of the whole missionary experience within nineteenth and twentieth century colonialism. Missionaries from that time, looking back, would share some of the understandings and perspectives of Metzler, Klassen, and Martin.

American Mennonite Mission to Vietnam clearly predated the Vietnam War. This fact was seen as a strength of the Mennonite presence there during the war. On the other hand, I remember well how O. O. Miller (then secretary of the Eastern Mennonite Board) explained his understanding of that presence in relation to the **pax americana** which, he said, "will, like the **pax romana,** be around for a long, long time, probably even longer than that of the **pax brittanica.**" Vatican II released the missiological rebound to the end of **pax romana** ecclesiology in the flowering of liberation theologies in Latin America. They are contextual but still too much in reaction to the Roman ecclesiastical imperium to be mature guides for the messianic community of the Suffering Servant.

An astute English observer of the past two centuries of British Christian missions has pointed out how the missions adopted British colonial and imperial policy, including the slogan "Christianity, civilization, and commerce." He concludes that U. K. missionary strategy today is largely related to the aftermath of decolonization. This means that the British counterpart to Rome's liberation theology is probably still a long way off. Mission and church and social and political historians and analysts will be telling us about this for a long, long time to come.

Yet over and over again, one hears from the fruits of Western missions of colonial times, "We regret so much of what was done when you were here; we're glad you

came." This painful contradiction recognizes honest
intentions along with a distorted dynamic which produced
unfortunate consequences. Given this reality, could we
see the Mennonite experience of Vietnam not just as a
replay of the past—thirty years too late—but rather as a
preview of what we American missionaries and our
supporting constituency are deeply involved in wherever
we are in mission outside the borders of the United States.
(The Canadian context differs because the role of Canada
in world politics differs.) The large increase in American
missionaries and mission funds (mostly from non-mainline
churches, as ourselves) since World War II—the
beginning of the **pax americana**—has not let up
substantially. Our own Mennonite missionary expansion
has been integrally related to that **pax americana.** But only
in Vietnam has that reality come and gone within half a
lifetime. Can those of us committed to mission today learn
from such a pre-run and thus avoid operating blindly
under the **pax americana?**

As you write in your "emerging lessons": "The
political context is important to mission. Missionaries
value security. A government which insures social and
political tranquility becomes an ally. Without government
goodwill a mission cannot continue to work. But does the
missionary barter his witness against injustice for
personal security?" When I asked a former Salvation
Army leader in the Congo about their response to the
Kimbanguist relations in the thirties and forties, the
simple response was, "If we had protested, we would
have lost our right to witness to Christ." The all-powerful
economic powers in North America reason this way and
become the allies and defenders (and, as in Vietnam,
sometimes the creators) of the "social and political
tranquility" necessary to maintain economic activity as
they define it.

The churches within the same areas experience the

throttling, and sometimes repression, that comes from the "social and political tranquility" which makes the **American** mission possible. (In the Congo, it was the **Belgian** mission as over against the Kimbanguist.) Americans seek the **privilege** of **American** missions (e.g., Rex Humbard's television ministry in Brazil), without sensing the real meaning of colonialism as the imposition of values and patterns and models which ultimately serve the top of the pyramids of power and wealth which in turn structure the future of those whose sacrifices construct them. Thus it is not strange when churches that grew out of the colonial period use neo-colonial language. But the relationship of neo-colonialism to the **pax americana** is that of muscle to bone.

U.S. policy in Vietnam had to be good for the Vietnamese because it was good for the U.S.; Everett Dirksen called it "our front line of defense." Today even Jimmy Carter's concern for "human rights" must be seen within such a context of muscle and bone. (A UPI release reported recently that when Jimmy Carter is no longer president he would like to become a Southern Baptist missionary to influence people somewhere "for God and our side.") In this context foreign missionaries and their constituency need to share a common critical perspective. Within the U.S., given its provincial self-understanding, the missionary constituency is hard-pressed to have any real critical perspective on "our best interests." It is hard to believe that our best interests might not be good for others, that our economic prosperity (and sometimes prodigality) is sometimes even bad—very bad—for others. And support for American foreign missionaries must come from those who earn within the structures, which do—inevitably—"what is in our best interests."

One of the beautiful chapters—recorded in many places—of the early nineteenth century missionary effort is the story of the way some missionaries' Christian messianism functioned to critique and even oppose colonial policy, strategy, and patterns. One historian points out the shift in late ninteenth century missions when missionaries moved from "opposition" to "**loyal** opposition" in one country. This happened in Gleboland when colonists kept criticizing missionaries for praying for **both** the Glebo "kings" **and** the Liberian authorities. The shift was crucial. (But the Glebo Christians could also wonder why the missionaries were more loyal to the outside invaders than to the centuries-old existing authority.)

How do missionaries live out the "opposition" stance of the suffering servant when their constituency is loyal to the **pax americana**? In the Vietnam paradigm the Mennonite constituency in the U.S. was often in the "opposition" or "loyal opposition," perhaps because Vietnam did not appear to be in the U.S.'s best interests. A vanguard of students, Peace Section specialists, and observant leaders gave another dimension, another "look" to a constituency which appeared to be basically loyal even in conscientious objection. If the **pax americana** is going to be around a long, long time (Vietnam and Watergate are indications that one does not change things "at the top"), and if the Mennonite experience in Vietnam is a preview for late twentieth century world mission of the American Mennonite church, a major **missionary** task confronts us. That task is the creation of a conscious "opposition" constituency which will support the "opposition" missionary, just as in the days of the slave trade and liquor traffic the missionary was supported by ground swell opposition in Britain.

Our Promethean technological assumptions and the current myth of personal fulfillment are both allied with American wealth and power, itself fortified with the conviction that history is on our side: this is the backdrop for the **pax americana.** American Mennonite world mission will be effective only to the extent that American Mennonites are able to learn what it means to be what you describe as "a messianic movement led by Jesus Christ [the Suffering Servant]. The missionary is the vanguard of the movement. The messianic kingdom presents an alternative to the present world order. The church does not seek to impose this order on the larger society but rather models the 'newness' of the messianic kingdom in its common life. The world perceives this as a judgment on itself and may even find the presence of the church intolerable." The working out of a policy **in the U.S.A.** which reflects this stance is the most crucial missiological issue facing American Mennonites, to say nothing of the thousands of American foreign missionaries of other denominations.

Is there hope? I will cite three signs:

1. The information which Mennonite Central Committee's **Washington Memo** gives its readers is a sign of hope for American Mennonite world mission. But how many people in our constituency **read** this? Of those who read, how many **identify** with the concerns? And of those who identify, how many really see **response** as essential to the worldwide mission of the church in the U.S.?

2. When Goshen Biblical Seminary examined the meaning of endowment funds for its future, it asked (a) what Christ's teaching had to say in this concern, and (b) what endowment funds meant for the relationship of our U.S. church to Third World churches. Here it was not simply assumed that what is good for our institution is somehow—by definition—good for the rest of the world church and its mission. This is a new dimension in the calculus of ethical, social, political decision, and a **sine qua non** of our world mission.

3. A growing number of people see the need to give at least one percent of their gross annual income as a (non-missionary) "restitution fund" for the Third World,

as a reminder that before we give to the mission of the church we must restore to those who have suffered from the "one-way flow" which capitalism requires and in which—by virtue of our residence—we are implicated.

These are signs of hope which indicate to foreign missionaries that their constituency in the "richest and most powerful nation in the world's history" is not simply justifying the **pax americana**, but is, in new and creative ways, offering its loyalty to Jesus Christ and living out its opposition to everything "at home" which tends to work against the good of brothers and sisters in Christ abroad.

Crucial Issues in Theological Education in Latin America

29

*Hugo
Zorrilla*

Introduction

In thinking about "crucial issues," two basic ideas occur to me—ideas which in latent form, determine the content of this study paper: (1) Theological education in Latin America finds itself in a critical period which reflects not only a Latin American, but a general worldwide crisis in education. (2) Theological education in our countries has not yet found its own identity. Rather it continues to be a blending of traditional secular education patterns in Latin America and theological education molds from North America—a pattern which responds neither to the genius of Latin American Protestantism nor to the mission which the church is called to fulfill on this continent.

The basic purpose of this paper is to show at a glance the most important aspects of theological training that are being discussed in Latin America and to show why it is necessary to look for contextualized alternatives in theological education that sidestep the traditional scholarly framework.

To think of theological education in Latin America is to confront ourselves with the role of the educator as a minister of the gospel; it is to put into action the function of educating in the educative process; it is to reexamine contents and methodological processes in this apostleship. In this sense we ask: What are the objectives of theological education in Latin America today? What is the place of the church in the various programs of theological education? What relation is there between the ministry and theology programs in the seminaries and institutes? In a context of marginality and oppression, with high rates of illiteracy, unemployment, militarism and violence, what does it mean to have programs of theological education? Many such questions distress us profoundly when we think of the teaching task. Something is not functioning correctly when we think of seminaries "producing" pastors as if they were just one more product of a consumer society. The title of a recent article serves as an example of this kind of thinking: "El Seminario Central, Fábrica de Sacerdotes"[1] (Central Seminary, Priest Factory). This is where the problem of theological education begins. How do we conceive education for the ministry? The theological and ideological framework that has defined theological education in the past 150 years in Latin America has presented the ministry of theological teaching as a "means of production" of pastors who, within the elite, direct the church.

Laying aside the historical perspectives of theological education in Latin America, I will limit my exposition strictly to teaching, based above all, on my experience in Colombia and Costa Rica. It is not in vain to say that I am neither a "technician" in education, nor a "specialist" in Latin American problems. I express my thoughts with a great desire for dialogue and a profound recognition of my limitations. These impel me to continue the theological task with my eyes fixed on Jesus, Lord and Teacher.

The Crisis in Theological Education

The crisis in theological education has become increasingly accentuated in Latin America during this decade of the 70s. In our countries, as in all modern societies, we live in critical times where nothing is taken for granted. Only after something has been questioned will it be accepted. Fundamental questions are being raised and basic changes are taking place in all areas of knowledge and human action. Education cannot escape this questioning, and of course, neither can the church and, with her, the pertinence of traditional theology. Furthermore, the questioning of the church touches upon the ministry and its relevance in a convulsive, revolutionary, and militarized America. The churches see with dissatisfaction that the labors of the seminaries and Bible institutes are not responding to their needs because they follow patterns inherited from the mission boards. The seminaries go in one direction while the church wrestles in another. Non-contextualized churches carry out a ministry not suited to their reality while seminaries perpetuate theologies, methods, and strategies best suited to churches in an opulent and wealthy society. The opposite case also appears—theological schools and churches which seek new alternatives in theological education and experiment with new programs for training leaders. Two examples are the Association of Bible Churches of the Caribbean on the northern coast of Colombia and the Peruvian Evangelical churches.

Some reasons for crisis inherent to theological education can be detected within the administrative and teaching structures of traditional seminaries and institutes. Before mentioning these reasons, it is necessary to underscore that all these questions of theological education have their theological bases. The problem is one of theology and one of dependence, so much so that the crisis that exists in the centers of theological education in North America and Europe have been accepted as crisis in Latin America. Any decision that affects the church in North America affects its organisms in Latin America or other nations called "mission fields." Many of the basic decisions in regard to the training of leaders are prepared and "cooked up" by the missionaries and the mission boards. This process has been the rule, even in the beginnings of the so-called theological-education-by-extension movement that carried the name of Guatemala to all parts of the world where there are missions.

Now let us turn to some of the reasons for this crisis in theological education which is, I repeat, a theological crisis.

1. **A borrowed theology.** Theological education in Latin America has rested upon the importation of theological content, the emphasis varying according to the mission to which the seminary belongs. Each mission board has duplicated its efforts in order to perpetuate its "biblical truth" with its own institute or seminary. This is why theological schools have proliferated, thus duplicating human forces, expenses, etc.[2] Theological education and through it, theology itself, has come forth as an implantation of academic and theological systems by the mission boards. As a matter of fact, this holy institutionalization has made the seminaries and institutes the centers that give the parameters so that the denomination determines who is and who is not a pastor. This type of academic environment results in (1) a people

of God passive in the education of their leaders and helping to perpetuate the dependency of the local church. In this sense, the people of God are not involved creatively in the preparation and evaluation of their leaders. (2) They maintain forms of worship, stereotyped theological categories, and "prepackaged" models of irrelevant ministries.

2. **Copied curricula.** Most seminary and institute programs follow the same curricula as in North America. Successful completion of large numbers of these courses supposedly guarantees both academic and ministerial excellence. Although it is not common today, there are theological schools in Latin America with identically the same curriculum as the theological school in the United States of that particular mission, or the same program that the missionaries and professors studied at Fuller, Moody, Dallas, etc.

3. **Materials.** Until recently it was difficult to find theological textbooks written by Latin Americans. Most materials used in theological education are translated texts. Usually each mission translates and publishes the textbooks that contain their "true theology." At the present time valuable books are appearing in the fields of ecclesiology, pastoral theology, youth ministries, hymnology, ethics, evangelism, missiology, etc., written by men of God who have their ministries in Latin America.

4. **Professors.** Most teaching personnel in theological schools are missionaries who have no social or cultural ties with the country in which they teach. This is the sad picture of the institutions in Colombia. Many seminary and Bible institute professors, missionaries or not, lack the methodology to allow the student to be a person who actively participates in the educational process. These

professors, who often equate their academic excellence and their titles with teaching effectiveness treat their students as a captive audience to be "domesticated,"as Paulo Freire, the Brazilian educator, says. On the other hand, these same professors live detached from the social reality of the peoples of which their students are a part, and from the context it is supposed that theological reflection is carried out.

From this panorama, limited to be sure, we find in Latin America much dissatisfaction with the results of traditional models of theological education. Since the beginning of this decade, theological-education-by-extension as a valid alternative in our context has been attempted, although this form of education is neither new nor the only alternative. The appearance of alternatives in theological education today offers us various options in the politics of theological education. (1) There are those who are wrestling to perpetuate the residential institutions, fortifying them with more academic resources and more missionary personnel. (2) Others believe that the solution for a more efficient ministry in the churches is found in abolishing the residence programs and dedicating all their efforts to theological education by extension. (3) For others, the solution is theological education by extension, but with a curriculum contextualized and open to the local needs. The reason for this is that many extension programs are nothing more than decentralized residence programs. The structure is different, but the curriculum of " canned courses" is the same. In short, it is "the same dog with a different chain." (4) Some within the framework of residential seminaries look for other alternatives such as correspondence, extension, or diversified education with an open curriculum.[3] (5) Others look for a form of continued education which is both experimental and at the same time integrated into the community. Rejecting traditional schooling, they offer an open curriculum, taking advantage of all the resources in the churches. The objectives of this kind of program are the objectives of the church in the community. Some Pentecostal churches follow this line.

Contextual Education

Contextual theological education points toward an incarnational or penetrating style of theologizing. It seeks more than a mere identification with the means by which the Holy Scriptures are reread. It is not a folklorism unintegrated with the reality of the church in this moment in Latin America. It is not adaptation, giving the attitude of a superior culture that "sacrifices" itself, identifying with the poor, or that "mimics" folklorically for the benefit of "those poor things." It is to incarnate and to accompany the community of faith in the search for solutions for transforming its reality of sin (called oppression, dependence, exploitation, vices, marginality, etc). Through incarnation contextual education co-operates in the Latin American churches' search for identity. In this process the following elements must be questioned.

1. **The teaching structure.** Most of these programs, whether residential or extension, are controlled by the mission boards or by missionary personnel. This has mythicized the idea that the seminaries will bring the solution to problems in the churches. Furthermore, it is believed that the seminary develops the pastor, that is, that the task of the seminary or institute is to "produce" pastors and leaders in Christian education since the

mission board provides everything else.

Here we ask the basic question: What is the role of the seminary? It is no secret that many seminaries and institutes are the most effective forms of sectarian control for the denomination. The crisis is greater if local churches are not in an economic condition to support a professional pastor. It is questionable for our pastors today to live on what the church pays them. The list of frustrated and bitter people in the ministry who have not had the opportunity of acquiring a trade or profession is endless. The attitude of the churches, of the seminaries, and of the missions in this respect is oppressive when they defend the myth that only he can be called pastor who is "full-time." Some theological institutions help their students study a profession or a trade. Latin America cannot afford the luxury of "desk" pastors. Churches which are in a position to support their pastors well are limited in number. The problem expands even more when one sees that in the last several years the number of married students with families entering theological education is greater than the number of single students. This implies that they should have a profession or a scholarship in order to succeed in their studies. The sad part is that churches continue to receive scholarships from missions so that they can continue paying "full-time" pastors.

2. **Curricula.** Previously I said that most of the content in seminary curricula has been imported. Many curricula in theological education have a limited function in the mission of the churches. In no way do they help the student develop his creativity and understandings of the historical moment in which his people live. Many programs lack basic objectives. If they are present, they are the same as those of other institutions in some North

Atlantic country (like branch offices).

Another criticism is that seminaries lack church-centered or student-centered curricula. If we took off our tinted glasses of traditional academe, we would see a wide range of possibilities and resources available in our churches which could be integrated into programs of ministerial training, that, on the one hand, would be contextualized, and, on the other hand, would incorporate the learning experiences acquired outside a traditional structure.

3. **Content.** Not only do many curricula in theological education in Latin America lack contextualized objectives, but the units of content respond to other situations. The theological content and materials have not changed even though there are sociopolitical factors that influence our ministry, even if we do not want them to. The "prepackaged" content of theological courses is one of the most discussed elements today in Latin America for those who look for other alternatives in prophetic training. A program is judged nonbiblical, and consequently heretical, if it doesn't have 60-70% biblical content, which consists of studies of memorized "neutral" biblical content without theological reflection or dialogue with the world to which it ministers. Nevertheless, in some seminaries, such as the Latin American Biblical Seminary and in extension programs such as that of the Presbyterian Seminary in Guatemala, an integration of courses is sought. For example, it has been shown that one can teach Bible content, exegesis, theology, and pastoral principles in a course based on I Corinthians.

The irrelevant situation causes us to think in terms of integrated content in which the social sciences together with biblical and pastoral theology respond together to the present reality. It is vitally important to take into account these factors that affect the focus of theological education in Latin America:

(1) demographic changes, the "tugurios" (miserable cottages resulting from immigration of rural people to the cities)

(2) urban agglomeration with its problems of alcoholism and prostitution, districts of "rural" colonies, or colonies of foreigners

(3) changes in social structure, as a result of industrialization and the growing middle class accompanied by changes in traditional values

(4) transition from societies with economies based on farms to societies based on consumer goods and including industrialized agriculture

(5) political changes within a revolutionary ferment; political conscience-raising of the people living under militarized and oppressive governments

(6) revolution in the means of communication

(7) increase in the educational level and professionalism of church members.

Faced with this panorama of Latin America, theological education should provide men and women of God with the necessary ministerial tools and methodological resources that help develop the abilities of the students in order that the church may fulfill its ministry.

I should point out that theological content in seminaries and Bible institutes is questioned because of heavy emphasis upon a theology of the past. The majority of the courses are informational and based on memorization. Few of them tackle the present realities which impinge upon the theological task of the church and in this sense alienates it from its genuine missionary task.

The topic presented in this paper is of a general order, and it has not been our intention to describe models of theological education that break away from the traditional ones. Nevertheless it is worth mentioning some basic principles to keep in mind when structuring a program of contextualized theological education:

(1) Define groups of students according to academic levels and ministerial interests.
(2) Establish the interests and abilities of the students.
(3) Feel out the needs and realities of the community or the area.
(4) Define with the churches their priorities and projections.
(5) Look for and coordinate sources of human and physical resources in the locality.
(6) Prepare an open and integrated curriculum that incorporates the above principles.

Conclusion

To sum up: What then is the panorama of theological education in Latin America? The truth is that churches do not look for any one and only formula fallen from heaven. They endeavor to obtain alternatives, various possibilities for the training of leaders, not just an elite, but the education of the people of God as a whole, so that the church can understand its world, and what God has for that world.

Why other alternatives? The traditional scholarity of the seminaries does not respond adequately to the needs felt by the church. It is well-known that many leaders are outside the present means of ministerial preparation. It is realized that it is necessary to educate in context and to combine theory with practice immediately. The missiological labor of the church is formed on the march, and in this labor one theologizes and educates, and only thus are abilities developed that form Christians capable of dialoguing with other theologies or ideologies, but submitted only to the authority of the Bible and the guidance of the Spirit of the Master. Finally, it is the Teacher who confronts us with the foolishness of the Cross in order to make of theological education in the church a risk, a lamentation, a foolishness for His glory, and for the edification of the people of God.

Notes

1. Eco Católico. Año XLIV. Tomo 74. No. 2365. San José, 10 de octubre 1976. p. 7.

2. According to ALET (Latin American Association of Theological Schools), in Mexico alone in 1975 there were 120 institutes and seminaries. From Ecuador to Mexico there were 220 institutes and seminaries.

The Theological Education Fund listed the following statistics of schools: In Central America there are 158, with Mexico (99) and Guatemala (23) having the most institutions. In South America there are 159, with Brazil (78), Colombia (27) and Ecuador (13) leading. These figures do not include the schools that did not respond to the Theological Education Fund questionnaire.

3. The Latin American Biblical Seminary in Costa Rica is the institution that has struggled most in this line of thinking. Its PRODIADIS (Diversified Program at a Distance) program promises much under the educational philosophy of the Open University of London and the Universidad a Distancia in Madrid.

Crucial Issues in Leadership Training: A Chinese Perspective

30

Jonathan T'ien-en Chao

My task is to identify and to articulate the most crucial issues in leadership training in Third World ministries. I represent two perspectives: 1. that of a student of Chinese Protestant church history with a special interest in the problems of indigenization and leadership training, and 2. that of an initiator and promoter of Chinese indigenous theological education in connection with the China Graduate School of Theology (CGST), now operating in Hong Kong.

A decade ago a few of us Chinese theological students in the United States first took up the problem of Chinese theological education seriously. During these ten years my own views on leadership training have undergone three stages of development. I would like to share them with you briefly, as these reflections will color my analysis of the topic at hand.

During the initial years of our movement (1966-1970), along with other members of the founding team, my compelling concern was how to upgrade the quality of the Chinese ministry. We concluded that the key to this problem was the training of university graduates in a graduate school of theology where they might be equipped to become learned pastors who could rightly expound the Scriptures and ably defend the Christian faith against liberal theology and modern secular thought. This was to be done by a committed team of Chinese scholars and supported primarily by the Chinese Christian community. The emphasis then was on academic excellence, and we began to recruit and train a Chinese faculty in advanced studies.

However, as I was sent to Asia for a short term of teaching ministry (1970-1972), I had occasion to travel and to study the various problems facing the Chinese church today. Consultations and interviews soon enabled me to see that leadership training for church ministries required different levels and varying programs in accordance with the diversities of local needs; that lower levels of training and lay training are equally important as graduate training; and that these levels must be coordinated to avoid unnecessary tension. Thus in 1972 CGST adopted the multilevel and multiprogram approach to Chinese theological education. The graduate school that has been opened in Hong Kong since 1975 is basically following the above ideals accrued from the first two stages of our reflection (1966-1974).

In 1974 when I began the task of program design for our school, I was soon faced with the challenge of integrating the academic, the practical, and the spiritual components of theological training within the context of a seminary. Studying the historical development of ministerial training in China since 1865 and reflecting upon it in the light of the biblical teachings on the Christian ministry, I have gradually come to see that no authentic integration can be brought about by mere program design, however perfect that might be. It can only be done, I venture to say, by conscientious identification with the life and ministry of Christ and by experiencing the efficacy of that identification spiritually within a community of believers (functioning as the body of Christ) who are committed to the practice of radical discipleship in the manner prescribed by Jesus Himself and the Apostles. This is the direction in which I hope our school will go in the future.

It is in the light of these reflections that I wish to discuss and identify some of the most crucial issues in leadership training for today's ministries in the Third World which, I am sure, will also have implications for ministries in America. But in order to sharpen our perception of current issues and to provide a larger context for our discussion, I will attempt to analyze issues in leadership training that arose from the experiences of the Christian mission in China as well as issues that are being perceived by theological educators in Asia today. From these surveys it will become evident to us that differing historical and cultural contexts and preconceived concepts of leadership training influence people's perception of issues.

I. Leadership Training in China (1842-1949)[1]

The development of Protestant ministerial training in China may be roughly divided into three stages of growth in mission work. The timing of these stages differs, of course, from region to region depending on when the pioneer work began and how densely the region was "occupied" by missions. In the coastal regions mission work began in the five treaty ports (Canton, Amoy, Foochow, Ningpo, and Shanghai) after 1842, following the conclusion of the Opium War (1839-1842). But in the interior cities like Tientsin, Peking, and Hankow, mission work did not begin until 1861-1865, following the second Anglo-Chinese War (1858-1860) in which China lost again, and through which treaty the right to missionary travel and propagation was secured. Regions in Western China were not occupied by missionaries until 1890-1900. Each of these stages of development usually took 25-30 years.

During the first stage of pioneering mission work, missionaries concentrated on field evangelism and medical work as "pre-evangelism." Missionaries carried out their leadership training through a "station plan." They would pick some of their converts to be their assistants and trained them on the job, supplementing this with Bible lessons given privately and through short-term instruction. Missionaries in those days were usually not university graduates, but many were spiritual giants, men of faith and of evangelistic passion. In their training of "native helpers," they emphasized the cultivation of spiritual life, growth in faith, and improvements in the art of speaking through street preaching.[2] The exigencies of their times required the training of personal assistants in preaching, in visitation, in hospital care, or in school teaching. These "native assistants" were paid, controlled, and supervised by missionaries. They were seen as extensions of the arms of the missionaries. Ministerial training was not understood in terms of "leadership training," though theoretically some missionaries hoped that eventually these assistants would become pastors and "native leaders."

The second stage of development usually came after some 25-30 years of intensive evangelistic cultivation and church planting so that a Christian community gradually emerged, including the incorporation of a growing number of "covenant children." By this time mission schools on the primary level began to become well established, secondary schools were beginning to be initiated, and dispensaries became hospitals. Missionaries became more interested in the development of the institutional aspects of their work, and more "native helpers" were needed to staff these institutions, some of whom required professional training in addition to general mission education. The rise of institutions demanded a new class of more educated missionaries. Under the inspiration of the Student Volunteer Movement in England and America in the 1890s,[3] a new influx of university and seminary graduates entered foreign service and met this demand.

As this group of younger elitist, intellectual missionaries arrived in China, they were usually given institutional responsibilities. Their passion for academic excellence soon made them critical of both the state of mission schools and of the style of ministerial training begun by their predecessors. These scholar-missionaries, therefore, began to crusade for upgrading the mission schools, establishing secondary schools, and opening theological institutes—all aimed at developing an educational system for the training of a "better qualified, learned native ministry." Thus ministerial training during the second stage assumed an institutional form patterned after the British model of theological colleges, which combined liberal arts and theology, and the American model of Bible schools and denominational seminaries.[4] This institutional approach was essentially an attempt to transplant the Western model of parish ministry and seminary style training into the Chinese context. During the heyday of Protestant missions in China, there were more than 64 such theological schools of varying levels under the supervision of some 130 missionary societies and boards.[5]

As was to be expected, the personnel, the finance, the contents, and the administration were all under denominational missionary control.

The third stage was usually ushered in after 50-60 years of mission work in cities or regions of heavy missionary concentration, such as the major cities Amoy, Shanghai, Tientsin, Peking, Hankow, and Canton. Stimulated by discussions on cooperation and union in the national missionary conferences of 1890 and 1907, missions in each region began to move in the direction of union theological schools. Missionary personnel and financing were shared by participating missions. Thus this third period was marked by the rise of union theological schools supported by most of the older missions. This resulted in a general upgrading of academic standards, the professionalization of staff and administration, and the erection of institutional buildings modeled after the university or seminary structures of their schools in the West.[6] As American missions began to take on more prominence in the number of personnel and financial power after 1900, these union schools were usually patterned after the American model of seminaries, where the ideal standard of admission was the liberal arts degree. But since the number of college graduates was rather limited in number and the need for workers remained high, most students admitted even in these union schools from 1912-1950 were high school graduates.[7]

A few crucial issues in leadership training can be observed from the above survey. Some of these were openly debated among the missionaries, others were questioned by Chinese Christians; but, as a rule, they were ignored by missionary educators.

The first crucial issue, which became an area of tension between older pioneering missionaries and younger educational missionaries, was whether the Chinese preacher should be trained by the "station plan" or the "school plan." Advocates of the former argued on the basis of Jesus' method of training the twelve and that of Paul's training of Timothy. They also argued that training men converted in their adulthood in the crucible of actual service produces rugged and faithful workers who know their people well. They despised the school plan whereby students were molded in the protected atmosphere of the mission school with subsidy. The educational missionaries criticized the station plan as incapable of producing Chinese preachers who are thoroughly grounded in the Scriptures and in "Christian civilization." They despised Chinese preachers trained under older missionaries as being "too Confucian" in their thinking, and hence not really thoroughly converted from Confucius to Christ. To them, this cultural conversion could not be done except by a long process of formation through the system of mission schools from the primary level to the theological school. Each side in this dogged debate did not seem to see the historical and regional differences under which each plan developed. In the end as older missionaries passed away and as "unoccupied regions" diminished, the school plan won the day. After the founding of the Republic in 1912, most missions unwittingly accepted the institutional model of leadership training as the standard form, and the apprenticeship model simply faded out of history.

A second crucial issue that remained unsolved was the goal of ministerial training. As already intimated, during the first stage ministerial training was not conceived in terms of "leadership training," but the training of second-class employed "helpers." There were medical helpers,

educational helpers ("teachers"), and evangelistic helpers ("native preachers" or "native evangelists"). These
were called "native assistants." During the second stage
the training of "Chinese preachers" was for the purpose
of staffing street preaching chapels, outstations, and
general evangelistic outreach under the direction of
missionaries. At a later stage experienced assistants were
occasionally ordained to the pastorate of a self-supporting
church. During the third stage union theological schools
aimed at producing pastors as well as evangelists and
various other posts within the mission and church system
of full-time service. The pastoral training model was used
for all types of ministry. In all of these, the goal of training
seems to have been based on the training of certain
professional skills for evangelistic or other types of
churchly activities. In other words, training was centered
on performance or knowledge related to performance
under a given system.

A third issue raised by a small minority of missionary
thinkers and also by Chinese Christians was whether the
Western institutional form of ministerial training was the
best for the Chinese situation. Inseparably connected with
this doubt were questions about the validity of the
Western model of the full-time paid professional clergy,
marked by a long process of professional training and
ecclesiastical ordination. The missionaries' right to
transplant the Western model of ministry and of training
was not seriously questioned, but their functional
effectiveness was.

John Nevius (1829-1893), Presbyterian Mission in
Shantung, advocated, and even successfully worked out, a
volunteer system of unpaid elders to whom he entrusted
the care of local stations.[8] His main point was to prove

that an alternative to "employment systems," and to the "school plan" was possible. But few of his fellow missionaries listened to him as those in Korea did.

Perhaps the most vocal challenge against the professional clergy and against the institutional form of training came from Chinese independent churches that separated themselves from foreign missions, especially the Little Flock (Watchman Nee group). These dissidents were against Western denominationalism, against missionary control, against rational theology, and against the entire structure of institutional Christianity. These independent churches developed their own form of training through the development of spiritual gifts within local churches.[9]

A fourth issue was the place of Chinese culture and social studies in a theological curriculum. This issue was raised by Chinese Christian intellectuals more vocally during the anti-Christian movement period of 1922-1927.[10] But being primarily discussion among Chinese with few Chinese Christian leaders occupying administrative positions in theological schools, the matter was not perceived by missionary educators as a crucial issue.

1949-76. Chinese theological education in Hong Kong, Taiwan, and Southeast Asia during the last 27 years has been more or less following the same institutional models of Bible schools (for junior high graduates), and of theological seminaries (high school graduates combined with some college graduates) as developed in China. In fact, many schools were simply transplanted from China to Hong Kong or Taiwan by foreign missions during the early 1950s. Most of these schools are still financed by foreign missions and, until recently, headed by missionaries. Thus issues in leadership training that arose in China 1912-1950 remain basically unsolved by church and mission operating in Taiwan and Hong Kong.[11] (More on this below.)

II. Analysis of Current Views on Crucial Issues in Leadership Training

I will present briefly four perspectives on theological training in the Asian context: 1. views of the Theological Education Fund directors, 2. views of ecumenical theological educators within the Northeast Asia and Southeast Asia Associations of Theological Schools, 3. evangelical views as expressed by the Asian Theological Association, and 4. Chinese evangelical views as expressed by the Association for Promotion of Chinese Theological Education.

Historical Shifts in TEF's Perception of Issues

The Theological Education Fund represents a concerted effort on the part of ecumenical churches and missions to deal with the problem of training for ministry in the Third World. Founded in Ghana in 1958 under the International Missionary Council, TEF's perception of issues underwent three stages of development during three "mandates." Their evolution in view is of great significance.[12]

During the first mandate period (1958-1964), TEF basically operated as a central agency of missionary concerns for theological education in the younger churches founded by the mainline denominational mission boards. In many cases these were union schools, like those formed in China. During this period TEF defined the chief issue to be how to raise the level of academic standards in Third World theological schools. Its goal was to improve academic excellence by providing grants to key schools for building construction, faculty training in the West, library development, and textbook production through translation projects and occasional original writing. At that time TEF did not question the Western character of those theological schools or the problem of continued missionary leadership in administration and teaching. TEF sought to make Third World theological schools like seminaries in the West, and it did so through foreign funding for institutional buildup. At the end of the first mandate, however, TEF realized that strengthening of academic standards externally did not necessarily bring about the indigenous theological education which they sought.[13]

During the second mandate period (1965-1970), the Third World experienced a resurgence of local religions and the emergence of urbanization and its accompanying problems. TEF, by then under the Commission on World Mission and Evangelism of WCC, began to devote its attention to the interpretation of the gospel in relation to local culture and society and saw the issue of theological education as how to do it within the context of local cultures. Emphasis was placed on the **milieu** in which the ministry was to be carried out. During this period TEF also encouraged the formation of regional associations of theological schools and intensified its program of faculty development for nationals. Over 400 individual grants were given to Third World nationals for advanced studies in the West leading to masters and doctoral degrees.[14] Presumably TEF's attempt was to develop relevant regional theological education through training national theological educators and teachers to the level of their Western counterparts. The model of excellence was taken from seminaries in the West. Qualifications for leadership training were measured by academic degrees.

While many nationals did receive advanced academic training in the West and some even returned, TEF efforts to develop faculty for Taiwan must be considered a failure because most of those trained eventually came back to America after a short period of service. They were reabsorbed into American Christian organizational structures for which they seemed to be better fitted than the church situation in Taiwan. It is doubtful whether TEF achieved its goal of providing relevant theological training for local cultural milieux. TEF did realize at the end of the mandate that advanced training in the West was not conducive to regionalization of ministerial training.

During the current mandate period (1971-1977), Third World churches and societies are faced with a crisis of faith and are searching for meaning in life in a post-Christian era. WCC is concerned with social justice, liberation, and human development. Within this context TEF began to ask a most fundamental question: "What is theological education?" But the stress is not so much on the "what" **per se** in terms of **content** as on "what is it **for**—in the context of the contemporary, revolutionary world?"[15] This concern leads to the quest for forms of theological training and ministry that are authentic to particular contexts within Asia, Africa, or Latin America. This quest marks the first breakthrough in the concept of ministry and theological training. It has given the green light to deviation from the Western model and even to questions about the validity of defining excellence merely in academic terms.[16] One way by which TEF is expressing this concern is to encourage the establishment of regional graduate schools of theology within local cultural contexts rather than always sending graduate students to the West. TEF is also encouraging research within each region, especially centers which redefine criteria of excellence in terms of local cultural settings and even non-degree programs. However, at this point, there is no convincing evidence that TEF or its associated regional associations are seriously questioning the Western model of paid professional trained ministry. Nor are they departing from the centrality of the academic curriculum as the heart of theological training. Until these two strong pillars are radically shaken, it seems unlikely that TEF can truly fulfill its third mandate.

However, there is a sign of hope. It may be found in Director Shoki Coe's thinking on theological education as a process of formation, an ongoing movement of discerning the place and role of the text (gospel) within the missiological context, which he calls "contextualization." Dr. Coe speaks of a threefold formation process: 1. Christian formation: "I live, yet not I, but Christ lives in me" (Gal. 2:20); 2. theological formation: "Let this mind be in you, which was also in Christ" (Phil. 2:5); and 3. ministerial formation: "I work, but not I, but the ministry of Christ works in me" (applying Gal. 2:20).[17] Thus far, this appears to be the most promising insight from TEF thinkers, though it is not yet evident that this threefold formulation has found its way into the programs of schools traditionally supported by TEF. It is my hope that these formation principles will become the theme for TEF's fourth mandate.

Asian Perspectives on Issues within the NEAATS and ATSSES

Asian ecumenical perceptions of crucial issues in theological training follow that of TEF's fairly closely because of the latter's influence through Shoki Coe and

Ivy Chou. According to Dr. Emerito P. Nacpil, current director of the Association of Theological Schools in Southeast Asia (ATSSEA), in the past member schools of the Association have pursued academic excellence. But now they are beginning to realize that such an approach has proven to be inadequate and even damaging to the spiritual aspect of their efforts. They are beginning to realize the need for moral and spiritual development. So the current crucial issue for them is: What form of spirituality goes hand in hand with academic excellence? The problem Nacpil faces is that ATSSEA does not know what kind of piety goes well with academic learning.[18]

Even the kind of academic excellence advocated by ATSSEA is now under question by its own constituencies. The tension between seminaries and churches appears to grow stronger. Thus the second issue raised by ATSSEA is: What sort of theological orientation would be most useful to the Asian churches at this time? By theological orientation Nacpil meant "a kind of theoretical knowledge that will provide concrete guidance in the management of Asian affairs."[19] In other words, it is a kind of practical knowledge for an activist type of contextual ministry.

The search for spirituality in theological training is also being voiced by educators in the Northeast Asia Association of Theological Schools (NEAATS). Speaking from the Taiwan situation, Dr. David Chen, former principal and professor of ethics at Taiwan Theological College, asked: How can we raise the moral and spiritual standards of the students, that is, how do we develop moral and spiritual sensitivity in terms of trust in God and love for neighbors?[20] In 1974 the NEAATS commissioned a committee in Taiwan to study the matter of spiritual development of theological students. The committee's report urged member schools to regard spiritual development as a central ingredient to the process of theological education and suggested a community approach to the problem.[21]

Speaking from a Korean perspective, Chung Choon Kim saw the issue as how to relate theological training to the mission of the church.[22]

Thus, taken together, theological educators within the ecumenical circle in Asia are raising a fundamental issue in current theological education: How to develop spirituality as a reaction to over-academicism. This is interesting from two perspectives. In the first place, it represents a significant form of Asian reaction against the Western pattern of academic emphasis even in schools which have traditionally been regarded as ignoring spiritual values in their pursuit of academic excellence. In the second place, Northeast Asians (Chinese, Koreans, and Japanese) are beginning to sense a lack of spirituality which used to be present in their traditional moral/religious systems, namely, Confucianism, Taoism, Buddhism, and Shintoism. Mere intellectual study of rational theology is proving unsatisfactory in the Asian quest for Christian spirituality.

Evangelical Asian Perspective (ATA)
The Asian Theological Association, which emerged out of the Theological Assistance Program-Asia (TAP-ASIA) consultation in Singapore in 1971, is currently dealing with issues considered by TEF during its first and second mandates. They are concerned with the development of national faculty, the formation of an accreditation system raising academic standards, and how to bring about an integration of the academic, the spiritual, and the

practical aspects of theological training.[23]

While evangelicals in Asia are conscious of their spiritual heritage, the goal that is being pursued is also academic excellence, and the model adopted is also the Western institutional form of ministerial training, namely, the seminary system, including Theological Education by Extension (TEE). Because of this unquestioning acceptance of the Western seminary model, like TEF's first two mandates, evangelicals are pursuing virtually the same goal as the ecumenical schools did, namely, to raise the academic level and to respond to the Asian situation. The basic difference is one of theological content, not the form of expression. As Asian ecumenicals follow Western liberal trends, likewise Asian evangelicals are basically following the pattern of American evangelicalism in their theological training. There is a basic dichotomy between evangelical pietism on the experiential level and evangelical theological education on a rational level. The academic, the spiritual, and the practical form a trichotomy and remain essentially compartmentalized. How to integrate these three aspects was the main issue discussed at the Third ATA Consultation in Hong Kong, December 27, 1973-January 4, 1974. Even though two papers were presented on this subject, there appeared to be no significant conceptual breakthroughs in the structure or form of integration.[24] While both papers acknowledged the difficulty of achieving effective integration and saw the need of training in community, neither of them provided any theological framework of the seminary community as the basis for integration. What was reiterated was the importance of personal contacts between the faculty and students (including living together) and among the students, chapels, retreats, dormitory life, and field work. The Confucian stress on the influence of the teacher's personal character was made. This problem of integration remains unsolved while every evangelical school seems to fear losing spiritual vitality and suffering from haphazard practical programs under the pressure of "academic excellence."

Chinese Evangelical Perspective

Chinese evangelicals in diaspora during the past 27 years since China became Communist have been developing in diverse forms.[25] In leadership training they vary from functional training through service on the local church level to Bible school-seminary model of training.

During 1972-1973 two consultations of Chinese theological educators and church leaders were held in Hong Kong and Baguio, the Philippines, respectively. We have not had further opportunity for sharpening our definition of issues. But from the two consultations two issues appear to stand out: (1) How to develop theological education according to the needs of the Chinese church. There has been a clear recognition that seminary style leadership training has not been successful in producing real leaders for the church and that relevant and effective models of training must be judged by their usefulness in fulfilling the needs of the church. (2) How to provide a continuing education program for ministers already pastoring churches, but who find themselves inadequately prepared for their ministry.[26]

The real problem among Chinese evangelicals is that we have not yet been able to analyze clearly in depth what the needs of the Chinese church are, or what the church's ministry should be other than the traditional evangelical concept of evangelism, church growth, and missions as we have inherited them from the West. The common lack of awareness of crucial issues in leadership training is clearly reflected in the "Covenant" of the Chinese Congress on World Evangelism held in Hong Kong, August 18-25, 1976, by its conspicuous absence. The section on "theological research and writing" deals with theological production in the Chinese language. Nor is the subject of leadership training mentioned elsewhere in the Covenant. This lack of sensitivity to the cruciality of leadership training is probably due to an unquestioning acceptance of the traditional pattern of the ministry and its concomitant style of ministerial training through theological schools.

III. The Fundamental Issue: Leadership Training or Shepherd Formation?

From the above analysis of issues as perceived by missionaries in China (1900-1950) and by theological educators in contemporary Asia (1951-1976), it becomes clear that there is a wide range of opinion as to how ministerial leadership should be trained and what constitute the most crucial issues. Opinions differ according to a few basic variables: (1) how the goal of the ministry is defined; (2) the socio-historical context; (3) the stage of growth of the Christian community involved in the ministry; and (4) the loyalty and background of those involved in leadership training. Correct discernment of one's particular situation in which leadership development is sought becomes, therefore, very important. Failure to discern correctly can, and often does, lead to absolutizing a particular historical variable, such as the acceptance of the Western model of the ministry and of its training style in the Third World.

These variables often become areas of tension, and many of the issues observed above arise from these tension situations. Some of the most frustrating and practically insoluble tensions may be seen in the inherent contradiction between the spiritual goals of the ministry which Third World churches read in the New Testament and the academic goals of training which are embedded in the seminary model imported from the West, and in the contradiction between professed goals of indigenization of the church and the persistent acceptance of the Western model of the professional clergy. It appears, therefore, that such fundamental problems cannot be solved in a piecemeal fashion by upgrading the academic level of a theological school, or looking for some kind of spirituality that goes well with academic excellence, or even attempts at integrating the academic, the spiritual, and the practical. All these perceptions assume the validity of the institutional model of ministerial training. They have failed to question the system as a whole on the level of the ministry itself and from the biblical perspective.

What Is the Ministry for Which Leaders Are Trained?
This is the most fundamental question,[27] for the style of training must be determined by the nature of the ministry. Ministry is the purpose and training is a means. A certain concept of the ministry will demand a certain kind of leaders which require a certain type of training. Studies in the development of the Christian ministry in India and in China have shown that the concept of the ministry that was introduced there in the nineteenth century and persists even now is the model of the

professional pastor from the English-speaking West. This model of a full-time paid ministry is basically a package deal. In it is included: 1. the system of institutional training with its inherent emphasis on academic learning and through it the internalization of secularism, 2. the concept of self-support in terms of a congregation's ability to support such a full-time clergy, and 3. the institutionalization and professionalization of the ministry as symbolized by licensure, ordination, and the myths of status, rank, and authority that go with them. The extent to which this institutional ministry still retains the spiritual character of the New Testament pattern of ministry is a debatable question and one which is increasingly being asked by Third World churches.

Herbert T. Mayer, professor of historical theology at Seminex, St. Louis, has succinctly outlined what may be called the transmutation of the Christian ministry since the fourth century.[28] He noted that ministry in the early church from Jesus to Tertullian was basically a ministry of small Christian communities, wherein believers ministered to each other, centering upon Jesus the Lord whose presence and gifts to the community were administered through the Holy Spirit. Leaders of the community were peers elected to be spiritual leaders in order to enhance the ministry of the community. They had two basic roles: serving and guiding. Leaders considered themselves to be imitators of Christ and guides for their fellow believers in the ongoing process of imitating Christ.

As congregations grew in number, however, the administrative role of a bishop, such as Cyprian of Carthage, began to take on more prominence. Spiritual guidance became transmuted into ruling and together

with it came administrative authority. With the accession
of Constantine in A.D. 312, there occurred a great influx
of people into the church, resulting in lowering the
standards of discipleship, infiltration of secular values
into the church, and breakdown of values held earlier by
Christian communities such as sacrifice, self-giving, love,
and commitment to justice and liberty. Ambrose,
therefore, began to advocate that church leaders practice
true discipleship. Monastic institutions began to develop
and gradually a dichotomy between clergy and laity also
emerged. A superior rank for the clergy was assumed
and their ruling role became even more prominent. But
the clergy among themselves sought to develop spirituality as small group communities, and the concept of
pastors as imitators of Christ still prevailed. Prior to the
seventeenth century the clergy still saw themselves as
preachers of God's goodness, grace, and forgiveness and
sought to preserve charity and justice in the society. But
after the Enlightenment the idea of the pastor as an
imitator of Christ gradually faded away. Today we are all
too familiar with the image of a pastor as a preacher, as a
full-time administrator, and as the leader of his
congregation. Thus there is a serious discrepancy
between the biblical concept of the ministry as practiced
by the early church and the modern concept as developed
by the Western church. The most fundamental issue
facing Third World churches is which model to adopt: the
early church model or the modern Western model of the
ministry. The mode of training will follow from that
choice.

Whose Ministry and Who Are the Trainers?
The "what" of the ministry can best be understood in

terms of "whose ministry is it?" In modern Protestant missions ministry is most commonly understood as denominational ministry. A man would often introduce himself as a minister of such and such denomination because his ordination comes from that denomination, which also determines the sphere of his ministry. Or, under the influence of various types of individualism, people often talk of "so and so's ministry." In most of these cases the ministry is defined in terms of organized activities.

But the New Testament interpretation of the ministry is that all Christian ministry is essentially Christ's own ministry, and our ministry is basically an extension of the ministry of Christ carried out in the power of the Holy Spirit. The Christian ministry is, therefore, essentially a pneumatic ministry that is Christ-directed and that directs to Christ. What does this imply for training? Does it not imply that Christ Himself is the chief trainer and the Holy Spirit is the dean of Christ's school of ministry? This calls for rethinking the role of Christ and of the Holy Spirit in every model of ministerial training.

The current institutional system of church leadership training assumes that only scholars with masters and doctoral degrees (usually obtained from the West) are the ones who are qualified to engage in leadership training for the Christian ministry. When examined under the light of New Testament teaching, this assumption is more than presumptuous; it is an usurpation of Christ's prerogatives. The presumptuous character of the situation is seen in the question: "Whose training goals? Christ's or the scholars' or that of a mission/church?"

What Is the Goal of Ministerial Training?

Goals for ministerial training in theological schools today are usually stated in the catalogs. These goals, in summary, are: to train men (and in some cases, women) for pastoral or other diversified ministries of existing institutional churches so that they can adequately perform their duties in preaching, teaching, visitation, and administration. In other words, to keep the institutional churches going and growing. This type of ministry requires a kind of training that only theological schools of significant stature can provide. Because the ministry has become so professional, ministers must be trained in a very professional manner. That is why theological schools must have highly trained scholars and experts in order to produce quality professionals. Once this elitist concept of a professional ministry is accepted, the goal of academic excellence in theological training becomes inevitable. In this search for academic excellence, at least three essential elements (or sub-goals) in ministerial training must be sacrificed: (1) spiritual development of the seminary community as a whole; (2) spiritual leaders who do not possess higher academic degrees; and (3) the development of new or spiritual forms of training which conflict with the institutional system or which threaten the pursuit of academic excellence. There are also built-in pressures from within the school system as well as from the churches for persisting in the pursuit of academic excellence. Both the school system and the church at large have so sanctified this secular value that they pursue it with a religious devotion, believing that it is all for Christ's glory. In spite of this blind devotion, however, a survey of Third World theological education would testify that most schools have failed to attain their goal of academic excellence. Meanwhile, both students and faculty suffer from spiritual starvation.

The New Testament does not seem to separate goals of the ministry from the goals of training. While interpretations may differ on this point, we can say that the overall goal of the New Testament concept of the ministry is for the new Messianic community to grow corporately into the likeness of Christ through the gifts of the Holy Spirit. It is a corporate mutual sharing or imparting of a variety of "grace" given by Christ for the upbuilding of the body of Christ. Even those whom we would call "leaders," are designated by their spiritual functions: apostles, prophets, evangelists, pastors, and teachers. Their common function was to "equip the saints for the work of the ministry, for the building up of the body of Christ" (Eph. 4:11-12). Training takes place in the acts of ministry within the community, and the actual exercise of gifts provides the occasion for growth.

The New Testament provides many images for those who are called into the ministry. But the dominant image seems to be that of a shepherd, an undershepherd to be sure, serving under the great shepherd of the flock. Christ's charge to Peter after the resurrection was precisely in terms of being a shepherd (John 21:15-19). The undershepherd is to go ahead of the flock in following Christ, in living out the death and resurrection of Christ in their midst and, if possible, to die for the flock. In the undershepherd is incarnated the meaning of the life and death of Christ, and in living example he is "to mediate the dying and living of Christ" to his flock.[29]

What does this concept of the ministry imply for

training goals? Does it not imply that the undershepherd knows the chief shepherd experientially, especially in the pathway of the cross which Jesus trod by way of union with His death and resurrection? Does it not imply that he receive a revelatory knowledge of "the unsearchable riches of Christ" and the "plan of the mystery hidden for ages in God" (Eph. 3:8-9)? Does it not mean that he should be learning a shepherd's heart that loves and cares for the flock? Does it not call for faithfulness to the chief shepherd and master in discharging his duties? In a word, the goals for training of such an undershepherd are none other than to **be** like Christ, to **think** like Christ, and to **serve** like Christ. It is submitting oneself to the Spirit so that Christ might be reproduced in the undershepherd, who then will minister to the flock so as to reproduce Christ in them. This is a work which no institutional school of higher theological learning can do. It is a work of the Holy Spirit, the great teacher of the truth, the only one who is able to form Christ in the very fiber of an undershepherd's life. It is not exactly training. It is spiritual **formation.**

How and Where Does Spiritual Formation Take Place?
Spiritual or personality formation always takes place within a living environment. It is a process of transformation that touches the depth of one's being, that reshapes his motivating values, and that produces an entirely different world view. That transformation involves a living model (Christ), a spiritual artist who is the molder (Holy Spirit), and a living organism within which transformation takes place (the Christian community). In the early church that community was the local church which practiced true discipleship as a living body

of Christ. Today a local church is usually a unit of organization that only partially practices discipleship, and often small groups have to be formed within a congregation to practice Christian community life in a spiritual manner. But whenever and wherever a group of believers gather together in the name of Jesus and function as a living body of Christ according to the New Testament model it becomes a living community. Wherever Christ rules and the Holy Spirit ministers is the spiritual community wherein spiritual transformation takes place. This implies that even a theological school, if it transforms itself into a living spiritual community and practices true discipleship as a local body of Christ, can bring about the kind of spiritual formation that the early church communities did. If this is attempted seriously, the problem of integration of the academic, the spiritual, and the practical would be solved naturally. The place of learned scholars and experts would also fall into their proper place within the body-life as varieties of natural as well as spiritual gifts. This is risky, however, because turning a theological school into a living spiritual community could mean a total transformation of earlier institutional values. But this is exactly what we are hoping for, isn't it?

Therefore, the issues are not how to make training more relevant to the cultural-historical context, not how to bring about integration of trichotomous values, not how to develop a type of spirituality that goes well with academic excellence, but rather how to de-secularize our concept of the ministry and its training style, and how to realize an authentic pneumatic identification with Christ and with His ministry. For overemphasis on the context often distracts our attention from the text, and undue concentration on the text often diverts our attention from the author of the text, resulting in a rational approach to the ministry and to the task of spiritual formation. Christ is not meant to be objectified by our rational "Christologies" but to be formed in the hearts and lives of those who have responded to His call. The text is not meant to be deified, nor its teachings to be dogmatized by human rational formulations, but to be incarnated in lives of those who behold its glory, transforming them into living texts that reflect the image of their author, even Jesus Christ, our Lord. This is what leadership training, or rather shepherd formation, is all about.

Notes

1. The following analysis comes primarily from my own research. For more source information, see "Selected Bibliography on Chinese Theological Education" compiled by me in 1974 (CGST, Inc., P.O. Box 267, Silver Spring, Maryland 20907.).

2. See Jonathan Lees (LMS, Tientsin), "The Best Method of Selecting and Training Native Preachers, etc." *Records of the General Conference of Protestant Missionaries of China* (Shanghai, 1890), 483-490.

3. See Clifton J. Phillips, "The Student Volunteer Movement and Its Role in China Missions, 1886-1920," in John K. Fairbank, ed., *The Missionary Enterprise in China and America* (Cambridge, 1974), 91-109.

4. See C. Stanley Smith, *The Development of Protestant Theological Education in China* (Shanghai, 1941), 54-55.

5. For a comprehensive listing of the 64 theological schools according to regions, see "Special Committee on Theological Education: Statistical Report of Theological Schools" compiled by Frank Price in *Proceedings of the Fifth Annual Meeting of the China Continuation Committee, Hangchow, April 27-May 2, 1917* (Shanghai, 1917), 45-49. The most comprehensive study on theological training in China was done by a special commission under the National Committee for Christian Religious Education in China

published under the title, *Training for Service in the Chinese Church: A Report* (Shanghai, 1935). See Appendix B: "Statistical Chart of Theological and Bible Schools, 1933-1934." There 57 schools were listed under four categories: those requiring high school preparation (13); those requiring junior high preparation(14); those requiring less than junior high (26); and unregistered primary and middle schools (4).

6. See C. S. Smith, *op. cit.,* 88-127, on cooperation and union in theological schools. The architecture of the LMS Theological Institute in Tientsin, for example, was modeled after that of St. John's College, Cambridge University. The Lutheran Seminary in Shekow, Hupeh, was a reproduction of the main building of the Lutheran Seminary in St. Paul.

7. Student enrollment for 1917 was: 128 college graduates, 402 high school and junior high graduates, and 1,331 primary graduates; for 1922: 99 college, 295 middle school; and for 1938: 36 college, 209 middle school; and in 1950: 56 college, 493 high school graduates, 97 junior high graduates—out of a total of 694. See Cheng Chih-yi, "The Past, Present and Future of Theological Education in the Chinese Christian Church," *Shen-hsüeh-chih* (Nanking Seminary Review), XXVI:1-2 (November 1950), 12 (Chinese journal).

8. See John L. Nevius, "Methods of Mission Work: Organization of Stations, Present and Prospective," *Chinese Recorder,* XVII:5 (1886), 165-178; Nevius, *The Planting and Development of Missionary Churches* (Grand Rapids: Baker Book House, 1958). The lecture was first delivered in Korea in 1890 and published in 1895. It exerted a significant influence upon pioneer missionaries in Korea.

9. Witness Lee of the Little Flock (also called Assembly Hall) has produced a training manual called *An Outline of the Training Course for Service* (Taipei, mimeographed and bi-lingual, n.d.), 95 pages. For a short description of the Little Flock, see Allen J. Swanson, *Taiwan: Mainline versus Independent Church Growth: A Study in Contrast* (South Pasadena: William Carey Library, 1970), 188-218.

10. Wang Chih-hsin, for example, argued for the indigenization of theological schools as the first step toward the training of indigenous church leaders for China. See Ying Yuan-tao, "The Background and Contents of Chinese Christian Thought, 1922-1927," in *Wen-she* Monthly (in Chinese), I:9-10 (September 1925), 18; see

also Wang Chin-shin, "Indigenous Church and Indigenous Writings," *Wen-she*, I:6 (May 1926), 1-17.

11. For an analysis of the situation, see my article, "Foreign Missions and Theological Education: Taiwan, a Case Study," *Evangelical Missions Quarterly* (Fall, 1972), 1-16.

12. See Shoki Coe, "In Search of Renewal in Theological Education," *Theological Education,* IX:4 (Summer 1973), 233-243, and James Berquist, "TEF and the Uncertain Future of Third World Theological Education," idem, 244-253.

13. Coe, idem, 234.

14. Berquist, idem, 245.

15. Coe, idem, 237.

16. This breakthrough was probably due to James A. Berquist's influence since he joined the staff of TEF in the early 1970's. Berquist and P. Kamber Manickam's study, *The Crisis of Dependency in Third World Ministries* (Madras: The Christian Literature Society, 1974), represents serious questioning of the professional ministry.

17. Coe, idem, 242-243.

18. Emerito P. Nacpil, "The Question of Excellence in Theological Education," *Southeast Asia Journal of Theology,* XVI:1 (1975), 55-59.

19. Idem, 57.

20. David S. C. Chen, "The Task of Theological Education in Northeast Asia Today; Viewed from a Theological Angle," *Northeast Asia Journal of Theology* (September 1971), 20.

21. T. F. Cole, P. G. Craighill, C. F. Hsiao, M. D. Wogstad, "Personality and Spiritual Development in Relation to Theological Education," *Theology and the Church,* XI:2 (April 1974), 1-13. This is a bi-lingual journal of the Tainan Theological College.

22. Chung Choon Kim, "Seeking Relevance in Methods of Theological Education," *NEAJT* (September, 1971), 39.

23. Development of ATA may be followed by subscription to *Asia Theological News,* published quarterly by the Association. Starting in

1977, ATA is also going to publish a semi-annual journal called *Asia Theological Bulletin*. (Contact Bong Rin Ro, Th.D., Executive Secretary, ATA, P.O. Box 28-4, Shihlin, Taipei 111, Taiwan, ROC.)

24. Noboru Yamaguchi and John Chongnahm Cho, "The Integration of the Academic, the Spiritual, and the Practical in Theological Training," in *Voice of the Church in Asia: Report of Proceedings, Asia Theological Association Consultation. Hong Kong. December 27, 1973-January 4, 1974* (Singapore, ATA, 1975), 81-90.

25. On a general summary of the development of the Chinese church in diaspora, see my article, "The Christian Mission to the Chinese People," *Lutheran World*, XXIII:4 (1976) 262-268.

26. See "Formation of the Association for Promotion of Chinese Theological Education," *Reformed Ecumenical Synod News Exchange*, IX:2 (Feb. 22, 1972), 769-772. The complete book-length proceedings of the 1972 and 1973 Consultation on Chinese Theological Education (Hong Kong and Baguio respectively) in Chinese may be ordered from APCTE office, 5 Devon Road, Kowloon, Hong Kong.

27. This question is also being asked in the West. See Daniel C. Batson and D. Campbell Wyckoff, "An Alternative Model for Ministerial Education," *Theological Education*, IX:2 (Winter 1973), 100-111. However, Batson still assumes the validity of the professional ministry and advocates two levels of training: sensitization to problems and providing tools for problem solving.

28. "Pastoral Roles and Mission Goals," *Currents in Theology and Mission*, III:5 (October 1976), 292-302.

29. A. T. Hanson, "Shepherd, Teacher and Celebrant in the New Testament Conception of the Ministry," in David Paton (ed.), *New Forms of Ministry* (London: Edinburgh House Press, 1965), 21.

The Plight of the Burned-Out Pastor

31

Dwight J. McFadden, Jr.

Urban pastor, urban church, urban ministry—the expectations are high and adequate resources to meet the challenge often lacking. The urban church must address itself to many needs. The urban pastor often becomes the means through which the congregation meets these needs. Yet the problems the pastor faces demand more than one person can give on a sustained level. The conditions and the needs of the people with whom the pastor deals tend to take an untimely toll of energy and gifts. The pastor wears down; he begins to suffer what some persons have labeled "burnout."

The symptoms which characterize "burned out" pastors include the following:

- The pastor may dehumanize the persons with whom he works by treating them as objects rather than human beings.
- The pastor may make light of stressful issues or problems being dealt with in the community or congregation.
- The pastor may frequently be unavailable to people and for meetings.
- The pastor becomes sick more frequently and tends to be depressed.

These are only a few of the symptoms which my occur. Little research has been done on this question, but clearly the urban situation poses unique problems. Dr. Christina Maslach, assistant psychology professor at the University of California, has done research in this area. Professor LeRoy Spanial of Boston University and colleague Shulamit Teck, director of Eastern Institute for Group and Family Theories, have done research specifically on the professional "burnout" syndrome. People in helping professions are most apt to suffer from burnout.

The Leader's Personal Needs

The leadership of an urban church must minister to the whole person. The pastor must have the sum total of his own needs met in the same way. Just as his ministry to people is inclusive—social, economic, psychological, physical, and spiritual—his needs in these areas must also be fulfilled adequately. The urban pastor has fellowship with members of the congregation, but he also needs to socialize with his peers in the ministry who are working at church building in the city. In many urban settings there are few colleagues of his own denomination with whom he can take counsel. Most pastors in the city do participate in interdenominational ministerial associations, but some pastors are unable to share with anyone the burdens they carry from ministering to their congregations. The pastor may think he is less than a leader if he cannot handle the problems facing the congregation, much less his own problems. He may forget that other urban pastors experience similar problems and can empathize and give counsel.

In the city we find that pastors do not always have sufficient resources. The cost of living is higher than in most nonurban areas. If a pastor has to worry about how he is going to make it through the week, he will have a hard time keeping his mind on his work. The tent-making ministry is usually a problem for pastors who work in urban areas. There is not enough time to give both to the work of the church and to a job. One of these obligations will suffer. If an urban pastor works hard at both ministry and self-support, he will find the strain producing an even quicker burnout. Mennonite urban pastors are not getting rich!

Mental fatigue is a common problem among urban pastors. High expectations by the congregation and/or sponsoring agencies provide an extra amount of pressure. It is usually not said, but it is understood that the urban pastor has a field to harvest in the city and he is expected to pick a record crop. The urban pastor is not always prepared to handle all of the areas of planting, nurturing, and harvesting. He may know the problems facing the community but is not able to deal with them. He may be able to deal with the problems but does not know the community. Either way the urban pastor is frustrated, even though he has one of these strengths. The advance of psychological strain is rapid when energies become frustrated.

Pastors put a great deal of mileage on their bodies in the urban community. They run themselves down physically. Attention to long-range planning slips away when the needs are immediate. The pastor may also lack the right kind of physical exercise. He wears himself out by running all over the community.

Urban pastors are so overwhelmed by their task that they forget that work can be delegated to others or that a team can handle the job better. And a team is not always available to help. Urban pastors frequently take on a superman role. They are often forced into this role by the expectation that they can do all things. A superman syndrome develops. The pastor thinks that no one can do the job as well as he can and that it needs immediate care and he should be responsible for it.

The pastor does not always find time to cultivate his spiritual life. He is concerned about the spiritual well-being of others and sometimes neglects his own spiritual life and that of his family. The urban pastor needs a significant person with whom he can talk about his and his family's spiritual welfare. It is easy to overlook needs close to home because he is preoccupied with his ministry to others.

Role Conflict

The urban pastor faces certain expectations by virtue of his position in the community. He is put in the situation where he is a general practitioner, but he must be a specialist in order to be a success. He must continually deal with these conflicting demands.

The effective urban minister must be oriented toward his church community, while success requires denominational orientation. These demands are sometimes in conflict. The urban pastor stands in a prophetic role, but if he acts as an advocate and speaks prophetically, he does not fit the model of the saint. In addition the urban pastor faces time conflicts: long hours of work compete with family obligations. He must deal with these varied and conflicting expectations and must at the same time develop an authentic ministry that preserves his personal integrity. The urban pastor who cannot move in and out of these many roles may be consumed by the stress and tension caused by role conflict.

Organizational Needs

The urban church's response to local opportunities may grow into an institutional program. The organization of this operation or institution becomes the responsibility of the pastor. Frequently the institution moves away from the church and runs parallel to it. The pastor's energies are divided between leading and fulfilling the job originally assigned by the congregation. The shift creates a gap and sometimes a conflict of expectations. The institution takes more of the pastor's time; the congregation as such gets less attention. The dilemma is real. While the purpose of the church is ministry, the institutional ministry replaces church. How is the purpose and program of the church kept in creative balance?

Where Do We Go from Here?

We have noted some of the problems and difficult situations the urban pastor faces—how do we work at solutions to some of these problems?

In a leadership seminar in Elkhart, Indiana, October 1977, a group of urban pastors and lay leaders worked through what it means to be a biblical community and fulfill our mandate. Reflection on this seminar may help to pinpoint some ways in which we as a church can work at the plight of the burned out pastor. The seminar included some models that may be helpful for pastoring in the urban setting.

A look at the nature of the believers church helps us draw a conclusion about our responsibility to our shepherds who are becoming burned out.

In relationship to Christ, as a believers church we are:
- A chosen race (I Pet 2:9-10)
- The body of Christ (Eph 6:15-16)
- The household of God (Eph 2:19-22)
- An eschatological community (Acts 1:11, Mt 25:14-30, I Thess 5:12)

In relationship to each other we share:
- Fellowship, love, and caring (Acts 2:43-47, Eph 4:15, I Cor 13)
- Admonition, forgiveness, convenanting (Mt 18:15-18, I Cor 5:3)
- A variety of gifts (I Cor 12)
- Local and universal completeness (Acts 15, Jn 17:21)

In relationship to the world we are:
- •Pilgrims and strangers (Mt 10:16ff, Jn 2:15)
- •Ministers of reconciliation (II Cor 5:17-20)
- •Witnesses and prophets (Acts)
- •Disciples and citizens (Rom 12:13, I Pet 2:4-17)

In looking at how we relate to each other as a believers church, we are made aware that a variety of gifts are given to us (I Cor 12). In the urban area it seems, logically, that we would have a **group ministry** or team ministry to apply the variety of gifts given to us. A group ministry would allow different members of the team to take on differing responsibilities in accord with their gifts. There would be built-in support systems with this kind of arrangement.

The group could carry the burden and the work load together rather than strapping down one person with the total responsibility. Members of the leadership team could take sabbaticals and breaks without undue interruption of the congregation's ministry. A senior pastor might oversee the work of the team which would function as a core group leading the congregation's internal and external ministry.

Ideally, a congregation will have increasing people resources from among its members to complement and extend the specialized functions of its leaders or shepherds. In looking at the development of people resources for urban churches, one model to consider we might call a **continuing education program.** This program would touch every area of the lives of people in the urban congregation—home, church, occupation, and school.

The continuing education program would function on all levels in the church. All members would be involved in the study of family life, the Bible, how to better prepare for a future occupation, how to be best prepared in the present occupation or school situation. The congregation would discern members' gifts and weaknesses and would provide counseling support for improvement and follow up on development and future support.

One example of how this method might work is the case of a fictitious person. John Brown has been a member of the church since he was 14 years old. John is now 23, and his family has since become a part of the church. The pastor counseled with John's parents and siblings during John's participation in the congregation. John was taught the Bible, has seen family life models and received tutoring on problems he had relating to school. The pastor challenged John to consider a particular profession.

John had not thought about college before he started attending church, but now the pastor had helped to plant a seed. John admired a psychologist the church had in to lead a number of seminars. John wanted to be a psychologist. One of the members on the leadership team helped John to find out what it takes to be a psychologist. They sent for catalogs and information for different colleges.

John wanted to attend a Christian college. The leadership team encouraged this move. The youth leader at church along with other members of the leadership team helped John apply at a Christian college. The pastor with John investigated the quality of education and the social atmosphere there. The pastor contacted the college and helped to work out a financial package. At college John received periodic visits from the pastor and members of the church. He was encouraged to maintain involvement with a local church.

John worked around home during summers and also participated as a leader in the youth group in his congregation.

John graduated from college. He is doing graduate work at the local university and is working there as well. He is helping the congregation as a member of the leadership team in youth counseling. John is being encouraged by the congregation to do more postgraduate study. The congregation is growing in ministry and developing potential along with John.

Following along with one of its members must be an invigorating experience for the leaders, too. The team by force of interest and involvement is challenged to grow to its potential.

Practical Pastoral Training

Urban pastors are in a position to take advantage of institutions of higher education in their local communities. They need to be motivated to continue their education, share gained knowledge, and get away from the demands of ministry for periods of time. The urban pastor should be required to do a specified number of hours of study credit per year in practical theology, urban ministry, urban studies, and other areas of need.

The pastor should take courses throughout the year and meet with two one-week periods of class time at a college or seminary away from home and one course at a local institution. Pastors could work toward a bachelor's degree in practical theology or in other areas. Pastors with BA's could work toward MA's in practical theology, religion, and so on. One would hope that the work could be done at a Mennonite college or seminary.

The pastor's motivation for self-improvement and a break from work would be one of the requirements that the congregation and sponsoring agencies and the conference would include as part of his job description. Apart from studies on campus, the pastor would maintain contact with a counselor for work on a project that would deal with some aspect of the congregational program.

Congregational Life Audit

A program could be set up whereby urban congregations could evaluate and report progress on the goals they set for themselves. Ways of developing skills needed to carry out the program for the church could be shared. The life audit could also be set up to report community trends. It might measure the influence of the congregation in the community. It could report the investment of money, time, and skills in a congregational project and the return on these investments even if they are very small. This report and audit would check the vital signs of a congregation.

The congregation would undertake a semiannual review. An outside resource person would be called on for one of the reviews and for asking hard questions. The review would help get at the church's ministry, its needs and the needs of the pastor, how to plan for the future and what traps to avoid.

How do we succeed in urban ministry and avoid burning out our leaders? We need to evaluate the conditions, change conditions, develop leadership models that have built-in support systems and see that leaders are adequately taken care of. This may mean that more planning and resources will have to be available for urban congregations.

32

Paul M. Miller

A Shape for the Congregation of the Future

A Survey of the Present Situation

Some new wine is stretching the old skins. What shape will the new churchly reality take?

An ever-deepening study of our New Testament and Anabaptist roots is forcing us to ask whether we have adequate structures for decision-making, appropriate settings for discerning one another's gifts, or the best ways to hear a new believer's request for baptism. Our theology calls emphatically for biblical preaching, but some advocates of house fellowships see little place for it in the small group setting. Our faith calls for mutual admonition and discipline, but the form of much of our congregational life does not encourage it. We need mutual aid, prophetic action, mission, and evangelism which fits our faith, but the forms and structures we have borrowed need some stretching.

The size of our "average" congregation seems stuck at the worst possible plateau, 80 to 100 members. This is much too large to experience the closeness, mutual discipline, sharing, and group decision-making which a good "house fellowship" can know. It is also much too small to enjoy the economies of scale, the employment of specialized ministers, the peer-group of youth, and many

of the other benefits which go with a "great congregation." In many of these smaller congregations members
wear out, using their time and energies trying to maintain
the machinery needed for the educational, fellowship, and
missionary ministries of a 400-member congregation.

Some of our most evangelistic and fastest growing
congregations have faced a serious crisis as they have tried
to plan ahead for adequate facilities. It was almost as if
they were being made to feel guilty because they were
growing. Some persons who saw primarily the need for
and advantages of the small house fellowship have hinted
darkly that it is a decadent and self-centered church which
spends money for church buildings. Others argued that
since the early church did not build specialized edifices for
their meeting houses, therefore the church throughout
history should not do so either!

In some recent discussions the existence of the
"meetinghouse" option was ignored and the assumption
made that believers choose between either of two options:
the house fellowship or the sanctuary church. This paper
does not consider a sanctuary church as an option at all,
and proposes a church made up of a number of house
fellowships united in a great congregation instead.

A new seriousness is evident among some of those who
seek to plan ahead for needed space for the shared
activities of the larger household of faith or great
congregation. New ways are being sought and found to
make full use of available facilities. The time-honored
concept of the meetinghouse is being reclaimed and used.
There is a new determination to embody careful
stewardship in all planning and to symbolize the faith of
the believers church in any meetinghouses which are
erected.

Some congregational committees are doing time-use-
cost studies to ascertain just how much per week per
member a meetinghouse will cost if amortized over the

years it may reasonably be expected to serve the congregation. A number of studies have disclosed that the amount members have spent for their meetinghouse has compared closely to what members have spent for their year's vacation trip or other expenses in comparable categories.

Churchly Realities and the Best Setting for Each

A. A part of churchly reality happens best in the house fellowship, such as:

1. Hearing the testimony of the "confessing man" (Matt 16:18) and affirming his readiness for baptism;
2. Binding and loosing as members help one another to follow Jesus in life (Matt 18:17);
3. "Greeting the brethren" and confronting in brotherly admonition and discipline (1 Tim 6:10);
4. Forgiving one another after failures (basin and towel, Jn 13:14), declaring absolution, in a vital brotherhood of service and forgiveness;
5. Specific day-by-day caring, sharing food, bearing one another's burdens, engaging in fellowship evangelism;
6. Discerning and affirming gifts by which the Holy Spirit creates body (1 Cor 12:18,23);
7. Praying for one another during "sendings" or prayers for healing (Jas 5:14).
8. Giving and receiving counsel concerning ethical issues encountered in the world;
9. Assisting one another in problems related to personal faith and faithfulness, vocational choice, marriage, change of jobs, retirement, etc;
10. Enriching family living through times of recreation, nature study, picnics, and wholesome fun on an intergenerational basis. The house fellowship may be wise to hold two kinds of services—one for

　　fellowship, and one for serious discussion and
　　decision;
11. Banding together to move out in evangelism, estab-
　　lishing a new house fellowship in another area;
　　expanding by planned division;
12. Sharing ecstatic experiences, creating and singing
　　of spiritual songs.

B. A part of churchly reality is best mediated through the
great congregation gathered in the meetinghouse,
such as:

1. The larger congregation can provide balance, the
   "multitude of counselors" and their wisdom. Small
   groups tend to suffer from one-sidedness (3 Jn 9).
   Seldom can an intense small group avoid bias,
   narrowness, or what group dynamics researchers
   call "group think."
2. The gifts God's Spirit places first seem given to the
   great congregation or meetinghouse group. These
   include the equipping gifts of apostle, prophet,
   evangelist, pastor-teacher (Eph 4:11). It appears
   that God's Spirit placed these first (1 Cor 12:28) and
   does so repeatedly (1 Tim 1:18).
3. The great congregation helps decide when small
   groups disagree (Acts 15).
4. The great congregation can ignite the inspiration
   for festivals, celebrations, thanksgivings, baptisms,
   covenant renewal, eucharists, protests, missionary
   thrusts, and mass evangelism.
5. The great congregation can provide exposition and
   teaching of the meaning of the Scriptures and God's
   mighty acts so that the pilgrim people can find their
   places in history.
6. The great congregation can train for and administer
   programs of relief, social action, mission, prophetic
   witness to principalities, and cooperate with the
   agencies of worldwide relief, mission, and action.

7. The great congregation can engage in interchurch conversation and fellowship.

Suggestions About the Shape Congregational Life Might Take

A. Congregations using large meetinghouses should seek an optimum size of 250 to 400 members. Small fellowships should consider banding together to form a great congregation.

B. All members should hold a single membership expressed in two levels of churchly reality: in the meetinghouse or great congregation, and in a house fellowship which is in a satellite and supporting relationship.

C. The name "church" should be reserved for membership and participation in the total churchly reality, both house fellowship and meetinghouse congregation.

D. Churchwide agencies should correspond with and relate primarily to the large meetinghouse or great congregation. Paul wrote letters to the entire area-church, the great congregation, at Ephesus, or Philippi, or Rome, or Thessalonica, rather than to every individual house fellowship. Obviously he sought to avoid the real possibility of every small house fellowship going its independent way. That same concern should be deeply felt today.

E. Each great congregation should be led by a team with a central or chief "Servant-of-the-Word," assisted by helpers or elders, one selected by each house fellowship. The chief Servant-of-the-Word should be ordained, whereas elders might be suitably commissioned. Ordination serves to symbolize the centrality of the Scriptures and their teaching.

F. The decisions about major policies, sanctions, positions, and prophetic pronouncements should be agreed upon by the great congregation gathered in the meetinghouse. The house fellowships may initiate discussion and submit proposals or serve as a task force for study.

G. Serious cases of discipline should be referred by the house fellowship, by and through their elder, to the leadership team and the great congregation for action.

H. Love-feasts should be held in the small house fellowship, as often and as spontaneously as the Spirit moves, while the more liturgical Lord's Supper should be observed in the great congregation gathered in the meetinghouse. Washing of the saints' feet may well be observed along with the house fellowship love feasts.

I. Instruction of each new believer (judging a person to be faithful to the Lord), and recommending him or her for baptism should be done by the house fellowship. The actual baptizing should be in charge of the elders and the house fellowship but performed in the midst of the great congregation.

J. Scrutinizing of one another's budgets and endorsing one another's giving intentions should be done in the house fellowship, but adoption of the congregational budget should be done in the great congregation after all the elders have brought in their report of the giving intentions of house fellowship members.

K. Church letters should be forwarded by the central office of the congregation, with the approval of all of the elders; but the actual letter, which includes a description of the member's gifts for ministry, should be countersigned by at least two-thirds of the members of his or her house fellowship.

L. The worship services of the house fellowship should emphasize sharing, praise, testimonies, decision-making, spontaneous mutual aid, love feasts, spiritual songs, laying on of hands, prayers for healing, giving and receiving of admonition, Bible study, intercessory prayer sessions, evangelistic conversation, mutual forgiveness and reconciliation, and hearing and discussing reports from the great congregation or church agencies. The worship services of the great congregation should emphasize expository preaching, choral readings, the use of majestic hymns and mass choirs, recital of creeds or confessions of faith, formulation of words of prophetic appeal to people in power, festivals appropriate to the Christian calendar, receiving of missionary challenge, evangelistic appeal, and hearing reports from house fellowships.

M. Ideally every member should attend at least two services of worship every week: one objective, ordered worship service in the great congregation; and one service of a more intimate and subjective character held in the house fellowship. The fellowship group may meet either during the Sunday school hour or on Sunday evening, or on a weekday evening in the home of one of the members. The Sunday morning hour should be reserved for the worship of the great congregation in the meetinghouse and for Christian education experiences for children. Each congregation should decide their own schedule.

N. Because of the heavy agenda of churchly realities which should occur in the small group or house fellowship, its services should be at least one and one-half hours in length. The great congregation's worship might be attempted in an hour, but more time will be required if and as all of the house fellowships send in their reports and suggestions as they ought to do.

O. The initiative for linking house fellowships and the great congregation should rest with equal urgency upon both. Every house fellowship should be reminded that it is in danger of becoming schismatic if it does not seek linkage with a great congregation. Likewise every great congregation should feel the imperative to reach out to welcome emerging fellowships, recent converts, immigrant groups of believers which are in the area, and to promise to take seriously any messages the house fellowship sends in. House fellowships should not merely seek ties with other small groups like themselves. House fellowships should organize their own inner life according to the gifts discerned in their midst.

P. Officers of the denominational district or conference should be given a mandate to help house fellowships and great congregations to work out a happy two-way flow of mutual support, admonition, interaction, discernment, and a program of united action.

Q. Buildings, supplies, and equipment could be under the administrative oversight of a resources committee of the large meetinghouse congregation, with constant concern that facilities are fully used and freely shared so that all possible funds can go to serve the poor and further world evangelism.

R. Membership records, including the location of each member in a house fellowship, should be maintained by the central office of the great congregation. Persons who are invalids, shut-ins, or those unable to attend meetinghouse or house fellowship services should be the special concern of the leadership team and of the house fellowship, and provision should be made for their nurture and fellowship.

S. Persons who desire only the great congregation experiences held in the meetinghouse, and who for any reason do not wish to be a part of a house fellowship, should be the special concern of the leadership team. It may be that a less demanding type of traditional prayer meeting can be arranged for them until they gain courage and readiness to venture into a house fellowship. After all, many of the successes being reported by house fellowships are those which serve primarily young people and their peers. Forming house fellowships which include the life span will likely be more difficult. Both the great congregation and the house fellowship shall be concerned about the Christian education of youth and children and each provide the portion of it best suited to that setting.

T. Funerals should be in charge of the leadership team of the congregation with special testimonies from the deceased person's house fellowship members. The sustained concern and listening love which grieving survivors always need should become the concern of the house fellowship.

U. Weddings should be in charge of the leadership team of the great congregation with special involvement of house fellowship members as this may be most appropriate. The great congregation may well appoint task forces to work at the strengthening of marriage relationships. House fellowships should seek to give counsel as they are able so that marriage may be truly a churchly experience.

V. The leadership team should offer leadership in long-range planning, in organizational development, in leadership development, in suggesting the person for the ordained Servant-of-the-Word, and in coming to aid of a house fellowship which experiences serious crisis.

W. The Board of Congregational Ministries of the denomination may well give counsel to small fellowships which emerge far removed from other house fellowships in order that they might find ways of banding together into a great congregation. The Board might well give continued study to the division of churchly activity between the small house fellowship and the great congregation.

Planning for Growth

33

Richard Showalter

In our time Christianity can truly make a practical claim to being the universal religion. Buddhism and Islam have been missionary and universal in their outlook from the beginning, but only Christianity *has now found a home in almost every country of the world; it has adherents among all the races of men, from the most sophisticated of westerners to the aborigines of the inhospitable deserts of Australia; and there is no religion of the world which has not yielded a certain number of converts to it. This is something that has never happened before in the history of the world* (Neill 1964:14f).

Furthermore, much of this expansion has taken place in our own lifetime. To me, a product of the college and university atmosphere of the 1960s, this seems almost miraculous! During the '60s, we were confronted on every side by evidences of the decay of the church. I had been reared by missionary parents, and I carried the vision of following in their train. But the overwhelming impression that I gained during my college and university years was one of profound pessimism about the contemporary church. The age of missions is over, we were told. (Sometimes what was meant by that was simply that the age of colonialism is over, but the message was not always clear.)

What we did not know was that while Western colonialism was collapsing, the churches which had been planted in Africa and Asia were growing vigorously. We did not realize that even while Western Christian students battled with secularism, independent churches were springing up in Africa. Today there are more than 6,000 such groups in Africa. Many of them are confined to a single ethnic group, but others are quite large and spread into more than one country. One of these groups with which Mennonites have had some contact is the Kimbanguist Church of Zaire which is a good deal larger than the world Mennonite brotherhood and impresses us with its Christian pacifism.

In short, we did not carry a vision of world Christianity. I speak for myself first of all, but I think that I also speak for a great majority of my generation. We were so caught up in the throes of Western civilization that we did not catch the vision of a world fellowship of Christians, a reality given by the Holy Spirit in the midst of the eclipse of the West.

African church growth has perhaps been most impressive. At the turn of the century there were approximately ten million Christians in Africa. By the mid-70s there were 130 million. Barrett's projection for the year 2000 A.D. is that Christians will comprise forty-six percent of Africa's population, about triple the present number (1970:47). Whether or not the projection is correct, the numerical expansion of the church in Africa in our own day is enough to cheer the heart of any believer.

The case of Latin America is somewhat more complex. The rapidly-expanding Latin Protestant church is growing largely at the expense of the Roman Catholics and so does not represent direct conversion from totally non-Christian society. The figures are impressive, nevertheless. At the turn of the century there were approximately 50,000

Protestants in Latin America. Today the number of Protestants has passed twenty million, with predictions of up to 100 million for 2000 A.D. Protestantism is growing numerically at a rate three times that of the population in general.

Statistically, Asia seems to be least encouraging, with more than two million people who will not even hear the gospel unless the word is carried by cross-cultural messengers. Yet even in Asia there have been movements of expansion which thrill Christians around the world. Indonesia now has something over six million Christians, and about fifteen percent of the population of South Korea has confessed Christ. There is much in India and China to give reason for optimism, though both contain millions of persons who have not bowed their knees to Christ. The Spirit must be yearning with a tremendous love over the lands which produced such saints as Sadhu Sundar Singh and Watchman Nee.

These figures indicate the growth of the **churches** in parts of the world other than Europe and North America. The number of **missionaries** sent by North America has also grown significantly, from 10,700 in 1945 to 35,070 in 1972.

But more significant than this is the growing number of missionaries now being sent by churches in such countries as Nigeria, India, Brazil, and the Philippines. In our day the idea of foreign missions is slowly but surely being separated from the notion of colonial exploitation; for this we can only praise God.

Missions in Anabaptist/Mennonite History
Modern American Mennonites consider their tradition to be essentially missionary. The Great Commission appears over and over in the confessions of faith and court testimonies of the sixteenth-century Anabaptists. Littell shows how the idea of the restitution of the early church

led to a recovery of a missionary vision which propelled missioners all over Europe. It was assumed that the Great Commission was binding upon all church members (1964:109-37).

The Anabaptist rejection of ties between church and state and the institution of believer's baptism were two theological corollaries of the mission they embraced. The view of the church as a voluntary community (against the state church concept) and the understanding of Christian commitment as "free and uncompelled decision" were the underlying presuppositions of a theology of the church which demanded obedience to the Great Commission as a fundamental aspect of Christian faithfulness (Yoder 1971:15f). In all these respects, the Anabaptists were distinguished from the Protestant reformers of their century. It remained for such Protestant groups as the Moravians, the Quakers, the Wesleyans, and the German Pietists to promote the free church concepts which led to the awakening of the Protestant conscience for obedience to the Great Commission.

It may also be pointed out that Anabaptist missionizing was both structured and unstructured. The Moravian Hutterite colonies were "perhaps the greatest missionary center of the sixteenth century," with deliberate strategy for planting congregations all over Europe (Littell 1964:120). In contrast, much of the early movement had been marked by spread through persecution, exile, merchant mobility, and more or less haphazard wandering by lay preachers. Yet it would be wrong to assume that the itineracy of such men as Blaurock and Denk was unplanned and dictated entirely by the circumstances of persecution. In fact, the famous "Martyr Synod" held at Augsburg August 20, 1527, was a strategy-forming meeting which led to dividing out the sections of Europe on a great map of evangelistic enterprise. All this took place in the face of opposition so intense that only two or three members of the Martyr Synod lived longer than five years after the meeting.

We can analyze the degrees of cross-cultural transmission of the gospel with the following scheme:

E_0 - taking the gospel to nominal Christians in our own culture

E_1 - taking the gospel to non-Christian neighbors in our own culture

E_2 - taking the gospel cross-culturally, but within the same "family" of cultures

E_3 - taking the gospel cross-culturally to a radically different culture than our own.

It is striking that when we think of the Anabaptists in light of this scheme, their evangelism was almost all E_0 or E_1. They were taking the gospel to neighbors who shared their language and culture. They were part of a "people movement" to Christ. We can only guess at whether they would have sent foreign missionaries if the persecution had not been so intense.

After the Thirty Years' War the descendants of the Anabaptists "disappeared." Hounded by the state authorities on account of refusal to give military service, they lived in withdrawn communities in Switzerland, South Germany, Moravia, and the Netherlands. Some moved eastward to Poland and Russia; others moved westward to colonial America. The missionary vision which had been such an explosive force in the congregations of the sixteenth century was largely snuffed out. The Constantinianism which they had rejected so steadfastly was reproduced on a smaller scale within their own communities, communities which became even more decisively separated from the dominant culture when they moved to Russia and America and continued speaking German for many generations. In short, they became a "tribe," distinguished from the populace by language, endogamous marriage and dress, as well as by a faith radical in implication but which was in some respects "sleeping" in the womb of a subculture.

Mennonite church growth was by then almost entirely biological. Parents gave birth to large families. Many children remained in the Mennonite Church, faithful to the teaching they received. During the eighteenth and nineteenth centuries, revival movements in the wider culture appealed to many Mennonite youth, and significant numbers joined other Protestant groups.

In the last quarter of the nineteenth century came the series of events which have been termed the "Mennonite Great Awakening" (Wenger 1966:14). Increased use of the English language opened the churches to greater contact with other Christian groups in America. Innovations such as the Sunday school and the protracted meeting were debated, then gradually accepted. A General Conference was formed in 1897, mission agencies were formed, and church schools were instituted.

With the establishment of mission agencies, North American Mennonites moved from a position of biological reproduction to an attempt to transplant the "tribe" in other places—American cities, then India, South America, and Africa. Of course, our first missions were not consciously considered "transplanting the tribe," but in many respects this would be the most accurate designation for what we went about doing. We intended to plant churches which would share in full our theological tradition—itself a Western tradition. We intended to plant churches which would have some success in transmitting the specific forms and symbols which had become meaningful to us in our North American subculture. For example, in 1929 a committee from the Virginia Conference presented criticisms to Mennonite Board of Missions which (among other things) asked for conforming the dress of the Indian missionaries to that of the home church (particularly in avoiding neckties) and outlawing the wearing of the moustache **by Indian Christians** (Lapp 1972:59-63). The manual of the Mission Board contained such proscriptions until the 1940s.

A wealth of documentation could be provided for this phase of missionary understanding, a phase which is not entirely past. Perhaps it is never completely past for any people. The missionaries themselves, of course, were among the first to realize that such "transplantation" would not be possible, but they were often hard put to explain that impossibility to people back home.

A third phase of missionary understanding might be described as the commitment to plant congregations without regard for tribal transplantation, recognizing the Western "at-homeness" of both our theological tradition and our forms and symbols. This happened first among Mennonite missionaries in India where they came under the influence of J. W. Pickett and others who were becoming aware of "people movements" as a powerful vehicle for evangelization. It happened in East Africa in the 1940s when the Mennonite missionaries were involved with the East African Revival movement and experienced the growth of the church on a new basis. It is happening now in Ethiopia. Of course the same awareness has entered the hearts and minds of Mennonite Christians in many other settings as well. Yet many of us are living too largely in phase one or two, paying only lip service to phase three.

Now look again at the E-scheme on the degrees of cross-cultural transmission of the gospel. It is striking that Mennonite missionizing in the twentieth century has been predominantly E_2 or E_3. North American Mennonites as a whole have never experienced on home soil the excitement of being part of a people movement, though we have engaged in quite a bit of cross-cultural missionary work—some of it quite "successful." Perhaps it is this which separates us most decisively from the history we claim, that of sixteenth-century Anabaptism and that of the early church. It may be that those who lived through the Mennonite Great Awakening or those who are involved today in the charismatic renewal have come closest to the experience of such a movement. But all this has taken place primarily **within** a Christian community.

What would be the difference between a mission agency which is born and lives in a growing movement and a mission agency which is born and lives in a brotherhood which reproduces mainly by the conversion of its own children?

North American Mennonite Church Growth

As noted above, Mennonite foreign missions have been fairly successful in the twentieth century. Churches have been planted in nearly forty countries outside North America and Europe, and many of these are now autonomous.

In North America, however, we cannot so easily point to a good record. We have never actually participated in the formation of rapidly growing churches on home soil except through biological growth. What explanations can be offered for this difference?

It may well be that the sociological answer is far more significant than we have recognized. There is an important sense in which nearly **all** Mennonite witness has been cross-cultural witness since we left Europe. Our ethnic heritage has remained strongly intact through many generations on American soil, even to the persistence in many localities of the use of a second language well into the twentieth century. Thus our "neighbors" have generally lived in a different world than we. However, we have often assumed that they are genuinely our neighbors in the sense of sharing a common culture, and so have not recognized that the same principles which have been used by our foreign missionaries in sharing the gospel must also be used at home. This is the sociological reason why it is "easy" for some Baptists to grow churches in America, while it is "hard" for Mennonites to do the same.

Personhood and Peoplehood in Church Growth

One of the most fruitful insights about the numerical growth of the church to have emerged with new power in recent years is that Christianity is passed from person to person along lines of friendship and kinship and within homogeneous social units. At first thought there may seem to be nothing new in such a statement. But when unpacked it is dynamite.

Our usual question in considering the communication of the gospel is, "How do people become Christians? This kind of question carries a highly individualistic focus; it is the question a psychologist asks, and rightly so. However, there is another question with a sociological orientation which is equally valid, but too often ignored: "How do peoples become Christian?"

The fact is that people do not become Christians in isolation from their social context. I am a believer today because my father and mother were earnest Christians. To put it another way, my **people** were nearly all believers.

It is easy enough for us to accept this for ourselves, but what does it mean for the person whose social context is un-Christian or anti-Christian? We have often gone to such persons with a message of "Come out from among them and be separate!" "Leave your father and mother!" "Give up your old friendships!" "Come join us!"

There is enough truth in this to make it plausible. It is true that Jesus calls us out of our old life into a new relationship with him. It is true that he calls us to give up everything for his sake. It is true that in him there is a new community, created by his grace.

Nevertheless, it is also true that our culture, like our personhood, is a beautiful gift from God and is not to be lightly cast aside. Jesus never called people to reject their human peoplehood. Sometimes Christians will be rejected by their people, but the reconciliation is always half-complete, for Christians have already forgiven those who have thus rejected them. Far from calling us to strip ourselves of our culture and peoplehood, Jesus calls us to a divine fulfillment of that very peoplehood, a salvation **within** the culture into which we were born.

In the realm of psychology this has been obvious to Christians. When Jesus asks us to "deny ourselves," we know that this does not mean the obliteration of personhood but rather the fulfillment of personhood in relation to our Creator. The same is true in the sociology of Christian experience. When Jesus asks us to "hate our father and mother," he is not calling us to the obliteration of our peoplehood but rather to the fulfillment of that peoplehood in relation to our Lord.

To some, these insights seem to be a denial of the universalism of the Christian message. However, the recognition of these sociological principles is really an argument **for** universalism. When the choice for or against Christ is made primarily on the basis of reasons for and against particular cultural options, it is not a real decision for or against Christ. When Jesus is introduced to people **within** their culture, they can respond to him for who he is rather than getting mixed up in questions of whether or not in receiving him they are denying their own peoplehood.

More important, it means that we renounce the posture of inviting people to come out from among their kinship and friendship structures in order to become Christians. We do not seek individual converts who are immediately isolated from the cultural setting in which they are at home. Rather, we interact with each person as a representative of a social group, with a view to the salvation of the whole. (Jesus' conversation with the Samaritan woman was not merely a one-to-one matter, for her husband was brought into the conversation soon after it started. The meeting ultimately led to the salvation of many people in her village. Jesus interacted with the woman as a representative of her **people.**)

Because we believe that culture, like personhood, is a divine gift, and because we do not believe that it is harder for God to speak Hindi or Swahili than Greek or English, we expect the Holy Spirit to speak to all people in the cultural language they know best. We hope in every situation to see the emergence of a fellowship which is at home in a given culture or subculture. Such fellowships become unilikely if we insist that our unity in Christ demands that we universalize every local congregation as far as possible as soon as possible. Our unity and our universality do not depend on attempts to include a wide cultural spectrum in every gathering. The more different is my cultural context from that of my brother and sister, the more difficult it will be for us to share in a way that builds a common life, but we are nonetheless brothers and sisters in Christ, and our ultimate treasure is complete oneness in him.

So, although our Lord transcends culture, we never do.

The individualistic, one-by-one approach to conversion may be called "Christianization by extraction," and it stands in contrast to the approach which anticipates conversion with a minimum of social dislocation. The enormous growth of new religious movements in our day, documented by such scholars as Gottfried Oosterwal, is one signal of the continuing relevance of understanding and applying the peoplehood principle in missions.

Oosterwal writes, *These people movements toward the Christian church are not merely a story out of the past. They continue to happen in Indonesia and Cambodia, in Thailand and India, in Africa and South America. Often unrecognized by mission leaders for what they are, the movements sometimes fizzle, or they develop into new* religions or prophet-movements. *Western missions with their individual-oriented approach, their institutionalism, and their lack of messianic expectations may be unable to absorb such people movements when they arise. This has been one of the real tragedies in missions in the last few decades* (1980:250).

Proposals for Planning

In light of all these factors, what should be our priorities for missions and evangelism at home and abroad? Does the "great new fact" of Christian churches established on every continent mean that our responsibility should shift from church planting to church "brothering"? Should we shift our focus from foreign missions to home missions in light of the fact that we seem to have been more successful abroad than at home in the twentieth century?

Let's take them one at a time.

In North America, we need a new recognition of (1) the pluralism of our society and (2) our own cultural particularity. North America is not nearly so much a "melting pot" as has often been imagined, and we need to learn to apply the principles of cross-cultural missions in many places at home as well as abroad. Furthermore, we need to provide members of culturally conservative congregations some basic training in cross-cultural witness because nearly **all** their witness will need to be cross-cultural to some degree. Otherwise they are subjected to the temptation of developing a guilt complex because they are not successful at adding "outsiders" to their congregations. They should not even expect to do so, any more than missionaries should expect to be able to "transplant the tribe" abroad.

What they **should** expect is simply that they can be used of the Lord to introduce persons to Christ and plant new churches among other "tribes" and "peoples" in North America. For members of Mennonite congregations who are culturally more liberal (i.e., closer to total assimilation to some American norm), we can focus more strongly on the possibility of E_0 or E_1 evangelism, encouraging them to expand their congregations with additions from the larger community as well as planting daughter congregations. Even with such congregations, however, we need to give more recognition to the cultural dynamics, developing greater sensitivity to the common problem of making new Christians feel like "outsiders" even as we invite them in.

In foreign missions, we need a new focus on the eighty-five percent of non-Christians who will never be introduced to Christ except by cross-cultural witnesses. For the past two decades we have been working at our relationships with the churches which have been planted in nearly forty countries as a result of our missions. This has been necessary, and it will continue to be necessary. It is right that we pay attention to brothering such churches. It may be even more important that we pay attention to brothering some of the independent churches which we did not plant.

However, in light of the eighty-five percent, the Great Commission is just as binding on us in the next twenty-five years as it ever was for our ancestors—either in partnership with national churches where such exist or in pioneer evangelism in groups which are wholly without a Christian witness. If it is true that the existence of younger churches is a "great new fact" of our times, it is also true that the need for cross-cultural missionaries is one of the great facts in the church of our generation. If we can, in light of this reality, deny our responsibility for cross-cultural evangelism, we are not children of our Anabaptist fathers.

An important qualification, though, must be made at this point. Any assumption that North America carries the **sole** responsibility or even the **chief** responsibility for sending missionaries, for directing the progress of world evangelization, or for creating missionary strategy and theory would be a denial of our heritage just as certainly as it would be wrong to disavow any continuing interest in church planting. We may do neither. Internationally as locally, the posture to which Christ calls us is that of brothers and sisters among each other.

Furthermore, any time we speak of strategy in missions, we do well to remember such scenes from church history as that of Watchman Nee and his band, poised in 1948 to claim all of China for Christ. Theirs was a noble vision, and probably few have been better prepared for such a task. Yet a curtain fell in January 1949 with the coming of Mao Tse-tung to Peking that thwarted the mission in its beginning, and Watchman Nee spent most of his remaining years in prison. Who knows but what a similar judgment may stand over any dreams we dream today; indeed, over all the North American dreams of worldwide missionary strategy? So we will continue to plan, but may it be with humility born of dependence upon the Holy Spirit.

References Cited

Barrett, David B.
   1970   "A.D. 2000: 350 Million Christians in Africa"
           International Review of Mission January LIX:233

Lapp, John A.
   1972   *The Mennonite Church in India* Scottdale, Pa.: Herald
           Press

Littell, Franklin H.
   1964   *The Origins of Sectarian Protestantism* New York:
           Macmillan & Co.

Neill, Stephen
  1964   *A History of Christian Missions:* New York:
          Penguin Books

Oosterwal, Gottfried
  1980   "New Religious Movements" *Mission Focus:*
          Current Issues Scottdale, Pa.: Herald Press

Wenger, J. C.
  1966   *The Mennonite Church in America* Scottdale, Pa.:
          Herald Press

Yoder, John H.
  1971   "The Recovery of the Anabaptist Vision" *Concern* #18

34 Church Growth Among Spanish-Speaking North Americans

José M. Ortiz

If we take a retrospective look at the Spanish Mennonite work, we must conclude that growth has taken place. A difficulty arises as we try to locate sources for research. Few written materials and reports exist which identify the determining factors that played major roles. In the absence of materials, quite often I will be tempted to do some free-lancing.

Internal growth of a congregation or a society is classified as organic, qualitative, and quantitative. We will discuss the last. The term implies the recruitment of persons for the kingdom of God by calling them to repentance and faith in Jesus Christ as Lord and Savior of their lives and incorporating them into a worshiping and a witnessing Christian community.[1] Once those numerical growth factors have been identified, they will provide a basis for entering into the more reflective areas of incarnational, organic, and conceptual growth. That will possibly set up the agenda for the Latin church for the coming 25 years.

These churches emerged out of Mennonite missionary commitment that was expressed in developing city missions, in setting up Spanish departments in Anglo congregations, and in redeploying missionary personnel who returned from Latin America and Voluntary Service units in needy communities. The first Spanish involvement took place in Chicago, Illinois, in the late thirties. The rest is history, and the following chart indicates the phenomenal numerical membership growth in new congregations. Membership increase for 1976 was 26 percent and Menolatino pastors have set a goal of 2,000 members in 50 established congregations by 1980.

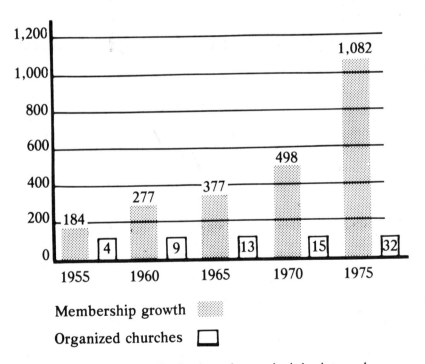

Orlando Costas, a Latin American missiologist, makes a pitch for incarnational growth. This calls for the involvement of the community of faith in the life and problems of the social environment. It is not imperialistic, nor alienating, for it is a means of the liberating action which generates hope and announces the advent of the kingdom of God. That emerges out of a group of believers who have experienced solidarity, covenant, and a sense of history as a part of the people of God. That ought to be the next chapter for the Menolatino church.

Why Growth?
Four brief reasons attempt a rationale for numerical growth.

1. Salvation Is the Agenda. Since the time of the Conquistadors, the Spanish have been known for two passions: a passion for acquiring land and a passion for winning souls.[2] The latter is still with us. Emerging new churches, as in the period of the Book of Acts, have the "kerygma" or proclamation spirit. The preaching of the Word is central, and all other church activities are satellites around the Great Commission. Once a group is consolidated, then the "didache" or teaching ministry emerges. At this point the Latin churches are still in the "kerygma" stage and salvation is the agenda. More developed churches *have increasingly sought to develop an array of inducements that would appeal to the widest range of potential members, yet with diminishing emphasis upon the one incentive unique to churches, that given preeminence by conservative churches: salvation. . . .*[3]

The church calendar does not follow a master plan on evangelism; it is determined by the Spirit ("where the wind blows"). As with the poet a message is provided "as you go." The altar is the place where the action is. In traditional churches the action takes place in the pew, the educational wing, the fellowship halls. The Corinthian church was polluted by the smell of wine; contemporary churches are polluted with the smell of coffee. Latino pastors tend to **make** their pulpits burning bushes where the fragrance of the presence of the Lord is felt. The altar is the place for conversion, vocational commitment, consecration, prayers for healing and forgiveness. There is a lot of "foot traffic" at the altar and quite often with the shoes off. The net result is the reconciling, retaining, and recycling of people.

Salvation is the agenda and people circle around that even when the altar is taken to more secular places such as the street corners, the condominium, parking lots, the factory, or hospital halls. A raw and uncamouflaged gospel is proclaimed. It speaks of a sinful person, God's saving grace, and the necessity of repentance in the spirit of John 3:16—and people still respond to the Christian persuaders. Possibly we have realized that at this stage in history our people cannot get fully involved in the great ills of society since we do not have the expertise, the personnel, nor the resources to meet those needs. But what we have received, that we share: the salvation experience at the personal level. If that agenda is diversified, possibly it will be reflected in the growth of the church.

2. Menolatino Pastors: "They Left Their Nets." The Caonabo Reyes family is a profile in courage. They felt called to establish a Spanish mission in Washington, D.C., and sought funds for support toward the close of the Mission Board's fiscal year. The options were to get in the waiting line, do the lobbying, or "leave their nets." They did the latter. They sold their house and moved to the new community. One year later a dozen persons have been baptized, and a church has emerged. The program includes radio spots, counseling help for illegal aliens, and Bible correspondence courses, in addition to the preaching and teaching ministries. It all started with a sense of call, without financial support, and without too much excess baggage. The money, the training, and the expertise emerged as they went.

This case repeats what happened in the Book of Acts. The Jews shared their religious traditions and the Greeks their philosophical heritage, but Peter and Paul (Acts 3:3) were able to share what they received from God. Our (Menolatino) pastors do likewise.

They have come from the production lines of factories, white collar jobs with the government, and "no collar" jobs in the farming fields. Now they are pulpit persons. They know the language of the sinner and the hurts and needs of the secular man. They can address his questions, possibly the very ones they held themselves prior to their calls to Christ.

If education means acquiring a diploma and the accumulation of credit hours, our Latin pastors have hardly any education. Only four pastors have shared their training in a Mennonite Bible school (The Mennonite Bible Institute of Puerto Rico); a few others have attended interdenominational or Pentecostal schools. The growth in their congregations cannot be attributed to formal education or being exposed to Mennonite evangelistic strategy.

If we take a panoramic view of pastoral cases, we might be able to survey and suggest the type of pastors that our congregations will need, thus giving us a clue for future pastoral training. It seems that the most suitable pastor to minister in our congregations is a breed of Pentecostal-oriented persons who can work within the free church tradition. I do not think those two traits mutually exclude each other. That kind of pastor can move the church to the stage where three basic elements of church life (generating leadership, self-funding, and developing new churches) are realized.

The Spanish church agenda is salvation. Present pastors have left their nets and are serving in a priestly fashion at the altar. On the basis of human knowledge, the kind of people they are handling are difficult agenda, but "God is giving the increase."

There are still Anglo personnel involved in Spanish churches, and if denominational policy is consistent with overseas missions, Anglo pastoral involvement will continue to decrease and phase out. That is called strategy; it simply means Latin pastors for Latin churches. That, I hope, will not be called radicalism.

3. A Favorable Sociology. The experts in people movements are saying that persons in transition are prime targets for conversion to Christianity. Latin mobility becomes a liability as persons and funds leave the community, but it becomes an asset as they get established in other communities as "beachheads" for new missionary outreach. Latins have been on the go, with no time to accumulate wealth, develop connections within the established social order, or professionalize their skills. True to the very nature of the gospel, it appeals to the dispossessed, the alienated, and the uprooted ones. Our churches are geared to serve that "clientele" and response is positive. That pattern was similar to primitive

Christianity, the people of "The Way" and "by the way."

This concludes the triad that has been developing: salvation is the agenda for clergy who have left their nets and are able to preach at the crossroads of a people's movement. Probably those are reasons enough why the churches have grown.

The statement above that people in transition are responsive to the gospel also creates a series of more serious questions that we cannot ignore if we want to claim some of the prophetic heritage. Some elements of change are entering the Latin scene; these must not be overlooked. Immigration laws are getting tighter, and if the unemployment picture in the USA continues, fewer Latins will be tempted to come to the USA and possibly some will return to their place of origin. Farming is becoming more and more mechanized and agribusiness will leave less room for the migrant laborer. Younger Latino parents are realizing the cost of wandering around the country. Following the harvest does not bring any security. Therefore, there is an urge to get established, learn some skills and integrate into a community. To those, becoming Protestants fosters the "americanization" process. The Latin population, now estimated at around 16 million and possibly exceeding the 25 million mark by the close of the century, will become more sophisticated, more established, more inclined to secure material goods, and thus increasingly less accessible for the gospel.

A second reaction to the earlier statement regarding the responsiveness of the dispossessed to the gospel should raise a red flag among affluent Christians. Does it mean that material wealth creates such a sense of security that people are tempted to live without God? In the Old

Testament the prevalent mentality was that economic progress was an indication of God's favor. Accumulation of wealth today seems very often the by-product of the exploitation of others. North Americans ought to have a sense of historical and moral judgment not to exploit the newcomer and then give them a Protestant creed. According to history it happened before to the Indians of both North and South America. That is the agony and the ecstasy of being evangelized in a society intoxicated with wealth.

4. A Theological Emphasis. Recent research into the theology expressed in the fastest growing churches indicates that "the theological thread that runs through the process is a very dogmatic fundamentalism in a charismatic setting. Seven pastors (out of eight surveyed) identified themselves as Charismatics."[4] According to the chart in this article, phenomenal growth is taking place in Menolatino congregations in the seventies, and most of the evangelism explosion has taken place in churches related to the Lancaster Spanish Council. José Santiago indicates that the reason is "because we give room for the Holy Spirit." Revival, manifestation of gifts of the Holy Spirit, prayer, fasting, and witnessing are part of the religious experience. Without apology some pastors freely acknowledge that their ministry is effective due to the "baptism of the Holy Spirit." There was a time that it was not "kosher" to speak that way and some went "underground." Now the tide is changing; speaking in those terms is fashionable.

This leads to a Latin "liturgy" that incorporates the existential dimension of the faith—what God is doing now. Christ becomes the object of praise and prayer in a very

subjective way. Salvation today tends to be liberation from
eternal damnation. There are indications that the pastoral
agenda is moving beyond that mentality, but it looks like
most of the congregations are operating at that point. The
present is the only possession; therefore the program
tends to be a now-oriented service in the light of the life to
come. If the trend continues, it can be safely stated that
the North American Latin experience has not lost affinity
with other Christians south of the border. In celebrating
what is happening now, rather than recollecting what God
did in the past, we may find an answer to why response
has been favorable.

Toward a Consolidation of Growth

It has been stated previously that present growth does
not necessarily mean response to an evangelization
strategy. It looks like a cartoon to speak of a master plan
when pastors are saying that the growth is due to the
Spirit and the Spirit blows where it pleases. Present Latin
church administrative patterns were a response to the
upheaval of the sixties and seventies when the issues were
social change and integration. That has at least given
the platform to discover more authentic expressions of
administration that will supplement and help facilitate the
congregation in its evangelism agenda at the local level. In
order to achieve that, pastors who minister successfully at
the altar must sit where denominational plans are shaped.
Otherwise the resources available could be directed to all
kinds of agenda. The consolidation stage is emerging,
and responsible planning must be designed to take care of
the developments.

Some projections have been made concerning the ideal
pastor to minister in Latin churches. Let us briefly picture

a church which could be a model. It is a church which grows numerically; identifies, sends, and gives partial support to its Bible school students; develops a "daughter church"; ministers among migrants; and its pastoral team (husband and wife) participates in the program of the larger church—whether the conference, the Latin Council, or the women's groups on a national level. That church is located in Moline, Illinois, and is pastored by Mac and Mary Bustos. That congregation expresses a balanced growth and possibly could set the model for congregational development.

Speaking of evangelism within the Mennonite Church in general is not easy. Joe Haines indicates that the three faces of evangelism are community, service, and proclamation[5] and warns of a proclamation without the other two elements. Glenn Brubacher in his article, "Evangelism: We Have No Common Understanding,"[6] struggles to verbalize the Mennonite tradition which is strong in being a caring community, but when it comes to evangelism on a person-to-person basis, is not there. The pastoral perspectives of Haines and Brubacher should challenge the Mennonite church worker to enter into the harvest and be as successful as the Mennonite farmer with his fields. Maybe the Latin Mennonites need to grow in being a community (koinonia) involved in service (diakonia) and the Anglo church must face the fact that kerygma is the Christian church agenda. Both mutually supplement each other's vision of what it means to be God's people today.

Notes

1. Clifton L. Holland, *The Religious Dimension in Hispanic Los Angeles* (South Pasadena, California: William Carey Library, 1974), pp. 445-446.

2. R. H. Bainton, *El Alma Hispana y el Alma Sajona* (Buenos Aires, Argentina: Editorial La Aurora, 1961), p. 21.

3. Dean Kelly, *Why Conservative Churches are Growing* (New York: Harper and Row, 1972), p. 92.

4. José M. Ortiz, "The Process of Incorporating New Members in Spanish Speaking Mennonite Churches" (unpublished dissertation, Doctor of Ministry Program, McCormick Theological Seminary, March 1976), p. 3.

5. Joseph Haines, "Evangelism's Three Faces," *Evangelical Visitor,* (June 10, 1976), pp. 4, 5.

6. Glenn Brubacher, "Evangelism: We Have No Common Understanding" *Mennonite Reporter* (September 30, 1974), p. 5.

Structures and Strategies for Interdependence in World Mission

35

Charles R. Taber

The vision of a truly equal, truly interdependent brother-hood of Christians in mission is not a new one. Neill, for instance, points out that Bishop A. R. Tucker of Uganda (1890-1908) "envisaged a Church in which African and foreigner would work together in true brotherhood, and on a basis of genuine equality" (1964:26). I do not think this dream was ever made explicit in the thinking of Rufus Anderson, Henry Venn, and John Nevius, though it is possible that it may have been implicit. But, as Neill says on the page already cited, "For the most part missionaries of almost all the churches were blind to this kind of possibility."

In recent years, a number of churches and missions have tried to give concrete expression to this vision. Most of these are very new, so that it is premature to make a final evaluation. But, though the designers retain their enthusiastic high hopes, I would anticipate problems as these schemes develop because I see in most of them signs that the factors which tended to perpetuate dependence and to inhibit interdependence are more intractable than had been thought. Part II of this paper will look briefly at some of these experiments. In the meantime, let us look at the background issues.

The Practical Dimensions of the Problem

I will consider the practical dimensions of the difficulties we encounter in trying to foster interdependence under three headings: history, our conception of the task, and cultural differences. These of course interpenetrate and reinforce each other, so that the solution will of necessity be more complex and all-embracing than we might guess at first look.

Historical background. It is of course true that the history within which we are forced to work, willy-nilly, is not of our making. But we cannot escape its far-reaching implications as the ground of many attitudes, formalized and institutionalized relationships, and entrenched patterns of behavior which constitute the obstacles to our efforts.

For over four centuries, Europeans systematically conquered and exploited the indigenous peoples, first of the New World, then of Africa and Asia. Starting from essentially similar levels of affluence, power, and technological development in the fifteenth century, Western and non-Western societies have since experienced vastly different histories: the West has become unimaginably wealthy and powerful, the non-West has stagnated or worse. The major factors in the present disparity of status were colonialism, slavery, mercantilism, and all of the other terrible expressions of the West's oppression of the Two-Thirds World. Once the initial advantage was gained via relatively small innovations in navigation and weaponry, it was expoited to the hilt to augment in every way possible the ways in which the West could enrich itself at the expense of its colonies.

As we have by now heard *ad nauseam*—though without necessarily realizing its full implications for us today—the missionary enterprise coincided not only in time, but also in point of origin, and even largely in attitudes, policy, and methods with the colonial enterprise. This was true even in the occasional cases where missionaries vocally and courageously protested the grosser abuses of colonialism. The indigenous cultures, native societies, and individual persons were summarily assumed to be inherently inferior to their Western counterparts. In *all* relationships between Westerner and non-Westerner, authority and initiative, as well as the relevant skills and financial resources, belonged by definition to the Westerner. This sprang from and reinforced in the Westerner a deep-seated arrogance, and in the non-Westerner led to a combination of excessive deference, dependency, self-denigration, and resentment. Since we are still today experiencing the difficulty of overcoming similar problems arising from analogous causes among various ethnic minorities in the U.S.A., we should be prepared to see why this heritage cannot be forgotten overnight.

The ostensible end of the colonial era (1945-1975, focusing about 1960) and the beginning of national independence led to hopes of "freedom at last"; but these hopes have been rudely shattered, as the West continues to dominate the Two-Thirds World by the power of its technological development and its enormous affluence. Working hand in glove, Western governments and Western corporations have established de facto control over the economies of the poorer nations. The mechanisms involved include the contrast between the highly unstable prices of the raw primary commodities produced by the poor nations and the escalating prices of the finished products sold by the rich nations; the granting of loans at high interest rates, which burdens the bare treasuries of the poor countries, and with strings which ensure their use for purposes favorable to the wealthy nations' interests; and even the outright overt or covert intervention to "destabilize" unfavorable governments (e.g. Chile) and to establish or prop up oppressive regimes that favor the interests of wealthy countries at the expense of their own citizens. The poor countries are faced essentially with Hobson's choice: either they accept Western so-called "aid" and the burdens and controls it entails, or they opt for a meager level of self-reliance. In either case they find themselves unable to provide the basic services their peoples desperately need. The joint voices of the poor nations in the United Nations give them a forum, but their power is effectively neutralized by the vetoes of the big powers in the Security Council. So far, petroleum is the only commodity whose producers have been able in some measure to turn the tables on the rich nations by operating unitedly.

I have emphasized this point at such length because we must face the fact that, whatever our own attitudes and practices, this is the context in which we operate. Christian leaders in other countries are bright enough and informed enough to diagnose the problem; they are also aware that, by and large, the American Christian public sees nothing wrong with the present system. We are therefore obliged to prove ourselves before we can really win the trust which is the only basis on which interdependence can work.

Our conception of the task. A second area which causes us difficulties is how we understand the task and how we go about organizing and pursuing our goals. Here, ironically, it is the very abundance of certain kinds of resources in our hands which blinds us to potentially more fruitful ways of approaching the job. These matters are so intertwined that I will treat them together. We need to consider at least three aspects of this complex.

a. First of all, in almost all instances **we assume from the outset that** *we* **know what the task is and what the goals are.** These are already defined in our minds and in our corporate deliberations and projections well before nationals are involved at all. After all, the mission has been working in a given area for many years; it has—at least one hopes so—well defined goals; and of course it has set in motion processes and founded institutions and structures designed to achieve these goals. Seldom does one really open up all of these basic questions *de novo* when the national church or its agencies become involved. It is expected that they will work enthusiastically towards the goals we have set and take over willingly all the machinery we have built to reach them. My observation is that under such circumstances nationals at best feel ill at ease with the foreign patterns and institutions, and at worst completely uninterested and uninvolved. It is precisely this in turn which leads missions to conclude that nationals have no vision or initiative! We are, it seems, in a vicious circle. Way back in 1947 J. Merle Davis said, "The Western Church has made the mistake of girding the Eastern David in Saul's armor and putting Saul's sword into his hands. Under these conditions the Church on the mission field has made a brave showing, but it is reasonable to expect that it will give a better account of itself by using its own familiar gear and weapons" (Davis 1947:108).

More recently, reflecting a Third-World perspective and 25 additional years of frustrating experience, Byang Kato wrote: "One mission complained about a national church that reluctantly accepted an elaborate medical program only to sell it to the government and use the money for the felt need. While one does not want to sit in judgment on such a case, it is apparent that local involvement was lacking at the beginning" (Kato 1972:199).

One could quite legitimately ask, Why *should* Third World church leaders simply take over from us without question all the precedents that we have established? Are we so nearly infallible, and they so ignorant, that completely unbroken continuity is the best way to save

God's mission? I doubt it.

b. Second, **our affluence has led us to develop the ecclesiastical analog of capital-intensive methods of work.** In *our* economy, the most expensive thing is human time, and any procedure or equipment which saves human time is an improvement. We have thus developed methods and techniques which require the large amounts of money we have at our disposal, and we unthinkingly give others the impression that is *the* way to do Christian work. In most of the rest of the world, equipment is prohibitively expensive, and the cheapest and most abundant resource is human time and strength. But we bypass the resource in which nationals are rich and major on the ones which we have in abundance. In such a "partnership" it is inevitable that the partner with the most highly valued resource will dominate.

This dominance is further buttressed by our conviction, to which we hold at least as firmly as we do to our doctrinal positions, that "he who pays the piper calls the tune" (Kalu 1975a:16). In other words, we accept without question the capitalist premise that in any operation the dominant factor is and ought to be the capital input rather than the labor input. Under the guise of "accountability" and encouraged by our stereotypes about the undependability of nationals in money matters, we insist on retaining control of projects which we fund—including the covert control arising from the possibility of funds being cut off, the power of the implicit veto. I know of no single obstacle to true partnership than this attitude which we find so hard to relinquish. It is invariably mentioned when Third World Christians discuss partnership or church-mission relations (Nacpil 1971; Costas 1973:415; Kalu 1975b: Kato 1972:197; see also Strong 1972:286; Taber 1976).

At the root of the problem, I think, is our materialism.

This can be seen among Western donors, who will far more readily give for a building or an airplane than for true human needs. It can be seen in our priorities in business meetings at all levels, from the local church to denominational conferences to the board meeting, where questions of money and property tend to dominate the agenda. And it is of course reflected in our ready judgment, conscious or unconscious, that people who are poor are less important than people who are rich, and that societies that do not major in the accumulation of material wealth are backward. That non-Westerners see this unlovely trait in us clearly is evident from two anecdotes. Loewen somewhere tells of a discussion with a group of Indians who told him that in their tradition the most important thing was spirits; but the Indians were learning from the missionaries to make money, not the Holy Spirit, the center of their lives. Some years ago, a missionary from Nigeria told me of a prominent American minister, well known in fundamentalistic circles, who visited Nigeria and spoke to a group of Nigerian ministers; the burden of his message was that because he served God, God had prospered him with a large salary, two cars, a big luxurious house, and so on. After the meeting, some of the Africans took my friend aside and asked him, "Is that man a Christian?"

c. Third is **our unbounded reliance on expertise, defined in technological terms and measured in years of formal schooling.** Our bemusement with expertise is reflected in our tacit assumption that *we* know how it ought to be organized, that *we* know how to plan and project and schedule. This, I think, is the reason we so spontaneously go about defining goals and methods unilaterally and only invite nationals to join in at a later stage. And if perchance we are willing to relinquish some of this technologically based power, it is because one or more of the nationals have been educated in the Western pattern and therefore have the same kind of expertise as we do. But not all missiologists are sure that this is a good idea. "Heaven save us," pleads John V. Taylor, "from an international Christian technocracy" (1971:337).

A subsidiary aspect of this attitude is our mania for specialization and compartmentalization. We have buildings which are used only on Sunday and other buildings which are never used on Sunday. By reflex the word "education" evokes for us a school, complete with specially designed building, specialized furniture and equipment, and specialized personnel. The word "worship," on the other hand, evokes a distinctive building, specialized furniture and equipment, and specialized personnel. This approach, especially as regards buildings and equipment, multiplies the cost of the total operation.

d. Fourth, **this bedazzlement with money and expertise has right from the start subverted true indigeneity in the church,** and it continues to do so. Huge areas of the work—education, health care, development programs, etc.—are without question and almost by definition beyond the effective control of local churches; they lack the funds to support them and the professionals to run them, and so by design or by default foreign funds support them and foreign experts control them. In at least one Mennonite field, Zaire, 80 percent of the church budget comes from overseas and is almost exclusively devoted to these para-church ministries and to the top-level administration of the church (Mutombo-Mpanya 1977). This situation, says Mutombo-Mpanya, results in tensions and jealousies between two classes of Christian workers: those engaged on local church ministries, who are supported at a modest level by their churches, and those engaged in the glamorous and heavily subsidized service or administrative ministries, who are supported at a much higher level by foreign funds.

While Dennis Clark was not writing specifically about this issue, his observations are, I think, extremely pertinent: **The national staff member of a foreign-controlled mission faces serious problems. Financed and directed by a society heavily dominated by Westerners, and whose first loyalty is to foreign supporters, he owes extraterritorial loyalties to that society. Often the result of this situation is alienation from local people. . . . It seems almost too late for Western societies to recruit the national because, with very few exceptions, the stigma of being labeled a "stooge" or "puppet" reduces usefulness. . . . The Western concept of "hiring and firing" overlooks the deep feeling of Christians in the Third World and can only attract "hirelings" who will flee when the wolf comes** (Clark 1971:207-208).

It is because of these difficulties that Kalu does not hesitate to call missionary education "an instrument of bondage" because "it bred marionettes in Church and State" (1975a:19).

To summarize: our approach to conceptualizing and organizing the task subverts true partnership because we unilaterally assume the right to define goals and methods, and because we rely on capital-intensive and technology-intensive patterns which put a premium on *our* resources rather than on the resources of the local church.

Cultural foundations. All of the problems I have already mentioned have cultural roots and cultural implications; however, I think it will be useful for us to isolate specifically four cultural factors which seem to me to be especially pertinent.

a. First is **our generally manipulative attitude toward our environment,** whether physical or social. We prize mastery, we reward the ambition to dominate, we regard

the solution of problems by subjugating their causes as the
best way to deal with them; "aggressive" is an adjective
with highly favorable connotation. Perhaps the best
metaphor for this attitude is the bulldozer. Three
quotations underline this point: **Far from considering
adjustments to environment a virtue, they (missionaries)
believe the efficiency of their work depends on bending
that environment** (Scott 1975:181). **Missionaries introduced a Western form of church based on a cash economy,
and since the form did not fit the Philippine economy, they
tried to fit the economy to the form by amateur aid
programmes and employment in miniature industries**
(Scott 1975:183).

**A significant example of the contrast in method
emerged during the preliminary planning of the first All
Africa Churches' Conference, held at Ibadan in 1958.
British and American "experts" had agreed that this was
to be Africa's conference run in Africa's way. But when it
appeared that the African leaders intended to have no
agenda but to allow the findings to emerge from free,
informal discussion, the experts felt constrained to take a
hand, and once again Western methods prevailed** (Taylor
1973:22n).

A special instance of this pragmatic, utilitarian,
triumphalistic attitude is our view of time, which leads us
to be extremely impatient. This no doubt springs from our
culturally conditioned understanding of such passages as
Ephesians 5:16 ("Redeeming the time. . . ," KJV) which
we interpret to mean that we should not "waste time" but
plow on ahead on a predetermined course no matter what.
It is not clear to me that this is a universally valid
interpretation; rather, it smacks of finding in the Bible
justification for our own haste.

b. Second, I think, is **our culturally induced bluntness of
manner,** our readiness to confront directly people with

whom we disagree and to push our ideas against theirs. This cannot help giving us an undue advantage over people who are culturally more polite, whose culture requires them to be more reticent and more oblique, who are expected to "save face" and to avoid confrontations. When a national fails to tell us to our faces that he disagrees with us, we too easily jump to the conclusion that he agrees with us, and we rush ahead with our plans. We are not tuned in to the far more subtle clues which other cultures provide when people disagree.

c. Not unrelated is the expectation, which we share with most nationals, that **when cooperative programs and partnerships are initiated, it is the nationals who will adjust** in matters of language, life-style, and so forth; they must for the best results become culturally Westerners. It is a tribute to their resiliency and flexibility that so many can make the adjustment and operate successfully on our turf without losing their bearings on their own. But why should programs and activities planned for and carried out in a non-Western society be designed in a Western setting and a Western idiom? Why should *we* not be the ones to adjust our cultural style? Yet it hardly ever happens; we live in our cultural cocoon, and when we invite nationals to work with us, we invite them to a limited participation in our cocoon rather than venturing out of it to meet them on their ground. Scott has some scathing words about this as he describes the cultural insulation of missionaries: "Unless he (the missionary) gets out of that spacesuit, he will never be able to cry on a Filipino shoulder, lock arms with a Filipino brother on a steep path, or taste the salt of Filipino tears" (1975:172).

d. Finally, I suggest that **the very title of our discussion reflects a Western bias:** *"Structures* and *strategies* for interdependence.'' Would not an African or an Asian look first to *relationships* between persons as the locus of success or failure? True, the relationships have been systematically undermined or destroyed by the factors of power and culture described above, and an African like Kalu recognizes this explicitly. And he would even insist that attention must be given to establishing a sounder systemic basis for fraternal relationships. But the systemic is the means to the relationship, not the other way around. What we should be seeking is *first,* a basis on which to build concrete and genuine expressions of our international *koinonia;* and *second,* approaches to doing a job.

Some Attempts at Solutions
I mentioned above that a number of attempts have been made recently to solve the problem and establish true partnership. At this point I will examine a few of these briefly.

United Methodist Church. The United Methodist effort is described by Harris and Patterson (1975). Under the rubric "Building Community in Mission," they mention nine programs or activities which their Board of Global Ministries and their churches are involved in: international itinerating teams in U.S. churches, recognition that education for mission is mission, involvement of U.S. ethnic minorities in global mission, development of more flexible patterns of U.S. missionary service, exploration of patterns for mission in the U.S., affirmation of the increased interest of the laity in missionary service, support for people in mission in their own countries, encouragement of the internationalization of the missionary presence, and participation in support of people's networks. All of these things are highly commendable; but aside from their being often expressions of aspiration rather than of reality, they reflect, as far as I can see, a totally unilateral view of the initiatives to be taken. There seems to be a minimum of involvement by non-Western

Christians in the planning of the effort and little wrestling with the deep level problems I have described.

The KKKMI. The KKKMI (Strong 1972) is a group of European agencies working in Indonesia. Strong actually lists a number of caveats and recommendations rather than describing an ongoing program. For instance, he differentiates between "partnerships where one partner is strong and one is weak; where one partner is silent; partnership with limited liability; and partnership where everything is held in common, such as a family with a joint banking account" (281). In discussing the slogan of the KKKMI ("Today we are partners"), he asks "whether it is a statement of fact or hope" (281). He points out that the very term "churches overseas" creates an unhelpful dichotomy (282). When a mission and a church are partners, he says, there will be tensions, since each has by definition a different focus of interest; it is necessary that each have a policy to guide its work, and both policies apply to the same arena; when the policies differ, which should prevail? The situation is exacerbated when a board insists on uniform policies in a number of fields where the churches may have different policies. Strong feels that the board secretary is in the crucial position to make or break the partnership. By means of a pointed question, he suggests that churches ought to be involved in the selection of missionaries. Finally, he emphasizes the difficulty involved when "we all want to receive unearmarked money but tend to want to pass it on earmarked" (286).

The Lutheran Church in America. Vikner (1974) describes the work of the LCA. He offers as a framework for the history of the LCA missions the usual three-stage model: missionary dominance, local autonomy, and interdependence. But he still clearly takes it for granted that the

LCA will unilaterally determine its role and its priorities in the world.

Conservative Baptists. Jacques (1973) outlines in some detail the approach of the Conservative Baptists in India, and especially in the Philippines. What emerged out of a history of tensions was a structure of "equal partnership" in which the mission and the fellowship of churches, each autonomous, agreed to work together through a system of committees in which they had equal representation (the "business committee," however, which is responsible for "the internal concerns of the mission, such as missionary housing, car, furlough and administration" remains unilaterally the prerogative of the mission). The two partners contribute financially as each is able to a joint budget. A lengthy document entitled "An Agreement for the Cooperative Stage of Nationalization of Conservative Baptist Work in the Philippines" spells out the name, the purpose, the goals, the members, the officers, the responsibilities, and so forth. Apparently the nationals were far more involved in the initial planning here than in the cases mentioned above. Though Jacques claims that the system works, it seems to me that there remains a good bit of insistence on the respective autonomy of the cooperating bodies, of keeping each other at arm's length, of leaning over backward to make sure each has exactly half of everything. To be sure, this is much better than fighting; but it is not true partnership in my understanding of the term. And the design of the whole scheme is extremely Western.

Joint Apostolic Action in Dahomey. Ayivi (1972) describes a cooperative effort called *L'Action Apostolique au Dahomey.* Proposed originally by Pastor Jean Kotto, general secretary of the Evangelical Church of Cameroun, it joins in a common project the Paris Missionary Society and a number of churches in francophone West Africa. The focus of the project was to send a joint team representative of the churches involved and incorporating a diversity of technical skills and specializations (theology, social work, education, nursing, agronomy, etc.), to one of the more resistant societies in West Africa, the Fon of Dahomey (now Republic of Benin). The threefold objectives were the development of the whole human being, the creation of a new form of Christian community, and to relate African culture to the gospel. I do not have detailed or recent information on this effort; but though Ayivi in 1972 was cautiously optimistic, it is my impression that the effort has lost its elan. It is possible that the continued resistance of Fon society was a factor; I have also heard that the members of the team were not fully able to coordinate their efforts to work toward well-understood joint goals. At any rate, the project today is not living up to original hopes.

The Latin America Mission. The fullest and most satisfactory definition of partnership I have seen is that of Roberts (1973) concerning the Latin American Mission. In some respects they had already achieved some of the positions that others only hoped for, but they were still not satisfied. Roberts points out that preparation for this advance went back to 1950 when the late Kenneth Strachan began insisting on eliminating racial discrimination between Latins and North Americans at all levels of the LAM. But, says Roberts, this was not enough: "Latin American leaders tended to become frustrated. Instead of the rest of us becoming more Latin American in our attitudes and administrative style, the Latin missionaries were forced to conform to North American standards of candidate screening, missionary support, deputation activities, executive procedures and administrative style" (338).

Finally, a joint consultation was held in January 1971 at which the majority were Latins. Roberts recalls, **Perhaps most important of all, . . . we learned . . . that the process of "latinamericanization" . . . did not consist simply in the recruitment of Latin Americans to serve side by side with us. We discovered that an organization might have 90 percent Latin Americans and still be a thoroughly "gringo" structure. . . . The key, we found, is in the decision-making process. This process must be shifted to Latin America and controlled by Latin Americans if the organization is to become truly autochthonous** (339-340).

One aspect of the overall reorganization is a high measure of decentralization, and the granting of a high degree of autonomy to the various specialized ministries and institutions formerly operated by the LAM. The umbrella organization is the Community of Latin American Evangelical Ministries.

Roberts discusses frankly problems involved in determining budgets, public relations (especially with the US supporting constituency), personnel, and the transfer of properties. He mentions a tendency for divisiveness among the components of CLAME and difficulty in establishing solid internal communications.

The weakest part of the scheme, from my perspective, and one which makes the model less useful than it might otherwise be, is failure to mention the role of *churches* in the whole operation. This is a failure one might expect from the "faith mission" context; yet it is in my view a grave weakness in the pattern.

Summary. As I read these accounts, I am struck by the persistence of the underlying difficulties. They seem to have numerous incarnations and to surface in many manifestations. In summarizing this section of my paper, I can do no better than quote three people who have faced the issues involved very concretely. After a discussion of the old-fashioned direct control via the purse strings, Orlando Costas says, "While much of this may be changing, there are signs that point in the direction of more subtle, indirect controls. This may be seen even among the most advanced and progressive mission organizations. Even though they may have handed over all administrative and strategic control, their leaders always manage somehow to get their way" (1973:414).

Tom Hanks, a student worker in Latin America vividly underlines the difficulty: **I had thought of paternalism as a deadly thing which I must be very careful not to create in my relations with students, instead of recognizing that it is the dominant, strangling pattern of relationships that exists in the church in Latin America. It is not that the student worker must be wise enough not to create such a monster. Rather he must be courageous enough to destroy the monster that now exists. . . . Anyone who has read or seen the film of Elsa, the lion who was "Born Free," knows it is infinitely easier to leave an animal free than to domesticate it and then try to teach it to be "indigenous." . . . You may even convince yourself that you have an indigenous student work—with students dashing all over putting your ideas into practice. Then dawns the day when you ask yourself, "But when was the last time they came up with a good original idea and carried it out?" and you realize it is not that they can't, it's that I'm dominating** (1972:153-154, 156, 157).

Finally, Emerito Nacpil explains why despair at this point led him to call for a moratorium on missionaries and foreign funds: **Of course, we can argue that we are not limited to these alternatives (with respect to whether the missionary serves mission or church, etc.). Instead, we can become partners—partners in obedience, joint participants in a common enterprise. But can we really? If we can, under present conditions, it can only be (and so far this seems to be the case) a partnership between the weak**

and the strong. And that means the continued dependence of the weak upon the strong, and the continued dominance of the strong over the weak, notwithstanding our efforts and protestations to the contrary. Under this kind of partnership, the missionary becomes the apostle of affluence, not sacrifice; cultural superiority, not Christian humility; technological efficiency, not human identification; white supremacy, not human liberation and community (1971:359).

I suppose one could sum up the whole matter in terms of the well-known recipe for elephant-rabbit stew: you take one elephant and one rabbit. It should not surprise us that the "50-50" stew in fact tastes more of elephant than of rabbit!

Dimensions of a Solution

I am not in a position to offer you a well-integrated model of the ideal form of interdependence. I can, however, suggest some features which I think will characterize any successful model.

Mutual trust. Fundamental to any success is a climate of mutual trust, respect, and genuine Christian love (i.e. love shorn of its paternalistic, condescending dimension), based on an understanding of the *koinonia* God intends for the whole body. Since this is basic, and since we easily confuse biblical ideals with concrete achievement, I want to quote Ogbu Kalu briefly: **It seems quite clear that no amount of tinkering with the present pattern will work. A missionary may be fully aware of the theological nature of the Church as the Body of Christ and the biblical pattern of interrelationships as one of mutual responsibility and interdependence. Yet he cannot avoid being paternalistic. The source of paternalism in mission is the structure of the enterprise itself** (1975b:143-144).

In other words, it is far from enough to realize fully the theological-biblical dimensions of a solution; we have to work in the concrete situation to find concrete expressions for the spiritual reality, which implies, for Kalu, the demolition of a system which inherently works at cross-purposes with the biblical pattern. It is this fact, according to Kalu, which underlies calls for moratorium, not in rejection of the Great Commission, but in explicit obedience to it. Only when the young churches are given breathing room, when the inherently oppressive presence of the mission is removed or relaxed, can they find their true role in the ministry of the total body.

Local decision making. It is crucial that decision making be focused in the place and on the persons who will be most directly involved. In other words, partnership involves each partner group having *primary* responsibility and authority in their own sphere, and *then* helping others in their spheres (Arias 1971:252). In other words, just as we do not expect African Christians to take unilateral or even primary initiatives with regard to churches in the U.S., so we should not arrogate to ourselves the right to initiate decisions and programs in other parts of the world. Kalu underlines this when he says, "The nature of the Universal Church means that aid relationships among churches must be different from aid relationships among nations. If there is to be real sharing-in-common, there must be sharing-in-common of power" (1975a:22).

As long as Westerners remain effectively in charge of designing the program, there will continue to be difficulties with the *model* of development used, and with the *mode* and *priority* of aid.

At this point I would like to comment on the suggestions of Calvin Shenk (1977) and Gerald Keener (1977). Shenk suggests the substitution of multilateral relations for bilateral ones. There is much value in this, but it is not by itself a full solution. The United Bible Societies entered into a radically centralized system called the World

Service Budget for the express purpose of obviating the patron-client relationship between the big societies and local offices and specific projects overseas. But it turned out that the dominance of the big societies remained securely in place, as Bible Society operations that received funds from the World Service Budget, even in countries with "autonomous" Bible Societies that were full members of the UBS, were subject to line-by-line review or veto by UBS executives, while the societies which were financially self-supporting did as they pleased. Efforts were made to modify this invidious distinction by making the financial operations of the big societies open for inspection, but there was never any question of bringing them under the tutelage of the UBS. The same distinction exists today in the appointment of senior personnel: ABS or BFBS can appoint whom they please to any internal post, but the Bible Society of Ghana cannot appoint a general secretary without the approval of the UBS.

Keener's proposal that *churches* enter into direct partnership across the seas is also good, but by itself a bit idealistic. Churches separated not only by thousands of miles but by enormous cultural gulfs need knowledgeable brokers to establish and maintain sound communications. Granting the fact that the churches are the fundamental reality, mission agencies can usefully serve this linking function if they are properly set up to do it.

Encouraging local initiative. Following from the above, we need to encourage nationals to take the lead in determining the most fundamental goals and methods of operation. We need to ask them, and press them for an answer. "What do *you* think are the tasks of the church?" And when they have sorted out *their* understanding of their mandate from God, we will need to encourage them to design methods which are appropriate to their setting and their resources. This will need to be done with all aspects of the work. If, for instance, they decide that the church needs to have educational activities, they need to be free to question whether this implies a school in our sense at all. In this game, we need to realize that by definition *they,* not we, are the experts; our expertise relates to a very different world, and is, as we have seen above, often a hindrance rather than a help when exported.

I realize that we cannot actually start with a blank slate on which to write beautiful new programs; we cannot at once eliminate all the mistakes of the past. At this point I can only repeat my advice in *The Other Side:* **A truly Christian approach in the field will begin with the mission taking the initiative. Mission boards need to approach their national churches with the following kinds of statements:**

1. We acknowledge and confess that our financial operations are sub-Christian. Please forgive us.

2. Let us together examine the whole program which we have instituted, most of which was instituted without consulting you. Let us prayerfully see which parts of the program have been genuinely helpful to you and which parts exist only because some missionary might be offended if they were discontinued. Let us see which parts of the program you would have instituted on your own initiative if we had not been in control.

3. Let us with all deliberate speed eliminate those programs which do not contribute sufficiently to the well-being of the church to justify their cost in money and freedom of action.

4. Let us plan how the remaining programs can reflect the Holy Spirit's leading in this specific sociocultural and historical situation. You take the initiative since this is your church under God. We are God's servants for your sake.

5. Finally, let's discuss finances honestly, see what is

needed, and discover together where it will come from—
how much from local sources, how much from outside. We
pledge to you that we will truly relinquish control (Taber
1976:43 -44).

Giving without strings. The last sentence spells out the
next feature of a successful partnership: that giving be
truly without strings. This was implicit in the quotation
from Kalu on church aid; it is underlined by this deeply
felt statement of Byang Kato: **If foreign aid is to help
rather than hinder the work of the Lord, it must be given
as unto the Lord and received as God's money. There must
be a strong element of trust all around. . . . Missionaries
. . . should have confidence in the nationals. The commonly heard phrase, "You cannot trust the national,"
must be dropped and humble repentance offered for the
past action** (1972:197).

The only way this can be put into effect, I think, is for us
to repent of and grow out of our materialism, that
materialism which leads us to grossly overestimate the
importance of the financial component of the operation
(what we contribute) and to underestimate the value of the
human component (what nationals contribute), the
materialism that in the name of "accountability" will not
relinquish control of programs to which we have given
money, the materialism that prevents us from trusting
nationals.

Can we become poor? Perhaps an even greater revolution
of values is called for. Weiser, in a tantalizing allusion
(1975:134), suggests that Jesus in Luke 9:3 ("Take
nothing with you for the trip . . .") had in mind a purpose
relevant to our discussion: "With all the necessary allow-
ances made for the different socioeconomic context
of the Gospels this injunction to the disciples seems to be
designed to put them into a state of extraordinary

powerlessness in any economic context.'' This raises the question for us: is it possible for us to really become functionally poor and weak in our dealings with Third World churches? What would we have to renounce in a very concrete way to free these churches from our overwhelming combination of powers which oppress them: the history of colonial relations, our financial affluence, our technological expertise, and our assumption—which they are in no position to deny effectively—that these powers give us the right to determine their destiny?

Epilogue

After the discussion of my paper in Hillsboro, I feel constrained to make explicit two points which were implicit in my thinking but which obviously did not come through to everyone.

First, the reason I shied away from becoming more specific in proposing solutions is precisely because, beyond the generalities I outlined, each situation is to a great extent unique, and solutions must be sought in *concrete* contexts and in interaction with *specific* persons and groups. There would have been a remainder of subtle imperialism in our sitting as a group of North Americans in Hillsboro and offering universal solutions to be applied. A crucial part of the solution is the dialogue process by which the solution is discovered and applied, and one cannot predict from a distance what will emerge. One must play it by ear (to speak in purely human terms), or be sensitive to the contextual guidance of the Holy Spirit (to use biblical categories); and the guidance must come to the persons and groups involved in *joint* prayer, confession, and discussion.

Second, in spite of my harping on problems and difficulties, I am essentially optimistic about *possibilities;* but my optimism is not based on our insight or our technical competence, but only on God's grace. I cannot be triumphalistic about solving problems through scholarship and expertise, because if I am, these will become yet more tools of manipulation. But I can and do have confidence in God to transcend our limitations and sins. The condition on our part is repentance for our sins. We have a tendency to want to pass through this stage quickly and to see in advance a blueprint for a happy outcome beyond the repentance to make it worthwhile; otherwise, we feel, the repentance will have been in vain! However, biblical repentance cannot be instrumental in that sense; it dare not be minimized or bypassed, and there is no guarantee of "success" on the other side. But we also need to see that *metanoia* is not self-flagellation or wallowing in guilt (which would lead to self-pity and eventually to self-congratulation!); rather, it is an honest facing up to our guilt, a repudiation of the sinful patterns (which will have systemic and structural consequences, as Kalu pointed out), and a determination to look ahead to the *possible* future God has in store for us (first person plural inclusive, i.e. Western and non-Western Christians). In other words, *metanoia* is a liberation from the shackles of past sins and *for* a better future. But we need to realize that our non-Western partners, not being able to see our hearts as well as God does, may take more convincing than God does that we mean what we say. So they may put us to the test in a variety of ways. But I firmly believe in the vision of "one new humanity" that John Toews so ably outlined for us.

Bibliography

Arias, Mortimer, 1971. "Mutual Responsibility," *International Review of Missions* 60.249-258

Ayivi, Emmanuel, 1972. "Joint Apostolic Action in Dahomey," *IRM* 61.144-149

Clark, Dennis E., 1971. "Receiving Churches and Missions," *Evangelical Missions Quarterly* 7.201-210

Costas, Orlando E., 1973. "Mission Out of Affluence," *Missiology* 1.405-423

Davis, J. Merle, 1947. *New Buildings on Old Foundations.* New York/London:SCM Press

Hanks, Tom, 1972. "Paternalistic—Me?" *EMQ* 8.153-159

Harris, Ruth M. & Patterson, Patricia J., 1975. "People in Mission: Toward Selfhood and Solidarity," *IRM* 64.137-142

Jacques, Edwin E., 1973. "An Equal Partnership Structure," *EMQ* 9.65-73

Kalu, Ogbu U., 1975a. "The Peter Pan Syndrome," *Missiology* 3.15-29

_____, 1975b. "Not Just New Relationship but a Renewed Body," *IRM* 64.143-147

Kato, Byang, 1972. "Aid to the National Church—When it Helps, When it Hinders," *EMQ* 8.193-201

Keener, Gerald H., 1977. "Critique of 'Internationalization of Mission,' " *The Seminarian* 7(5).3

Mutombo-Mpanya, 1977. "Problems of the Churches in Central Africa," paper delivered at the Symposium on "The Church in Africa," Milligan College, 31 March 1977. To be published.

Nacpil, Emerito P., 1971. "Mission but not Missionaries," *IRM* 60.356-362

Neill, Stephen C., 1964. *A History of Christian Missions.* Middlesex/Baltimore: Penguin

Roberts, W. Dayton, 1973. "Mission to Community—Instant Decapitation," *IRM* 62. 338-345

Shenk, Calvin E., 1977. "Internationalization of Mission," *The Seminarian* 7(5).1-3

Strong, Robbins, 1972. "Practical Partnership with Churches Overseas," *IRM* 61.281-287

Taber, Charles R., 1976. "Money, Power and Mission," *The Other Side,* March-April 1976, 28-34, 43-44

Taylor, John V., 1963. *The Primal Vision.* London: SCM Press

_____, 1971. "Small is Beautiful," *IRM* 60.328-338

Vikner, David L., 1974. "The Era of Interdependence," *Missiology* 2.475-488

The Authors

R. Pierce Beaver has written widely on missionary history. In 1971 he retired as professor of missions and chairman of the Church History Field at the University of Chicago Divinity School.

Don Blosser teaches Bible and is director of the Center for Discipleship at Goshen (Indiana) College. He did his doctoral research on the jubilee concept.

George R. Brunk, III, is assistant professor of New Testament and dean at Eastern Mennonite Seminary, Harrisonburg, Virginia.

J. Lawrence Burkholder has been president of Goshen (Indiana) College since 1971. He served in China from 1945-48 as a representative for Mennonite Central Committee and Church World Service. He has been instrumental in negotiating a student exchange program with a Chinese university in 1980.

Jonathan T'ien-en Chao is director of Chinese Research Center, Hong Kong. He was born in Manchuria during the Japanese occupation and left China in 1948.

Howard H. Charles is professor of New Testament at Goshen Biblical Seminary, Elkhart, Indiana.

John Driver serves with Mennonite Board of Missions in Barcelona, Spain. He formerly served in Puerto Rico from 1951-66 and in Uruguay from 1966-74.

Michael Garde, an Irish Mennonite, gives leadership to the Mennonite witness in Dublin, Ireland.

J. D. Graber (1900-78) served as a missionary in India from 1925-42, as a relief commissioner in China from 1943-44, and as general secretary and secretary for overseas missions at Mennonite Board of Missions from 1944-67.

James Klassen served in Vietnam under Mennonite Central Committee from 1972-76. He teaches Vietnamese at Wichita (Kansas) State University and serves as a Vietnamese language consultant for Mennonite Central Committee.

C. Norman Kraus serves in Japan with Mennonite Board of Missions. He taught religion at Goshen (Indiana) College from 1952-79 and was director of the Center for Discipleship there.

Dwight J. McFadden, Jr., is associate general secretary of the Mennonite Church General Board Office of Black Concerns in Elkhart, Indiana.

Luke S. Martin served in Vietnam from 1962-75 with Eastern Mennonite Board of Missions and Charities. In 1976 he headed the Vietnam Study Project and prepared a report on the Mennonite mission and service work in Vietnam. He is pastor of Allentown (Pennsylvania) Mennonite Church.

James E. Metzler served in Vietnam from 1963-68 and in the Philippines from 1970-76 with Eastern Mennonite Board of Missions and Charities.

Paul M. Miller is professor of practical theology at Goshen Biblical Seminary, Elkhart, Indiana.

Gottfried Oosterwal is chairman of the Department of World Mission, Andrews University, Berrien Springs,

Michigan, and missions consultant for the Seventh-Day Adventist Church. He served as a missionary in New Guinea and the Philippines.

José M. Ortiz is associate general secretary of the Mennonite General Board Office of Latin Concerns in Elkhart, Indiana.

Robert L. Ramseyer serves in Japan with the Commission on Overseas Mission of the General Conference Mennonite Church and is director of the Overseas Mission Training Center, Elkhart, Indiana.

Sue Richard has been a self-supported missionary in Japan with Mennonite Board of Missions since 1963.

David A. Shank serves with Mennonite Board of Missions in Ivory Coast, West Africa. He served in Belgium from 1950-73.

Wilbert R. Shenk is secretary for overseas missions at Mennonite Board of Missions.

Richard Showalter pastors a new congregation at Mechanicsburg, Ohio, and chairs the Evangelism/Church Growth Resource Team sponsored jointly by the Mennonite Board of Missions Home Missions Division and Mennonite Board of Congregational Ministries.

Roger C. Sider is associate professor of psychiatry at University of Rochester (New York) School of Medicine and Dentistry. He served as a medical missionary in Rhodesia from 1967-69.

Willard M. Swartley is associate professor of New Testament, director of the Institute of Mennonite Studies, and dean of Associated Mennonite Biblical Seminaries, Elkhart, Indiana.

Charles R. Taber teaches at Emmanuel School of Religion, Milligan College, Tennessee. Earlier he was a missionary in Central African Republic and linguistic consultant for the United Bible Societies in West Africa.

John E. Toews is associate professor of New Testament and dean of Mennonite Brethren Biblical Seminary, Fresno, California.

Virgil Vogt serves as a pastor at Reba Place Fellowship, Evanston, Illinois.

A. F. Walls is the founding head of the Department of Religious Studies at the University of Aberdeen, Scotland. Prior to that he taught in Sierra Leone and Nigeria.

Hugo Zorrilla recently resigned as dean of the Latin American Biblical Seminary, San José, Costa Rica, to pursue advanced studies in Spain.

Index